Creative Leadership

There has never been a better time to study, practice, and experience creative leadership. In the fluid and turbulent economic and social environments of the 21st century, creative leadership has become a cardinal force in the creation and evolution of adaptive organizations. In the last two decades, organizational science has witnessed a rapid increase in the number of studies on the nature, skills, and processes of creative leadership. The resulting accumulated body of knowledge has remained for many years dispersed and fragmented across multiple strands of organizational research. This volume seeks to foster the cross-fertilization of scientific knowledge and insight by bringing together authoritative contributions from leading scholars whose work is located in different strands of creative leadership research.

Creative Leadership: Contexts and Prospects builds upon a recently introduced multi-context framework that integrates metatheoretically three conceptualizations of creative leadership found in the extant literature: Facilitating employee creativity; Directing the materialization of a leader's creative vision; and Integrating heterogeneous creative contributions. These three conceptualizations reflect essential differences in the enactment of creative leadership across various collaborative contexts of creative work, and they underlie the intellectual efforts of different research strands.

The collection of chapters in *Creative Leadership: Contexts and Prospects* offers the latest thinking on creative leadership in facilitative, directive, and integrative contexts, and a stimulating set of ideas for crafting the next generation of nuanced theories and empirical studies in the field.

Charalampos Mainemelis is Professor of Organizational Behavior and Director of the SEV Center of Excellence in Creative Leadership at ALBA Graduate Business School, The American College of Greece, Greece.

Olga Epitropaki is Professor of Management at Durham University Business School, UK.

Ronit Kark is Associate Professor of Organizational and Leadership Studies at the Department of Psychology at Bar-Ilan University, Israel.

Routledge Studies in Leadership Research

Responsible Leadership
Realism and Romanticism
Edited by Steve Kempster and Brigid Carroll

CSR, Sustainability, and Leadership
Edited by Gabriel Eweje and Ralph J Bathurst

Revitalising Leadership
Putting Theory and Practice into Context
Suze Wilson, Stephen Cummings, Brad Jackson, and Sarah, Proctor-Thomson

Women, Religion and Leadership
Female Saints as Unexpected Leaders
Edited by Barbara Denison

"Leadership Matters?"
Finding Voice, Connection and Meaning in the 21st Century
Edited by Chris Mabey and David Knights

Innovation in Environmental Leadership
Critical Perspectives
Edited by Benjamin W. Redekop, Deborah Rigling Gallagher, and Rian Satterwhite

After Leadership
Edited by Brigid Carroll, Suze Wilson, and Josh Firth

Creative Leadership
Contexts and Prospects
Edited by Charalampos Mainemelis, Olga Epitropaki, and Ronit Kark

For a full list of titles in this series, please visit www.routledge.com

Creative Leadership

Contexts and Prospects

Edited by
Charalampos Mainemelis,
Olga Epitropaki, and Ronit Kark

Routledge
Taylor & Francis Group
LONDON AND NEW YORK

First published 2019 by Routledge

2 Park Square, Milton Park, Abingdon, Oxon, OX14 4RN
605 Third Avenue, New York, NY 10017

Routledge is an imprint of the Taylor & Francis Group, an informa business

First issued in paperback 2020

Library of Congress Cataloging-in-Publication Data
A catalog record for this book has been requested

ISBN: 978-1-138-55986-8 (hbk)
ISBN: 978-0-367-73363-6 (pbk)

Typeset in Sabon
by Apex CoVantage, LLC

We dedicate this book to our children,
Lydia, Iris Ioanna, and Gianluca Mainemelis;
Alexandros and Manolis Mylonopoulos; and
Omer, Ofri, and Clil Kark,
in the hope of a better and more creatively led future.

Contents

Preface

Seven years ago, a series of stimulating conversations propelled us to defamiliarize a familiar question: *What do creative leaders do?* The question appeared embarrassingly simple, considering that the three of us have devoted our academic careers to researching and teaching creativity and leadership. It turns out, however, that we found it hard to come up with a mutually agreed concise answer. What made the task of answering the question difficult was not the shortage of knowledge but the profusion of it. We realized that far beyond our shared knowledge base on the subject, each one of us had accessed in the past additional reservoirs of scientific knowledge that the other two were, at best, only mildly familiar with. We eventually reached the conclusion that creative leadership was the focus of investigation of a large number of research streams—larger than what each one of us had initially thought—and that most of those streams had rarely engaged with one another in any form of intellectual exchange.

Upon reflecting on the distinctive properties of these research streams and on the potential benefits of pulling their knowledge stocks together, we submitted an article proposal to the *Academy of Management Annals*, with the stated purpose of developing a unified framework of creative leadership. An anonymous reviewer commented, "*Overall, my core concern is that you are proposing a review for a literature that really doesn't exist to any significant degree.*" We replied by providing a sample list of 100 recently published articles on creative leadership, noting that this was just a subset of the body of research that we were going to examine. In the final article, we reviewed over 200 scholarly works culled from over 60 academic journals. By the time the article was published, we were certain that any researcher who had examined in-depth the link between creativity and leadership would be intimately familiar with at least one-third of these works. At the same time, we now had more and more solid reasons to believe that even researchers who were considered experts in their respective research streams might have never read (or even heard of) other clusters of articles included in this body of research.

Our article, which was a finalist for the *Academy of Management Annals* 2015 Best Article Award, was the first attempt to connect the dispersed and fragmented body of research on creative leadership. We believe that the multi-context framework that we proposed offers a fertile conceptual springboard for crafting more nuanced theories and empirical studies of creative leadership in the future. What is more important to the field, however, is not the framework itself, but the underlying motivation to connect distal research streams.

The purpose of this volume is to build upon this recent metatheoretical framework in order to foster the cross-fertilization of knowledge and insight among different research strands of creative leadership. The chapters in this book are authored by scholars who have made in the past outstanding contributions to research on creative leadership in their respective streams, or/and are currently conducting novel and interesting research in the area. By bringing together in this volume exemplar contributions from diverse bodies of scientific work, we seek to trigger fertile exchanges and recombinations of knowledge about creative leadership. We feel that the time is ripe for such a scholarly endeavor, considering that research on creative leadership is rapidly growing and the practice of creative leadership is spreading and gaining in importance across different types of organizational contexts.

Charalampos Mainemelis, Olga Epitropaki,
and Ronit Kark

Figures

Tables

Contributors

Isabelle Bouty is Full Professor of Management and Organization at University Paris Dauphine PSL, Paris, France.

Julia Buck is a doctoral student in Industrial and Organizational Psychology at the University of Oklahoma, USA.

Filomena Canterino is Assistant Professor at the School of Management, Politecnico di Milano, Italy.

Stefano Cirella is Assistant Professor in Management at the Essex Business School, University of Essex, UK.

Jean-Francois Coget is Professor and Chair of the Management, Human Resources, and Information Systems area at the Orfalea College of Business, California Polytechnic State University, San Luis Obispo, USA.

Colleen Durban is a doctoral student in industrial and organizational psychology at the University of Oklahoma, USA.

Olga Epitropaki is Professor of Management at Durham University Business School, Durham University, UK.

Nicole Flocco is a PhD candidate at the School of Management of Politecnico di Milano, Italy.

Lucy L. Gilson is Professor and the Management Department Head at the University of Connecticut, USA.

Marie-Léandre Gomez is Associate Professor of Management Control at ESSEC Business School, Paris, France.

Yash Gujar is a doctoral student in industrial and organizational psychology at the University of Oklahoma, USA.

Sarah Harvey is Associate Professor in the School of Management at University College London, UK.

Maria Kakarika is Associate Professor of Organizational Behavior at NEOMA Business School, Paris, France.

Ronit Kark is Associate Professor of Organizational and Leadership Studies at the School of Psychology at Bar-Ilan University, Israel.

Chia-yu Kou is Assistant Professor of Organizational Behavior at School of Business, University College Dublin, Ireland.

Ho Kwong Kwan is Department Head in Organizational Management at School of Economics and Management and Professor at the Advanced Institute of Business Research, Tongji University, China.

G. James Lemoine is Assistant Professor of Organization and Human Resources at the University of Buffalo (SUNY) School of Management, USA.

Robert C. Litchfield is Associate Professor in the Department of Economics and Business at Washington & Jefferson College, USA.

Elizabeth Long Lingo is Assistant Professor of Organization Studies and Creative Enterprise at Foisie Business School at Worcester Polytechnic Institute, USA.

Robert G. Lord is Professor of Leadership at Durham University Business School, Durham University, UK.

Charalampos Mainemelis is Professor of Organizational Behavior and Director of the SEV Center of Excellence in Creative Leadership at ALBA Graduate Business School, The American College of Greece, Greece.

Jennifer Mueller is Associate Professor of Management at the University of San Diego School of Business, USA.

Michael D. Mumford is the George Lynn Cross Distinguished Research Professor of Psychology at the University of Oklahoma, USA.

Christina E. Shalley is the Sharon M. and Matthew R. Price Chair and Professor of Organizational Behavior at the Scheller College of Business at the Georgia Institute of Technology, USA.

Abraham B. (Rami) Shani is Professor of Management and Organization Behavior at the Orfalea College of Business, California Polytechnic State University, San Luis Obispo, USA.

Robert J. Sternberg is Professor of Human Development at Cornell University, USA, and Honorary Professor of Psychology at Heidelberg University, Germany.

Marc Stierand is Associate Professor of Service Management and Director of the Institute of Business Creativity at Ecole Hôtelière de Lausanne, HES-SO/University of Applied Sciences Western Switzerland, Switzerland.

Silviya Svejenova is Professor of Leadership and Innovation at the Department of Organization at Copenhagen Business School, Denmark.

E. Michelle Todd is a doctoral student in industrial and organizational psychology at the University of Oklahoma, USA.

Wenxin Xie is a PhD student in the School of Management at University College London, UK.

Xiaomeng Zhang is Associate Dean for executive education, Co-Director of Leadership and Motivation Research Centre, and Associate Professor of Organizational Behavior at Cheung Kong Graduate School of Business, China.

Acknowledgments

We thank David Varley at Routledge for approaching us two years ago with the idea for this book. We also thank Brianna Ascher, Mary Del Plato, and the editorial team at Routledge for their support throughout the book's development process. Last but not least, we are grateful to all of our colleagues who accepted our invitation to author a chapter for this volume. Their past work on creative leadership inspired our own metatheoretical work a few years ago. We hope that their present work in this book will stimulate the next generation of theories and empirical studies in the field.

Part I

Foundations of Creative Leadership

1 Introduction

Connecting Creative Leadership's Strands of Research

Charalampos Mainemelis, Olga Epitropaki, and Ronit Kark

Introduction

The concept of creative leadership was introduced in the 1950s by Selznick (1984) in an attempt to differentiate the more generative manifestations of leadership from both technical administration and artificial intelligence systems (Stark, 1963). By 2018, creative leadership has become more important and relevant than ever before. With the advent of the global, digital, and knowledge-based economy, leaders require creativity in order to build and develop adaptive organizations. Moreover, as creativity and innovation are now business imperatives for many types of organizations, the ability to foster the creativity of employees has become an important aspect of many leadership jobs. Furthermore, the explosion of creative industries has created a vast sector of economic activity in which the notion of leadership is often virtually indistinguishable from the notion of creative leadership. Last, but not least, as breakthrough advancements in artificial intelligence threaten to render many traditional forms of management obsolete, creative leadership becomes increasingly important as a source of some cardinal leadership qualities that intelligent machines do not possess (at least not yet), such as the ability to solve creatively highly complex social problems.

Recently, we proposed a metatheoretical integration of research on creative leadership conducted between 1957 and 2014 (Mainemelis, Kark, & Epitropaki, 2015). We observed that research on creative leadership has grown substantially in the last 15 years and that various streams of organizational, psychological, and sociological inquiry have examined the relationship between creativity and leadership, albeit using slightly different names such as 'creative leadership', 'leading for creativity and innovation', and 'managing creatives'. We found that across all strands of research *creative leadership refers to leading others toward the attainment of a creative outcome*. However, different research strands tend to give different meanings to what it actually means to lead others toward the attainment of a creative outcome.

We identified in the literature three conceptualizations of creative leadership that are not mere artifacts of diverse paradigmatic or methodological choices, but rather, they reflect actual differences in the enactment of creative leadership across organizational and social contexts. Moreover, these three conceptualizations are not exclusive properties of any given research strand, but rather, each conceptualization underlies the intellectual efforts of two or more research strands in the organizational and larger social science literature.

We observed that across all social and work contexts where the production of work is collaborative and non-solitary, creativity depends not only on one or more individuals' creative contributions, such as generating and refining new ideas, but also on other people's supportive contributions, such as providing psychological, social, and material support for creativity. Although supportive contributions do not constitute creative contributions, past research has consistently shown that they play a pivotal role in stimulating and sustaining the creative performance of other members in the collaborative context (e.g., Amabile et al., 1996, 2004; Koseoglu, Liu, & Shalley, 2017; Lin, Mainemelis, & Kark, 2016; Madjar, Oldham, & Pratt, 2002; Oldham & Cummings, 1996; Zhang & Bartol, 2010). The three conceptualizations that we discerned in the extant body of research differ primarily in terms of the relative ratios of the creative and supportive contributions that leaders and followers make in the creative process *in contextually patterned ways*. We integrated these conceptualizations into a metatheoretical framework of three collaborative contexts of creative leadership: *Facilitating* employee creativity; *Directing* the materialization of a leader's creative vision; and *Integrating* heterogeneous creative contributions, as shown in Figure 1.1.

The first conceptualization, *Facilitating*, focuses on the leader's role in fostering the creativity of followers in the organizational context. In Facilitative contexts, leaders are expected to make more supportive contributions, on balance, so that followers can make in turn more creative contributions to the final work product. In such contexts, higher degrees of creative leadership refer to higher degrees of leader supportive contributions, which, all other things being equal, result in higher degrees of follower creative contributions. This conceptualization was originally developed within a social-psychological strand of organizational creativity research that examines contextual influences on employee creativity, and later it expanded into a strand of leadership research that examines the influences of various leadership styles on employee creativity. These two research strands focus on how leaders foster or hinder employee creativity, and they have been the most prolific contributors to creative leadership research to date (e.g., Amabile et al., 2004; George & Zhou, 2007; Liao, Liu, & Loi, 2010; Lin, Mainemelis, & Kark, 2016; Oldham & Cummings, 1996; Mumford et al., 2002; Shin & Zhou, 2003, 2007; Tierney, Farmer, & Graen, 1999; Zhang & Bartol, 2010).

The second conceptualization, *Directing*, portrays the creative leader as the primary source of creative thinking and behavior (e.g., Sternberg,

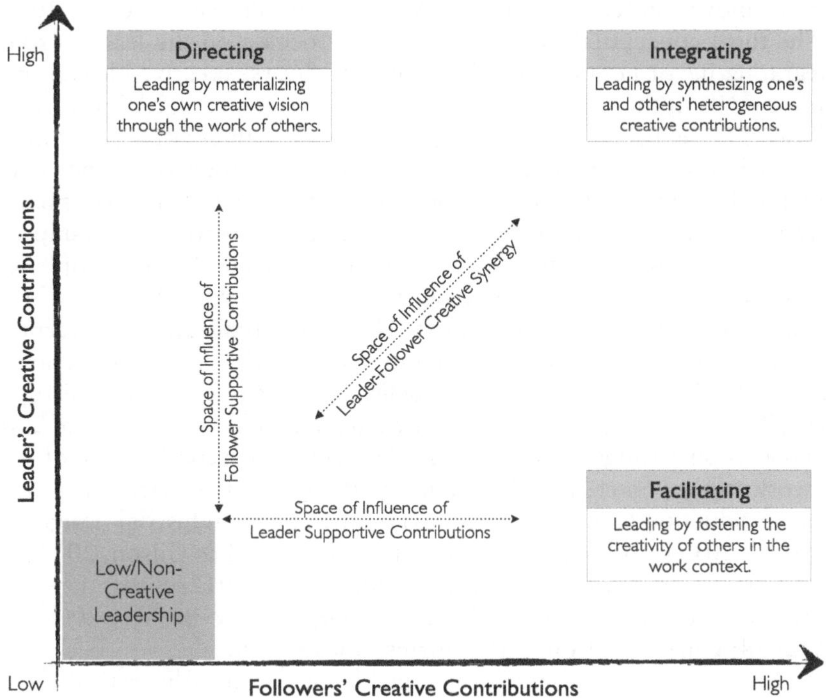

Figure 1.1 The Multi-context Model of Creative Leadership
(Reproduced with permission from Mainemelis, Kark, & Epitropaki, 2015: 401)

Kaufman, & Pretz, 2003). In Directive contexts, followers are expected to make more supportive contributions so that the leader can make in turn more creative contributions. In such contexts, higher degrees of creative leadership refer to higher degrees of leader creative contributions, which all other things being equal, depend on the leader's ability to inspire and elicit higher degrees of follower supportive contributions. Creative leadership in Directive contexts refers, therefore, to materializing a leader's creative vision through other people's work. This conceptualization has been associated with research conducted in contexts where the leader is an institutional entrepreneur or otherwise a master-creator who both creates and manages his or her creative enterprise. This conceptualization of creative leadership is evident in three strands of research that have produced a set of case studies of creative haute cuisine chefs (e.g., Bouty & Gomez, 2010; Gomez & Bouty, 2011; Stierand, 2015; Svejenova, Mazza, & Planellas, 2007; Svejenova, Planellas, & Vives, 2010), a set of studies on orchestra conductors (e.g., Hunt, Stelluto, & Hooijberg, 2004; Marotto, Roos, & Victor, 2007), and a set of studies on creative leadership in the context of top-down corporate innovation (e.g., Eisenmann & Bower, 2000; Vaccaro et al., 2012).

The third conceptualization, *Integrating*, focuses on the leader's role in integrating his or her creative ideas with the diverse creative ideas of other professionals in the work context. In Integrative contexts, both leaders and followers are expected to make high degrees of both creative and supportive contributions. However, as these inputs are heterogeneous, the creative leader is charged with the responsibility of synthesizing them into a final creative product. In such contexts, higher degrees of creative leadership refer to higher degrees of creative synergy among the leader's (or multiple leaders') creative vision and the heterogeneous creative contributions of other members of the collaborative context. This conceptualization is evident in a stream of studies on creative leadership in cinematic (e.g., Coget, Haag, & Gibson, 2011; Epitropaki & Mainemelis, 2016; Mainemelis & Epitropaki, 2013; Perretti & Negro, 2007), theatrical (e.g., Dunham & Freeman, 2000), and television settings (Murphy & Ensher, 2008); a second stream of social network studies on creative leadership in the form of creative brokerage in music production (e.g., Lingo & O'Mahony, 2010), industrial design (e.g., Obstfeld, 2012), and museum settings (e.g., Litchfield & Gilson, 2013); and a stream of research on dual (e.g., Hunter et al., 2012; Sicca, 1997) and shared (e.g., Davis & Eisenhardt, 2011; Hargadon & Bechky, 2006; Harvey, 2014; Harvey & Kou, 2013) forms of leadership.

An alarming observation that emerged from our metatheoretical integration of research is that the sharing of scientific knowledge and insight has been highly constrained and even nonexistent among research strands that embrace different conceptualizations of creative leadership. We believe that each of these research streams has made important independent contributions to our understanding of creative leadership, to date. We also believe, however, that each of these research streams has something valuable to gain from increasing its exposure to the research questions, conceptual frameworks, methodological approaches, and conclusions of other strands of creative leadership research. By bringing together in this edited volume exemplar contributions from each of these bodies of work, we seek to trigger fertile exchanges and novel recombinations of knowledge about creative leadership.

The book is organized in four parts. Part I, Foundations of Creative Leadership, entails two chapters (following the present one) that discuss aspects of creative leadership that generalize across all contexts. Part II, III, and IV includes chapters that focus on creative leadership in, respectively, Facilitative, Directive, and Integrative contexts. Next, we provide a brief overview of each chapter in the volume.

Part I: Foundations of Creative Leadership

Following this chapter, which briefly introduces the multi-context model, Chapter 2 argues that creative leadership research should pay more attention to the role of contextual variability. In Chapter 2, Charalampos Mainemelis suggests that, despite the fact that the manifestations of creative leadership vary substantially across contexts, creative leadership research is still troubled by low degrees of contextual sensitivity. He observes that although both styles and contexts exert significant influences on the emergence, unfolding, and consequences of creative leadership, to date research has over-emphasized the role of contextually invariable styles and has sidelined the role of variable contexts. He suggests that while increasing the degree of contextualization of future research is a question of revisiting the way that we build theories and design empirical studies in the field, increasing the field's general level of awareness of the importance of contextual variability requires a metatheoretical approach of systematically comparing and synthesizing the similarities and differences observed across a number of studies that are conducted in different contexts.

Mainemelis proposes that the tripartite multi-context model can be used as a metatheoretical tool for revealing significant patterns of contextual variability in creative leadership research. Drawing on past research on the role of context in organizational research in general and in leadership research in particular, he discusses what constitutes context in creative leadership; its levels, dimensions, and configurations; and the main organizational sources of contextual variability that affect the manifestation of creative leadership.

In Chapter 3, Olga Epitropaki, Jennifer Mueller, and Robert Lord observe that in the socio-cognitive domain of leadership perceptions and schemas, leadership and creativity remain not only separate but also contradictory notions. Examining points of convergence and divergence in established Implicit Leadership and Implicit Creativity Theories (ILTs vs. ICTs), they observe that despite certain trait similarities between ILTs and ICTs (such as 'intelligence'), a substantial number of traits are different or even antithetical. They note that this is true especially about traits related to the dark side of creativity, such as 'disobedient', 'poor at business', and 'extreme', that are contradictory to notions of leadership that highlight 'decision making', 'structure', and such traits as 'decisive', 'hard-working', 'helpful' and 'understanding'.

Epitropaki, Mueller, and Lord suggest that connectionist models proposed in the ILTs literature offer a pathway to convergence as they highlight the context-sensitive, dynamic, and flexible nature of schemas and allow for both stability and flexibility of implicit theories. They reason that creativity will be automatically activated as a salient trait of leadership in organizational contexts where creativity is a desired quality, innovation is a key strategic objective, positive emotions prevail, and organizational actors see themselves as creators. They suggest that this is more likely in Directive and Integrative creative leadership contexts, where the leader has a strong creator identity, visible creative contributions, and creativity and innovation are key strategic objectives of the work contexts. They also note that they expect little convergence between creativity and leadership in Facilitative contexts of creative leadership where there is limited requirement for creative contributions on behalf of the leader.

Part II: Creative Leadership in Facilitative Contexts

In Chapter 4, Michael Mumford, Colleen Durban, Yash Gujar, Julia Buck, and Michelle Todd make three observations that are indispensable to understanding the progress that research in Facilitative contexts of creative leadership has made during the last 20 years. First, they remind us that, to the surprise of many, an early literature review by Mumford et al. (2002) concluded that effective leadership is strongly related to the initiation and success of creative efforts in firms. Second, they suggest that while it has traditionally been thought that leaders of creative efforts do not themselves need to be especially creative, more recent research suggests that this assumption is not well founded. Finally, they argue that, while the field has assumed that if one could lead elsewhere, one could also lead creative efforts, their present work in Chapter 4 contradicts this assumption.

Building upon an earlier model proposed by Mumford and his colleagues, Mumford, Durban, Gujar, Buck, and Todd focus in Chapter 4 on three dimensions of functions that creative leaders must execute: leading the work (which includes scanning, theme identification, project creation, planning, mission definition, evaluation and feedback, monitoring, and learning), leading the people (which includes team formation, climate creation, and follower interactions), and leading the firm (which entails resource acquisition, support acquisition, and expertise/technology importation). Next, Mumford, Durban, Gujar, Buck, and Todd identify five sets of skills that creative leaders must possess in order to execute these functions effectively: creative thinking skills, forecasting, causal analysis skills, constraint analysis skill, and wisdom. Reflecting on the number and complexity of these functions and skills, they conclude with an important observation: that leading creative efforts may be one of the most—if not the most—demanding forms of leadership in organizations.

While Chapter 4 focuses on the functions and skills leaders must possess in order to lead effectively creative collectives, Chapter 5 focuses on the different ways or styles leaders may employ in order to foster the creativity of others. In Chapter 5, Christina E. Shalley and G. James Lemoine observe that leadership may be the most examined contextual predictor of creativity in the extant literature, and that the related findings have been fairly consistent across empirical studies. Shalley and Lemoine offer a critical review of research on the relationship between leadership behaviors and employee creativity. They discover in the literature five main categories of leadership styles and behaviors that influence followers' creativity: transformational, charismatic, and transactional; participative (which includes participative, inclusive, and empowering leadership); power focused (authoritative and directive); moral/immoral (authentic, ethical, servant/abusive); and a final category that includes general leadership behaviors not connected to style. Shalley and Lemoine discuss several moderating or otherwise intervening conditions in all five categories. They conclude that participative, transformational/charismatic, moral, and general approaches all positively predict creativity, whereas more authoritarian, directive, and abusive behaviors suppress employee creativity.

Shalley and Lemoine emphasize that, given that the field has long assumed that creativity is infrequent or even rare, it seems contradictory to conclude that virtually anything a leader does fosters employee creativity. In order to shed light on this paradox, Shalley and Lemoine offer three possible explanations: first, creativity may not be as rare as the field has thought, especially in contexts where most cases of employee creativity represent incremental forms of creativity. The second explanation is a methodological halo-like effect, where evaluations of leaders' behaviors inadvertently tap creative characteristics or processes themselves. A third explanation is that the outcomes of leadership and the antecedents of creativity are very similar. Shalley and Lemoine conclude that all three views have some merit, and they urge future research to focus more sharply on whether, when, and under which conditions a specific leader behavior might impact followers' creativity.

Chapter 6 focuses sharply on one of the leadership behaviors reviewed in Chapter 5, empowering leadership. In Chapter 6, Xiaomeng Zhang and Ho Kwong Kwan observe that, despite the fact that contemporary work organizations rely increasingly on team creativity in an attempt to stay competitive in the global marketplace, to date most research on the relationship between empowering leadership and employee creativity has been conducted at the individual level of analysis. In order to address this issue, Zhang and Kwan present in their chapter an empirical study about the relationship between empowering leadership and team creativity in the context of R&D teams in an information technology organization in China.

Building upon Amabile's (1988) componential model of creativity and Yukl's (2013) contingency perspective of leadership, Zhang and Kwan develop and test a conceptual model that links empowering leadership to team creativity via three intervening mechanisms: team creative efficacy, team learning behavior, and team task complexity. They find that empowering leadership is positively associated with team creativity; that this relationship is mediated by team creative efficacy and team learning behavior; and that these relationships are moderated by team task complexity. Zhang and Kwan conclude that empowering leadership facilitates cooperation among team members in acquiring task-relevant knowledge (i.e., team learning behavior); creates favorable conditions that promote team members' shared belief in their ability to produce something new and useful (i.e., team creative efficacy); and has a greater impact on team processes, emergent states, and outcomes when teams face demanding situations (e.g., high level of task complexity), which require team leaders to play a greater role.

While Chapter 6 examines the role of team task complexity as a link in the relationship between leadership and team creativity, Chapter 7 examines another dimension of team complexity, namely team diversity. In Chapter 7,

Maria Kakarika observes that, to date, research on diversity has been propelled by four theories that focus on diversity as information processing, as social categorization, as disparity/(in)justice, and as access to external networks. She also observes that many studies on the relationship between diversity and creativity have yielded inconsistent empirical findings. Kakarika argues that these mixed results indicate the need to craft more complex models, by paying greater attention to the selection of the appropriate diversity variable among various available diversity variables, and by paying attention to the mechanisms through which diversity achieves its effect on creativity.

Building upon a recently introduced metatheoretical framework of team diversity (Mayo et al., 2017), Kakarika develops in Chapter 7 a conceptual framework of creative leadership in the context of diverse teams that takes into account complex interactions among various dimensions of diversity and specifies different leader behaviors that can channel diversity into higher degrees of creativity. She suggests that while in social categorization contexts leaders may foster creativity by engaging in emotional conflict management and by creating a superordinate group identity, in information-processing contexts leaders may foster creativity by enabling information flow and promoting healthy degrees of cognitive conflict. In addition, while in disparity contexts leaders may foster creativity by engaging in emotion management and by reducing feelings of injustice, in variety of access contexts leaders may foster creativity by allowing the team to connect with various external sources of information and political support. Kakarika concludes by offering three general guidelines that integrate the mutually enforcing effects of the four diversity contexts.

Part III: Creative Leadership in Directive Contexts

In Chapter 8, Robert J. Sternberg reminds us that, because creativity has dark and potentially disastrous sides, what matters is not only whether creativity is used but also how it is used. He suggests that creativity is important for effective leadership because it is the component whereby one generates the ideas that others will follow. A leader who lacks creativity, writes Sternberg, may get along and get others to go along, but he or she may get others to go along with inferior or stale ideas. At the same time, Sternberg argues that creativity may be a necessary but not sufficient condition for great leadership. Considering that leaders often fail because they lack ethics rather than creativity or intelligence, Chapter 8 poses the question, what characteristics, in addition to creativity, are needed in order to protect against dangerous leaders?

Sternberg discusses this question in relation to the WICS (wisdom, intelligence, creativity, synthesis) model that he and his colleagues have developed over the years. He argues that leadership that is both good and effective is in large part a function of creativity in generating ideas, analytical intelligence in evaluating the quality of these ideas, practical intelligence in implementing the ideas and convincing others to value and follow them, and wisdom to ensure that the decisions and their implementation help to achieve a common good for all stakeholders. Sternberg discusses ten main elements of a creative attitude toward leadership; eight types of creative leadership contributions; academic and practical components of intelligence; the role of wisdom in leadership; and the synthesis among the wisdom, intelligence, and creativity components.

While Chapter 8 makes use of a few high-magnitude examples of creative leadership in politics (e.g., Nelson Mandela), Chapter 9 focuses on high-magnitude cases of creative leadership in haute cuisine. In Chapter 9, Isabelle Bouty, Marie-Léandre Gomez, and Marc Stierand observe that the majority of past theories and empirical studies in the field have focused on how the average person engages creatively with a task in a work context that usually does not depend primarily on creativity. Drawing on and aggregating the insights that each one of them has accumulated over the years from conducting empirical research in the field of haute cuisine, Bouty, Gomez, and Stierand propose a theoretical foundation that is more sensitively attuned to the practices of highly creative leaders in work contexts requiring substantial degrees of creativity. Their data-driven reflexive interpretation of their past empirical investigations carries special weight, considering that over the years the three of them have penetrated in unusually deep and prolonged (for researchers) ways into the reality of the creative practices, chefs, teams, and organizations that constitute the world of haute cuisine.

Following a reflexive transversal analysis, Bouty, Gomez, and Stierand suggest that chefs direct their team through enabling (configuring the creative space to set the conditions of creative work), orientating (managing creative work to keep it abounded and focused), and complying (assessing ideas to select those that fit). The chapter highlights that even though creative chefs rarely perform the necessary legwork of creative production themselves, they strictly control it to be in line with their overall creative vision. Bouty, Gomez, and Stierand argue that the three creative leadership practices of enabling, orientating, and complying are interrelated in nonlinear, non-stable, and often 'fuzzy' ways.

While Chapter 9 focuses on exceptional creativity in the field of haute cuisine, Chapter 10 focuses on exceptional creativity in the arts. In Chapter 10, Silviya Svejenova observes that whereas original forms of expression may abound in the arts, radical innovation is rare and hard to foresee. She argues that in the context of artistic innovation the emphasis is less on leading others and more on leading time. Svejenova poses the question, "how does creative leadership unfold in time in contexts of artistic innovation?" The purpose of her chapter is to explore not merely the long-term effects of creative leadership, but, most importantly, the connection between structural and dynamic aspects of time in the emergence and stabilization of novelty, and its materialization into a 'creative world', a distinctive universe of signs and symbols that is fertile and hence able to inspire future generations of audience and creators.

Svejenova explores empirically these issues through an analysis of the case of Joan Miró, who is recognized as one of the greatest art innovators of the 20th century for establishing a novel visual language and aesthetics. Her analysis distinguishes between two different enactments of Miró's creative leadership: time patterning, the temporal infrastructure of the artist's creative practice that entails different tensions; and temporality work, which involves cultivating serendipity and surprise, extending events' duration, stepping into new temporalities, and considering potentiality. Svejenova argues that time patterning provides a scaffolding for steady creative work and experimentation, whereas temporal work ensures the materialization of a creative world of novel signs, symbols, and forms.

Part IV: Creative Leadership in Integrative Contexts

In Chapter 11, Sarah Harvey, Chia-yu Kou, and Wenxin Xie observe that although creative groups face a variety of coordination challenges, past research has often studied them as if they were leaderless. Building on a recent model that describes collective creativity as a process of creative synthesis (Harvey, 2014), Harvey, Kou, and Xie discuss in their chapter how creative leaders can shape and help materialize a vision by drawing out and then enabling integration of group members' diverse inputs. Their process model of leading for creative synthesis consists of three phases: marshaling resources, helping groups to engage in the process facilitators through leader behaviors (which includes inciting action for enacting ideas, directing collective attention, and identifying overlaps for building on similarities), and facilitating feedback from the external environment.

Harvey, Kou, and Xie's model departs from past research in notable ways. Instead of emphasizing how leaders can set the vision themselves (as it is usually the case in Directive contexts), or how leaders can create an environment where many diverse new ideas arise from followers (as it is usually the case in Facilitative contexts), the model that they present in Chapter 11 focuses on how leaders use constraints, boundaries, and other variability-reduction practices to help the group generate and integrate ideas. Moreover, by defining creative synthesis as a dialectic process in which group members integrate their diverse inputs to develop a shared understanding of a task, their model places a strong emphasis on collective leadership and on what individual leaders can do to enable collective leadership.

While Chapter 11 examines creative leadership in less dispersed and more temporally stable organizational groups, Chapter 12 examines creative leadership in the context of shorter creative projects undertaken by temporary and dispersed networks of heterogeneous professionals. In Chapter 12, Elizabeth Long Lingo notes that in Integrative contexts creative leadership requires generating, eliciting, and synthesizing new ideas into a cohesive whole; it involves the formation of a constellation of creative content contributors from across a network as opposed to a single organization or unit; and it often lacks formal authority over those involved. She also observes that in such contexts creative leaders face three types of ambiguity: ambiguity over quality, or what constitutes success; ambiguous occupational jurisdictions, or control over decisions or whose expertise should prevail; and ambiguity regarding process, or how the collective creative work should proceed. Lingo argues that integrative creative leaders navigate these tensions by engaging a distinct form of brokerage, creative brokerage, that weaves together both tertius gaudens and tertius iungens approaches in order to manage the three types of ambiguity, elicit creative contributions, and maintain the commitment of those involved.

Building upon the study of Nashville country music producers by Lingo and O'Mahony (2010), Lingo offers in Chapter 12 a focused conceptualization of the role of the integrative creative leader through four primary phases of the collective creative process: resource gathering, defining project boundaries, creative production, and final synthesis. She discusses in detail the key challenge faced by creative leaders in each of the four phases; the key result that triggers the (nonlinear) transition to the next phase; the type and content of the ambiguity present in each phase; and the creative brokerage practices that creative leaders use by combining tertius iugens and tertius gaudens approaches in order to effectively navigate the various tensions, challenges, and objectives.

While Chapters 11 and 12 focus on how creative leaders synthesize their and others' heterogeneous creative contributions into a final creative product, Chapter 13 focuses on how creative leaders achieve higher level synthesis by rearranging others' individual creative products into novel creative collections. In Chapter 13, Robert C. Litchfield and Lucy L. Gilson observe that museum curators bring together the creative works of others, aggregate them into collections, and then take samples of these collections and present them as a form of new work labeled exhibitions. The extent that curators themselves are creative does not lie in the individual works, but in the curators' ability to combine works into a new (novel) and coherent (useful) exhibitions. Using museum curators as an analogy, Litchfield and Gilson propose that curatorial leaders might logically aim to assemble ideas that represent different types of creativity from the perspective of their general business operations, and that alternate framings may serve to alter these creative profiles in ways that can reveal new value propositions.

Elaborating upon their earlier work (e.g., Litchfield & Gilson, 2013; Gilson & Litchfield, 2017), Litchfield and Gilson analyze in Chapter 13 the comparative advantages of curatorial creative leadership over the idea championing and the portfolio management perspectives. They illustrate their arguments with the analytical example of curatorial creative leadership in the context of a boutique hotel chain that seeks to cross-reference ideas collected from employees by domain (e.g., lobby, bar, maid service, guest services/concierge) and creative type (i.e., foolish, disruptive, radical, or breakthrough).

While Chapters 11, 12, and 13 explore commonalities of creative leadership in Integrative contexts, Chapter 14 explores sources of variability among integrative creative leaders. In Chapter 14, Nicole Flocco, Filomena Canterino, Stefano Cirella, Jean-Francois Coget, and Abraham B. (Rami) Shani note that filmmaking is a par excellence Integrative context of creative leadership, where the film director has to elicit, orient, and integrate the highly heterogeneous inputs of multiple non-similar professionals into a coherent whole, the final cut. They observe that while the final cut is a collective effort, the act of integrating heterogeneous inputs itself is not necessarily so: integration could be done solely by the director, in an autocratic manner, or it could be shared with others, in a democratic manner. Flocco, Canterino, Cirella, Coget, and Shani examine the factors that can help explain why different directors occupy different 'locations' on the autocratic-democratic continuum. In doing so, they offer a rare juxtaposition of context and styles approaches to studying creative leadership.

Analyzing a range of secondary sources, they contrast and compare the cases of six film directors: Christopher Nolan, George Lucas, John Lasseter, Lars von Trier, Quentin Tarantino, and Richard Linklater. Flocco, Canterino, Cirella, Coget, and Shani conclude that the seven film directors vary considerably in the extent to which they integrate heterogeneous contributions in an autocratic vs. a democratic manner. They also propose seven factors that appear to be associated with this variation: the personalities of the directors, in particular, their apparent need for control; the temporality of involvement of others in crafting the vision (early vs. late); secrecy, or the extent to which directors protect the creative process from others vs. leave it open; directors' tendency to work with the same crew and cast across different movies or not; consolidation of roles by the director; technology, in particular how high vs. low tech the movie is, as indicated by the extent and complexity of special effects or animation in the filmmaking process; and the organization of the filmmaking process, such as whether rehearsals occur or not, or time is allotted for creative reorientation during the filmmaking.

Discussion

Discovering Similarities

In a recent critical reading of the creative leadership literature, we suggested that the field needs "to develop more nuanced, more accurately bounded, and more synthetic perspectives about creative leadership" (Mainemelis, Kark, & Epitropaki, 2015: 451). The collection of scholarly contributions in this book responds to this call with a set of nuanced insights about the context, content, emergence, variations, and consequences of creative leadership. We discern four central themes in the contributions that the chapters make: revealing complexity, synthesizing key dimensions, suggesting novel directions, and capturing dynamic processes.

Some chapters analyze the multidimensionality and complexity of creative leadership in relation to contextual variability (Chapter 2), implicit theories (Chapter 3), and leader behaviors (Chapter 5). Some chapters synthesize different aspects related to creative leadership into more complex conceptualizations, including common functions and skills (Chapter 4), types of team member diversity (Chapter 7), and wisdom, intelligence, and creativity (Chapter 8). Some chapters propose novel extensions to our understanding of creative leadership, specifically, from the individual to the team level of analysis (Chapter 6); from short to long time frames (Chapter 10); from idea generation to the assembly of idea collections (Chapter 13); and from focusing on either context or styles to juxtaposing both the context and styles orientations in studying creative leaders (Chapter 14). Last, but not least, some chapters shed light on creative leadership as a fluid and dynamic process of recursive creative practices (Chapter 9), creative synthesis (Chapter 11), and creative brokerage (Chapter 12).

We note next that the collection of chapters reveals important methodological and theoretical differences among different research streams. That said, we invite the reader to consider that most of these differences are not unbridgeable in metatheoretical terms, and that many basic assumptions, definitions, or/and concepts about creativity and leadership are shared by most or all chapters in the book. We believe that it is important to preserve such fundamental commonalities because they are essential to sustaining and developing the intellectual exchange among different research strands.

Discovering Differences

A comparison among the chapters composing Parts II, III, and IV sheds new light on some key differences among the Facilitative, Directive, and Integrative creative leadership contexts that we identified in Mainemelis, Kark, and Epitropaki (2015).

The three chapters in the Directing context set the *magnitude of creativity* much higher than the chapters in the Facilitating and Integrating contexts. In Chapter 9, Bouty, Gomez, and Stierand identify as a limitation of past research the tendency "to focus more on the average person's engagement in a creative task rather than on the practices of highly creative leaders." Their chapter concerns highly creative leaders in haute cuisine. Svejonova as well notes in Chapter 10 that

> whereas original and distinctive forms of expression may abound, only a limited number of artists or social groups, usually denoted as avant-garde, . . . precursors, . . . or rebels, . . . achieve breakthrough novelty and open up new domains of knowledge through their work.

In order to examine the creation and evolution of radically new forms, aesthetics, techniques, and subject matters that change the world of art, Svejenova analyzes the case of legendary artist Joan Miró. Although Sternberg's propulsion model identifies creative contributions of variable magnitudes, his discussion in Chapter 8 of "great leadership" points to higher-than-average cases of creative leadership.

In contrast, the chapters in the Facilitating and Integrating contexts do not restrict the magnitude of creative contributions to high levels. For example, in Chapter 13, Litchfield and Gilson discuss a broad range in the degrees of novelty and utility of creative products. Similarly, in Chapter 5, Shalley and Lemoine wonder whether creativity is not "as rare as some have expected" and that "radical creativity might be far less prevalent in organizations than incremental creativity." If that were true, it would support the conclusion that we reached in Mainemelis, Kark, and Epitropaki (2015): contextual variability is largely responsible for the variability in the approaches, conceptualizations, and findings of research conducted in the three contexts. Put another way, at one extreme, research in the Directing context is selective and studies notable 'master-creators' in contexts where radical master-creators exist; at another extreme, research in the Facilitating context is inclusive and usually studies lower magnitude cases of creative leaders and creative employees in a variety of organizations where most creativity is not radical.

Furthermore, the three chapters in the Directive context set the creative leader's *level of responsibility* much higher than research in the other two contexts. We note earlier that the notion of creative leadership was introduced in 1957 by Philip Selznick (1984) in his book *Leadership in Administration*. The concept of creative leadership appears on page 149, in the last subsection of the book titled "Creative Leadership." A few pages earlier, on page 142, there is the penultimate subsection of the book titled "Responsible Leadership." The proximity of the two subsections is not accidental: for Selznick, responsible leadership and creative leadership are fundamental components of great leadership and work in unison to create a better, more secure, and more creative future. Among the 14 chapters in this volume, the chapter that comes closer to portraying creative leadership in similar terms is Chapter 8, in which Sternberg suggests that great leadership is leadership that shapes a better future for all:

> We need creative leaders. But we also need leaders with analytical intelligence, common sense, and wisdom. We have few of those. If the world does not acquire more of them soon, our future will be compromised or perhaps, worse, eliminated.

While the other two chapters in the Directing context do not link creative leadership with the future of the society or the world at large, they associate the actions and decisions of the Directive creative leader with the evolution of the field in which he or she functions, be it haute cuisine (Chapter 9) or the arts (Chapter 10). In contrast, the chapters in the Facilitating and Integrating contexts tend to examine the creative leader's responsibility and ultimately impact within the boundaries of a specific project (Chapters 4, 11, 12, and 14) or regular, continuous organizational work (Chapter 5, 6, 7).

A corollary issue concerns the *time frame* used to examine the consequences of creative leadership. At one extreme, Svejenova, in Chapter 10, employs a very long time frame that goes well beyond the life of the creator. Creative leadership, she notes, is about "leading time" by crafting a "creative world" that offers "inspiration for others and, thereby, projects the novel artwork into the future." In the creativity literature, it is well established that the ultimate value of radical creative products in the arts is better judged in long time frames. Svejenona's use of a long time frame brings to the field of creative leadership research a fresh angle of leading others indirectly—that is, by inspiring and mobilizing people in the long future through one's creative work. Although the other chapters in the Directing context do not use such long time frames, we note earlier that they associate creative leadership with the long-term evolution of their respective fields. At another extreme, the chapters in the Integrating context work with the much shorter time frames observed in intense organizational projects (Chapter 11 by Harvey, Kou, and Xie), music production projects (Chapter 12 by Lingo), and filmmaking projects (Chapter 14 by Flocco, Canterino, Cirella, Coget, and Shani). Tellingly, the chapters in the Facilitating context do not have clear time frames as they focus more on continuous organizational activities or/and temporally static relationships among variables.

In addition, the chapters composing this book reveal different preferences for conducting research in *permanent or temporary structures*. Research in Integrative contexts tends to take place either in temporary organizations, such as music production projects (Chapter 12) and filmmaking projects (Chapter 14), or in temporary projects that take place within permanent organizational structures (Chapters 11 and 13). In contrast, most chapters in the Facilitating (Chapters 5, 6, and 7) and the Directing (Chapters 8, 9, and 10) contexts focus more on ongoing forms of creative collaboration within permanent organizational structures.

Another pattern of differences concerns the relative emphasis given to *variance or process approaches* to studying creative leadership. Consistent with an earlier observation about the shortage of process-based studies in research in Facilitating contexts (Mainemelis, Kark, & Epitropaki, 2015), the four chapters in the Facilitating context show the strongest preference for variance-based research, especially Chapter 5 on leadership behaviors (Shalley & Lemoine), Chapter 6 on empowering leadership (Zhang & Kwan), and Chapter 7 on team diversity (Kakarika). Mumford, Durban, Gujar, Buck, and Todd's model of functions and skills in Chapter 4 as well is based on discrete variables and relationships among discreet variables that are grounded in past variance-based research. However, because their model integrates these variables under an overarching stage-orientated conceptual structure, it could propel in the future the development of more process-based empirical studies. In contrast, chapters in the Directing and Integrating contexts embrace a more pluralistic mix of approaches, and four of them embrace process-based methodologies: Bouty, Gomez, and Stierand's recursive process model of creative practices in Chapter 9; Svejenova's dual temporal analysis of Miró's creative process in Chapter 10; Harvey, Kou, and Xie's process model of leading creative synthesis in Chapter 11; and Lingo's process model of creative leadership as creative brokerage in Chapter 12.

Learning From Research in the Other Two Contexts

What could research in each of the three contexts of creative leadership learn from research in the other two contexts? Although there are several things to consider, let us conclude with an intellectually playful note on what research in each context could discover about itself by reflecting on how it looks through the lens of research in the other two contexts.

Seen through the lens of research in the Directing and Integrating contexts, research in the Facilitating context could be described as the static study of anonymous leaders helping anonymous followers to generate anonymous creative products in anonymous organizations, whereby the creativity of the product is usually average, creativity is usually not seen as being very important in the organization, and the study usually focuses on variance-based relationships that have no particular beginning, end, duration, or any other temporal marker. Seen through the lens of research in the Facilitating and Integrating contexts, research in the Directing context could be described as the elitist study of famous creative leaders generating famous creative products in famous creative organizations, whereby the famous creative leaders are members of a small minority of celebrated heroes in a famous creative field, the famous creative field and the famous creative organization are highly atypical of most fields and most organizations in the world, and most of the hard implementation work in the creative process is done by non-famous followers who aspire to become at some point famous creative leaders. Seen through the lens of research in the Facilitating and Directing contexts, research in the Integrating context could be described as a 'road-trip-story' type of study about how one or more creative leaders who know how to do well one thing look around for other creative professionals who know how to do well various other types of things so that at some point they can all get together to synthesize their different crafts into a new creative product, whereby the gathering happens in a usually short-lived occasion and takes place within a collaborative context that, more often than not, did not exist the day before and will not exist the day after.

These playful portrayals of the three research orientations are, of course, exaggerated. However, they are not unfounded in empirical reality. They express real differences that, in our view, are systematically generated to a significant extent by patterned differences among the contexts where the three research orientations conduct their studies. From this point of view, the pluralism of orientations in the field of creative leadership research is not merely normal or expectable, but most importantly necessary to capturing the full range of the manifestations of the phenomenon. Equally important is the additional step of connecting metatheoretically the knowledge stocks of these research orientations so as develop broader and more accurate views about creative leadership and its manifestations across different contexts.

Bringing together multiple research strands may also have beneficial implications for their developmental trajectories. Reflecting on the earlier discussion, we believe that the main implication for research in the Facilitating context is the need to embrace more the dimensions of time and temporality, to incorporate more process-based approaches into its theories and empirical designs (e.g., Langley & Tsoukas, 2016), and to pay more attention to the identity and specificity of the people, contexts, and products that it studies. The main implication for research in the Directing context is to become more inclusive and more experimental in its sampling and site-selection methods, so as to better identify and possibly expand the usually narrow limits of the generalizability of its findings. Considering that research in the Integrative context is historically the younger among the three (Mainemelis, Kark, & Epitropaki, 2015), the main implication for it is related to growing in two directions: working backward to identify what happens in individuals' creative process before they come together to synthesize their ideas and inputs; and working forward to shed light on the sources of collaborative continuity that may persist among the members of the collective long after the temporary organization or the temporary project within a permanent organization dissolve. We invite the reader to discover that the chapters in this volume offer novel and nuanced insights that can propel the evolution of their respective research streams toward those directions.

References

Amabile, T. M. 1988. A model of creativity and innovation in organizations. *Research in Organizational Behavior*, 10: 123–167.

Amabile, T. M., Conti, R., Coon, H., Lazenby, J., & Herron, M. 1996. Assessing the work environment for creativity. *Academy of Management Journal*, 39: 1154–1184.

Amabile, T. M., Schatzel, E. A., Moneta, G. B., & Kramer, S. J. 2004. Leader behaviors and the work environment for creativity: Perceived leader support. *Leadership Quarterly*, 15: 5–32.

Bouty, I., & Gomez, M-L. 2010. Dishing up individual and collective dimensions in organizational knowing. *Management Learning*, 41: 545–559.

Coget, J. F., Haag, C., & Gibson, D. E. 2011. Anger and fear in decision-making: The case of film directors on set. *European Management Journal*, 29: 476–490.

Davis, J. P., & Eisenhardt, K. M. 2011. Rotating leadership and collaborative innovation: Recombination processes in symbiotic relationships. *Administrative Science Quarterly*, 56: 159–201.

Dunham, L., & Freeman, R. E. 2000. There is business like show business: Leadership lessons from the theatre. *Organizational Dynamics*, 29: 108–122.

Eisenmann, T. R., & Bower, J. L. 2000. The entrepreneurial M-form: Strategic integration in global media firms. *Organization Science*, 11: 348–355.

Epitropaki, O., & Mainemelis, C. 2016. The "genre bender": The creative leadership of Kathryn Bigelow. In C. Peus, S. Braun, & B. Schyns (Eds.), *Leadership lessons from compelling contexts, monographs in leadership and management, Vol. 8*: 275–300. Bigley, UK: Emerald Group Publishing Limited.

George, J. M., & Zhou, J. 2007. Dual tuning in a supportive context: Joint contributions of positive mood, negative mood, and supervisory behaviors to employee creativity. *Academy of Management Journal*, 50: 605–622.

Gilson, L. L., & Litchfield, R. C. 2017. Idea collections: A link between creativity and innovation. *Innovation: Organization & Management*, 19: 80–85.

Gomez, M-L., & Bouty, I. 2011. The emergence of an influential practice: Food for thought. *Organization Studies*, 32: 921–940.

Hargadon, A. B., & Bechky, B. A. 2006. When collections of creatives become creative collectives: A field study of problem solving at work. *Organization Science*, 17: 484–500.

Harvey, S. 2014. Creative synthesis: Exploring the process of extraordinary group creativity. *Academy of Management Review*, 39: 324–343.

Harvey, S., & Kou, C. 2013. Collective engagement in creative tasks: The role of evaluation in the creative process of groups. *Administrative Science Quarterly*, 58: 346–386.

Hunt, J. G., Stelluto, G. E., & Hooijberg, R. 2004. Toward new-wave organization creativity: Beyond romance and analogy in the relationship between orchestra-conductor leadership and musician creativity. *Leadership Quarterly*, 15: 145–162.

Hunter, S. T., Cushenbery, L., Fairchild, J., & Boatman, J. 2012. Partnerships in leading for innovation: A dyadic model of collective leadership. *Industrial and Organizational Psychology: Perspectives on Science and Practice*, 5: 424–428.

Koseoglu, G., Liu, Y., & Shalley, C. E. 2017. Working with creative leaders: Exploring the relationship between supervisors creativity and their employees' creativity. *The Leadership Quarterly*, 28: 798–811.

Langley, A., & Tsoukas, H. 2016. *Process studies handbook*. London: Sage Publications.

Liao, H., Liu, D., & Loi, R. 2010. Looking at both sides of the social exchange coin: A social cognitive perspective on the joint effects of relationship quality and differentiation on creativity. *Academy of Management Journal*, 53: 1090–1109.

Lin, B., Mainemelis, C., & Kark, R. 2016. Leaders' responses to creative deviance: Differential effects on subsequent creative deviance and creative performance. *Leadership Quarterly*, 4: 537–556.

Lingo, E. L., & O'Mahony, S. 2010. Nexus work: Brokerage on creative projects. *Administrative Science Quarterly*, 55: 47–81.

Litchfield, R. C., & Gilson, L. L. 2013. Curating collections of ideas: Museum as metaphor in the management of creativity. *Industrial Marketing Management*, 42: 106–112.

Madjar, N., Oldham, G. R., & Pratt, M. G. 2002. There's no place like home? The contributions of work and nonwork creativity support to employees' creative performance. *Academy of Management Journal*, 45: 757–767.

Mainemelis, C., & Epitropaki, O. 2013. Extreme leadership as creative leadership: Reflections on Francis Ford Coppola in The Godfather. In C. Giannantonio & A. Hurley-Hanson (Eds.), *Extreme leadership: Leaders, teams, and situations outside the norm*: 187–200. Northampton, MA: Edward Elgar Publishing.

Mainemelis, C., Kark, R., & Epitropaki, O. 2015. Creative leadership: A multi-context conceptualization. *Academy of Management Annals*, 9: 393–482.

Marotto, M., Roos, J., & Victor, B. 2007. Collective virtuosity in organizations: A study of peak performance in an orchestra. *Journal of Management Studies*, 44: 388–413.

Mayo, M., Kakarika, M., Mainemelis, C., & Deuschel, N. T. 2017. A metatheoretical framework of diversity in teams. *Human Relations*, 70(8): 911–939.

Mumford, M. D., Scott, G. M., Gaddis, B., & Strange, J. M. 2002. Leading creative people: Orchestrating expertise and relationships. *Leadership Quarterly*, 13: 705–750.

Murphy, S. E., & Ensher, E. A. 2008. A qualitative analysis of charismatic leadership in creative teams: The case of television directors. *Leadership Quarterly*, 19: 335–352.

Obstfeld, D. 2012. Creative projects: A less routine approach toward getting new things done. *Organization Science*, 23: 1571–1592.

Oldham, G. R., & Cummings, A. 1996. Employee creativity: Personal and contextual factors at work. *Academy of Management Journal*, 39: 607–634.

Perretti, F., & Negro, G. 2007. Mixing genres and matching people: A study in innovation and team composition in Hollywood. *Journal of Organizational Behavior*, 28: 563–586.

Selznick, P. 1984. *Leadership in administration*. Berkeley, CA: University of California Press (Originally published 1957).

Shin, S. J., & Zhou, J. 2003. Transformational leadership, conservation and creativity: Evidence from Korea. *Academy of Management Journal*, 46: 703–714.

Shin, S. J., & Zhou, J. 2007. When is educational specialization heterogeneity related to creativity in research and development teams? Transformational leadership as a moderator. *Journal of Applied Psychology*, 96: 1709–1721.

Sicca, L. M. 1997. Management of Opera Houses: The Italian experience of the "Enti Autonomi". *International Journal of Cultural Policy*, 4: 201–224.

Stark, S. 1963. Creative leadership: Human vs. metal brains. *Academy of Management Journal*, 6: 160–169.

Sternberg, R. J., Kaufman, J. C., & Pretz, J. E. 2003. A propulsion model of creative leadership. *Leadership Quarterly*, 14: 455–473.

Stierand, M. 2015. Developing creativity in practice: Explorations with world-renowned chefs. *Management Learning*, 46: 598–617.

Svejenova, S., Mazza, C., & Planellas, M. 2007. Cooking up change in haute cuisine: Ferran Adrià as an institutional entrepreneur. *Journal of Organizational Behavior*, 28: 539–561.

Svejenova, S., Planellas, M., & Vives, L. 2010. An individual business model in the making: A chef's quest for creative freedom. *Long Range Planning*, 43: 408–430.

Tierney, P., Farmer, S. M., & Graen, G. B. 1999. An examination of leadership and employee creativity: The relevance of traits and relationships. *Personnel Psychology*, 52: 591–620.

Vaccaro, I. G., Jansen, J. J. P., Van Den Bosch, F. A. J., & Volberda, H. W. 2012. Management of innovation and leadership: The moderating role of organizational size. *Journal of Management Studies*, 49: 28–51.

Yukl, G. 2013. *Leadership in organizations* (8th ed.). Essex, UK: Pearson.

Zhang, X., & Bartol, K. M. 2010. Linking empowering leadership and employee creativity: The influence of psychological empowerment, intrinsic motivation, and creative process engagement. *Academy of Management Journal*, 53: 107–128.

2 On the Relationship Between Creative Leadership and Contextual Variability

Charalampos Mainemelis

Introduction

Twelve years ago, Porter and McLaughlin (2006: 559) revisited a long-standing question about research on leadership in organizations:

> Leadership in organizations does not take place in a vacuum. It takes place in organizational contexts. The key issue, therefore, is whether, and to what extent, the organizational context has been front and center in recent leadership literature. That is, does a relative void still exist in the research literature on the impact of the organizational context on leadership?

Searching for an empirical answer, Porter and McLaughlin analyzed 373 articles about leadership published in 21 major journals between 1990 and 2005. They measured organizational context as a constellation of elements, such as culture/climate; goals, strategies, and missions of individuals, teams, and organizations; demographic and capability features of people; organizational states and conditions (e.g., stability, crisis, resources); size, shape, type, and elements of structure; and dimensions of time. Although their measure of organizational context was rich and included a multitude of dimensions, Porter and McLaughlin found that 65% of the articles in their sample did not place any emphasis on organizational context, 19% placed a slight emphasis, and only 13% placed a moderate-to-strong emphasis on organizational context. They concluded that future research could be improved by "making a concerted effort to focus directly on the nature of the organizational context as a primary object of interest, rather than treating it as almost an afterthought" (573).

We recently reached similar conclusions about creative leadership research (Mainemelis, Kark, & Epitropaki, 2015). In our case, our initial intention was not to stress the role of context, but to integrate findings and insights from various research strands. We discovered, however, that the conceptualization of creative leadership varies significantly across research strands, not because of unbridgeable epistemological or methodological discrepancies among them, but because of essential differences among the contexts wherein creative leadership is enacted. In other words, we found that contextual variability generates conceptual variability in creative leadership research.

After analyzing the sources of contextual variability that we found in the creative leadership literature, we crafted a metatheoretical model that entails three distinct collaborative contexts: *Facilitating*, *Directing*, and *Integrating* (Mainemelis, Kark, & Epitropaki, 2015). To date, we have witnessed perplexing instances where other researchers engage with the multi-context model as if the terms 'Facilitating', 'Directing', and 'Integrating' in it referred to individual styles and not to collaborative contexts. We have even come across the baffling idea that any leader can move into any context at any time and impose ab initio his or her own favorite stylistic mix—e.g., "a bit of facilitating, a bit of directing, and a bit of integrating". After all, the extant leadership literature suggests that contexts constrain what leadership behaviors are considered prototypical (e.g., Liden & Antonakis, 2009: 1589; Lord et al., 2001: 314; Osborn et al., 2002: 798; see also Chapter 3 in this volume by Epitropaki, Mueller, and Lord). After all, we explicitly called the three contexts "collaborative *contexts*"; we clearly labeled the model "multi-*context* model"; we even gave the article the title "Creative Leadership: Towards a Multi-*Context* Conceptualization". Why would anyone ignore context even when context tries so hard to be noticed?

There are many reasons that context is often ignored or sidelined in organizational research. Context defies broad generalization because it exposes the boundary conditions and other limitations of a theory (Bacharach, 1989; Liden & Antonakis, 2009). Ironically, instead of treating context as an opportunity to strengthen the sophistication and predictive validity of theories, research tends to accumulate evidence as if context did not matter (Johns, 2006; Sergeeva & Andreeva, 2016). Furthermore, researchers need to invest considerable time and effort in order to become familiar with the intricate and unique aspects of any given context (Mowday & Sutton, 1993). This is important because "apparently trivial contextual stimuli sometimes have marked effects" (Johns, 2006: 387). For example, in Chapter 9 of this volume, Bouty, Gomez, and Stierand note that in order to construct more refined interpretations about creative leadership in haute cuisine, they had to invest years in becoming "highly acquainted with their empirical field" (in fact, one of them has been a chef in haute cuisine). Most researchers, however, rarely become immersed in the context; instead, they treat it as a 'constant' in their study (Johns, 2006).

The paradoxical implication is that, when a number of studies on a subject claim to take into account their empirical context but in effect they treat it only as a 'constant', context ends up playing little or no role in the resulting findings across those studies, even when the studies are conducted in diverse contexts. For example, Thomson, Jones, and Warhurst (2007: 636) criticized the tendency of research to treat the creative industries as a single type of work context, noting that "the distinctive characteristics of creative labor are best understood within particular sector and market contexts." Consider also that the empirical studies that we reviewed in the Facilitating context in Mainemelis, Kark, and Epitropaki (2015) have produced largely convergent findings despite the fact they were conducted in diverse organizational contexts such as an oil field services company, an information technology company, a steel company, a cereals company, high technology firms, R&D departments, an industrial design firm, a telecommunications organization, a confectionery company, media firms, advertising agencies, management consulting firms, a non-for-profit hospital, a for-profit hospital, a petroleum drilling equipment company, an helicopter company, and a lunar design consultancy, to name a few.

Even research that pays attention to context usually focuses only on measuring a few discrete variables across contexts. This approach has many benefits, including generalization (Liden & Antonakis, 2009). For example, studies conducted in Facilitative contexts have shown that higher degrees of leader support are associated with higher degrees of employee creativity (Anderson, Potočnik, & Zhou, 2014; Mainemelis, Kark, & Epitropaki, 2015). Despite its merits, however, this approach has some limitations. Because it is not concerned with how the selected variables interact with other variables in the focal context to form complex configurations, it ends up studying a set of variables in a context rather the context itself (Rousseau & Fried, 2001). As Johns (2006) noted, it "is not that context is never studied. Rather, it is that its influence is often unrecognized or underappreciated". In other words, research that focuses on measuring discrete contextual variables across contexts ends up highlighting the primacy of contextual invariability instead of shedding light on the intricate role of contextual variability.

Moreover, this approach relies on standard quantitative tools that cannot easily capture essential qualitative differences among contexts. For instance, consider the difference between the normative expectations for a leader to be a 'master-creator' vs. a 'facilitator' of others' creativity. This difference is not merely a question of degree that can be reliably assessed with a standard Likert-type scale. It is also a question of kind and embeddedness in social structure (Mainemelis, Kark, & Epitropaki, 2015) and requires thus more context-sensitive forms of assessment. Finally, research that measures discrete contextual variables across contexts usually focuses more on what Heath and Sitkin (2001) called 'Big-B' variables, which emphasize interesting behavior that may be relevant for organizations, and 'Contextualized-B' variables, which emphasize behavior that occurs in an organizational context, and less on 'Big-O' variables that emphasize behavior that is central to organizing. The tendency to ignore the 'Big-O' often leads to conclusions that may be elegant and valid in psychological or sociological terms, but they often leave one quarreling as to what exactly is 'organizational' about them (see also Blair & Hunt, 1986; Porter & McLaughlin, 2006).

I operate here under the assumption that most of us have conducted in the past research of low contextual sensitivity. It is beyond my purpose in the present chapter to suggest ways for strengthening the contextualization of future studies (see Blair & Hunt, 1986; Liden & Antonakis, 2009; Rousseau & Fried, 2001). Instead, I discuss how the multi-context model can be used as a metatheoretical tool for revealing significant patterns of contextual variability in the extant creative leadership literature. Drawing on past analyses of the role of context in organizational research in general, and in leadership research more specifically, I highlight the critical role that context plays in our capacity to understand the pluralistic manifestations of creative leadership in organizations. Building on the multi-context model, I also propose a set of insights about what constitutes context in creative leadership; its levels, dimensions, and configurations; and some key organizational sources of contextual variability in creative leadership.

What Constitutes Context?

"The term 'context' comes from a Latin root meaning 'to knit together' or 'to make a connection'" (Rousseau & Fried, 2001: 1). In social science, context generally refers to "stimuli and phenomena that surround and thus exist in the environment external to the individual, most often at a different level of analysis" (Mowday & Sutton, 1993: 198). With regard to behavior in organizations, context refers to "situational opportunities and constraints that affect the occurrence and meaning of organizational behavior as well as functional relationships between variables" (Johns, 2006: 386). In more specific reference to leadership, context "is the milieu—the physical and social environment—in which leadership is observed" (Liden & Antonakis, 2009: 1587).

Understanding a given context requires in-depth investigation and thick description of its essential properties (Rousseau & Fried, 2001: 7; Sergeeva & Andreeva, 2016: 256). Seminal examples of delicately contextualized creative leadership research include Bouty and Gomez's (2010) study of the evolution of creative practices under three different head chefs in a Michelin-starred restaurant in France over an eight-year period; Lingo and O'Mahony's (2010) study of the creative brokerage of 23 independent music producers in the Nashville music industry; Marotto, Roos, and Victor's (2007) study of the performance of an Eastern European orchestra under four different conductors; and Murnighan and Conlon's (1991) study of leadership and team dynamics in 20 string quartets in Great Britain. These studies went beyond testing or extending known theories, models, or relationships: they all revealed, in quite vivid and compelling ways, how creative leadership is related to specific exigencies of practice, intricate elements of the social structure, and other aspects of the focal context.

While understanding any given context requires focused investigation, understanding contextual variability requires a different approach. Exploring why and how the manifestations of a phenomenon vary across different contexts requires the identification of a few fundamental contextual dimensions in order to craft a metatheoretical framework for contrasting, comparing, and integrating the findings of research studies conducted in different contexts (Johns, 2006: 391; Liden & Antonakis, 2009: 1594). In order to develop such a framework, we recently posed the question, *which contextual dimensions are particularly relevant to understanding the manifestations of creative leadership across contexts*? (Mainemelis, Kark, & Epitropaki, 2015). Searching for a response that was grounded in the extant literature, we reasoned that a proper metatheoretical framework must meet two criteria. First, it must specify contextual aspects that have been solidly theorized as being central to the phenomena of creativity, leadership, and creative leadership; and second, sufficient empirical evidence should exist that the variable configurations of those contextual aspects are related to the variable manifestations of creative leadership.

With regard to the first criterion, we found that there is substantial agreement in the literature that creativity in organizational contexts requires both creative contributions (e.g., generating and developing new ideas), and supportive contributions (e.g., providing psychological, social, or/and material support for creativity) (Amabile, 1988; Amabile et al., 1996; Ford, 1996; Madjar, Oldham, & Pratt, 2002; Oldham & Cummings, 1996; Simonton, 2002, 2004a, 2004b). With regard to the second criterion, we discovered in the empirical literature three manifestations of creative leadership, which differ in terms of the ratio of leader/follower creative contributions and in terms of the corresponding ratio of leader/follower supportive contributors.

We proposed hence a multi-context model of three collaborative contexts of creative leadership: *Facilitating employee creativity, Directing the materialization of a leader's creative vision, and Integrating heterogeneous creative contributions*. In the Facilitative context, creative leadership focuses on eliciting and supporting followers' creative contributions. In the Directive context, creative leaders act as primary (but not lone or sole) creators who elicit and use followers' supportive contributions. In the Integrative context, creative leadership focuses on eliciting heterogeneous creative contributions from followers and synthesizing them with the leader's own creative contributions (Mainemelis, Kark, & Epitropaki, 2015; see also Figure 1.1 in Chapter 1). We also clarified that whether creative leadership will be manifested in the form of Facilitating, Directing, or Integrating ultimately depends on a dynamic confluence of cultural, industry, organizational, professional, personal, and task characteristics. In the next section, I discuss how this model can help us understand the tendency of different research strands to focus on different levels of the organizational context.

Levels and Configurations of Context

Johns (2006) portrayed context as entailing two levels, the omnibus and the discrete. The omnibus context refers broadly to an entity that entails many features and particulars. He noted that research about the omnibus context should tell a 'story' that describes *what* (substantive content of the study), *who* (occupational and demographic elements), *where* (location of region, culture, industry), *when* (absolute and relative time), and *why* (rationale for the conduct of the study). The discrete context refers to the particular contextual variables or levers that shape behavior or attitudes, and includes the task context (e.g., autonomy, uncertainty, accountability, resources), the social context (social density, social structure, and direct social influence), and the physical context (e.g., temperature, light, the built environment, and décor). Johns (2006: 391) suggested,

> Discrete can be viewed as nested within omnibus context such that the effects of omnibus context are mediated by discrete contextual variables. . . [which] provide the explanatory link between more descriptive and general omnibus context and specific organizational behavior and attitudes.

Similarly, Rousseau and Fried (2001: 4) suggested,

> Whether circumstances intersect in ways that are fortuitous, fearful, or somewhat in between, a configuration of facts may be necessary to understand their meaning. A set of factors, when considered together, can sometimes yield a more interpretable and theoretically interesting pattern than any of the factors would show in isolation. All studies omit variables. But when neglected variables are causally significant, their omission creates problems in interpreting results. . . . Taking a richer slice of the organizational setting, its practices, and how people react to them is necessary to identify effects that derive from configurations and more detailed descriptions of settings and their distinct features can help us identify what those configurations comprise.

This view leads to a second question: *is creative leadership located in the omnibus context, the discrete context, or in one of their configurations?* Theoretically, all leadership must ultimately belong to a complex configuration that spans and connects the two levels of the context and the behaviors and attitudes that they influence (Blair & Hunt, 1986; Heath & Sitkin, 2001; Johns, 2006). For example, Osborn et al. (2002: 798) suggested that leadership

> is socially constructed in and from a context where patterns over time must be considered and where history matters. Leadership is not only

the incremental influence of a boss toward subordinates, but most important it is the collective incremental influence of leaders in and around the system.

More often than not, however, creative leadership research takes into account only selected contextual aspects. Research on Facilitative creative leadership focuses on the discrete context, especially the social context. This body of research treats employee creativity as the dependent variable and works backward to identify personal and contextual characteristics that affect it (Zhou & Shalley, 2008: 351). Creative leadership is viewed as one of the most important elements of the social context that affects employee creativity (Amabile et al., 2004; Anderson, Potočnik, & Zhou, 2014; Hunter, Bedell, & Mumford, 2007; Zhou & Shalley, 2008). This approach is consistent with interactionist theories of creativity (e.g., Amabile, 1988; Ford, 1996; Woodman, Sawyer, & Griffin, 1993) and with the observation that employee creativity is related more strongly to proximal contextual factors than to distal ones (Shalley, Gilson, & Blum, 2000). Furthermore, by usually focusing sharply on a set of elements in the discrete context, research on Facilitative creative leadership tends to explain with greater psychological precision several micro-dimensions of creative leadership.

On the other hand, this approach does not shed sufficient light on how Facilitative creative leadership is related to the omnibus context. Besides a few seminal exceptions that have addressed aspects of the omnibus context (e.g., organizational downsizing, Amabile & Conti, 1999; cultural values, Shin & Zhou, 2003; educational specialization heterogeneity, Shin & Zhou, 2007; and diversity, Kakarika in Chapter 7 of this volume), most studies in the Facilitative context focus only on the proximal social context and the task context. Creative leadership, however, cannot be fully understood if studied only as an isolated antecedent of employee creative behavior. Put another way, if creative leadership is part of the social context of employee creativity, what constitutes the social and organizational context of creative leadership itself? Engaging with this question; addressing the associated 'who', 'where', and 'when' elements of the omnibus context; and exploring more carefully the links among the omnibus and the discrete levels are important steps toward increasing the contextual sensitivity of this stream of research.

In contrast, research on Directive creative leadership emphasizes the omnibus context. Directive creative leadership is usually manifested in work contexts where there is a substantial overlap between the identity of the organization and the identity of the leader, or/and where the creative leader's personal mark is otherwise visible or recognizable in the final creative product (Mainemelis, Kark, & Epitropaki, 2015). Not surprisingly, many elements of the omnibus context, especially the 'who' of leadership, play a central role in this body of research. Unlike studies in Facilitative contexts, in which the 'who' is nearly always anonymous, studies in Directive contexts provide vivid accounts of eponymous 'who', for example, chefs Ferran Adrià (Svejenova, Planellas, & Vives, 2010), Bernard Loiseau (Paris & Leroy, 2014), Alain Passard (Gomez & Bouty, 2011), René Redzepi (Messeni Petruzzelli, & Savino, 2014), Moreno Cedroni, Davide Scabin (Slavich, Cappetta, & Salvemini, 2014), Daniel Boulud (Inversini, Manzoni, & Salvemini, 2014), Fergus Henderson, Raymon Blanc, Michel Troisgos (Stierand, 2015), and architects Corbusier, Walter Gropius, Sir Edwin Lutyens, Ludwig Mies van de Rohe, Frank Lloyd Wright (Jones, 2010) and Frank Gehry (Bennis, 2003). Even when such studies keep the 'who' anonymous, they usually discuss in detail the leader's professional role, for example, "orchestra conductor" (Faulkner, 1973a; Marotto, Roos, & Victor, 2007) or "Michelin-star chef" (Fauchart & von Hippel, 2008). Because Directive collaborative contexts are usually associated with institutionalized and stratified settings with well-defined statuses and roles (Mainemelis, Kark, & Epitropaki, 2015), professional roles usually convey a wealth of information about the leader and the context wherein s/he operates (Johns, 2006).

In order to link the omnibus context with a focal set of behaviors or attitudes, research on Directive creative leadership usually pays attention to various dimensions of the discrete context as well. Although the resulting research may not always have the sharp focus or/and the psychological precision of research in Facilitative contexts, it tends to be more configurational (cf. Rousseau & Fried, 2001) and more informative about the vital connections among intrapersonal, interpersonal, organizational, and institutional factors (see, for example, Faulkner, 1973b; Marotto, Roos, & Victor, 2007; and Stierand, 2015). On the other hand, because research on Directive creative leadership is often conducted in settings described as institutionalized or/and stratified, the generalizability of its findings is often more limited or/ and not always clear.

Finally, research on Integrative creative leadership tends to focus more on configurations of omnibus and discrete elements. In Integrative contexts, creativity depends upon the creative synthesis of multiple and heterogeneous creative contributions made by the leader and the followers (Mainemelis, Kark, & Epitropaki, 2015). Research on Integrative creative leadership often examines temporary projects (e.g., filmmaking, opera, theater, video game production), where the leader is directly involved in forming the temporary collective and thereafter managing its relationships with internal and external constituencies. This body of research pays attention to dynamic processes and network exchanges that run through the omnibus and discrete levels and the external environment as well. In fact, creative leadership in this literature is often portrayed as a grand effort to configure human, symbolic, and technical capital sourced from inside and outside the organization (e.g., Lampel & Shamsie, 2003; Obstfeld, 2012; Perretti & Negro, 2007). For example, Lingo and O'Mahony's (2010) study of nexus practices illustrates how creative leaders form novel creative collectives that encompass various omnibus, discrete, and other external elements; and how they later utilize the power associated with their position in the temporary network in order to navigate relational tensions and other challenging professional exchanges.

Other studies focus more on collective forms of creative leadership in Integrative contexts. In this case, the integration of heterogeneous creative inputs into a final creative product is not an act of single leadership, but an act of dual (e.g., Alvarez & Svejenova, 2002; Hunter et al., 2012; Sicca, 1997), rotated (e.g., Barrett, 1998; Davis & Eisenhardt, 2011), or shared leadership (e.g., Hargadon & Bechky, 2006; Harvey, 2014; Harvey & Kou, 2013). In any case, this research stream tends to focus more on fluid processes and their configurations and less on static elements of either the omnibus or the discrete context. Although research in Integrative contexts is more process-orientated and less static than research in Facilitative contexts, the generalizability of its findings is often more limited due to the temporary, less traditional, and often idiosyncratic nature of the work contexts where it is usually conducted.

Organizational Sources of Contextual Variability

Johns (2006: 386) observed that when empirical results surprise us, it is often because "of our failure to consider contextual influence when doing research". Paying attention to context is therefore essential to understanding the variable exigencies of organizational practice and the variable realities of social structure that influence the phenomena that we investigate (Osborn et al., 2002). This leads to a third question: *which contextual factors influence whether creative leadership will be manifested as Facilitating, Directing, or Integrating?* Put another way, which factors influence the ratios of leader/follower creative contributions and leader/follower supportive contributors? Organizational contexts fall on a continuum from "weakly" to "strongly" structured in terms of how the opportunities for making creative contributions are distributed among the members of the collective (Mainemelis, Kark, & Epitropaki, 2015). The stronger the organizational context, the more *ex-ante* influences it imposes on how creative leadership will be manifested.

Let me return at this point to Porter and McLaughlin's (2006: 573) call for "a concerted effort to focus directly on the nature of the organizational context as a primary object of interest, rather than treating it as almost an afterthought". The three contexts of creative leadership are not organizational contexts themselves, but contexts of creative collaboration nested within organizational contexts (Mainemelis, Kark, & Epitropaki, 2015). What exactly is 'organizational' then about Facilitating, Directing, and Integrating? I suggest next that the three contexts are shaped by different configurations of organizational conditions, as summarized in Table 2.1.

Table 2.1 Organizational Sources of Contextual Variability in Creative Leadership

Organizational Dimensions	*Creative Leadership Contexts*		
	Facilitating	*Directing*	*Integrating*
Strategic role of creativity	Usually not central to the organization	Central to the identity of the organization	Central to the products of the organization
Functional role of creativity	Problem searching and problem solving; more creative ideas, more often, by more people	Craft, maintain, and evolve an authentic creative identity	Creative synthesis of multiple heterogeneous contributions
Key learning mode	Separation	Codification and teachability	Recombination
Structure	Usually permanent, usually hierarchical	Usually permanent, usually institutionalized or/and stratified	Usually temporary, often networked, often egalitarian
Size	Any	Usually small	Usually small
Key location in the social structure	Organizational positions	Usually professional roles	Usually professional roles
Perceived importance of creativity in leadership	Creativity is usually not seen as essential to leadership	Creativity is usually seen as essential to leadership	Creativity is usually seen as essential to leadership
Ex-ante normative expectations about creative leadership	More creative contributions from the followers, more supportive contributions from the leader	More creative contributions from the leader, more supportive contributions from the followers	Creative and supportive contributions from both the leader(s) and the followers, synthesis from the leader(s)

Some organizations (e.g., movie companies, music companies, theaters, video game companies) depend on the ongoing creation of new products that are complex and require substantial degrees of creativity (e.g., movies, music records). Because these products require distinct creative contributions made by different professionals, creativity usually takes the form of a higher order synthesis of heterogeneous creative inputs. In such organizations, learning is usually achieved through the recombination of human capital (Grabher, 2004), work takes the form of a temporary project that is usually small in size and often has a networked form, professional roles tend to be more important than fixed organizational positions (Bechky, 2006), collaborative climate is often egalitarian, and leadership may take the form of a single leader (e.g., Lingo, 2010; Mainemelis & Epitropaki, 2013), dual (e.g., Hunter et al., 2012; Sicca, 1997), rotated (e.g., Davis & Eisenhardt, 2011), or shared leadership (e.g., Harvey, 2014; Harvey & Kou, 2013). In such organizational contexts, creativity is usually seen as essential to leadership, regardless of whether leadership is single, dual, rotated, or shared. When these factors are present in the organizational context, it is more likely that the collaborative context will be Integrative, that is, it will place *ex-ante normative expectations* upon the leader(s) and the followers to make both creative and supportive contributions, and upon the leader(s) to be in charge of the synthesis of the heterogeneous inputs.

In contrast, in other organizations creativity is central not only to the products but also to the identity of the organization, and, furthermore, there is often a close relationship between the identity of the creative leader and the identity of the organization (Jones, Anand, & Alvarez, 2005). The functional role of creativity in such organizational contexts (e.g., haute cuisine, boutique architectural firms) is not to produce diverse new ideas per se, but rather, to strengthen the development and maintenance of an authentic creative identity that permeates all aspects of the organization's existence. The key organizational learning modes, codification, and teachability, ensure that the creative vision and personal 'signature' of the creative leader are replicated in all products generated by the followers in the work context (Slavich, Cappetta, & Salvemini, 2014; see also Chapter 9 in this volume). Such organizational contexts tend to be highly institutionalized or/and stratified, more hierarchical than egalitarian, small and permanent in structural terms, and professional roles in them tend to be more important than organizational positions. Creativity in such organizational contexts is usually perceived as essential to leadership. When these factors are present in the organizational context, it is more likely that the collaborative context will be Directive; that is, it will place *ex-ante normative expectations* upon the leader to make more creative contributions and upon the followers to make more supportive contributions.

Finally, in many organizations creativity is not central to the identity of the organization or its products, although it might be important in some of its units or operations. Creativity here takes the more free-flowing form of problem-searching and problem-solving through enhanced autonomy (e.g., Amabile et al., 1996), and/or the form of more structured organizational practices, such as brainstorming (e.g., Sutton & Hargadon, 1996) and idea suggestions schemes (e.g., Frese, Teng, & Wijnen, 1999). Such organizational contexts seek to elicit more creative ideas, more often, by more people in the work context. In order to increase the number of creative ideas, such organizations cannot depend only on the leader or any other given individual. Rather, they have to promote creativity more broadly among employees. These contexts tend to be permanent; more hierarchical; and in them organizational positions tend to be more important than professional roles. Such contexts tend to pursue creativity by separating people so that they can be creative through different pathways (Grabher, 2004). More often than not, leader creativity in such contexts is not seen as essential to leadership, however, leadership is often seen as essential to fostering employee creativity. When these factors are present in the organizational context, it is more likely that the collaborative context will be Facilitative, that is, it will place *ex-ante normative expectations* upon the leader to make more supportive contributions and upon the followers to make more creative contributions.

Table 2.1 summarizes the organizational sources of contextual variability in creative leadership. I clarify that by calling them 'organizational' I do not mean to understate the influences of the larger contexts wherein organizations and their members are embedded, such as industries, fields, and professions. Rather, I assume that these influences are absorbed to some extent by the organizational context; they interact with other unique factors in it, such as elements of the organizational culture; and they are exerted upon the collaborative dynamics of creativity in the organizational context in uniquely patterned ways. In addition, I do not mean to underplay the importance of personal factors in shaping the emergence of the three collaborative contexts. Rather, I assume that the 'stronger' the organizational context, the less likely that the personal characteristics of the leader will determine ex-ante whether the collaborative context will take the form of Facilitating, Directing, and Integrating. I also assume that there is substantial between-person variability within the same context and that individual leadership styles play a role in this respect, as Chapter 14 in this volume suggests. That said, I wish to emphasize, first, the role of the organizational context as a source of variability in creative leadership, and second, the fact that, as the organizational structure becomes stronger, the emergence of the three collaborative contexts is shaped more by a set of variable contextual factors and less by a set of contextually invariable leadership styles.

Conclusion

In light of recent evidence that the manifestations of creative leadership vary substantially across contexts, I have argued that creative leadership research needs to improve both the degree of contextualization of its studies and its overall awareness of the role of contextual variability. With regard to the latter, I have suggested that the multi-context model offers a metatheoretical platform for analyzing and integrating patterns of contextual differences observed in the literature. I have offered a set of insights about what constitutes context in creative leadership, its level and configurations, and the basic organizational sources of variability in creative leadership.

Although the arguments summarized in Table 2.1 are grounded in the extant literature (see Mainemelis, Kark, & Epitropaki, 2015), future research should examine empirically their validity, and develop and further refine them. For example, while Chapters 11 and 12 in this volume examine

Integrative creative leadership, they focus on different structural configurations: the former focuses more on stable structures and the latter more on temporary structures. Future research could enhance our understanding of creative leadership by examining in more fine-grained ways such differences within and between the three contexts. In addition, while I have focused more on organizational sources of variability, future research could elaborate on the multi-context model in order examine other contextual and personal differences within and among the three contexts.

In conclusion, Porter and McLaughlin (2006: 574) argued that research should pay more attention to the dynamic aspects and processes of organizational contexts. As they put it, "In effect, there is a need to build more movies rather than just snapshots" (574). In this chapter, I have suggested that the multi-context model offers to creative leadership researchers a metatheoretical conceptual tool that they can use in order to make such composite 'movies' out of numerous research snapshots.

References

Alvarez, J. L., & Svejenova, S. 2002. Symbiotic careers in movie making: Pedro and Augustin Almodovar. In M. Peiperl, M. Arthur, & N. Anand (Eds.), *Career creativity: Explorations in the remaking of work*: 183–208. New York: Oxford University Press.

Amabile, T. M. 1988. A model of creativity and innovation in organizations. *Research in Organizational Behavior*, 10: 123–167.

Amabile, T. M., & Conti, R. 1999. Changes in the work environment during downsizing. *Academy of Management Journal*, 42: 630–640.

Amabile, T. M., Conti, R., Coon, H., Lazenby, J., & Herron, M. 1996. Assessing the work environment for creativity. *Academy of Management Journal*, 39: 1154–1184.

Amabile, T. M., Schatzel, E. A., Moneta, G. B., & Kramer, S. J. 2004. Leader behaviors and the work environment for creativity: Perceived leader support. *The Leadership Quarterly*, 15: 5–32.

Anderson, N., Potočnik, K., & Zhou, J. 2014. Innovation and creativity in organizations: A state-of-the-science review, prospective commentary, and guiding framework. *Journal of Management*, 40: 1297–1333.

Bacharach, S. B. 1989. Organizational theories: Some criteria for evaluation. *Academy of Management Review*, 14: 496–515.

Barrett, F. J. 1998. Creativity and improvisation in jazz and organizations: Implications for organizational learning. *Organization Science*, 9: 605–622.

Bechky, B. A. 2006. Gaffers, gofers, and grips: Role-based coordination in temporary organizations. *Organization Science*, 17: 3–21.

Bennis, W. 2003. Frank Gehry: Artist, leader, and "neotenic". *Journal of Management Inquiry*, 12: 81–87.

Blair, J. D., & Hunt, J. G. 1986. Getting inside the head of the management researcher one more time: Context-free and context-specific orientations in research. *Journal of Management*, 12: 147–166.

Bouty, I., & Gomez, M-L. 2010. Dishing up individual and collective dimensions in organizational knowing. *Management Learning*, 41: 545–559.

Davis, J. P., & Eisenhardt, K. M. 2011. Rotating leadership and collaborative innovation: Recombination processes in symbiotic relationships. *Administrative Science Quarterly*, 56: 159–201.

Fauchart, E., & von Hippel, E. 2008. Norms-based intellectual property systems: The case of French chefs. *Organization Science*, 19: 187–201.

Faulkner, R. R. 1973a. Orchestra interaction: Some features of communication and authority in an artistic organization. *The Sociological Quarterly*, 14: 147–157.

Faulkner, R. R. 1973b. Career concerns and mobility motivations of orchestra musicians. *The Sociological Quarterly*, 14: 334–349.

Ford, C. M. 1996. A theory of individual creative action in multiple social domains. *Academy of Management Review*, 21: 1112–1142.

Frese, M., Teng, E., & Wijnen, C. J. 1999. Helping to improve suggestion systems: Predictors of making suggestions in companies. *Journal of Organizational Behavior*, 20, 1139–1155.

Gomez, M-L., & Bouty, I. 2011. The emergence of an influential practice: Food for thought. *Organization Studies*, 32: 921–940.

Grabher, G. 2004. Temporary architectures of learning: Knowledge governance in project ecologies. *Organization Studies*, 25: 1491–1514.

Hargadon, A. B., & Bechky, B. A. 2006. When collections of creatives become creative collectives: A field study of problem solving at work. *Organization Science*, 17: 484–500.

Harvey, S. 2014. Creative synthesis: Exploring the process of extraordinary group creativity. *Academy of Management Review*, 39: 324–343.

Harvey, S., & Kou, C. 2013. Collective engagement in creative tasks: The role of evaluation in the creative process of groups. *Administrative Science Quarterly*, 58: 346–386.

Heath, C., & Sitkin, S. B. 2001. Big-B versus Big-O: What is organizational about organizational behavior? *Journal of Organizational Behavior*, 22: 43–58.

Hunter, S. T., Bedell, K. E., & Mumford, M. D. 2007. Climate for creativity: A quantitative review. *Creativity Research Journal*, 19: 69–90.

Hunter, S. T., Cushenbery, L., Fairchild, J., & Boatman, J. 2012. Partnerships in leading for innovation: A dyadic model of collective leadership. *Industrial and Organizational Psychology: Perspectives on Science and Practice*, 5: 424–428.

Inversini, M., Manzoni, B., & Salvemini, S. 2014. Daniel Boulud: The making of a successful creative individual business model. *International Journal of Arts Management*, 16: 55–63.

Johns, G. 2006. The essential impact of context on organizational behavior. *Academy of Management Review*, 31: 386–408.

Jones, C. 2010. Finding a place in history: Symbolic and social networks in creative careers and collective memory. *Journal of Organizational Behavior*, 31: 726–748.

Jones, C., Anand, N., & Alvarez, J. L. 2005. Manufactured authenticity and creative voice in cultural industries. *Journal of Management Studies*, 42: 893–899.

Lampel, J., & Shamsie, J. 2003. Capabilities in motion: New organizational forms and the reshaping of the Hollywood movie industry. *Journal of Management Studies*, 40: 2189–2210.

Liden, R. C., & Antonakis, J. 2009. Considering context in psychological leadership research. *Human Relations*, 62(11): 1587–1605.

Lingo, E. L., & O'Mahony, S. 2010. Nexus work: Brokerage on creative projects. *Administrative Science Quarterly*, 55: 47–81.

Lord, R. G., Brown, D. J., Harvey, J. L., & Hall, R. J. 2001. Contextual constraints on prototype generation and their multilevel consequences for leadership perceptions. *Leadership Quarterly*, 12: 311–338.

Madjar, N., Oldham, G. R., & Pratt, M. G. 2002. There's no place like home? The contributions of work and nonwork creativity support to employees' creative performance. *Academy of Management Journal*, 45: 757–767.

Mainemelis, C., & Epitropaki, O. 2013. Extreme leadership as creative leadership: Reflections on Francis Ford Coppola in The Godfather. In C. Giannantonio & A. Hurley-Hanson (Eds.), *Extreme leadership: Leaders, teams, and situations outside the norm*: 187–200. Northampton, MA: Edward Elgar Publishing.

Mainemelis, C., Kark, R., & Epitropaki, O. 2015. Creative leadership: A multi-context conceptualization. *Academy of Management Annals*, 9: 393–482.

Marotto, M., Roos, J., & Victor, B. 2007. Collective virtuosity in organizations: A study of peak performance in an orchestra. *Journal of Management Studies*, 44: 388–413.

Messeni Petruzzelli, A., & Savino, T. 2014. Search, recombination, and innovation: Lessons from haute cuisine. *Long Range Planning*, 47: 224–238.

Mowday, R. T., & Sutton, R. I. 1993. Organizational behavior: Linking individuals and groups to organizational contexts. *Annual Review of Psychology*, 44: 195–229.

Murnighan, J. K., & Conlon, D. E. 1991. The dynamics of intense work groups: A study of British string quartets. *Administrative Science Quarterly*, 36: 165–186.

Obstfeld, D. 2012. Creative projects: A less routine approach toward getting new things done. *Organization Science*, 23: 1571–1592.

Oldham, G. R., & Cummings, A. 1996. Employee creativity: Personal and contextual factors at work. *Academy of Management Journal*, 39: 607–634.

Osborn, R. N., Hunt, J. G., & Jauch, L. R. 2002. Toward a contextual theory of leadership. *Leadership Quarterly*, 13: 797–837.

Paris, T., & Leroy, F. 2014. Managing transition in an artistic company with entrepreneurial management: A case study of Groupe Bernard Loiseau. *International Journal of Arts Management*, 16: 42–53.

Perretti, F., & Negro, G. 2007. Mixing genres and matching people: A study in innovation and team composition in Hollywood. *Journal of Organizational Behavior*, 28: 563–586.

Porter, L. W., & McLaughlin, G. B. 2006. Leadership and the organizational context: Like the weather? *Leadership Quarterly*, 17: 559–576.

Rousseau, D. M., & Fried, Y. 2001. Location, location, location: Contextualizing organizational research. *Journal of Organizational Behavior*, 22: 1–13.

Sergeeva, A., & Andreeva, T. 2016. Knowledge sharing research: Bringing context back in. *Journal of Management Inquiry*, 25(3): 240–261.

Shalley, C. E., Gilson, L. L., & Blum, T. C. 2000. Matching creativity requirements and the work environment: Effects on satisfaction and intentions to leave. *Academy of Management Journal*, 43: 215–223.

Shin, S. J., & Zhou, J. 2003. Transformational leadership, conservation and creativity: Evidence from Korea. *Academy of Management Journal*, 46: 703–714.

Shin, S. J., & Zhou, J. 2007. When is educational specialization heterogeneity related to creativity in research and development teams? Transformational leadership as a moderator. *Journal of Applied Psychology*, 92: 1709–1721.

Sicca, L. M. 1997. Management of Opera Houses: The Italian experience of the "Enti Autonomi". *International Journal of Cultural Policy*, 4: 201–224.

Simonton, D. K. 2002. Collaborative aesthetics in the feature film: Cinematic components predicting the differential impact of 2,323 Oscar-nominated movies. *Empirical Studies of the Arts*, 20: 115–125.

Simonton, D. K. 2004a. Film awards as indicators of cinematic creativity and achievement: A quantitative comparison of the Oscars and six alternatives. *Creativity Research Journal*, 16: 163–172.

Simonton, D. K. 2004b. Group artistic creativity: Creative clusters and cinematic success in feature films. *Journal of Applied Social Psychology*, 34: 1494–1152.

Slavich, B., Cappetta, R., & Salvemini, S. 2014. Creativity and the reproduction of cultural products: The experience of Italian haute cuisine chefs. *International Journal of Arts Management*, 16: 29–41.

Stierand, M. 2015. Developing creativity in practice: Explorations with world-renowned chefs. *Management Learning*, 46(5): 598–617.

Sutton, R. I., & Hargadon, A. 1996. Brainstorming groups in context: Effectiveness in a product design firm. *Administrative Science Quarterly*, 41: 685–718.

Svejenova, S., Planellas, M., & Vives, L. 2010. An individual business model in the making: A chef's quest for creative freedom. *Long Range Planning*, 43: 408–430.

Thomson, P., Jones, M., & Warhurst, C. 2007. From conception to consumption: Creativity and the missing managerial link. *Journal of Organizational Behavior*, 28: 625–640.

Woodman, R. W., Sawyer, J. E., & Griffin, R. W. 1993. Toward a theory of organizational creativity. *Academy of Management Review*, 18: 293–321.

Zhou, J., & Shalley, C. E. 2008. Expanding the scope and impact of organizational creativity research. In J. Zhou & C. E. Shalley (Eds.), *Handbook of organizational creativity*: 347–368. New York: Lawrence Erlbaum Associates.

3 Unpacking the Socio-cognitive Foundations of Creative Leadership

Bridging Implicit Leadership and Implicit Creativity Theories

Olga Epitropaki, Jennifer S. Mueller, and Robert G. Lord

Introduction

In their review of creative leadership, Mainemelis, Kark, and Epitropaki (2015) observed a literature paradox with regard to creativity and leadership. On the one hand, prior studies (e.g., Mumford et al., 2000; Sternberg, 2007) and practitioner literature have highlighted the importance of creativity for leadership; on the other hand, dominant leadership schemas do not include creativity as an attribute of leadership (e.g., Epitropaki et al., 2013; Lord, Foti, & DeVader, 1984; Offermann Kennedy, & Wirtz, 1994) and studies have shown that creativity may even harm an individual's chances to be promoted to leadership positions (e.g., Mueller, Goncalo, & Kamdar, 2011). But has the relationship between creativity and leadership always been so tenuous? Interestingly no. Early studies have seen creativity and leadership as two sides of the same coin: 'genius'. In his book *Genius, Creativity and Leadership*, D. K. Simonton (1984: 1) viewed creativity and leadership as the two main paths toward greatness and making history. He characteristically noted,

> History . . . is molded by the personalities and accomplishments of certain exceptional individuals. These outstanding historical figures make history in one of two major ways. On the one hand there are the *creators*, who make lasting contributions to human culture, whether as scientists, philosophers, writers, composers or artists. Creators of the stature of Einstein, Sartre, Joyce, Stravinsky and Picasso have left a durable impression on the thoughts and sensitivities of innumerable men and women. On the other hand there are *leaders*, who transform the world by their deeds rather than by their ideas or emotional expressions. Leaders of the calibre of Hitler, Stalin, Franklin D. Roosevelt and Mao Tse-tung have made a permanent mark upon the course that history has taken.

One of the earliest attempts to explore the commonalities between leadership and creativity can be traced back to Thorndike's (1950) work on *creators* and *leaders*. By examining 91 historical figures on 48 characteristics, four dimensions emerged: industriousness, extraversion, aggressiveness and intelligence. Two out of these four dimensions were found to be identical (and transhistorically invariant) across both *leaders* and *creators*: intelligence and aggressiveness (Simonton, 1991). Simonton (1991) further highlighted the commonalities between the two constructs and suggested that "sometimes creativity and leadership combine into a unified phenomenon, such as *creative leadership*" (68). He further declared, "If creativity and leadership reach extraordinary dimensions, a single term may be applied to both—*genius*" (68). Despite these early attempts to bridge creativity and leadership, the two research streams gradually grew apart, leading Simonton to comment in 1991, "It has become customary to treat creativity and leadership as if they are rather separate behavioral phenomena" (67). Thirty years later, this gap still prevails.

In the socio-cognitive domain of leadership perceptions and schemas in particular, leadership and creativity remain not only separate but even contradictory notions. There is a striking absence of the trait 'creative' from existing operationalizations of leadership schemas (e.g., Epitropaki & Martin, 2004; Epitropaki et al., 2013; Lord, Foti, & De Vader, 1984; Offermann, Kennedy, & Wirtz, 1994), and creative individuals are less likely to emerge as leaders (Kark et al., 2014; Mueller, Goncalo, & Kamdar, 2011). Interestingly enough, in Lord, Foti, and De Vade's (1984) list of prototypical attributes, the trait "creative" was included in the *non-leader* attributes list, which clearly implies that creativity is not perceived as a core characteristic of leadership (Epitropaki et al., 2013). Even in the context of creative industries where creativity is a salient attribute, the roles of the *leader* and the *creator* are many times kept separate. It is not uncommon for creative organizations to separate the creator and manager roles purposefully so that creators can specialize in generating novel ideas and managers can decide whether these ideas are going to be implemented (Benner & Tushman, 2003; Berg, 2016). As Berg (2016) notes, we many times observe an interesting oxymoron in creative settings: "many managers get promoted into management positions based on their success as creators [and] once they become managers, they often spend more time evaluating others' ideas than generating their own" (436). How can we, thus, resolve this incongruity and bridge the seemingly separate worlds of leadership and creativity?

In this chapter, we will argue that socio-cognitive approaches to leadership (e.g., Epitropaki & Martin, 2004; 2005; Epitropaki et al., 2013; Lord & Maher, 1991; Lord, Foti, & DeVader, 1984; Shondrick, Dinh, & Lord, 2010; Shondrick & Lord, 2010) and creativity (e.g., Christensen, Drewsen, & Maaløe, 2014; Hass, 2014; Mueller, Goncalo, & Kamdar, 2011; Sternberg, 1985) may help us resolve the observed creative leadership contradictions in the extant literature and managerial practice. We will first examine Implicit Leadership and Creativity Theories (ILTs vs. ICTs) content to examine points of convergence vs. divergence. We will then discuss recent dynamic views of cognitive structures and schemas that allow for higher context-sensitivity and plasticity and conclude the chapter by discussing implications for creative leadership.

Implicit Theories of Leadership and Creativity

Implicit theories are generally defined as a constellation of ideas individuals hold about a particular construct or lay beliefs about a particular phenomenon (e.g., Sternberg & Davidson, 1986). In the leadership field, ILTs have been defined as cognitive structures that are developed through socialization processes and specify the traits and attributes that characterize leaders (Lord, Foti, & DeVader, 1984; Lord & Maher, 1991). Lord, Foti, and DeVader (1984) were the first to generate a pool of 59 leader attributes (e.g., intelligent, honest, educated and dedicated) and further found that these traits differed in the level of prototypicality—i.e., the degree they matched the image of a leader participants had in mind. Some traits, such as *intelligent, honest, understanding, determined, decisive* were highly prototypical, others such as *happy, high achiever* were neutral while another category of traits such as *authoritarian* and *dishonest*, were antiprototypical. They further identified 26 non-leader attributes such as *easy going*, *investigative* and *creative*. Thus, in this first ILTs list, creativity is explicitly identified as a non-leader trait. Later, studies identified factors of positive or prototypical traits including intelligence, sensitivity, dedication, strength, attractiveness, charisma and dynamism (Epitropaki & Martin, 2004; Offermann, Kennedy, & Wirtz, 1994), as well as factors of negative or antiprototypical traits such as tyranny and masculinity (Offermann, Kennedy, & Wirtz, 1994). The GLOBE study in 62 different countries (House et al., 1999, 2004) identified six global dimensions of Culturally Implicit Leadership Theories (CILTs), namely, Charismatic/Value-Based, Team-Oriented, Self-Protective, Participative, Humane and Autonomous. They also listed 21 universal positive leader attributes (e.g., honest, dynamic, intelligent, motive arouser, etc.), eight universal negative leader attributes (e.g., loner, ruthless, dictatorial, etc.) and 35 specific leader characteristics that are viewed as positive in some cultures and negative in others—i.e., they are culturally contingent (e.g., ambitious, individualistic, compassionate, domineering, etc.). Once again, creativity does not appear as a leadership characteristic (neither emic or etic) in the GLOBE study. Only certain creativity-related traits such as *risk taker*, *provocateur* and *unique* are found in the list of leader attributes that vary across cultures (Den Hartog et al., 1999).

The importance of these leadership prototypes for the exercise of leadership in real-world contexts is critical. According to leader categorization theory (Lord & Maher, 1991), perceivers compare stimuli from the target individual (e.g., their direct manager, their CEO or a political leader) to the attributes of the abstract leadership prototype. If there is a *perceived match* between the target person and the leadership prototype the follower holds in memory, then the target is more likely to be seen as a leader that deserves the follower's respect and trust. The follower will also be more willing to make the extra effort to develop high quality of exchanges with the leader and deliver superior organizational outcomes (Epitropaki & Martin, 2005). The absence of *creativity* (or of similar traits) as a salient trait of the abstract leader prototype (and its existence in the non-leader category) suggest two possible outcomes with regard to leader categorization: creativity will either be totally discounted by perceivers when they evaluate leaders or will influence them negatively.

A relevant study in this context is that conducted by Mueller, Goncalo, and Kamdar (2011) who tested whether the expression of a creative idea would indeed negatively relate to perceptions of leadership potential. They first showed that engineers working in a company where creativity was encouraged and desired, who were rated as generating more creative ideas by their supervisors, were also rated as having lower leadership potential by these same supervisors. To address directionality (e.g., whether expressing creative ideas influenced perceived leadership potential, or perceived leadership potential influenced expressing creative ideas) the authors conducted a laboratory experiment where university students were randomly assigned to pitch either a creative or practical idea to observers, who then assessed the students' leadership potential. The authors showed that those instructed to pitch a creative idea were seen as having lower leadership potential relative to those instructed to pitch a practical idea. It was only when the "charismatic" leader prototype was activated in a third study that the authors showed that leadership perceptions were not completely incompatible with expressing a creative idea. When participants were primed to think of a charismatic leader relative to a leader, they viewed a fictional person expressing a creative idea as having higher levels of leadership potential.

Let us now examine more closely dominant creativity schemas or Implicit Creativity Theories (ICTs). ICTs have been described as the "unique theories of the causal nature and structure in describing creativity and creative persons" (Lee et al., 2013: 77). Research has generally shown that people have implicit theories that creative people have positive traits. For example, Sternberg (1985) showed that most groups believed creative people were *intelligent* and *wise*. Runco and colleagues (Runco & Bahleda, 1986; Runco & Johnson, 2002; Runco, Johnson, & Bear, 1993) have conducted numerous studies showing that while some of the specific traits might differ across domain (e.g., in the arts vs. science), creative people were viewed as having a host of positive traits including (but not limited to): *open-minded*, *imaginative*, *intelligent*, *curious* and *resourceful*. Hass (2014) found evidence that across different domains (e.g., science and the arts), creative people were seen to have the ability to integrate disparate information, to be intellectual and productive as well as possess a high IQ level. Christensen and colleagues found that across many different job advertisements in an

English and Danish sample, people associated "openness to experience" with being a creative person (Christensen, Drewsen, & Maaløe, 2014).

However a closer look at the research also shows a second, albeit much less consistent pattern—a dark side of being seen as creative. First, while Sternberg (1985) noted that while professors in philosophy, physics and art viewed wisdom as positively related to creativity, professors in business viewed wisdom as negatively related to creativity. Other classical work has shown that those with a creative personality have many wonderful traits such as being *clever, insightful*, and *resourceful*, are also viewed as *egotistical snobbish* and *unmannerly* (Gough, 1979). Elsbach and Kramer (2003) identified that, for the most part, creative people were viewed positively except for those categorized as "artists" who were seen as *brilliant* but also *obscure, poor at business, extreme* and *quirky*. Runco and Johnson (2002) showed cross-cultural evidence that people believe creative students have a host of largely positive traits, except that they are also *impulsive*. And while some work shows that teachers say they value creativity and teaching creative students, they also view students who perform well on creative thinking tests as *disobedient* and *unpleasant to teach* (Westby & Dawson, 1995). This dark side of creativity schemas may help us understand the observed gap between creativity and leadership. Traits such as *impulsive, disobedient, poor at business* and *unmannerly* are clearly antithetical to notions of leadership that highlight decision making, structure, task and people orientation.

In the ICTs literature another interesting idea has been explored: while we know that people have implicit beliefs about creative people, do they also have implicit beliefs about creative ideas? Scholars widely agree that creative ideas are defined as products or processes that are both novel and useful (Amabile, 1996). However, the question remains whether the average lay person also agrees with this scientific definition of creativity. The discussion of implicit theories of creative ideas has early roots in work by Teresa Amabile who in her classical paper on the "social psychology of creativity" introduces the conceptual assessment technique—a gold standard approach to measuring creativity (Amabile, 1982). When describing the method she notes, "basically, the method requires that all judges be familiar enough with the domain to have developed, over a period of time, some implicit criteria for creativity, technical goodness and so on" (1002). In this way, Amabile introduces the idea that there can be scholarly definitions of creativity that are explicit and that we may assume that these explicit scholarly definitions also reflect implicit beliefs people have about creativity. In later years, when research began to discover that people can disagree about whether certain idea cues indicate creativity (Paletz & Peng, 2008), this provided the first evidence that people's explicit and scholarly conceptualizations of creativity may not match people's implicit beliefs about creativity. Indeed, Loewenstein and Mueller (2016) attempted to map out a comprehensive model of the implicit theories seen to indicate creativity in the United States and China. The authors noted that these implicit beliefs bore relatively little resemblance to the explicit scholarly theories in the creativity literature. Indeed, some participants viewed the fact that an idea has 'mass market appeal', or 'technology' as indicative of creativity—neither feature reflects whether ideas are novel or useful. This finding is reminiscent of classical work in the domain of ILTs finding that people viewed a person's height as indicative of leadership—even though whether or not a person was tall bore no resemblance to scholarly conceptual definitions of leadership (Blaker et al., 2013).

Just as there is evidence that expressing a creative idea can harm a person's perceived leadership potential (Mueller, Goncalo, & Kamdar, 2011), there is also evidence that the mere fact that an idea is novel can harm the likelihood the idea is accepted and embraced. A burgeoning number of studies have identified that people engaged in idea evaluation activities who explicitly purport to desire novelty, reject novel ideas (Boudreau et al., 2016; Criscuolo et al., 2017; Mueller, 2014), without sufficient consideration (Siler, Lee, & Bero, 2015), even when novel ideas are also high in quality (Boudreau et al., 2016). To address the puzzle of why people desire but reject creative ideas, Mueller, Melwani, and Goncalo (2012) identified that participants primed with a mindset around uncertainty intolerance explicitly stated that they valued creativity, similar to participants primed with a mindset around uncertainty tolerance. However, those primed with uncertainty intolerance also showed faster reaction times when pairing words like 'vomit' with creativity and words like 'heaven' with practicality, and, subsequently, downgraded an idea as being less 'creative' relative to participants in the uncertainty tolerance condition. Said differently, participants in the uncertainty tolerance condition exhibited positive explicit and implicit associations with creativity. In contrast, participants in the uncertainty intolerance condition showed evidence of positive explicit attitudes toward creativity and negative implicit attitudes toward creativity, and had a harder time recognizing a creative idea. In sum, it follows that if people experience a bias against creativity because they are in a mindset that prioritizes certainty and correctness in decision making, they may be more likely to have an automatic negative association with creativity and so downgrade creative ideas.

What are the implications for these implicit theories of creative ideas for leadership perceptions and the exercise of leadership? As noted in prior sections, prototypical leaders are expected to promote group order and diminish uncertainty by emphasizing shared goals (Phillips & Lord, 1981). Indeed, prototypical leadership traits involve being seen as "decisive" and "directive" and so knowing answers to problems (Lord, Foti, & de Vader, 1984). In contrast, creative ideas have uncertain feasibility and unproven value (Klein & Knight, 2005; Van de Ven, 1988); hence, expressing creative ideas, one hallmark of being seen as a creative person, may actually introduce ambiguity or uncertainty into the group, something which runs contrary to the prototypical views of leadership.

In sum, when we closely examine the content of ILTs as well as of ICTs and implicit theories of creative ideas, we get a better understanding of the tension between the two concepts. Whereas novelty, esthetic taste and imagination, as well as nonconformity and ambiguity prevail in the world of ICTs, structure, reliability, results and people focus are found in the world of ILTs, making the two worlds hard to converge. One possibility that creativity can relate positively to perceptions of leadership was shown but only when people have already demonstrated prototypical leadership traits (e.g., charisma). Correspondingly, the relationship between expressing a creative idea and leadership perceptions might be dependent upon whether the person expressing the idea is already in a leadership role, as those in leadership roles may be seen as already having demonstrated success, and so may not evoke the same level of uncertainty in others minds when they express an idea that is new and unproven (Kark et al., 2014). Mueller, Goncalo, and Kamdar (2011), examined "leadership potential"—instances when study participants and vignette actors were not yet in a leadership role, and so cannot speak to the possibility that having a positive track record (e.g., being in a leadership position) might shift whether people view the expression of a creative idea as a positive indicator of leadership. Another boundary condition of the Mueller, Goncalo, and Kamdar (2011) study is that they examined idea expression—not whether participants had a reputation of being creative generally. In an unpublished study, Mueller and Goncalo identified that participants viewed a job applicant as more leader-like when the applicant's resume stated he/she was creative versus when the applicant's resume stated he/she was practical. This finding suggests that having a reputation as a being a creative person might help a person achieve a leadership role.

Dynamic Views of Implicit Theories and Schemas

New theoretical developments in the implicit theories literature can perhaps offer a basis for a higher level of convergence between creativity and leadership domains. The *connectionist perspective* (Brown & Lord, 2001; Hanges, Lord, Godfrey, & Raver, 2002; Lord, Brown, & Harvey, 2001) is an advancement to previous theoretical interpretations of ILTs due to its focus on the schema activation process. Lord, Brown, and Harvey (2001) argued that leadership categories are *context-sensitive, dynamic* and *flexible* mental representations that can be generated in real-time ("on the fly") as a response to contextual factors (e.g., task, organization or industry related). Connectionist networks are "networks of neuron-like processing units that continuously integrate information from input sources and pass on the resulting activation (or inhibition) to connected (output) units" (314). An important aspect of these models is that leadership prototypes, which are recurrent networks in which each attribute is connected to other prototypical attributes, serve as integration devices. That is, they are simultaneously influenced by top-down constraints from context (e.g., leaders, followers, groups, affect, culture) and bottom-up features such as the attributes and behaviors of a potential leader. As they become activated, these recurrent networks find the best representation or interpretation of all sources of activation. Because these systems usually complete processing before conscious attentional processes can be activated (Dinh, Lord, & Hoffman, 2014), it is likely that leadership prototypes are constructed in response to stimuli and contextual features primarily through automatic processes.

An important advantage of connectionist networks is that they allow both for stability and for flexibility of schemas. Stability comes from the pattern of connections among prototypical attributes, which changes slowly with experience, whereas flexibility comes from the different patterns of top-down constraints and bottom-up features that activate these networks (Foti, Knee, & Backert, 2008; Sy et al., 2010). They thus allow for a generic leadership schema (that is generalizable across different contexts) existing and of different node activation of the generic schema in different contexts. It is also helpful to consider the role of connectionist systems in explaining creativity in general. Researchers who investigate the operation of complex, adaptive systems (e.g., Page, 2007) emphasize that it is the integration of information from various sources that creates new structures. For example, affective reactions, general knowledge, and episodic memories may be integrated to create new thoughts or visions, which are qualitatively different than their constituent elements. Dehaene (2014) explains that the brain produces such integration all the time as it constructs conscious meaning from the activation of localized units and then feeds this meaning back to tune local units to the global, contextualized interpretation. Consciousness, then, is an emergent output of the interaction of lower level units connected by a global neuronal network. This process directly parallels social perceptions in general (see Freeman & Ambady, 2011) and leadership perceptions in specific, as the meaning created by an integrative connectionist system in each case. It seems reasonable, then, for creativity to follow similar processes.

Connectionist networks are also likely to tune creative processes to particular emotions or patterns of emotions. For example, Bledow, Rosing, and Frese (2013), found that self-reported creativity at the end of an actual work day was enhanced by a pattern of negative emotions in the morning followed by positive emotions later in the day. They explained this effect by noting that negative emotions focus group members on specific details, while positive emotions broaden people's thoughts and the actions they consider (Fredrickson, 2001). Each of these effects can be viewed in terms of emotions setting constraints on how one's context was interpreted, through the general process previously discussed (e.g., Dehaene, 2014). Bledow et al. also replicated these results using an experimental manipulation based on recalling and writing a short essay about an experience that made them feel "afraid, distressed, or nervous" or "happy, inspired, or enthusiastic".

Visser et al. (2013) used an emotional contagion manipulation in which leaders displayed either happy or sad emotions, and then groups performed either analytic or creativity tasks. In two studies using this design, they found that analytic performance was better in the sad conditions, but creative task performance was better in the happy conditions. Moreover, these effects were mediated by follower reports of happy or sad emotions. Again, we might expect that connectionist networks automatically tuned motivational and information processing strategies to the emotions felt by participants. It is not only task and organizational characteristics but also emotions can influence the salience of creativity as a core trait in a leadership connectionist network.

Although, to the best of our knowledge, connectionist models have not been applied in creativity research, there is consistent evidence for domain variation and context-sensitivity of ICTs (e.g., Hass, 2014; Paletz & Peng, 2008). For example, Hass (2014) found differences in creativity trait profiles among artists and scientists and studies have shown cultural variations (e.g., Paletz & Peng, 2008). Mueller, Melwani, Lowenstein, and Deal (2018) recently proposed the *social context model of creative idea recognition*, which notes that a person's social context (e.g., roles, culture) can evoke certain goals (e.g., uncertainty intolerance), which then shapes the kind of features or cues people believe indicate creativity of an idea. Given that people's mindsets can guide the extent to which they label ideas as creative, it is also possible that the question of whether or not expressing a creative idea is viewed as a positive or negative indicator of leadership could also be partially determined by the mindset experienced by the person doing the evaluating. Further, both the traits of the target in question and the mindset of the evaluator may play a joint role. For example, evaluators primed with an intolerance to uncertainty relative to a tolerance to uncertainty might only view the expression of a novel idea as creative and so indicative of leadership if the person in question was already in a leadership role or had proven success. Along similar lines, in their connectionist model, Lord, Brown, and Harvey (2001) highlighted the role of observers' self-schemas, i.e., organized collections of information about some aspect of the self, that can color the interpretations of a target's behavior. If a person views themselves as creative and creativity is a salient trait of their self-schema, they will be more likely to also view creativity as a desired trait of an observed leader.

If context, self-schemas, mindsets and emotions matter for prototype activation, then in organizational contexts where creativity is a desired quality, innovation is a key strategic objective (e.g., creative industries, high technology), positive emotions prevail (e.g., via fun and playful work environments) and organizational actors see themselves as creators, creativity will be automatically activated as a salient trait of leadership. Mainemelis, Kark, and Epitropaki (2015) discussed filmmaking as an interesting context where creativity and leadership coexist. The creative leader, i.e., the director has to generate and communicate a creative vision to the team, inspire creativity from others and synthesize the creative inputs of the team. In certain cases (e.g., F.F. Coppola), the creative product (i.e., the film) is achieved via extreme, unconventional behavior on behalf of the creative leader who deliberately induces tension and destabilizes the team in order to achieve radical innovation (Mainemelis & Epitropaki, 2013). If we think of creativity as movement from a familiar to a novel attractor in a dynamic system, then such destabilization is consistent with dynamic representations of change. For example, Stephen, Dixon, and Isenhower (2009) found that periods of instability and high uncertainty (high entropy in their terms) preceded the emergence of new problem-solving structures.

In other cases (e.g., Kathryn Bigelow), the director/creative leader effectively manages the creativity-leadership paradoxes by exhibiting ambidextrous leadership behaviors with balanced business (e.g., budget, efficiency) and innovation outcomes (Epitropaki & Mainemelis, 2016). Haute cuisine is also another interesting example where creativity is an undeniable characteristic of leadership (e.g., Mainemelis, Kark, & Epitropaki, 2015). Haute cuisine is a highly institutionalized field where one can observe a very clear hierarchical structure. The *creator*, i.e., the chef, is at the top of the hierarchy and is the one that generates the creative ideas and provides direction and leadership to their team to ensure the impeccable reproduction of the new recipes by second chefs and cooks. Other examples of contexts where creativity and leadership converge include the opera, top-down innovation (e.g., Steve Jobs) and entrepreneurship (e.g., Elon Musk). In such environments, creativity will be perceived as a desired quality of leadership (instead of a negative or non-leader trait) and one would expect creativity to be rapidly activated in perceivers' connectionist network of leadership prototypes.

But what happens in traditionally non-creative contexts? Can we observe recent changes in the general ILTs? There is evidence that in addition to the contextual activation of creativity in specific organizational settings, the general leadership prototypes are also changing and recent conceptualizations include creativity as a trait. For example, Offermann and Coats (2018) very recently replicated the original ILTs factor structure of Offermann, Kennedy, and Wirtz (1994) scale but also found a new creativity factor emerging that included four traits: *creative*, *innovative*, *clever* and *courageous*. Offermann and Coats (2018) attributed the emergence of creativity as an ILTs factor in the new samples to the "U.S. economic forces emphasizing innovation as the cure for previous economic malaise, and the role of leaders in developing climates that encourage and promote discovery and invention" (9). In a recent unpublished MSc dissertation, Mueller (2017) explored the implicit leadership theories of millennials and found creativity as an ILTs factor encompassing four traits: *creative*, *innovative*, *visionary* and *unconventional*. When prompted for business *leader exemplars*, participants frequently named business leaders such as Steve Jobs, Bill Gates and Mark Zuckerberg, whom they thought were "revolutionary", "built an empire from nothing" and were "innovative". Lord (2018) explains such effects by noting that each new generation learns ILTs in different historical, technical and cultural contexts. It would be surprising if content didn't change for millennials compared to individuals who grew up in the 1960–1990s and where the original samples from which ILTs were derived. It should be stressed that such differences are structural and represent differences in the content and associations of ILTs elements; not merely the dynamic adjustment of ILTs to new contexts, which is another source of change.

Toward a 'Unified Creative Leadership' Concept

The question remains: "are we getting closer to the unified notion of creative leadership that Simonton envisioned in the 1990s?" Recently, Mainemelis, Kark, and Epitropaki (2015) attempted such a convergence by integrating the dispersed and fragmented literature on leadership and creativity into a unified multi-context framework of creative leadership. They suggested that creative leadership generally refers to leading others toward the attainment of a creative outcome and that it is manifested across various work contexts in three different ways: *Facilitating*, where the creative leader focuses on fostering the creativity of employees; *Directing*, where the creative leader focuses on materializing his or her creative vision through the work of employees; and *Integrating*, where the creative leader focuses on synthesizing his or her creative work with the heterogeneous creative works of other organizational members. As already discussed in the previous section on dynamic views of implicit theories and schemas, these three contexts have implications for the salience of creativity as a characteristic of leadership. We expect automatic activation of creativity as a leadership trait in both the *Directing* (e.g., haute cuisine and top-down innovation) and *Integrating* contexts (e.g., filmmaking) where the leader has a strong creator identity, visible creative contributions and creativity and innovation are key strategic objectives. Still, we expect little convergence between creativity and leadership in *Facilitating* contexts where there is limited requirement for creative contributions on behalf of the leader. Mainemelis, Kark, and Epitropaki (2015) further observed that leadership research undertaken in traditional work settings (i.e., permanent organizations with stable employment and position-based coordination) often fails to capture the unique aspects of leadership in the more fluid creative industries. Creativity is often examined as one of many possible employee outcomes (such as job performance and work attitudes) of various leadership behaviors (e.g., transformational leadership, authentic leadership etc.) and the intricacies of the creative leadership phenomenon are not further examined. Mainemelis, Kark, and Epitropaki (2015) stressed that creative leadership may differ substantially from traditional forms of leadership, and as a result, it requires fresh theoretical and empirical approaches.

Socio-cognitive approaches offer us the opportunity to examine the foundational perceptual blocks of creative leadership and have a look inside the 'black box' of automatic processes that guide leadership and creativity perceptions. For a unified creative leadership construct to emerge, our prototypes of leadership and creativity must also change to reflect that convergence. Such change can take place via two routes: via intrapersonal prototype change and via contextual changes that make the links between leadership and creativity more salient. On the intrapersonal level, two interventions could potentially change leadership and creativity schemas: Conditioning and Selective Prototype Activation (Dasgupta & Asgari, 2004; Epitropaki et al., 2013; Gawronski & Sritharan, 2010; Martin, Epitropaki, & O'Broin, 2017). Conditioning involves pairing a concept (e.g., leader) with a new association (e.g., creator). Prior studies have used conditioning to reduce implicit gender stereotyping (Blair, Ma, & Lenton, 2001) as well as implicit race bias (Dasgupta & Greenwald, 2001). Selective Prototype Activation is another possible intervention that assumes that individuals hold multiple (positive, negative and neutral) implicit theories (Hanges, Lord, & Dickson, 2000; Lord & Shondrick, 2011). A Selective Prototype Activation intervention would involve repeated cueing of positive prototypes involving leadership and creativity such that they become chronically accessible (Kruse & Sy, 2011; Srull & Wyer, 1979).

Furthermore, given the context-sensitivity and dynamic nature of schemas suggested by the connectionist models (Lord, Brown, & Harvey, 2001), contextual changes can also help strengthen the salience of creativity as a core attribute of leadership. Organizational environments that acknowledge creativity as a key organizational value, allow free expression of ideas, encourage risk-taking, have organizational structures and systems supportive of creativity and organizational leaders who facilitate creativity or are creators themselves (e.g., Amabile, 1998; Andriopoulos & Gotsi, 2002; Robinson & Stern, 1997) will strengthen the positive and minimize the negative implicit theories of creativity.

Conclusion

In this chapter, we attempted a closer look at creative leadership from a socio-cognitive perspective. We specifically examined Implicit Leadership and Implicit Creativity Theories in order to understand the observed literature paradox that views creativity as an important but at the same time antithetical notion to leadership (Epitropaki et al., 2013; Mainemelis, Kark, & Epitropaki, 2015). Our analysis showed that despite certain trait similarities between ILTs and ICTs (such as intelligence), a substantial number of traits are different or even antithetical, especially traits related to the dark side of creativity such as *disobedient*, *poor at business*, *extreme* are clearly contradictory to notions of leadership that highlight decision making, structure, task and people orientation such as *decisive, hard-working, helpful* and *understanding*. The connectionist models proposed in the ILTs literature (e.g., Brown & Lord, 2001) offer a pathway to convergence as they highlight the context-sensitive, dynamic and flexible nature of schemas and allow for both stability and flexibility of implicit theories. Depending on contextual, task-, organization- or industry-related characteristics (e.g., R&D teams, creative industries) creativity can be activated as a salient trait of leadership and thus mental representations of creative leadership can be automatically constructed—'on the fly'. Furthermore, recent ILTs scale development studies (e.g., Offermann & Coats, 2018) provide evidence for schema change of the general ILTs prototype and emergence of creativity as a key factor of ILTs in younger generations. We may thus see higher levels of convergence between leadership and creativity in the near future and Simonton's (1991) notion of a 'unified creative leadership' construct may be within reach.

References

Amabile, T. M. 1982. Social psychology of creativity: A consensual assessment technique. *Journal of Personality and Social Psychology*, 43(5): 997–1013.

Amabile, T. M. 1996. *Creativity in context: Update to the social psychology of creativity*. Boulder, CO: Westview Press.

Amabile, T. M. 1998. How to kill creativity. *Harvard Business Review*, 76(5): 76–87.

Andriopoulos, C., & Gotsi, M. 2002. Lessons from a creative culture. *Design Management Journal (Former Series)*, 13(2): 57–63.

Benner, M. J., & Tushman, M. L. 2003. Exploitation, exploration, and process management: The productivity dilemma revisited. *The Academy of Management Review*, 28(2): 238–256.

Berg, J. M. 2016. Balancing on the creative highwire: Forecasting the success of novel ideas in organizations. *Administrative Science Quarterly*, 61: 433–468.

Blair, I. V., Ma, J. E., & Lenton, A. P. 2001. Imagining stereotypes away: The moderation of implicit stereotypes through mental imagery. *Journal of Personality and Social Psychology*, 81: 828–841.

Blaker, N. M., Rompa, I., Dessing, I. H., Vriend, A. F., Herschberg, C., & Van Vugt, M. 2013. The height leadership advantage in men and women: Testing evolutionary psychology predictions about the perceptions of tall leaders. *Group Processes & Intergroup Relations*, 16(1): 17–27.

Bledow, R., Rosing, K., & Frese, M. 2013. A dynamic perspective on affect and creativity. *Academy of Management Journal*, 56: 432–450.

Boudreau, K. J, Guinan, E. C., Lakhani, K. P., & Riedl, C. 2016. Looking across and looking beyond the knowledge frontier: Intellectual distance, novelty, and resource allocation in science. *Management Science*, 62(10): 2765–2783.

Brown, D. J. & Lord, R. G. 2001. Leadership and perceiver cognitions: Moving beyond first order constructs. In M. London (Ed.), *How people evaluate others in organizations: Person perception and interpersonal judgment in I/O psychology*: 181–202. Mahwah, NJ: Lawrence Earlbaum.

Christensen, B. T, Drewsen, L. K., & Maaløe, J. 2014. Implicit theories of the personality of the ideal creative employee. *Psychology of Aesthetics, Creativity, and the Arts*, 8(2): 189.

Criscuolo, P., Dahlander, L., Grohsjean, T., & Salter, A. 2017. Evaluating novelty: The role of panels in the selection of R&D projects. *Academy of Management Journal*, 60: 433–460.

Dasgupta, N., & Asgari, S. 2004. Seeing is believing: Exposure to counter-stereotypic women leaders and its effect on the malleability of automatic gender stereotyping. *Journal of Experimental Social Psychology*, 40: 642–658.

Dasgupta, N., & Greenwald, A. G. 2001. On the malleability of automatic attitudes: Combating automatic prejudice with images of admired and disliked individuals. *Journal of Personality and Social Psychology*, 81: 800–814.

Dehaene, S. 2014. *Consciousness and the brain: Deciphering how the brain codes our thoughts*. New York: Penguin Group.

Den Hartog, D., House, R., Hanges, P., Ruiz-Quintanilla, S., & Dorfman, P. 1999. Culture specific and cross-culturally generalizable implicit leadership theories: Are attributes of charismatic/transformational leadership universally endorsed? *The Leadership Quarterly*, 10: 219–256.

Dinh, J. E., Lord, R. G., & Hoffman, E. 2014. Leadership perception and information processing: Influences of symbolic, connectionist, emotion, and embodied architectures. In D. V. Day (Ed.), *The Oxford handbook of leadership and organizations*. New York: Oxford University Press.

Elsbach, K. D., & Kramer, R. M. 2003. Assessing creativity in Hollywood pitch meetings: Evidence for a dual-process model of creativity judgments. *Academy of Management, Journal*, 46(3): 283–301.

Epitropaki, O., & Mainemelis, C. 2016. The "genre bender": The creative leadership of Kathryn Bigelow. In C. Peus, S. Braun, & B. Schyns (Eds.), *Leadership in compelling contexts: Monographs in leadership and management series*: 275–300. Bingley: Emerald Group Publishing Limited.

Epitropaki, O., & Martin, R. 2004. Implicit leadership theories in applied settings: Factor structure, generalizability and stability over time. *Journal of Applied Psychology*, 89: 293–310.

Epitropaki, O., & Martin, R. 2005. From ideal to real: A longitudinal study of Implicit Leadership Theories, Leader-Member Exchanges and employee outcomes. *Journal of Applied Psychology*, 90: 659–676.

Epitropaki, O., Sy, T., Martin, R., Tram-Quon, S., & Topakas, A. 2013. Implicit leadership and followership theories "in the wild": Taking stock of information-processing approaches to leadership and followership in organizational settings. *Leadership Quarterly*, 24: 858–881.

Foti, R. J., Knee, R. E., Jr., Backert, R. S. G. 2008. Multi-level implications of framing leadership perceptions as a dynamic process. *Leadership Quarterly*, 19: 178–194.

Fredrickson, B. L. 2001. The role of positive emotions in positive psychology: The broaden-and-build theory of positive emotions. *American Psychologist*, 56: 218–226.

Freeman, J. B., & Ambady, N. 2011. A dynamic interactive theory of person construal. *Psychological Review*, 118: 247–279.

Gawronski, B., & Sritharan, R. 2010. Formation, change and contextualization of mental associations: Determinants and principles of variations in implicit measures. In B. K. Payne & B. Gawronski (Eds.), *Handbook of implicit social cognition: Measurement, theory and applications:* 216–240. New York: Guilford Press.

Gough, H. G. 1979. A creative personality scale for the adjective check list. *Journal of Personality and Social Psychology*, 37(8): 1398–1405.Hanges, P. J., Lord, R. G., & Dickson, M. W. 2000. An information-processing perspective on leadership and culture: A case for connectionist framework. *Applied Psychology: An International Review*, 49: 133–161.

Hanges, P. J., Lord, R. G., Godfrey, E. G., & Raver, J. L. 2002. Modeling non-linear relationships: Neural networks and catastrophe analysis. In S. Rogelberg (Ed.), *Handbook of research methods in industrial/organizational psychology*: 431–455. Oxford: Blackwell.

Hass, R. W. 2014. Domain-specific exemplars affect implicit theories of creativity. *Psychology of Aesthetics, Creativity, and the Arts*, 8: 44–52.

House, R. J., Hanges, P. J., Ruiz-Quantilla, S. A., Dorfan, P. W., Javidan, M., Dickson, M., Gupta, V., & the GLOBE Co-ordinating Team. 1999. Cultural influences on leadership and organizations: Project GLOBE. In W.H. Mobley (Ed.), *Advances in global leadership*, 1: 171–233. Stamford, CT: JAI Press, Inc.

Kark, R., Miron-Spektor, E., Gorsky, R., & Kaplun, A. 2014. *Two roads diverge in a yellow wood: The effect of exploration and exploitation on creativity and leadership development*. Working paper, Bar-Ilan University, Israel.

Klein, K. J., & Knight, A. P. 2005. Innovation implementation: Overcoming the challenge. *Current Directions in Psychological Science*, 14(5): 243–246.

Kruse, E. T., & Sy, T. 2011. *Manipulating implicit theories through inducing affect*. Presented at the Academy of Management, San Antonio, TX.

Lee, H., Kim, J., Ryu, Y., & Song, S. 2013. Do people use their implicit theories of creativity as general theories? *Journal of Creative Behavior*, 49: 77–93.

Loewenstein, J., & Mueller, J. 2016. Implicit theories of creative ideas: How culture guides creativity assessments. *Academy of Management Discoveries*, 2: 320–348.

Lord, R. G. 2018. Leadership in the future and the future of leadership research. In B. Schyns, P. Neves, & R. Hall (Eds.), *Handbook of methods in leadership research*. Cheltenham, UK: Edward Elgar Publishing.

Lord, R. G., Brown, D. J., & Harvey, J. L. 2001. System constraints on leadership perceptions, behavior and influence: An example of connectionist level processes. In M. Hogg & R. Tinsdale (Eds.), *Blackwell handbook of social psychology, Vol. 3. Group processes*: 283–310. Oxford: Wiley-Blackwell.

Lord, R. G., Foti, R. J., & De Vader, C. L. 1984. A test of leadership categorization theory: Internal structure, information processing, and leadership perceptions. *Organizational Behavior and Human Performance*, 34: 343–378.

Lord, R. G., & Maher, K. J. 1991. *Leadership and information processing: Linking perceptions and performance*. Boston, MA: Unwin Hyman.

Lord, R. G., & Shondrick, S. J. 2011. Leadership and knowledge: Symbolic, connectionist, and embodied perspectives. *Leadership Quarterly*, 22, 207–222.

Mainemelis, C., & Epitropaki, O. 2013. Extreme leadership as creative leadership: Reflections on Francis Ford Coppola in the Godfather. In C. Giannantonio & A. Hurley-Hanson (Eds.), *Extreme leadership: Leaders, teams, and situations outside the norm:* 187–200. Northampton, MA: Edward Elgar Publishing.

Mainemelis, C., Kark, R., & Epitropaki, O. 2015. Creative leadership: A multi-context conceptualization. *Academy of Management Annals*, 9: 393–482.

Martin, R., Epitropaki, O., & O'Broin, L. 2017. Methodological issues in leadership training: In pursuit of causality. In K. J. Sund, R. J. Galavan, & G. P. Hodgkinson (Eds.), *Methodological challenges and advances in managerial and organizational cognition*: 73–94. Emerald Group Publishing Limited.

Mueller, E. 2017. *Implicit leadership theories of the generation Y: A mixed-method approach*. Unpublished MSc Dissertation, Durham University Business School, Durham University, UK.

Mueller, J. S., Goncalo J. A., & Kamdar, D. 2011. Recognizing creative leadership: Can creative idea expression negatively relate to perceptions of leadership potential? *Journal of Experimental Social Psychology*, 47: 494–498.

Mueller, J. S., Loewenstein, J., & Deal, J. 2014. Managers reject ideas customers want. *Harvard Business Review*, 92(7/8): 30–31.

Mueller, J. S., Melwani, S., & Goncalo, J. 2012. The bias against creativity: Why people desire yet reject creative ideas. *Psychological Science*, 21(1): 13–17.

Mueller, J., Melwani, S., Loewenstein, J., & Deal, J. J. 2018. Reframing the decision-makers' dilemma: Towards a social context model of creative idea recognition. *Academy of Management Journal*, 61(1): 94–110.

Mumford, M. D., Zaccaro, S. J., Harding, F. D., Jacobs, T. O., & Fleishman, E. A. 2000. Leadership skills for a changing world: Solving complex social problems. *The Leadership Quarterly*, 11: 11–35.

Offermann, L. R., & Coats, M. 2018. Implicit theories of leadership: Stability and change over two decades. *The Leadership Quarterly*. doi.org/10.1016/j.leaqua.2017.12.003.

Offermann, L. R., Kennedy, J. K., & Wirtz, P. W. 1994. Implicit leadership theories: Content, structure, and generalizability. *Leadership Quarterly*, 5: 43–58.

Page, S. W. 2007. *The difference: How the power of diversity creates better groups, firms, schools, and societies*. Princeton, NJ: Princeton University Press.

Paletz, S. B. F., & Peng, K. 2008. Implicit theories of creativity across cultures: Novelty and appropriateness in two product domains. *Journal of Cross-Cultural Psychology*, 39: 286–302.

Phillips, J. S., & Lord, R. G. 1981. Causal attributions and perceptions of leadership. *Organizational Behavior & Human Performance*, 28(2): 143–163.

Robinson, A. G., & Stern, S. 1997. *Corporative creativity: How innovation and improvement actually happen*. San Francisco, CA Berrett-Koehler Publishers.

Runco, M. A., & Bahleda, M. D. 1986. Implicit theories of artistic, scientific, and everyday creativity. *The Journal of Creative Behavior*, 20(2): 93–98.

Runco, M. A., & Johnson, D. J. 2002. Parents' and teachers' implicit theories of children's creativity: A cross-cultural perspective. *Creativity Research Journal*, 14(3–4): 427–438.Runco, M. A., Johnson, D. J., & Bear, P. K. 1993. Parents' and teachers' implicit theories of children's creativity. *Child Study Journal*, 23(2): 91–113.

Shondrick, S. J., Dinh, J. E., & Lord, R. G. 2010. Developments in implicit leadership theory and cognitive science: Applications to improving measurement and understanding alternatives to hierarchical leadership. *Leadership Quarterly*, 21: 959–978.

Shrondrick, S. J., & Lord, R. G. 2010. Implicit leadership and follower theories: Dynamic structures for leadership perceptions, memory, and leader-follower processes. *International Review of Industrial and Organizational Psychology*, 25: 1–34.

Siler, K., Lee, K., & Bero, L. 2015. Measuring the effectiveness of scientific gatekeeping. *Proceedings of the National Academy of Sciences*, 112(2): 360–365.

Simonton, D. K. 1984. *Genius, creativity, and leadership: Historiometric inquiries*. Cambridge, MA: Harvard University Press.

Simonton, D. K. 1991. Personality correlates of exceptional personal influence: A note on Thorndike's (1950) creators and leaders. *Creativity Research Journal*, 4(1): 67–78.

Srull, T. K., & Wyer, R. S. 1979. The role of category accessibility in the interpretation of information about persons: Some determinants and implications. *Journal of Personality and Social Psychology*, 37: 1660–1672.

Stephen, D. G., Dixon, J. A., & Isenhower, R. W. 2009. Dynamics of representational change: Entropy, action, and cognition. *Journal of Experimental Psychology: Human Perception and Performance*, 35: 1811–1832.

Sternberg, R. J. 1985. Implicit theories of intelligence, creativity and wisdom. *Journal of Personality and Social Psychology*, 49: 607–627.

Sternberg, R. J. 2007. A systems model of leadership: WICS. *American Psychologist*, 62: 34–42.

Sternberg, R. J., & Davidson, J. E. (Eds.). 1986. *Conceptions of giftedness*. New York: Cambridge University Press.

Sy, T., Shore, L. M., Strauss, J., Shore, T. H., Tram, S., Whiteley, P., Ikeda-Muromachi, K. 2010. Leadership perceptions as a function of race-occupation fit: The case of Asian Americans. *Journal of Applied Psychology*, 95: 902–919.

Van de Ven, A. H. 1988. Central problems in the management of innovation. In M. L. Tushman & W. L. Moore (Eds.), *Readings in the management of innovation* (2nd ed.): 103–122. New York: Ballinger Publishing Co and Harper & Row Publishers, Inc.

Visser, V. A., van Knippenberg, D., van Kleef, G. A., & Wisse, B. 2013. How leader displays of happiness and sadness influence follower performance: Emotional contagion and creative versus analytic performance. *Leadership Quarterly*, 24: 172–188.

Westby, E. L., & Dawson, V. L. 1995. Creativity: Asset or burden in the classroom? *Creativity Research Journal*, 8(1): 1–10.

Part II

Creative Leadership in Facilitative Contexts

4 Leading Creative Efforts

Common Functions and Common Skills

Michael D. Mumford, Colleen Durban, Yash Gujar, Julia Buck, and E. Michelle Todd

Introduction

For many years, we all believed creative work in firms did not need effective leadership (Mumford et al., 2002). In part, this view reflects the "value" placed on creativity in many firms (Dess & Pickens, 2000). In part, however, it reflects the distinct autonomy of creative people and their unwillingness to accept direction from others (Feist & Gorman, 1998). What has become clear in recent years, however, is that the long-term survival and success of firms depends on sustained innovation—the development and fielding of new products and services (Benner & Tushman, 2003). Innovation, however, ultimately depends on peoples' skills in solving—producing original, high quality, and elegant solutions—the kind of novel, complex, ill-defined—or poorly structured—problems (Mumford & Gustafson, 2007) that call for creative thought.

To the surprise of many, Mumford et al. (2002), in a review of the available studies (e.g., Barnowe, 1975; Pelz & Andrews, 1966; Tierney, Farmer, & Graen, 1999), concluded effective leadership is strongly ($r \cong 0.40$), related to the initiation and success of creative efforts in firms, proving positively related to invention disclosures, publications, schedule performance, budget performance, and market share (e.g., Atwater & Carmeli, 2009; Tierney & Farmer, 2002). The strong relationship between leader effectiveness and creative performance in firms has led to the proposal of a number of substantive models intended to describe how the effective leadership of creative efforts occurs, including product championing (Howell & Boies, 2004), leader climate definition (Isaksen, 2017; West & Sacramento, 2012), leader support for creative self-efficacy (Tierney & Farmer, 2011), leader management of team processes (Zhang & Bartol, 2010), leader authenticity (Černe, Jaklič, & Škerlavaj, 2013), and transformational leadership (Shin & Zhou, 2003), to mention a few.

One approach that appears to have some promise for understanding how leaders contribute to the success of creative efforts in firms may be found in the Functional Model of creative leadership proposed by Mumford and his colleagues (Mumford et al., in press; Mumford et al., in press; Mumford, Peterson, & Robledo, 2013; Robledo, Peterson, & Mumford, 2012).

Indeed, this model appears capable of accounting for the performance of eminent scientific leaders (Vessey et al., 2014). In the present effort, we will examine the key functions held to be executed by those asked to lead creative efforts. Subsequently, we will examine some of the critical skills leaders of creative efforts must possess to execute these functions—skills such as causal analysis, constraint analysis, forecasting, and wisdom.

Functions

The Functional Model of creative leadership proposed by Mumford and his colleagues is based on five key assumptions. First, because creative problems are complex, novel, and ill defined (Mumford & Gustafson, 2007), leaders must induce structure on followers' creative problem-solving efforts. Put differently, leaders must define and plan the work to be done (Hemlin, 2009). Second, work on creative projects is typically done by teams (Chen, Chang, & Hung, 2008). And leaders must structure team interactions in such a way as to promote creative work in teams (Carmeli & Paulus, 2015). Third, creative work in firms is costly, requiring acquisition of resources, both fiscal and personnel resources, with costs increasing as new ideas about products and services move from initial development to fielding (Mumford, Bedell-Avers, & Hunter, 2008). Thus, leaders must acquire the resources needed to support creative work. Fourth, leaders play a key role both in providing feedback on project work and in helping team members deal with emergent crises or shifts in the demands posed by project work (Drazin, Glynn, & Kazanjian, 1999; Farris, 1972). Fifth, and finally, as leaders address all these requirements, they must encourage learning on the part of the team, the firm, and the profession (Hitt, Ireland, & Lee, 2000).

Figure 4.1 presents the model describing the key functions to be executed by leaders of creative efforts as proposed by Mumford and colleagues (e.g., Mumford et al., in press; Mumford, Peterson, & Robledo, 2013). It should be noted that this model is domain general, applying to scientific fields as well as those in the arts. This model begins with the proposition that leaders scan the professional environment and the firm's concerns to identify key themes worth exploring. Theme identification provides a basis for project creation, project planning, and definition of the mission to be given to project teams. Mission definition provides a basis for evaluation and feedback to followers, as well as ongoing monitoring of project work, which may lead to either reconfiguration of project work or fielding of the new product. Put somewhat more globally, this vector of leadership functions holds that leaders of creative efforts must lead the work.

To lead the work, however, leaders must have people to do the work. This observation implies leaders must recruit followers and establish the environment they must work in. Shared perceptions of the work environment (or climate) allows team members to interact effectively—a climate, in part, established by how leaders interact with followers. This vector of leadership

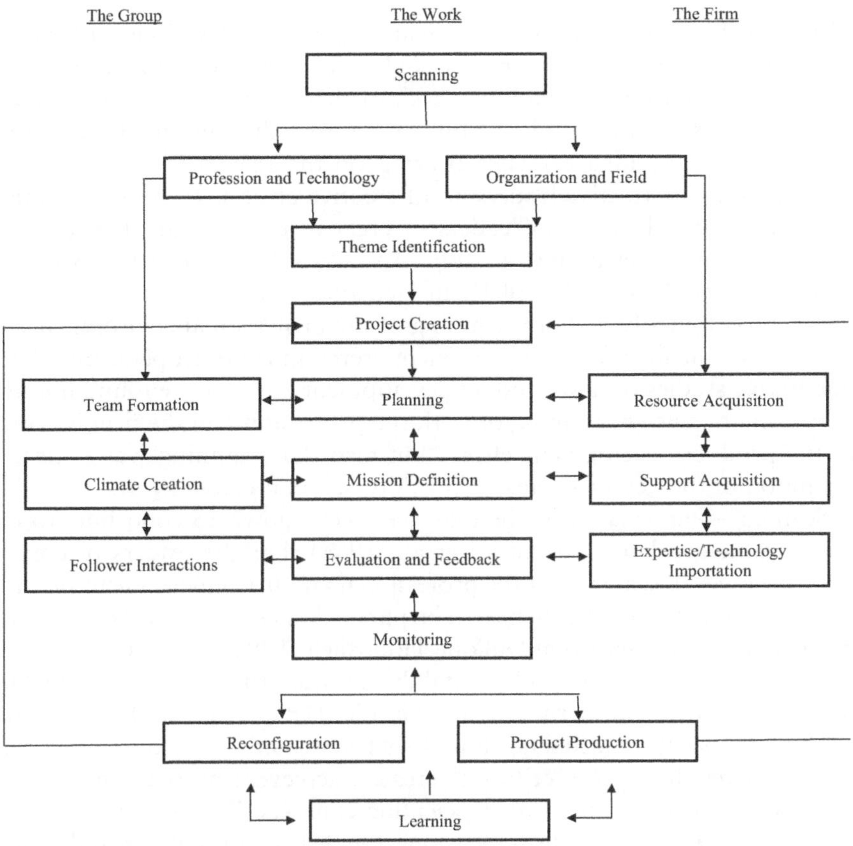

Figure 4.1 Model of Critical Leadership Activities

Note: Figure drawn from Robledo, Peterson, and Mumford (2012) with permission.

functions, of course, implies leaders of creative efforts must lead the group, or team, doing the work.

To allow team members to do the work, however, requisite resources must be obtained from leaders of the firm. Not only must leaders establish the legitimacy of the creative efforts to obtain resources and support from top management, but also they must build support in other institutional units likely to be involved in the development and fielding of the new product or services—often recruiting members of these units based on the skills needed for product development. These within firm sales and educational activities become more critical as project work becomes more cross-functional in nature and proceeds to the fielding of the new product or service. This vector is leadership functions is noteworthy because it implies the leaders of creative efforts must also lead the firm.

Leading the Work

Although this model appears to provide a plausible description of the key functions to be executed by those asked to lead creative efforts, one might ask what evidence is available for each of these functions. Over the years, a number of scholars, scholars employing rather different methods in their studies, have provided evidence bearing on the relevance of these varied activities on the effective leadership of creative efforts. To begin, a number of studies have shown that leaders of creative efforts scan their environment to acquire relevant information (Ancona & Caldwell, 1992; Kickul & Gundry, 2001; Unsworth, 2001). In fact, these scanning activities may be rather broad, involving both scanning of the professional environment and scanning of the firm for problems encountered in routine operations. Thus, qualitative studies of new product development efforts have found not only that open, extensive scanning of both the profession and the firm is critical in the product development efforts but also that scanning was critical to definition of the key problems to be addressed in creative efforts.

Scanning—information gathering—has been shown to contribute to creative problem solving (Mumford et al., 1996). For the leaders of creative efforts, however, scanning of the professional and firm environment provides a basis for identifying the themes to be pursued in creative efforts. For example, in a study of scientists at DuPont, Hounshell (1992) found that sustained, consistent exploration of fundamental themes was critical to innovation. Similarly, Root-Bernstein, Bernstein, and Garnier (1995), in a study of scientific leaders (Nobel Prize winners), found that systematic, sustained work with respect to key themes was critical to creative achievement. Scanning is just as relevant in artistic contexts as in scientific contexts. For example, a painter scans and takes notice of the dimensions, the texture, the color, and the materials of a canvas, identifying themes for product development. Therefore, creative leadership is structured with respect to a limited set of key issues.

Theme identification, and the acquisition of expertise with respect to these themes, provides a basis for project creation and project planning—with project planning influencing both recruitment of staff and acquisition of resources. The importance of planning to effective leadership of creative efforts was examined in a study by Hemlin (2009). More specifically, Hemlin (2009) conducted a critical incident study where the creative efforts of 84 research and development groups in universities and biotechnology firms were examined. He found that leaders were unwilling to delegate project planning activities—viewing project planning as their critical duty. Additionally, it has been found that teams led by leaders with greater planning skills perform more successfully on creative problem-solving tasks (Marta, Leritz, & Mumford, 2005).

Planning is, of course, a complex activity involving identification and management of obstacles. In fact, Caughron and Mumford (2008) found, in another experimental study, that the identification and management of obstacles in planning was critical to the success of leaders' creative problem-solving efforts. Plans, moreover, provide leaders with the basis for defining the mission to be given to the group. Hunter, Bedell-Avers, and Mumford (2007), in a meta-analytic study, found that definition of challenging professional missions was a noteworthy, positive influence on real-world creative accomplishment. In fact, Partlow, Medeiros, and Mumford (2015) have shown that effective articulation of viable missions is critical to performance on a creative problem-solving task requiring formation of a plan for leading an experimental secondary school.

Plans and missions are noteworthy because they provide a basis for appraising the work of followers. Farris (1972) has shown followers, followers working in research and development teams, actively seek feedback from leaders in initial definition of team assignments and after some work has been completed. In a study of idea evaluation, Lonergan, Scott, and Mumford (2004) presented undergraduates with ideas for marketing a new product—the 3-D holographic television. These ideas, ideas drawn from Redmond, Mumford, and Teach (1993), were of either established quality or established originality. Prior to reviewing these ideas, participants were asked to assume the role of a manager (the leader), review followers' ideas and prepare for a final campaign—campaigns appraised for quality and originality. In addition, manipulations were made to encourage evaluation of these ideas with respect to operating efficiency and innovation standards. It was found that the most original and highest quality campaigns were obtained when high-quality ideas were appraised with respect to innovation standards and highly original ideas were appraised with respect to operating efficiency. Thus, leaders are active, expert participants in followers' creative efforts seeking to compensate for deficiencies in their work. Indeed, other studies by Gibson and Mumford (2013) and Licuanan, Dailey, and Mumford (2007) have shown leaders must think, and think deeply, when evaluating others' ideas.

When ideas "pass inspection" and implementation begins, new crises and new creative problems emerge (Gordon, 2017). As a result, leaders cannot simply evaluate and improve ideas—they must be actively involved in product development and fielding. Drazin, Glynn, and Kazanjian (1999) conducted a qualitative study on the development of a new aircraft. They found that leaders not only actively monitored project work but also played a key role in helping project teams address the crises that routinely emerge in creative efforts. The way these crises are addressed, however, provides a basis for organizational learning—learning facilitated by self-reflection (Strange & Mumford, 2005). As Isaksen (2017) has pointed out, however, it is important for leaders of creative efforts to both learn from failure and success.

Leading the People

Of course, leaders must have someone to lead. Most creative work, however, is done by professionals—professionals who have a strong sense of autonomy (Feist & Gorman, 1998). As a result, leaders of creative efforts must in a sense recruit team members. In a qualitative study of a new product development firm information technology, Kidder (1981) found that it is project leaders who are responsible for recruiting and retaining key staff. This finding is of some importance because it implies leaders must know the work, the professions, and the workforce, appraising potential worker skills with respect to the demands made by a project.

Although more research is needed on how leaders execute the recruitment function, three key points should be kept in mind. First, leaders may recruit people with different perspectives on issues to ensure productive technical conflict (Fay et al., 2006; Hülsheger, Anderson, & Salgado, 2009). Second, in recruitment, leaders must anticipate how the project and project work could contribute to professional development and professional accomplishment (Zuckerman, 1977). Third, in recruiting team members, leaders must communicate project plans and missions in such a way that team members have a shared understanding, a shared mental model, of the nature of the work at hand (Day, Gronn, & Salas, 2004). It is important to note that in some cases, in musical orchestras for example, it is the creative team that actually recruits the leader to lead the team. However, even in these cases, the leader must still perform the aforementioned recruitment functions to encourage productive conflict, professional development, and a shared understanding of the work.

Not only must leaders recruit team members with requisite skills, but also they must establish the procedures and processes by which team members will work together. Thus, Mitchell et al. (2015) found that leader inclusiveness, the leaders valuing different points of view, enhances the creative performance of teams in part by bringing technical issues to fore and in part by establishing a shared sense of identity. Other work indicates leaders should encourage participation by team members (Baer & Frese, 2003; Kerr & Murthy, 2004), ensure feelings of psychological safety among group members (Carmeli et al., 2014; Kessel, Kratzer, & Schultz, 2012), and establish contingencies and work conditions that encourage active collaboration, especially collaborative efforts that result in the elaboration of and refinement of ideas (Mathieu et al., 2008).

James, James, and Ashe (1990) argued that these, and other actions by leaders, are the key variables that shape peoples' perceptions of their work environments, and more specifically, their perceptions of work climate. Over the years, a number of models have been proposed in attempts to account for the work climate leaders should establish to encourage creativity and innovation, with models being framed with respect to team interventions (West et al., 2003), the unique needs, or personalities, of creative people

(Feist, 1999); the motives of creative people (Amabile et al., 1996); organizational resources (Abbey & Dickson, 1983); and requirements for new product development (Thamhain, 2003).

Hunter, Bedell, and Mumford (2005) reviewed the various models of creative climate that have been proposed. They identified 19 dimensions commonly proposed in models of creative climate: (1) positive peer group, (2) positive supervisor relations, (3) resources, (4) professional challenges, (5) mission clarity, (6) autonomy, (7) positive interpersonal exchange, (8) intellectual stimulation, (9) top management support, (10) reward orientation, (11) flexibility and risk-taking, (12) product emphasis, (13) participation, and (14) organizational integration. In a later study, Hunter, Bedell, and Mumford (2007) conducted a meta-analytic investigation to assess the impact of these climate variables on individual and team creative performance.

Although it was found that all of these attributes of peoples' perceptions of their work environment were positively related to creativity, three climate dimensions produced especially strong effects: (1) positive interpersonal exchange ($d = 0.91$), (2) intellectual stimulation ($d = 0.88$), and 3) professionally challenging work ($d = 0.85$). These findings are, or course, consistent with earlier work showing that transformational leadership contributes to creativity (Sosik, Kahai, & Avolio, 1999). By the same token, they indicate leaders must establish a challenging, intellectually engaging work environment where peer support can be expected for work contributing to the mission. As Isaksen (2017) points out, involving others in goal setting, recognizing achievement, resolving technical conflict, discounting personal conflict, and encouraging team members to explore the implications of ideas are all leader behaviors that will give rise to these climate perceptions.

Of course, climate perceptions, in part, arise from leaders' interactions with followers. Tierney, Farmer, and Graen (1999) examined positive leader-follower exchange among research and development chemists. They found that both publications and invention disclosures are positively related to positive interactions between leaders and followers. These positive exchange relationships, however, appear most beneficial when the leader seeks to build feelings of creative self-efficacy among followers. Thus, Tierney and Farmer (2002) and Tierney and Farmer (2011) have shown that feelings of creative self-efficacy, feelings in part established through interactions with leaders, contribute to the creative accomplishments of followers.

Leading the Firm

What has long been clear is that creative efforts in firms require both financial support and legitimation (Dougherty & Hardy, 1996)—financial support and legitimation, which is provided by the support of top management teams. For example, Wang and Hsieh (2013), in a survey study, found that active engagement of a firm's senior management in creative efforts was critical to the success of new product introductions. Additionally, in a qualitative study of the adoption of a new technology it was shown that engagement of top management, or policy agencies, was critical to the success of this technology ensuring not only requisite resources were available but also that other key stakeholders (e.g., customers) were aware of and supportive of the effort.

The need for resources and support implies that the leaders of creative efforts must be able to "sell" their projects to top management. In fact, a series of studies by Howell and Higgins (1990), Markham and Griffin (1998), and Markham and Smith (2017) all indicate that successful leaders of creative efforts are able to "sell" or champion creative efforts. In particular, Howell and Boies (2004) have provided us with some evidence about how leaders go about championing new projects. They interviewed 19 matched pairs of champions and non-champions involved in one of 29 new product development efforts. Interviews were content analyzed to assess knowledge, idea promotion, idea packing, and selling. They found that contextual knowledge (knowledge of firm strategy and operations) was a powerful influence on both the packaging of ideas and the selling of ideas to others. These findings suggest that to champion projects, leaders of creative efforts must have a real understanding of both the firm and/or profession—and, be able to explain how the project will contribute to advancing the firm's strategy and achieving key goals of the firm.

Not only must the leaders of creative efforts be able to sell to top management, but also they must build support for the efforts among other vested stakeholders or units in the firm. Jelinek and Schoonhoven (1990) conducted a qualitative study of a failed new product development effort—chip marking of shipping containers. It was known the prototypic chip marker worked, and the project had top management support, yet it failed—largely because other relevant organizational units refused to support the effort. Thus, leaders of creative efforts not only must sell to top management, but also they must sell the project to other relevant organizational units. As Mumford et al. (in press), note, however, such "sales" efforts may be as much about educating other institutional units about the project "as sales" per se. And, if necessary, providing these units with the technical support needed to resolve problems in their functional area breached by the creative effort. In this sense, those asked to lead creative efforts must become teachers—teachers actively trying to help other units understand, and hopefully support, the creative effort. Note that the earlier discussion of leading the firm does not mean that leaders of creative efforts must actually *lead* the firm in terms of holding a top management position such as CEO. Rather, leaders of creative efforts must lead the firm in the sense that they must lead the firm to accept the creative idea or product put forth through championing and building firm support.

Leader outreach to other key constituencies in a firm is not simply a nice thing to do. Leaders in the course of these efforts themselves learn about the capabilities of these units and the staff working in these units. This knowledge may, in fact, prove crucial because as projects move from development to fielding new expertise and skills, often expertise and skills drawn from other organizational units, will be required. Accordingly, Keller (2001) and Thamhain (2003) have provided evidence indicating that cross-functional teaming, at least appropriately timed cross-functional teaming, contributes to successful new product introductions, as well as schedule and budget performance.

What should be recognized here, however, is the introduction of new expertise and skills, particularly skills drawn from different units, may prove disruptive to creative teams. Due to potential disruption, leaders must help these cross-functional team members understand, or make sense of, the creative effort at hand (Drazin, Glynn, & Kazanjian, 1999). Leaders, moreover, must act to recognize the unique contributions of outsiders to the project and encourage recognition of their potential contributions by team members (Bird & Sherwin, 2005). Finally, leaders must manage group processes and climate, recognizing that introduction of "outside" perspectives often disrupts creative efforts (Friedrich & Mumford, 2009). As a result, leaders of creative efforts must lead efforts to import expertise into creative teams.

Skills

Although additional evidence bearing on Mumford and his colleagues' (e.g., Mumford et al., in press; Mumford, Peterson, & Robledo, 2013; Robledo, Peterson, & Mumford, 2012) model of the key functions that must be executed by those asked to lead creative efforts is needed, the evidence available at this point (e.g., Vessey et al., 2014) does suggest this model is at least plausible. Functional models of this sort, however, are of interest not only because they describe key "work" activities but also because they point to the key capacities people need to execute these activities (Fleishman et al., 1991; Mumford et al., 2000). Accordingly, in the following section, we will briefly examine the implications of the model for the skills leaders must possess to lead creative efforts. A more extensive explanation of each of the following skills may be found in Mumford et al. (2017).

Creative Thinking Skills

With regard to the leadership of creative efforts, it has traditionally been thought that leaders of creative efforts do not themselves need to be especially creative. However, the model of functional leadership presented earlier suggests this assumption is not well founded. For example, how can someone seek to compensate for deficiencies in ideas—often a lack of originality—if they are not capable of creative thought (Lonergan, Scott, & Mumford, 2004)? The available evidence indicates that leaders' creative thinking skills are in fact critical to the effective leadership of creative efforts (Connelly et al., 2000; Mumford et al., 1998; Mumford, Medeiros, & Partlow, 2012; Mumford, Vessey, & Barrett, 2008). Although these skills develop over time as leaders acquire experience (Zaccaro et al., 2015), possession of creative thinking skills early in their careers has been found to be critical to career performance in leading creative efforts.

Forecasting Skill

Many of the functions specified in Mumford's (e.g., Mumford et al., in press; Robledo, Peterson, & Mumford, 2012) model seem to require forecasting skill. For example, leaders must plan, and planning, or the mental simulation of future actions, is commonly held to require forecasting (Mumford, Mecca, & Watts, 2015; Mumford, Schultz, & Van Doorn, 2001). Leaders, moreover, must be able to envision (or forecast) the potential implications of the themes being perused (O'Connor, 1998). And, in providing evaluative feedback, leaders must anticipate both followers' reactions and the impact of the feedback provided. Although forecasting was once discounted as a viable cognitive skill (Pant & Starbuck, 1990), more recent research indicates that leaders can make accurate forecasts and that more effective leaders forecast (Beeler et al., 2010; Byrne, Shipman, & Mumford, 2010; Dailey & Mumford, 2006; Shipman, Byrne, & Mumford, 2010). Although other examples of this might be cited, the foregoing observations seem sufficient to make our point: leadership of creative efforts requires forecasting skill.

Causal Analysis Skill

The model of creative leadership points to another skill likely to prove important to the leadership of creative efforts: causal analysis skill. In planning, leaders of creative efforts must not only identify critical causes that need to be controlled in the effort but also identify the causes of performance in a product or service that must be investigated further (Bird & Sherwin, 2005). Moreover, to identify viable projects, leaders must think about the causes of both good and poor product performance within a system. Causal analysis skill, however, is not simply a matter of leading the work. In championing ideas (or selling ideas) to top management, they must be able to demonstrate how a project would cause (or contribute to) a firm's strategic objectives. And, in recruiting team members and establishing climate, they must anticipate the importance and significance of the key causes they have identified (Kidder, 1981). Some initial support pointing to the importance of causal analysis skills has been provided in Hester et al. (2012) and Marcy and Mumford (2007). Thus, there is reason to expect leader causal analysis skills would contribute to effective execution of many of the key functions to be executed by the leaders of creative efforts.

Constraint Analysis Skill

Traditionally, creative work, and presumably the leadership of creative efforts, was held to be inhibited by constraints. More recent work, however, indicates that creative thinking is enhanced as people seek to identify and "work around" or "work within" constraints (Haught, 2015; Haught-Tromp, 2017; Onarheim & Biskjaer, 2015; Stokes, 2009). For example, leaders who are better able to identify and work with monetary and task objective constraints have been shown to perform better on a creative problem-solving task (Medeiros, Partlow, & Mumford, 2014). This observation, in turn, suggests that constraint analysis skills might also be critical to the effective leadership of creative projects.

Wisdom

The functions that must be executed by those asked to lead creative efforts are not only complex but also require judgment. Leaders must know when and how to try to sell a creative effort to top management. They must be able to balance different points of view in conflict over technical approaches to the problems being addressed in a creative effort. They must also be able to appraise the impact of importing expertise, or technology, on team processes. All these requirements suggest that those asked to lead creative efforts must be wise (McKenna, Rooney, & Boal, 2009).

Wisdom, as a skill, has been defined in different ways by different investigators (Arlin, 1990; Orwell & Perlmutter, 1990; Sternberg, 1985, 1990). Despite these definitional differences, most agree wisdom involves appraising the merits of solutions in context. As a result, wisdom is held to require awareness of solution fit, systems perception, systems commitment, judgment under uncertainty, self-objectivity, and self-reflection (Zaccaro, Mumford et al., 2000). In fact, Zaccaro et al. (2000) have provided evidence indicating wisdom is related not only to leader performance but also to leader creative thinking. There is still much research on wisdom that needs to be done; however, recent research investigating attributes of wisdom (e.g., Mumford et al., 2000) points to wisdom being an important skill for leaders of creative efforts.

Conclusion

Before turning to the broader conclusions from the present effort, certain limitations should be noted. To begin, in the present effort we have focused only on one model describing the requirements for leading creative efforts—the Functional Model proposed by Mumford and his colleagues (Mumford et al., in press; Mumford, Peterson, & Robledo, 2013; Robledo, Peterson, & Mumford, 2012). Although this model appears to provide a viable, plausible basis for describing the key functions that must be executed by those asked to lead creative efforts, it should be recognized that this is only one model of how those asked to lead creative efforts actually lead. Moreover, it should be recognized that this model does not necessarily rule out, or compete with, other models such as transformational leadership (Sosik, Kahai, & Avolio, 1999) or leader-member exchange (Tierney, Farmer, & Graen, 1999) that have been used to account for the leadership of creative efforts. Positive leader-follower exchange, like transformational leadership, may contribute to execution of many of these key functions.

This Functional Model of the requirements for leading creative efforts is of interest because it points to the kind of skills leaders must acquire if they are to lead creative efforts effectively. In the present effort, based on the Functional Model, we identified five skills needed for the effective leadership of creative efforts: creative thinking skill, causal analysis skill, forecasting skill, constraint analysis skill, and wisdom. Indeed, evidence has been presented indicating that each of these skills influence peoples' ability to solve creative leadership problems. Nonetheless, it should be recognized that this list of skills may not be exhaustive—other skills may well exist that influence leaders' ability to solve creative problems and lead creative initiatives, such as networking skill (Mumford et al., in press). Moreover, it should be recognized that much of the research considered herein has examined experimental studies of leaders' performance in solving creative problems. Thus, the question arises as to how these skills are applied in real-world settings where the leaders of creative efforts must interact with multiple teams and multiple team members to turn new ideas into viable products.

Finally, in the present effort, we have focused on the key functions and key skills needed by those asked to lead creative efforts. As a result, little has been said about what leaders must know (i.e., what kind of knowledge and experience must leaders possess) to execute these skills. This point is of some importance because prior research has shown effective execution of skills depends on the availability of substantial and well-structured knowledge (Mumford, Medeiros, & Partlow, 2012). And, clearly, experience and deliberative practice will contribute to the acquisition of this knowledge, as well as effective skill execution (Ericsson, 2009).

With this said, we believe the present effort has noteworthy conclusions. To begin, the work required of those asked to lead creative efforts is hard and exceptionally complex. Leaders of creative efforts must lead the work, they must lead the people doing the work, and they must lead the firm. Each of these three global functions is associated with a number of other complex activities. In leading the work, leaders must scan multiple sources, define viable work themes, formulate project plans, define team missions, evaluate followers' products, respond adaptively to crises, and monitor team work activities. In leading the people doing the work, leaders must recruit team members, establish a work environment, and interact effectively with followers. In leading the firm, leaders must sell the project to top management, build support for the project among stakeholders in the firm, and import requisite expertise from relevant stakeholder groups. The multiple functions required of those asked to lead creative efforts, and the complex nature of all these functions, suggests that leading creative efforts may be one of the most—if not the most—demanding forms of leadership we see in firms.

At a substantive level, this observation is noteworthy for another reason. Each of these functions is of sufficient importance to understanding effective leadership of creative efforts that studies are warranted examining how each function contributes to effective leadership of creative efforts. Although many studies have examined leader-follower interactions (e.g., Tierney, Farmer, & Graen, 1999), we need more work on how leaders go about recruiting team members. We need more work on how leaders plan creative work. We also need more work on how leaders build support for creative projects among other vested stakeholders in a firm. Additionally, we need more work on how leaders learn from both project success and project failure.

Not only have we historically underestimated the functional work demands made on the leaders of creative efforts, we also have underestimated exactly what is needed by the people leading these efforts. Put differently, we have assumed if you could lead elsewhere, then you could lead creative efforts. Our observations in the present effort clearly contradict this assumption. It is not enough for the leaders of creative efforts to be able to lead. The leaders themselves must be able to think creatively. Indeed, given that leaders of creative efforts must compensate for deficiencies in others' work in evaluation (Lonergan, Scott, & Mumford, 2004), the level of creative thinking skill required of those who prove successful in leading innovative programs may, in fact, be exceptional.

Unto itself, creative thinking skills on the part of leaders will not guarantee the success of a creative project. Leaders of creative efforts must also be able to analyze and act on both key causes and key constraints—often in real-time. They must be able to forecast the downstream implications of their actions. Additionally, they must be able to evaluate their options in a wise fashion. These skills indicate the leaders of creative efforts must be something more than just technically creative people—they must have the skills and experience that allow them to plan and act in a complex institutional system on projects where success, however valuable, is not assured.

The complex array of skills needed to lead creative efforts, however, points to a larger concern. We need to know more, far more, about how these skills develop and the type of developmental interventions (either assignments or educational training programs) most likely to prove of value in encouraging the development of these skills (Scott, Leritz, & Mumford, 2004). Evidence bearing on viable developmental interventions may with time provide a basis for formulating successful programs that will provide leaders with the skills needed to lead creative efforts and provide firms with viable new products and success. We hope the present effort provides an impetus for future work along these lines.

Acknowledgments

We would like to thank Sam Hunter, Roni Reiter-Palmon, Rich Marcy, and Kelsey Mederios for their contributions to the present effort.

References

Abbey, A., & Dickson, J. W. 1983. R & D work climate and innovation in semiconductors. *Academy of Management Journal*, 26: 362–368.

Amabile, T. M., Conti, R., Coon, H., Lazenby, J., & Herron, M. 1996. Assessing the work environment for creativity. *Academy of Management Journal*, 39: 1154–1184.

Ancona, D. G., & Caldwell, D. F. 1992. Demography and design: Predictors of new product team performance. *Organization Science*, 3: 321–341.

Arlin, P. K. 1990. Wisdom: The art of problem finding. In R. J. Sternberg (Ed.), *Wisdom: Its nature, origins, and development*: 230–243. New York: Cambridge University Press.

Atwater, L., & Carmeli, A. 2009. Leader—member exchange, feelings of energy, and involvement in creative work. *The Leadership Quarterly*, 20: 264–275.

Baer, M., & Frese, M. 2003. Innovation is not enough: Climates for initiative and psychological safety, process innovations, and firm performance. *Journal of Organizational Behavior*, 24: 45–68.

Barnowe, J. T. 1975. Leadership and performance outcomes in research organizations: The supervisor of scientists as a source of assistance. *Organizational Behavior and Human Performance*, 14: 264–280.

Beeler, C. K., Antes, A. L., Wang, X., Caughron, J. J., Thiel, C. E., & Mumford, M. D. 2010. Strategies in forecasting outcomes in ethical decision-making: Identifying and analyzing the causes of the problem. *Ethics & Behavior*, 20: 110–127.

Benner, M. J., & Tushman, M. L. 2003. Exploitation, exploration, and process management: The productivity dilemma revisited. *Academy of Management Review*, 28: 238–256.

Bird, K., & Sherwin, M. J. 2005. *American prometheus: The triumph and tragedy of J. Robert Oppenheimer*. New York: Vintage Books.

Byrne, C. L., Shipman, A. S., & Mumford, M. D. 2010. The effects of forecasting on creative problem-solving: An experimental study. *Creativity Research Journal*, 22, 119–138.

Carmeli, A., & Paulus, P. B. 2015. CEO ideational facilitation leadership and team creativity: The mediating role of knowledge sharing. *The Journal of Creative Behavior*, 49: 53–75.

Carmeli, A., Sheaffer, Z., Binyamin, G., Reiter-Palmon, R., & Shimoni, T. 2014. Transformational leadership and creative problem-solving: The mediating role of psychological safety and reflexivity. *The Journal of Creative Behavior*, 48: 115–135.

Caughron, J. J., & Mumford, M. D. 2008. Project planning: The effects of using formal planning techniques on creative problem-solving. *Creativity and Innovation Management*, 17: 204–215.

Černe, M., Jaklič, M., & Škerlavaj, M. 2013. Authentic leadership, creativity, and innovation: A multilevel perspective. *Leadership*, 9: 63–85.

Chen, M. H., Chang, Y. C., & Hung, S. C. 2008. Social capital and creativity in R&D project teams. *R & D Management*, 38: 21–34.

Connelly, M. S., Gilbert, J. A., Zaccaro, S. J., Threlfall, K. V., Marks, M. A., & Mumford, M. D. 2000. Exploring the relationship of leadership skills and knowledge to leader performance. *The Leadership Quarterly*, 11: 65–86.

Dailey, L., & Mumford, M. D. 2006. Evaluative aspects of creative thought: Errors in appraising the implications of new ideas. *Creativity Research Journal*, 18: 385–390.

Day, D. V., Gronn, P., & Salas, E. 2004. Leadership capacity in teams. *The Leadership Quarterly*, 15: 857–880.

Dess, G. G., & Pickens, J. C. 2000. Changing roles: Leadership in the 21st Century. *Organizational Dynamics*, 28: 18–34.

Dougherty, D., & Hardy, C. 1996. Sustained product innovation in large, mature organizations: Overcoming innovation-to-organization problems. *Academy of Management Journal*, 39: 1120–1153.

Drazin, R., Glynn, M. A., & Kazanjian, R. K. 1999. Multilevel theorizing about creativity in organizations: A sense making perspective. *Academy of Management Review*, 24: 286–329.

Ericsson, K. A. (Ed.). 2009. *Development of professional expertise: Toward measurement of expert performance and design of optimal learning environments.* Cambridge: Cambridge University Press.

Farris, G. F. 1972. The effect of individual role on performance in innovative groups. *R & D Management*, 3: 23–28.

Fay, D., Borrill, C., Amir, Z., Haward, R., & West, M. A. 2006. Getting the most out of multidisciplinary teams: A multisample study of team innovation in health care. *Journal of Occupational and Organizational Psychology*, 79: 553–567.

Fiest, G. J. 1999. The influence of personality on artistic and scientific creativity. In R. J. Sternberg (Ed.), *Handbook of creativity*: 273–296. Cambridge: Cambridge University Press.

Feist, G. J., & Gorman, M. E. 1998. The psychology of science: Review and integration of a nascent discipline. *Review of General Psychology*, 2: 3–47.

Fleishman, E. A., Mumford, M. D., Zaccaro, S. J., Levin, K. Y., Korotkin, A. L., & Hein, M. B. 1991. Taxonomic efforts in the description of leader behavior: A synthesis and functional interpretation. *The Leadership Quarterly*, 2: 245–287.

Friedrich, T. L., & Mumford, M. D. 2009. The effects of conflicting information on creative thought: A source of performance improvements or decrements? *Creativity Research Journal*, 21: 265–281.

Gibson, C., & Mumford, M. D. 2013. Evaluation, criticism, and creativity: Criticism content and effects on creative problem solving. *Psychology of Aesthetics, Creativity, and the Arts*, 7: 314–331.

Gordon, R. G. 2017. *The rise and fall of American growth: The U.S. standard of living since the civil war.* Princeton, NJ: Princeton University Press.

Haught-Tromp, C. 2015. The role of constraints in creative sentence production. *Creativity Research Journal*, 27: 160–166.

Haught-Tromp, C. 2017. The Green Eggs and Ham hypothesis: How constraints facilitate creativity. *Psychology of Aesthetics, Creativity, and the Arts*, 11: 1–8.
Hemlin, S. 2009. Creative knowledge environments: An interview study with group members and group leaders of university and industry R & D groups in biotechnology. *Creativity and Innovation Management*, 18: 278–285.
Hester, K. S., Robledo, I. C., Barrett, J. D., Peterson, D. R., Hougen, D. P., Day, E. A., & Mumford, M. D. 2012. Causal analysis to enhance creative problem-solving: Performance and effects on mental models. *Creativity Research Journal*, 24: 115–133.
Hitt, M. A., Ireland, R. D., & Lee, H. U. 2000. Technological learning, knowledge management, firm growth and performance: An introductory essay. *Journal of Engineering and Technology Management*, 17: 231–246.
Hounshell, E. A. 1992. Invention in the industrial research laboratory: Individual or collective process. In R. J. Weber & D. N. Perkins (Eds.), *Inventive minds: Creativity in technology*: 273–291. New York: Oxford University Press.
Howell, J. M., & Boies, K. 2004. Champions of technological innovation: The influence of contextual knowledge, role orientation, idea generation, and idea promotion on champion emergence. *The Leadership Quarterly*, 15: 123–143.
Howell, J. M., & Higgins, C. A. 1990. Champions of technological innovation. *Administrative Science Quarterly*: 317–341.
Hülsheger, U. R., Anderson, N., & Salgado, J. F. 2009. Team-level predictors of innovation at work: A comprehensive meta-analysis spanning three decades of research. *Journal of Applied Psychology*, 94: 1128–1145.
Hunter, S. T., Bedell-Avers, K. E., & Mumford, M. D. 2005. Dimensions of creative climate. *The International Journal of Creativity & Problem Solving*, 15: 97–116.
Hunter, S. T., Bedell-Avers, K. E., & Mumford, M. D. 2007. The typical leadership study: Assumptions, implications, and potential remedies. *The Leadership Quarterly*, 18: 435–446.
Isaksen, S. G. 2017. Leadership's role in creative climate creation. In M. D. Mumford & S. Hemlin (Eds.), *Handbook of research on leadership and creativity*: 131–158. Cheltenham, UK: Edward Elgar Publishing.
James, L. R., James, L. A., & Ashe, D. K. 1990. The meaning of organizations: The role of cognition and values. In B. Schneider (Ed.), *Organizational climate and culture*: 40–84. San Francisco, CA: Jossey-Bass.
Jelinek, M., & Schoonhoven, C. B. 1990. *The innovation marathon: Lessons learned from high technology firms*. Oxford: Wiley-Blackwell.
Keller, R. T. 2001. Cross-functional project groups in research and new product development: Diversity, communications, job stress, and outcomes. *Academy of Management Journal*, 44: 547–553.
Kerr, D. S., & Murthy, U. S. 2004. Divergent and convergent idea generation in teams: A comparison of computer-mediated and face-to-face communication. *Group Decision and Negotiation*, 13: 381–399.
Kessel, M., Kratzer, J., & Schultz, C. 2012. Psychological safety, knowledge sharing, and creative performance in healthcare teams. *Creativity and Innovation Management*, 21: 147–157.
Kickul, J., & Gundry, L. K. 2001. Breaking through boundaries for organizational innovation: New managerial roles and practices in e-commerce firms. *Journal of Management*, 27: 347–361.
Kidder, T. 1981. *The sole of a new machine*. New York: Avon.

Licuanan, B. F., Dailey, L. R., & Mumford, M. D. 2007. Idea evaluation: Error in evaluating highly original ideas. *The Journal of Creative Behavior*, 41: 1–27.

Lonergan, D. C., Scott, G. M., & Mumford, M. D. 2004. Evaluative aspects of creative thought: Effects of idea appraisal and revision standards. *Creativity Research Journal*, 16: 231–246.

Marcy, R. T., & Mumford, M. D. 2007. Social innovation: Enhancing creative performance through causal analysis. *Creativity Research Journal*, 19: 123–140.

Markham, S. K., & Griffin, A. 1998. The breakfast of champions: Associations between champions and product development environments, practices and performance. *Journal of Product Innovation Management*, 15: 436–454.

Markham, S. E., & Smith, J. W. 2017. How can we advise Achilles? A rehabilitation of the concept of the champion for leadership. In M. Mumford & S. Hemlin (Eds.), *Handbook of research on leadership and creativity*: 59–81. Cheltenham, UK: Edward Elgar Publishing.

Marta, S., Leritz, L. E., & Mumford, M. D. 2005. Leadership skills and the group performance: Situational demands, behavioral requirements, and planning. *The Leadership Quarterly*, 16: 97–120.

Mathieu, J., Maynard, M. T., Rapp, T., & Gilson, L. 2008. Team effectiveness 1997–2007: A review of recent advancements and a glimpse into the future. *Journal of Management*, 34: 410–476.

McKenna, B., Rooney, D., & Boal, K. B. 2009. Wisdom principles as a meta-theoretical basis for evaluating leadership. *The Leadership Quarterly*, 20: 177–190.

Medeiros, K. E., Partlow, P. J., & Mumford, M. D. 2014. Not too much, not too little: The influence of constraints on creative problem solving. *Psychology of Aesthetics, Creativity, and the Arts*, 8: 198–210.

Mitchell, R., Boyle, B., Parker, V., Giles, M., Chiang, V., & Joyce, P. 2015. Managing inclusiveness and diversity in teams: How leader inclusiveness affects performance through status and team identity. *Human Resource Management*, 54: 217–239.

Mumford, M. D., Baughman, W. A., Supinski, E. P., & Maher, M. A. 1996. Process-based measures of creative problem-solving skills: II. Information encoding. *Creativity Research Journal*, 9: 77–88.

Mumford, M. D., Bedell-Avers, K. E., & Hunter, S. T. 2008. Planning for innovation: A multi-level perspective. In *Multi-level issues in creativity and innovation*: 107–154. Emerald Group Publishing Limited.

Mumford, M. D., & Gustafson, S. B. 2007. Creative thought: Cognition and problem solving in a dynamic system. *Creativity Research Handbook*, 2: 33–77.

Mumford, M. D., Higgs, C., Todd, E. M., & Martin, R. In Press. Leading creative groups: What must leaders think about? In P. Paulus & B. Nijstad (Eds.), *Group creativity*. Oxford: Oxford University Press.

Mumford, M. D., Marks, M. A., Connelly, M. S., Zaccaro, S. J., & Johnson, J. F. 1998. Domain-based scoring in divergent-thinking tests: Validation evidence in an occupational sample. *Creativity Research Journal*, 11: 151–163.

Mumford, M. D., Marks, M. A., Connelly, M. S., Zaccaro, S. J., & Reiter-Palmon, R. 2000. Development of leadership skills: Experience and timing. *The Leadership Quarterly*, 11: 87–114.

Mumford, M. D., Martin, R., Elliott, S., & McIntosh, T. In Press. Leading for creativity: A tripartite model. In J. Kaufman & R. Sternberg (Eds.), *Cambridge handbook of creativity*. Cambridge: Cambridge University Press.

Mumford, M. D., Mecca, J. T., & Watts, L. L. 2015. Planning processes: Relevant cognitive operations. In M. D. Mumford & M. R. Frese (Eds.), *The psychology of planning in organizations: Research and applications*: 9–30. New York: Routledge.

Mumford, M. D., Medeiros, K. E., & Partlow, P. J. 2012. Creative thinking: Processes, strategies, and knowledge. *The Journal of Creative Behavior*, 46: 30–47.

Mumford, M. D., Peterson, D. R., & Robledo, I. C. 2013. Leading scientists and engineers: Cognition in a socio-technical context. In S. Hemlin, C. M. Allwood, B. Martin, & M. D. Mumford (Eds.), *Creativity and leadership in science, technology, and innovation*: 29–57. London: Routledge.

Mumford, M. D., Schultz, R. A., & Van Doorn, J. R. 2001. Performance in planning: Processes, requirements, and errors. *Review of General Psychology*, 5: 213–240.

Mumford, M. D., Scott, G. M., Gaddis, B., & Strange, J. M. 2002. Leading creative people: Orchestrating expertise and relationships. *The Leadership Quarterly*, 13: 705–750.

Mumford, M. D., Todd, E. M., Higgs, C., & McIntosh, T. 2017. Cognitive skills and leadership performance: The nine critical skills. *The Leadership Quarterly*, 28: 24–39.

Mumford, M. D., Vessey, W. B., & Barrett, J. D. 2008. Commentary: Measuring divergent thinking: Is there really one solution to the problem? *Psychology of Aesthetics, Creativity, and the Arts*, 2: 86–88.

Mumford, M. D., Zaccaro, S. J., Harding, F. D., Jacobs, T. O., & Fleishman, E. A. 2000. Leadership skills for a changing world: Solving complex social problems. *The Leadership Quarterly*, 11: 11–35.

O'Connor, G. C. 1998. Market learning and radical innovation: A cross case comparison of eight radical innovation projects. *Journal of Product Innovation Management*, 15: 151–166.

Onarheim, B., & Biskjaer, M. M. 2015. Balancing constraints and the sweet spot as coming topics for creativity research. In L. J. Ball (Ed.), *Creativity in design: Understanding, capturing, supporting*: 1–18. Copenhagen: Technical University of Denmark.

Orwell, L., & Perlmutter, M. 1990. The study of wise persons: Integrating a personality perspective. In R. J. Sternberg (Ed.), *Wisdom: Its nature, origins, and development*: 160–177. New York: Cambridge University Press.

Pant, P. N., & Starbuck, W. H. 1990. Innocents in the forest: Forecasting and research methods. *Journal of Management*, 16: 433–460.

Partlow, P. J., Medeiros, K. E., & Mumford, M. D. 2015. Leader cognition in vision formation: Simplicity and negativity. *The Leadership Quarterly*, 26: 448–469.

Pelz, D. C., & Andrews, F. M. 1966. Autonomy, coordination, and stimulation, in relation to scientific achievement. *Systems Research and Behavioral Science*, 11: 89–97.

Redmond, M. R., Mumford, M. D., & Teach, R. 1993. Putting creativity to work: Effects of leader behavior on subordinate creativity. *Organizational Behavior and Human Decision Processes*, 55: 120–151.

Robledo, I. C., Peterson, D. R., & Mumford, M. D. 2012. Leadership of scientists and engineers: A three-vector model. *Journal of Organizational Behavior*, 33: 140–147.

Root-Bernstein, R. S., Bernstein, M., & Garnier, H. 1995. Correlations between avocations, scientific style, work habits, and professional impact of scientists. *Creativity Research Journal*, 8: 115–137.

Scott, G., Leritz, L. E., & Mumford, M. D. 2004. Types of creativity training: Approaches and their effectiveness. *The Journal of Creative Behavior*, 38: 149–179.

Shin, S. J., & Zhou, J. 2003. Transformational leadership, conservation, and creativity: Evidence from Korea. *Academy of Management Journal*, 46: 703–714.

Shipman, A. S., Byrne, C. L., & Mumford, M. D. 2010. Leader vision formation and forecasting: The effects of forecasting extent, resources, and timeframe. *The Leadership Quarterly*, 21: 439–456.

Sosik, J. J., Kahai, S. S., & Avolio, B. J. 1999. Leadership style, anonymity, and creativity in group decision support systems: The mediating role of optimal flow. *The Journal of Creative Behavior*, 33: 227–256.

Sternberg, R. J. 1985. Implicit theories of intelligence, creativity, and wisdom. *Journal of Personality and Social Psychology*, 49: 607–627.

Sternberg, R. J. (Ed.). 1990. *Wisdom: Its nature, origins, and development*. New York: Cambridge University Press.

Stokes, P. D. 2009. Using constraints to create novelty: A case study. *Psychology of Aesthetics, Creativity, and the Arts*, 3: 174–180.

Strange, J. M., & Mumford, M. D. 2005. The origins of vision: Effects of reflection, models, and analysis. *The Leadership Quarterly*, 16: 121–148.

Thamhain, H. J. 2003. Managing innovative R & D teams. *R&D Management*, 33: 297–311.

Tierney, P., & Farmer, S. M. 2002. Creative self-efficacy: Its potential antecedents and relationship to creative performance. *Academy of Management Journal*, 45: 1137–1148.

Tierney, P., & Farmer, S. M. 2011. Creative self-efficacy development and creative performance over time. *Journal of Applied Psychology*, 96: 277–293.

Tierney, P., Farmer, S. M., & Graen, G. B. 1999. An examination of leadership and employee creativity: The relevance of traits and relationships. *Personnel Psychology*, 52: 591–620.

Unsworth, K. 2001. Unpacking creativity. *Academy of Management Review*, 26: 289–297.

Vessey, W. B., Barrett, J. D., Mumford, M. D., Johnson, G., & Litwiller, B. 2014. Leadership of highly creative people in highly creative fields: A historiometric study of scientific leaders. *The Leadership Quarterly*, 25: 672–691.

Wang, D. S., & Hsieh, C. C. 2013. The effect of authentic leadership on employee trust and employee engagement. *Social Behavior and Personality: An International Journal*, 41: 613–624.

West, M. A., Borrill, C. S., Dawson, J. F., Brodbeck, F., Shapiro, D. A., & Haward, B. 2003. Leadership clarity and team innovation in health care. *The Leadership Quarterly*, 14: 393–410.

West, M. A., & Sacramento, C. 2012. Creativity and innovation: The role of team and organizational climate. In M. Mumford (Ed.), *Handbook of organizational creativity*: 359–385. New York: Academic Press.

Zaccaro, S. J., Connelly, S., Repchick, K. M., Daza, A. I., Young, M. C., Kilcullen, R. N., & Bartholomew, L. N. 2015. The influence of higher order cognitive capacities on leader organizational continuance and retention: The mediating role of developmental experiences. *The Leadership Quarterly*, 26: 342–358.

Zaccaro, S. J., Mumford, M. D., Connelly, M. S., Marks, M. A., & Gilbert, J. A. 2000. Assessment of leader problem-solving capabilities. *The Leadership Quarterly*, 11: 37–64.

Zhang, X., & Bartol, K. M. 2010. Linking empowering leadership and employee creativity: The influence of psychological empowerment, intrinsic motivation, and creative process engagement. *Academy of Management Journal*, 53: 107–128.
Zuckerman, H. 1977. *Scientific elite: Nobel laureates in the United States*. New York: Free Press.

5 Leader Behaviors and Employee Creativity

Taking Stock of the Current State of Research

Christina E. Shalley and G. James Lemoine

Introduction

There have been a number of empirical studies focused on leadership behaviors and creativity. In fact, leadership may be the very most examined contextual predictor of creativity in the literature, and fairly consistent findings have emerged across empirical studies. In this chapter, we first review research representative of the major findings concerning how leader behaviors can facilitate employee creativity. This review is not exhaustive, but we believe it is reflective of the research that has been conducted to date on individual level creativity. Recently, Mainemelis, Kark, and Epitropaki (2015) precisely conceptualized creative leadership, and in reviewing prior research, they categorized it into three main conceptualizations. Their first conceptualization, which they labeled Facilitating, dealt with how leaders can help to foster or hinder employee creativity. Our piece fits squarely within this conceptualization. As Mainemelis and colleagues (2015) pointed out, central to the Facilitating conceptualization is what leaders can do to foster employee creativity, as well as how leaders can support employees' creativity.

The leadership literature features many different 'styles' or 'approaches' to leadership, each with their own relevant leader behaviors. In organizing this brief review, we first categorize the various leadership styles common in the literature, and then we discuss some of the major empirical findings for each of these categories. We discovered five main categories of leadership styles and behaviors within which research on creativity as an outcome has been conducted. The first category has received the most research attention and encompasses the transformational and charismatic paradigms, including transactional leadership as a component of the 'full-range leadership model' (Bass, 1985). Another subset of research, which we call 'participative leadership,' involves leadership behaviors aimed at activating subordinate involvement and initiative, such as participative, inclusive, and empowering leadership. Contrarily, a third category of leadership behaviors represents styles which maintain power for the leader him or herself, including authoritarian and directive leadership. The fourth category involves morally focused leadership behaviors, which include both normatively moral (i.e., authentic, ethical, and servant) and immoral (i.e., abusive) leader styles. The final category emerging in our review involves more general leadership behaviors, unconnected to any specific style.[1]

After providing an overall summary of the general findings across these categories, we discuss implications of the collective body of work on leader behavior and employee creativity, and derive from our review some potential new research questions and directions.

Transformational/Charismatic Leadership

Research in this stream often contrasts a 'transformational leader' or a charismatic individual who serves as a motivating and developing role model for employees, with a 'transactional leader,' which might involve contingent reward leadership based on incentives or punishments, or might alternatively represent the absence of leadership altogether (Bass, 1985). Of these leadership types, by far the most work has emerged linking creativity to transformational leadership. In general, transformational leadership is positively associated with creativity, and it has been suggested that organizations may want to train managers to be more transformational in how they lead their employees or use personality testing to identify those who are more likely to serve as transformational leaders (e.g., Jyoti & Dev, 2015). Given that the results of two meta-analyses revealed the positive association between transformational leadership and employee creativity (Hammond et al., 2011; Wang et al., 2011), much of the more recent empirical work has been focused on identifying mediators and moderating conditions of this relationship. For example, Qu, Janssen, and Shi (2015) sought to identify why and when transformational leadership is positively related to employee creativity. They hypothesized that employees' relational identification with leaders could be an underlying mechanism, which might vary by the employees' perceptions of leaders' creativity expectations. Using a Chinese field sample they found support for these hypotheses. Shin and Zhou (2003), in a multi-organizational field design, found that transformational leadership was positively related to employee creativity, and that followers' conservation (i.e., a value) moderated this relationship. They also found that intrinsic motivation mediated the interaction of transformational leadership and followers' conservation, and partially mediated the contribution of transformational leadership to employee creativity.

As for other contingencies, Jyoti and Dev (2015) argued and found a moderating role played by learning orientation in the relationship between transformational leadership and employee creativity. Cheung and Wong (2011) hypothesized that leaders' task and relational support would moderate the relationship between transformational leadership and followers' creativity, and their results indicated that when there was high leader task and relational support, this positive effect was strengthened.

Some research has simultaneously examined the effects of transformational and transactional leadership on creativity. For example, in an experimental study Herrmann and Felfe (2014) tested the moderating effects of task novelty and personal initiative on the relationships between transformational and transactional leadership and creativity. They found that transformational leadership precipitated higher creativity than transactional leadership, and high-task novelty produced higher creativity than low task novelty. They also found that the positive effect of transformational leadership on creativity was stronger when the task was highly novel and personal initiative was high.

In a promising and different approach, Eisenbeiss and Boerner (2013) argued that attention to the positive effects of transformational and charismatic leadership had obscured our understanding of potential negative effects on creativity for these forms of leadership. They tested this idea in a field study involving R&D workers. Developing an integrative framework on the parallel positive and negative effects of transformational leadership and employee creativity, their results indicated that transformational leadership is positively associated with employee creativity. However, it also increases employees' dependency on their leader, which can subsequently reduce their creativity.

One study that focused on transactional leadership by Hussain and colleagues (2017) examined its impact on organizational creativity through the underlying mechanism of knowledge sharing behavior between leaders and employees. Using a field telecom sample, they investigated the effect of offering a contingent reward for knowledge sharing, and they found that knowledge sharing mediated the positive association between transactional leadership and organizational creativity.

Similar results have emerged in studies of charismatic leadership, which generally find that leaders who act as role models and clearly articulate visions tend to boost creative performance. For instance, in an experimental study, Lovelace and Hunter (2013) found that charismatic leaders stimulate subordinate creative performance over and above pragmatic or ideological leaders on middle-stage creative tasks as opposed to early or later stage creative tasks.

Participative Leadership

Other leadership behaviors focus on getting employees involved and supporting their initiative, which may be particularly relevant for creativity. Tung and Yu (2016) examined the role of participative and supportive leadership for enhancing employee creativity through the mediating mechanism of enhanced employee promotion focus. They further argued that instrumental leadership would induce a prevention focus that also would enhance employee creativity. Their Taiwanese field study supported these arguments, suggesting that leaders with very different styles were all able to enhance creativity through distinct mechanisms.

Zhang and Bartol (2010) examined the effect of empowering leadership on employee creativity. They viewed empowering leadership as a process that creates a work context in which employees feel that they can share power with their managers. They stated that empowering leaders give employees autonomy, indicate that they have confidence in their ability to perform their work, try to remove any obstacles that could prevent them from performing effectively, and stress the meaning and importance of the work. In a study of IT professionals and their supervisors in China, they found that empowering leadership positively affected psychological empowerment, impacting both intrinsic motivation and creative process engagement, and in turn increasing employee creativity. They also found that empowerment role identity moderated the link between empowering leadership and psychological empowerment, and leaders' encouragement of creativity moderated the connection between creative process engagement and psychological empowerment.

Using an interesting contingent contextual approach, Harris and colleagues (2014) conducted two studies that focused on newcomers to the organization. Specifically, they examined how empowering leaders, newcomer trust in these leaders, and organizational support for creativity were associated with employee creativity. In their first study they found relationships between empowering leadership and creativity, which became stronger contingent upon perceived organizational support for creativity. In Study 2, however, they discovered that this perceived organizational support for creativity was a less important moderator of creative process engagement than the amount of trust the newcomers had in management. In a related finding, Zhang and Zhou (2014) found that empowering leadership had the strongest relation to employee creativity when the employees trusted their supervisors, and they had high uncertainty avoidance, with creative self-efficacy mediating this effect.

Taking a different approach, Dong and colleagues (2015) found that customers' empowering behaviors, such as their placing faith in employees and supporting their autonomy, were positively related to service employees' creativity, and this effect was mediated through service employees' state promotion focus. They also found that both customers' and supervisors' empowering behavior worked synergistically in their relationship with employee creativity.

Inclusive leaders who are open, accessible, and available to their employees have also been shown to facilitate employee creativity. For example, Carmeli, Reiter-Palmon, and Ziv (2010) found that inclusive leadership was positively related to employees' perceptions of psychological safety, which contributed to greater employee involvement in their creative work.

Authoritarian/Directive Leadership

In general, 'controlling supervision' styles such as authoritarian or directive leadership have been found to be negatively associated with employee creativity (e.g., Oldham & Cummings, 1996), although such research is somewhat rare. Much of this work has focused more on supportive or non-controlling supervision rather than controlling supervision. An interesting study by Wang and colleagues (2013) focused on how authoritarian and benevolent leadership styles interacted with the sex of the leaders. They studied a predominantly male R&D department and contrasted it with a predominantly female customer service division. They found that the negative relationship between an authoritarian leadership style and subordinate performance, including task performance, creativity, and citizenship behavior, was stronger for female rather than male leaders. On the other hand, they found that benevolent leadership was positively related to employee performance and this effect was stronger for male leaders as opposed to female leaders.

Moral Leadership

A fourth stream of leadership research deals with behaviors and styles centered on morality (or the lack thereof) in which leaders are guided primarily by their moral identities (Aquino & Reed, 2002). Ethical leadership, for instance (Brown, Treviño, & Harrison, 2005), is commonly viewed as a positive predictor of creativity, and most research on this relationship has sought to identify its underlying mechanisms. For example, two studies have investigated the mediating role of psychological empowerment in the relationship between ethical leadership and follower creativity. Both studies were in the Pakistani context: one of doctors in a large public hospital (Chughtai, 2016) and one of supervisor-subordinate dyads working in hotels (Javed et al., 2017). Both found mediated relationships of ethical leadership on creativity through psychological empowerment, with the latter also finding support for leader-member exchange as a full mediator.

Voice and knowledge sharing serve as other salient precursors of creativity, similar to empowerment in that if employees do not feel empowered, they may not speak up or share knowledge. Chen and Hou (2016) proposed that the voice behavior of employees serves as an underlying mechanism in the relationship between ethical leadership and employee creativity. In a Taiwanese R&D sample, they found that there was a positive relationship between employee perceptions of ethical leadership and employees' voice behavior. Voice behavior was related to employee creativity, and the indirect effect of ethical leadership on creativity through voice behavior was stronger when the employees worked in a more innovative climate. Finally, Ma et al. (2013) examined the mediating role of knowledge sharing and self-efficacy in the relationship between ethical leadership and employee creativity in a Chinese field study. They found support for knowledge sharing and self-efficacy as mediating mechanisms.

Servant leadership (Liden et al., 2008) represents an alternative approach to moral leadership focused on stakeholders. Liden and colleagues (2014) tested a model in which servant leaders developed a 'serving culture' and found that this type of culture had a positive effect on employee creativity. Neubert and colleagues (2008) hypothesized and found support for employees' promotion focus as a mediator of the relationship between servant leadership and employee creative behavior. Eight years later, Neubert and his colleagues (2016) once again found that servant leadership was positively related to employees' creative behavior and that the organizational structure moderated this relationship through employee satisfaction.

There is also support for relationships between creativity and authentic leadership, which focuses on the leader's own self-awareness and self-concordance (Gardner et al., 2005). For example, Rego et al. (2012, 2014) found support for psychological capital, its component of hope, and positive affect as mediators linking authentic leadership and employee creativity. Similarly, Semedo and colleagues (2016, 2017) concluded that authentic leadership boosted creativity through affective well-being and resourcefulness.

On the opposite end of the moral leadership spectrum, abusive supervision reflects an immoral approach to leadership (Tepper, 2007). Research linking abusive supervision with creativity is somewhat rare, but what does exist points to its negative effect. For example, Liu and colleagues (2016) identified two sequential mechanisms underlying the effect of abusive supervision on employee creativity. In a multi-source, time lagged study, they found support for their proposition that abusive supervision worked through psychological safety, which then affected organizational identification, which in turn impacted creativity. In a very novel study, Liu, Liao, and Loi (2012) focused on how and when department leaders' abusive supervision can flow down organizational levels to undermine employee creativity. They found that team leaders' abusive supervision mediated the negative relationship between department leaders' abusive supervision and individual team members' creativity. They hypothesized and found that team leaders' and members' attributions for their own supervisors' motives for being abusive (i.e., performance-promotion and injury-initiation) determined the extent to which team leaders' abusive supervision explained the effect of department leaders' abusive supervision on employee creativity.

General Leadership Behaviors

There have been a number of studies that have not focused specifically on any particular leadership style, but instead examined the general role of leaders' behaviors for facilitating employees' creativity. For example, broadly supportive leadership has been found to be related to employee creativity. This type of leadership can take a number of forms (e.g., clearly specifying the goals for their job or offering help) and seems to operate through enhancing employees' intrinsic motivation, positive affect, or their feelings of psychological safety (e.g., George & Zhou, 2007; Madjar, Oldham, & Pratt, 2002; Zhang & Bartol, 2010). For example, in a longitudinal study of knowledge workers using daily surveys, Amabile and colleagues

(2004) examined both the positive (e.g., conveying intellectual and technical competence) and negative (e.g., close monitoring) leadership behaviors that were associated with employee creativity. Similarly, Oldham and Cummings (1996) found that employees that were supervised in supportive and non-controlling ways had higher levels of creativity than those supervised in a more controlling fashion.

Carmeli, Gelbard, and Reiter-Palmon (2013) in two studies demonstrated that leader supportive behaviors impacted employee creativity, both directly and indirectly through facilitating knowledge sharing and employee creative problem solving. Wu and colleagues (2008) found that leaders' promotion focused behaviors were positively related to employee creativity. Redmond, Mumford, and Teach (1993) experimentally manipulated three leader behaviors that they hypothesized would facilitate their followers' creativity. These behaviors contributed to employee problem construction, developing learning goals, and building their feelings of self-efficacy. They found that leader behaviors that contributed to problem construction and feelings of self-efficacy increased follower creativity. Venkataramani and colleagues (2014) found that leaders' social networks affected their employees' radical creativity. Specifically, they argued that when the leader is a critical liaison (i.e., between-centrality) in information exchange and interactions, this can facilitate their employees' creativity. Finally, Tierney and Farmer (2004) focused on the Pygmalion process for the creativity of R&D employees. They found that when supervisors had higher expectations for employee creativity, their employees perceived that they were more supportive of creativity, and creative self-efficacy mediated the effect of supervisor expectations, supervisors' behaviors and employees' views on creative performance.

There have been a few studies that have looked at the role of leaders' creativity as predictors of employees' creativity (e.g., Mathisen, Einarsen, & Mykletun, 2012). For example, Koseoglu, Liu, and Shalley (2017) used role identity theory to argue that leaders who are creative themselves can serve as potential role models for their employees' creativity via helping to enhance their employees' creative role identity. They examined this in a Chinese sample and their hypotheses were supported, indicating that the creative behaviors of leaders themselves are worthy of further attention. In an interesting experimental study, Jaussi and Dionne (2003) looked at the relationship of leaders' unconventional behavior (e.g., standing on furniture) and their followers' creativity. They found that unconventional behavior positively and significantly interacted with followers' perceptions of their leader as being a role model to positively predict their creativity.

Implications for Leader Behaviors and Creativity, and Future Research Directions

Overall, our review of the extant empirical literature suggests that leaders not only have a positive impact on employee creativity, but virtually *any* marginally positive leadership behavior seems to precipitate creativity. It seems that a leader can be charismatic or transactional; empowering or focused on ethical compliance; servant, educational, or creative themselves; and any of these behaviors (and many others) increase employee creativity. With few exceptions, the research reviewed painted a positive picture of leader behavior and creativity, with very few studies proposing or finding negative, mixed, or nonsignificant relationships. Given the long-standing proposition by theorists of creativity being infrequent, unusual, and even rare (Sternberg & Lubart, 1991; Vincent & Kouchaki, 2016), it seems somewhat contradictory to conclude that virtually anything a leader does might serve to substantially increase employee creativity. Although leadership is expected to have meaningful effects on employee attitudes and behaviors, does this conclusion stretch the power of leadership too far?

One resolution for this question might be to conclude that creativity is not as rare as some have expected. Indeed, some scholars have concluded that this is the case, arguing that whereas individuals capable of truly groundbreaking creativity are seldom encountered, creativity exists in the everyday sense in 'normal people' as well (Mayer, 1999). This might be best captured by research distinguishing 'radical' or breakthrough creativity of wholly new processes and products, from 'incremental' or minor creativity providing relatively small tweaks and edits (Madjar, Greenberg, & Chen, 2011). Some scholars have suggested that radical creativity might be far less prevalent in organizations than incremental creativity (Lemoine, Shalley, & Xu, 2017), and if this is true, it's plausible that most leader behaviors have their strongest impact on incremental creativity. Which leader behaviors, then, might affect groundbreaking radical creativity?

A second explanation for the question of how virtually every leader behavior might impact creativity would be a methodological effect, not dissimilar to a 'halo effect' in which evaluations of leader behaviors inadvertently tap creative characteristics or processes themselves. For instance, van Knippenberg and Sitkin (2013) have argued that studies of charismatic/transformational leadership should be interpreted while considering the items used to measure it, as those items are often conflated with outcomes. In the case of creativity, the MLQ (the most common operationalization of charismatic/transformational leadership) features items indicating that the leader "gets me to look at problems from many different angles" and "suggests new ways of looking at how to complete assignments," (Bass & Avolio, 1989) both of which sound very much like part of the creative process. Other leadership operationalizations may feature similar issues in that leadership is measured as itself featuring creativity or known antecedents of creativity, such as items from empowering leadership scales like "encourages work group members to exchange information with one another" (Arnold et al., 2000) or servant leadership items such as "my manager can solve work problems with new or creative ideas" (Liden et al., 2008). If leadership measures themselves reflect creative processes, then the widespread relationship of leaders' behaviors to creativity becomes less surprising; instead, it suggests tautology.

A third possible reason for these ubiquitous relationships might be that theory on the outcomes of leadership, and the antecedents of creativity, are often quite similar. Intrinsic motivation, for example, is often positioned as both one of the most salient outcomes of effective leadership (Burns, 1978), and as one of the three most important individual predictors of creativity (Amabile, 1996). Is it surprising, then, that leadership would impact creativity? If effective leadership creates trust, learning, and enhanced communication, all of which are established antecedents of creativity, then the idea that leadership and creativity might be linked becomes intuitive. This perspective would support the widespread results found in this review, as the exact content of the leader behaviors would matter much less than the simple question of whether or not exposure to the leader created motivation, trust, learning, and so on. In this case, it becomes intuitive that leadership should precipitate creativity.

This suggests the potential for a broad theoretical perspective of leadership and creativity, which might help to explain all of these research results. Such a theory-based approach could also shed light on the numerous mediators revealed in our review. Many of the mediators in these studies are either well-known antecedents of creativity or are themselves arguably components of collective creativity. We found that mediators in these studies are, overall, quite similar to one another, with many papers investigating mediators connected to (for instance) efficacy, empowerment, psychological safety, identification, trust, and commitment. Research studying these mediating mechanisms, or mediating mechanisms which are themselves part of creativity such as creative process engagement or speaking up, constitute nearly the entirety of the process models we reviewed. These similarities would seem to indicate an underlying theory: when conditions are created for enhanced efficacy and resources, or when they strengthen connections between the employee and their organization, enhanced creativity should result, as efficacy, resources, and connections should all provide the intrinsic motivation needed for creativity to flourish.

We expect that there is some truth to all three of these explanations helping to explain the results of our review, and consequently suggest that additional research merely indicating links between leader behaviors and creativity may have limited theoretical or practical value. Instead, we suggest scholars dive deeper into questions of which leader behaviors may more strongly precipitate creativity than others; when supposedly positive leader behaviors might hamper creativity or feasibly negative behaviors might enhance it; or what types of creativity certain leader behaviors might most strongly promote. Are any of these leader behaviors, for instance, truly capable of driving groundbreaking creativity in times of crisis? Does leadership, when operationalized in a manner devoid of inherent creative content and measured in a way accounting for any halo effects, still correlate with employee creativity? Perhaps most importantly, is there a simple underlying theory that might explain the links between all of these leader behaviors and creativity? We expect there is, and we repeat our suspicion here that perhaps we have missed the forest for the trees. It may well be that in general, positive leader behaviors build self-efficacy, increase resource availability, and enhance positive affect, in general and toward the organization, team, coworkers, and leader. All of these would be expected to boost an employee's intrinsic motivation (Vroom, 1964), which in turn would motivate creativity (Amabile, 1996).

One promising avenue to build the 'when' of such a theory (Whetten, 1989) might be to consider that 'when' literally, and examine how leadership and creativity might affect each other temporally. This does not merely indicate potential for reciprocal effects of follower creativity on leader behaviors, although such an investigation might be promising in its alignment with recent developments in followership theory and the 'co-production' of leadership (Uhl-Bien et al., 2014). If followers can influence their leaders' behaviors, would those changed leadership behaviors continue to promote creativity to the same degree that the original behaviors did? Would changes to leadership behaviors last, or fade over time? Temporal investigations might also examine, for instance, whether continued exposure to the same leadership behaviors continue to increase creativity beyond the initial amount, or if their effects on creativity diminish over time. Could a follower become so accustomed to an empowering leader, for example, that the leader's impact on creativity fades? Or could the empowering leader have exponential effects over time, inspiring subordinates to redouble their creative efforts? Alternatively, do creativity-supported leader behaviors need to be maintained, or would relatively limited exposure be sufficient to drive some forms of creativity? How does exposure to multiple styles of leadership, or dramatically different leadership behaviors, affect creativity over time, and does the order of the behaviors, or the degree to which they are repeated, matter? Application of temporal theories and perspectives (Bluedorn & Denhardt, 1988; Mitchell & James, 2001) offer many promising and practically meaningful new research directions that might expand our understanding of how and when leadership behaviors impact creativity.

Our review of empirically investigated moderators of leadership's effect on creativity revealed opportunities to more deeply explore contextual contingencies. The large majority of moderators we identified were personal rather than contextual, including followers' individual differences, trust, ability, and emotion. Quite often, these moderators mirrored antecedents of creativity such as learning, motivation, and well-being. A much smaller number of studies examined contextual variables as potentially impacting the effectiveness of leadership in driving creativity. Although it is well established that both leadership and context affect creativity, and that their joint effects are important to consider (see Shalley & Gilson, 2004, for a review), little empirical work has investigated this promising area. Further, what work does exist accounting for contextual factors in the relationship between leadership and creativity most often examines similarly broad moderators such as 'creativity climate' or 'climate for innovation.' We suggest that there is a need to move beyond such panoptic and creativity-centric moderators to examine other contextual factors important for leadership to effectively grow creativity. Some evidence of this was found in our review; for instance, Li and colleagues (2016) found that task interdependence might enhance some negative effects of transformational leadership on individual innovation, and Murphy and Ensher's (2008) qualitative examination of television production teams revealed that the organization's structure, in terms of follower distance from leaders, represents an important contingency. It is likely that certain leadership behaviors are more effective at driving creativity in times of crisis than others and that job roles, or task and team characteristics, might render certain leadership behaviors more useful at certain times. Also, we may see differences across industries and nationalities. The joint effects of leadership and context are a promising area for further exploration, offering the potential for building more practically useful knowledge.

This deeper examination of leadership and creativity might also mandate an emphasis placed on the potential 'dark side' of leadership, to balance the overwhelmingly positive view of leadership and creativity that emerges in the current body of literature. We see this as having to do with investigating when seemingly positive forms of leadership can lead to unintended consequences, sometimes forming an unexpected paradox. Mainemelis and colleagues (2015) suggested that the examination of paradoxes in creativity research remain a relatively unexplored area. Some promising work within this stream has recently emerged, such as Shalley and Gilson's (2017) investigation of the need for balancing standardization and creativity, and research on creative deviance which has found complex and varied relationships between different leader responses and subsequent creative behaviors (Lin, Mainemelis, & Kark, 2016). Eisenbeiss and Boerner's (2013) work on the negative side effects of transformational leadership on employee creativity also fits within this general direction, and there are a number of avenues that could be examined to pursue similar ideas. When might leader charisma or creativity hinder subordinate creativity? Could well-intentioned leadership result in followers taking the wrong path, attempting a creative project too grand or sweeping for their abilities or authority, or engaging in processes which hinder rather than help creativity? For instance, leadership is often credited with building follower efficacy (e.g., Redmond, Mumford, & Teach, 1993) and self-esteem (Greenleaf, 1977). It is plausible that at very high levels of such variables, followers might resist creative endeavors, thinking that they already possess the needed answers. Similarly, the high levels of cohesion thought to result from positive leadership (e.g., Waldman & Yammarino, 1999) could lead teams to engage in 'groupthink' processes harmful to creativity. Even leadership's positive impact on organizational commitment (e.g., Leroy, Palanski, & Simons, 2012) might cause followers to resist change, forgoing opportunities to creatively improve processes due to their belief that the organization is desirable in its existing state. An empowered team might not be motivated to use their autonomy to engage in creativity, or a team featuring shared leadership may not feel the authority to engage in creativity. In this manner, positive leader behaviors might, at certain times or at certain levels, suppress subordinate creativity.

Compilations of leader behaviors, as popularized in leadership 'styles,' might also have unintended consequences for creativity. Ethical leadership, for instance, prioritizes follower compliance with organizational norms, rules, and standards (Brown, Treviño, & Harrison, 2005). Although this form of leadership has been linked to creativity (e.g., Ma et al., 2013), it seems reasonable to conclude that a focus on compliance and rules might stifle divergent thought in some situations. Of course, research has indicated that some structure and standardization is beneficial for creativity (Gilson et al., 2005); with this in mind, could the more free-wheeling autonomy of participative and empowering leadership imply some limitations on creative outcomes? When might a leader's moral focus, as exemplified by authentic, ethical, or servant leadership, hinder or even conflict with creative processes or outcomes? Given a certain context, which of the many leader behaviors outlined here would most effectively drive creative performance, and why?

In conclusion, the research linking leader behaviors to employee creativity is large and quite varied. We do not question that this body of literature as a whole has made meaningful contributions to our theoretical and conceptual understandings of how leadership and creativity relate. We argue, however, that we may now possess sufficient knowledge of leadership behaviors' widespread positive impact on creativity and why they occur. Now is the time for more advanced theory building and operational refinement to determine not whether leadership impacts creativity, but under what conditions might leader behavior *best* impact creativity, and when.

Note

1 We did not include studies on leader-member exchange (LMX) in this review, as LMX research tends to focus on relationship quality between the leader and follower, rather than specific behaviors undertaken by a leader that might impact creativity.

References

Amabile, T. M. 1996. *Creativity in context*. Boulder, CO: Westview Press.

Amabile, T. M., Schatzel, E. A., Moneta, G. B., & Kramer, S. J. 2004. Leader behaviors and the work environment for creativity: Perceived leader support. *The Leadership Quarterly*, 15: 5–32.

Aquino, K., & Reed, A., II. 2002. The self-importance of moral identity. *Journal of Personality and Social Psychology*, 83(6): 1423–1440.

Arnold, J. A., Arad, S., Rhoades, J. A., & Drasgow, F. 2000. The empowering leadership questionnaire: The construction and validation of a new scale for measuring leader behaviors. *Journal of Organizational Behavior*, 21(3): 249–269.

Bass, B. M. 1985. *Leadership and performance beyond expectations*. New York: Free Press.
Bass, B. M., & Avolio, B. 1989. *Manual for the multifactor leadership questionnaire*. Palo Alto, CA: Consulting Psychologists Press.
Bluedorn, A. C., & Denhardt, R. B. 1988. Time and organizations. *Journal of Management*, 14(2): 299–320.
Brown, M. E., Treviño, L. K., & Harrison, D. A. 2005. Ethical leadership: A social learning perspective for construct development and testing. *Organizational Behavior and Human Decision Processes*, 97(2): 117–134.
Burns, J. M. 1978. *Leadership*. New York: Harper & Row, Publishers, Inc.
Carmeli, A., Gelbard, R., & Reiter-Palmon, R. 2013. Leadership, creative problem-solving capacity, and creative performance: The importance of knowledge sharing. *Human Resource Management*, 52: 95–121.
Carmeli, A., Reiter-Palmon, R., & Ziv, E. 2010. Inclusive leadership and employee involvement in creative tasks in the workplace: The mediating role of psychological safety. *Creativity Research Journal*, 22: 250–260.
Chen, A. S. Y., & Hou, Y. H. 2016. The effects of ethical leadership, voice behavior and climates for innovation on creativity: A moderated mediation examination. *The Leadership Quarterly*, 27: 1–13.
Cheung, M. F., & Wong, C. S. 2011. Transformational leadership, leader support, and employee creativity. *Leadership and Organization Development Journal*, 32: 656–672.
Chughtai, A. 2016. Can ethical leaders enhance their follower's creativity? *Leadership*, 12: 230–249.
Dong, Y., Liao, H., Chuang, A., Zhou, J., & Campbell, E. M. 2015. Fostering employee service creativity: Joint effects of customer empowering behaviors and supervisory empowering leadership. *Journal of Applied Psychology*, 100(5): 1364–1380.
Eisenbeiss, S. A., & Boerner, S. 2013. A double-edged sword: Transformational leadership and individual creativity. *British Journal of Management*, 24: 54–68.
Gardner, W. L., Avolio, B. J., Luthans, F., May, D. R., & Walumbwa, F. 2005. "Can you see the real me?" A self-based model of authentic leader and follower development. *Leadership Quarterly*, 16(3): 343–372.
George, J. M., & Zhou, J. 2007. Dual tuning in a supportive context: Joint contributions of positive mood, negative mood, and supervisory behavior to employee creativity. *Academy of Management Journal*, 50: 605–622.
Gilson, L. L., Mathieu, J. E., Shalley, C. E., & Ruddy, T. M. 2005. Creativity and standardization: Complementary or conflicting drivers of team effectiveness? *Academy of Management Journal*, 48(3): 521–531.
Greenleaf, R. K. 1977. *Servant leadership: A journey into the nature of legitimate power and greatness*. Mahwah, NJ: Paulist Press.
Hammond, M. M., Neff, N. I., Farr, J. L., Schwall, A. R., & Zhao, X. 2011. Predictors of individual-level innovation at work: A meta-analysis. *Psychology of Aesthetics, Creativity and the Arts*, 5: 90–105.
Harris, T. B., Li, N., Boswell, W. R., Zhang, X. A., & Zie, Z. 2014. Getting what's new from newcomers: Empowering leadership, creativity and adjustment in the socialization context. *Personnel Psychology*, 67: 567–604.
Herrmann, D., & Fefe, J. 2014. Moderators of the relationships between leadership style and employee creativity: The role of task novelty and personal initiative. *Creativity Research Journal*, 25: 172–181.

Hussain, S. T., Abbas, J., Lei, S., Haider, M. J., & Abrams, T. 2017. Transactional leadership and organizational creativity: Examining the mediating role of knowledge sharing behavior. *Cogent Business & Management*, 4: 136–163.

Jaussi, K. S., & Dionne, S. D. 2003. Leading for creativity: The role of unconventional leader behavior. *The Leadership Quarterly*, 14: 475–498.

Javed, B., Khan, A. A., Bashir, S., & Arjoon, S. 2017. Impact of ethical leadership on creativity: The role of psychological empowerment. *Current Issues in Tourism*, 20: 839–851.

Jyoti, J., & Dev, M. 2015. The impact of transformational leadership on employee creativity: The role of learning orientation. *Journal of Asia Business Studies*, 9: 78–98.

Koseoglu, G., Liu, Y., & Shalley, C. E. 2017. Working with creative leaders: Exploring the relationship between supervisors creativity and their employees' creativity. *The Leadership Quarterly*, 28: 798–811.

Lemoine, G. J., Shalley, C. E., & Xu, N. 2017. *Individual and team creativity: An interactionist examination of creativity in different contexts*. Paper presented at the Academy of Management Annual Meeting, Atlanta, GA.

Leroy, H., Palanski, M. E., & Simons, T. 2012. Authentic leadership and behavioral integrity as drivers of follower commitment and performance. *Journal of Business Ethics*, 107(3): 255–264.

Li, V., Mitchell, R., & Boyle, B. 2016. The divergent effects of transformational leadership on individual and team innovation. *Group & Organization Management*, 41(1): 66–97.

Liden, R. C., Wayne, S. J., Liao, C., & Meuser, J. D. 2014. Servant leadership and serving culture: Influence on individual and unit performance. *Academy of Management Journal*, 57: 1434–1452.

Liden, R. C., Wayne, S. J., Zhao, H., & Henderson, D. 2008. Servant leadership: Development of a multidimensional measure and multi-level assessment. *The Leadership Quarterly*, 19(2): 161–177.

Lin, B., Mainemelis, C., & Kark, R. 2016. Leaders' responses to creative deviance: Differential effects on subsequent creative deviance and creative performance. *The Leadership Quarterly*, 27(4): 537–556.

Liu, D., Liao, H., & Loi, R. 2012. The dark side of leadership: A three-level investigation of the cascading effect of abusive supervision on employee creativity. *Academy of Management Journal*, 55(1): 1187–1212.

Liu, W., Zhang, P., Liao, J., Hao, P., & Mao, J. 2016. Abusive supervision and employee creativity: The mediating role of psychological safety and organizational identification. *Management Decision*, 54: 130–147.

Lovelace, J. B., & Hunter, S. T. 2013. Charismatic, ideological, and pragmatic leaders' influence on subordinate creative performance across the creative process. *Creativity Research Journal*, 25: 59–74.

Ma, Y., Cheng, W., Ribbens, B. A., & Zhou, J. 2013. Linking ethical leadership to employee creativity: Knowledge sharing and self-efficacy as mediators. *Social Behavior and Personality: An International Journal*, 41: 1409–1419.

Madjar, N., Greenberg, E., & Chen, Z. 2011. Factors for radical creativity, incremental creativity, and routine, noncreative performance. *Journal of Applied Psychology*, 96(4): 730–743.

Madjar, N., Oldham, G. R., & Pratt, M. G. 2002. There's no place like home? The contributions of work and nonwork support to employees' creative performance. *Academy of Management Journal*, 45: 757–767.

Mainemelis, C., Kark, O., & Epitropaki, O. 2015. Creative leadership: A multi-context conceptualization. *The Academy of Management Annals*, 9: 393–482.

Mathisen, G., Einarsen, S., & Mykletun, R. 2012. Creative leaders promote creative organizations. *International Journal of Manpower*, 33: 367–382.

Mayer, R. E. 1999. Fifty years of creativity research. In R. Sternberg (Ed.), *Handbook of creativity*: 449–460. New York: Cambridge University Press.

Mitchell, T. R., & James, L. R. 2001. Building better theory: Time and the specification of when things happen. *Academy of Management Review*, 26(4): 530–547.

Murphy, S. E., & Ensher, E. A. 2008. A qualitative analysis of charismatic leadership in creative teams: The case of television directors. *The Leadership Quarterly*, 19(3): 335–352.

Neubert, M. J., Hunter, E. M., & Tolentino, R. C. 2016. A servant leader and their stakeholders: When does organizational structure enhance a leader's influence? *The Leadership Quarterly*, 27: 896–910.

Neubert, M. J., Kacmar, K. M., Carlson, D. S., Chonko, L. B., & Roberts, J. A. 2008. Regulatory focus as a mediator of the influence of initiating structure and servant leadership on employee behavior. *Journal of Applied Psychology*, 93: X–1220.

Oldham, G. R., & Cummings, A. 1996. Employee creativity: Personal and contextual factors at work. *Academy of Management Journal*, 39: 607–634.

Qu, R., Janssen, O., & Shi, K. 2015. Transformational leadership and follower creativity: The mediating role of follower relational identification and the moderating role of leader creativity expectations. *The Leadership Quarterly*, 26: 286–299.

Redmond, M. R., Mumford, M. D., & Teach, R. 1993. Putting creativity to work: Effects of leader behavior on subordinate creativity. *Organizational Behavior and Human Decision Processes*, 55: 120–151.

Rego, A., Sousa, P., Marques, C., & Pina e Cunha, M. 2012. Authentic leadership promoting employees' psychological capital and creativity. *Journal of Business Research*, 65: 429–437.

Rego, A., Sousa, P., Marques, C., & Pina e Cunha, M. 2014. Hope and positive affect mediating the authentic leadership and creativity relationship. *Journal of Business Research*, 67: 200–210.

Semedo, A. S. D., Coelho, A. F. M., & Ribeiro, N. M. P. 2016. Effects of authentic leadership, affective commitment and job resourcefulness on employees' creativity and individual performance. *Leadership & Organization Development Journal*, 37(8): 1038–1055.

Semedo, A. S. D., Coelho, A. F. M., & Ribeiro, N. M. P. 2017. Authentic leadership and creativity: The mediating role of happiness. *International Journal of Organizational Analysis*, 25(3): 395–412.

Shalley, C. E., & Gilson, L. L. 2004. What leaders need to know: A review of social and contextual factors that can foster or hinder creativity. *The Leadership Quarterly*, 15: 33–53.

Shalley, C. E., & Gilson, L. L. 2017. Creativity and the management of technology: Balancing creativity and standardization. *Production and Operations Management*, 26: 605–616.

Shin, S. J., & Zhou, J. 2003. Transformational leadership, conservation, and creativity: Evidence from Korea. *Academy of Management Journal*, 46: 703–714.

Sternberg, R. J., & Lubart, T. I. 1991. An investment theory of creativity and its development. *Human Development*, 34(1): 1–31.

Tepper, B. J. 2007. Abusive supervision in work organizations: Review, synthesis, and research agenda. *Journal of Management*, 33(3): 261–289.

Tierney, P., & Farmer, S. M. 2004. The Pygmalion process and employee creativity. *Journal of Management*, 30(3): 413–432.

Tung, F. C., & Yu, T. W. 2016. Does innovation leadership enhance creativity in high-tech industries? *Leadership and Organization Development Journal*, 37: 579–591.

Uhl-Bien, M., Riggio, R. E., Lowe, K. B., & Carsten, M. K. 2014. Followership theory: A review and research agenda. *The Leadership Quarterly*, 25(1): 83–104.

Van Knippenberg, D., & Sitkin, S. B. 2013. A critical assessment of charismatic-transformational leadership research: Back to the drawing board? *The Academy of Management Annals*, 7(1): 1–60.

Venkataramani, V., Richter, A., & Clarke, R. 2014. Creative benefits from well-connected leaders? Leader social network ties as facilitators of employee radical creativity. *Journal of Applied Psychology*, 99: 966–975.

Vincent, L. C., & Kouchaki, M. 2016. Creative, rare, entitled, and dishonest: How commonality of creativity in one's group decreases an individual's entitlement and dishonesty. *Academy of Management Journal*, 59(4): 1451–1473.

Vroom, V. H. 1964. *Work and motivation*. New York: Wiley-Blackwell.

Waldman, D. A., & Yammarino, F. J. 1999. CEO charismatic leadership: Levels-of- management and levels-of-analysis effects. *Academy of Management Review*, 24(2): 266–285.

Wang, G., Oh, I. S., Courtright, S. H., Colbert, A. E. 2011. Transformational leadership and performance across criteria and levels: A meta-analytic review of 25 years of research. *Group and Organization Management*, 36: 223–270.

Wang, A. C., Chiang, J. T. J., Tsai, C. Y., Lin, T. T., & Cheng, B. S. 2013. Gender makes a difference: The moderating role of leader gender on the relationship between leadership styles and subordinate performance. *Organizational Behavior and Human Decision Processes*, 122: 101–113.

Whetten, D. A. 1989. What constitutes a theoretical contribution? *Academy of Management Review*, 14(4): 490–495.

Wu, C., McMullen, J. S., Neubert, M. J., & Yi, X. 2008. The influence of leader regulatory focus on employee creativity. *Journal of Business Venturing*, 23: 587–602.

Zhang, X., & Bartol, K. M. 2010. Linking empowering leadership and employee creativity: The influence of psychological empowerment, intrinsic motivation, and creative process engagement. *Academy of Management Journal*, 53: 107–128.

Zhang, X., & Zhou, J. 2014. Empowering leadership, uncertainty avoidance, trust, and employee creativity: Interaction effects and a mediating mechanism. *Organizational Behavior and Human Decision Processes*, 124: 150–164.

6 Empowering Leadership and Team Creativity

The Roles of Team Learning Behavior, Team Creative Efficacy, and Team Task Complexity

Xiaomeng Zhang and Ho Kwong Kwan

Introduction

As one way of coping with rapid technological change and fierce global competition, many organizations rely heavily on employee creativity, which can substantially contribute to organizational innovation, productivity, and survival (Liu et al., 2017; Shalley, Zhou, & Oldham, 2004). To ignite the creative spark of employees, organizations are increasingly using team-based structures (Paulus, 2008). New ideas are proposed and pursued by work teams through interaction among team members, and such creative collaboration is shown to pay considerable dividends (Hülsheger, Anderson, & Salgado, 2009). Therefore, it is important to understand the conditions that contribute to team creativity (Shalley, Zhou, & Oldham, 2004), which refers to the production of novel and potentially useful ideas about products, services, processes, and procedures by a group of employees (Shin & Zhou, 2007).

A number of scholars theorize that the empowering behavior of team leaders plays a key role in giving team members latitude, thus stimulating creative action by the team (Amabile et al., 2004). Indeed, Zhang and Bartol (2010) theorized that empowering leadership addresses the underlying nature of creative work and they, for the first time, empirically found that empowering leadership has a positive influence on individual employees' creativity. More recently, Zhang and Zhou (2014) also found that perceptions of empowering leadership are positively associated with employee creativity. Because organizations now rely heavily on team creativity to remain competitive, it is theoretically important and empirically necessary to extend the relationship between empowering leadership and creativity to a team level. Empowering leadership at the team level is defined as team leader behaviors that facilitate the sharing of power with and enhance the work motivation of team members (Srivastava, Bartol, & Locke, 2006). Moreover, Marks and colleagues' team effectiveness model has theorized that team leader behaviors influence team effectiveness through the simultaneous mediating effects of team processes and emergent states (Marks,

Mathieu, & Zaccaro, 2001). Therefore, a major purpose of this study is to build on and extend Amabile's (1983, 1996) componential model of creativity and Amabile and Pratt's (2016) dynamic componential theory of creativity to theorize a conceptual model that bridges empowering leadership with team creativity via the necessary mediation mechanisms.

Moreover, the contingency perspective of leadership (Liden & Antonakis, 2009; Yukl, 2013) holds that leadership is a social construct and cannot be fully understood when examined in isolation from the context in which it occurs. That is, a team leader's role is salient only within a specific context (Zhang & Zhou, 2014). A few studies of creativity suggest that a promising direction for future research is to examine how leadership style interacts with other contextual variables in influencing the creative outcomes of teams (Wang, Kim, & Lee, 2016; Zhou & Hoever, 2014). Shalley and colleagues (2004) called for research into the interaction effects of supervisory style and task complexity—two key characteristics of the organizational context that have long been considered to be important contributors to creativity. Team task complexity refers to the extent to which a team task has a high level of information-processing requirements and few set procedures (Man & Lam, 2003). Based on the notion that a high level of team task complexity requires team leaders to play a greater role (Morgeson, 2005), we propose that empowering leadership has a greater impact on team learning behavior and team creative efficacy, and, ultimately, team creativity, when the level of task complexity is high.

In sum, this chapter makes a number of contributions. First, we extend both the leadership and the creativity literature by investigating the connection between empowering leadership and creativity in a field setting. Second, we consider team learning behavior and team creative efficacy (as the team process and the team emergent state, respectively) simultaneously to investigate their mediating effects on the empowering leadership-team creativity relationship. Third, we explore the moderating influence of team task complexity on the aforementioned relationships to identify the boundary condition for the effectiveness of empowering leadership.

Theory and Hypotheses

Empowering Leadership and Team Creativity

According to the studies of Arnold et al. (2000) and Srivastava, Bartol, and Locke (2006), there are five dimensions of empowering leader behavior: *leading by example*, which reflects a leader's commitment to his or her own work and the work of team members for the achievement of better performance; *coaching*, which refers to actions that educate team members and help them to become more efficient and self-reliant; *participative decision making*, which encourages the sharing among team members of ideas and opinions in group decision making, and facilitates the recognition of valuable inputs from members; *informing*, which promotes the company-wide dissemination of information, resulting in team members who are more likely to understand the compelling mission and expectations of their leader, and thus to work cooperatively to fulfill collective goals; and *showing concern*, which includes the support and fair treatment of subordinates by a team leader in the form of trust, concern for their well-being, and willingness to help.

Conceptually, through leading by example, empowering leaders demonstrate their own commitment to the work and to the team to achieve better performance, and thus act as role models for subordinate team members, who will try in different ways to achieve the team goals related to creative outcomes. Through coaching, empowering leaders boost the confidence and facilitate the ability of team members to challenge the status quo and increase the level of self-reliance and efficiency of the latter in accomplishing tasks. Enhanced team confidence and abilities will help the team develop new ideas, resulting in more creative outcomes (Amabile & Pratt, 2016).

Furthermore, by encouraging participation and enhancing perceived autonomy in decision making, empowering leaders enable team members to make decisions and implement actions without direct intervention by their leaders (Bass, 1985). As a result, team members are empowered to engage in a process in which they can explore diverse alternatives, which leads to higher levels of team creativity (Gilson & Shalley, 2004). By providing information and clarifying expectations, empowering leaders communicate motivational direction. Research shows that leaders elicit creativity by setting creativity-specific expectations (Shalley, Zhou, & Oldham, 2004; Shin & Zhou, 2007). Finally, empowering leaders demonstrate their concern for followers by showing them consideration, offering them support, and treating them fairly. These forms of behavior facilitate collaboration among team members and help them overcome the fear of challenging the status quo, which leads to greater team creativity (Hirst, van Knippenberg, & Zhou, 2009). Therefore, we posit the following hypothesis:

> *Hypothesis 1:* Empowering leadership is positively related to team creativity.

The Mediating Roles of Team Learning Behavior and Team Creative Efficacy

Amabile's (1983, 1996) componential model of creativity and Amabile and Pratt's (2016) dynamic componential theory of creativity identify the learning of domain-relevant skills and creativity-relevant skills as the key components necessary for creativity. Domain-relevant skills comprise an individual's complete set of response possibilities from which the new response is to be synthesized. This component can be considered as a set of cognitive pathways for generating a solution or solving a problem. The larger the set, the more the numerous alternative responses will be available to create something new. Creativity-relevant skills include a cognitive-perceptual style that is characterized by "a facility in understanding complexities and an ability to break set during problem-solving" (Amabile, 1996: 88). That is, it is important for individuals to learn to break a perceptual and cognitive set and understand complexities of the task or situation and perceive it creatively to produce creative work. Therefore, the learning of the task and related subjects (domain-relevant skills) expands the scope of cognitive pathways, and the learning of cognitive set breaking abilities (creativity-relevant skills) enhances the flexibility with which cognitive pathways are explored (Amabile & Pratt, 2016).

Creativity scholars recently have argued in favor of the concept of creativity in teams as a learning process that energizes team member behaviors to produce creative outcomes (Wang, Kim, & Lee, 2016). This is because creativity involves generation of something new for which the necessary strategies often have yet to be learned (Hirst, Van Knippenberg, & Zhou, 2009). Team learning behavior is defined as an ongoing process of collective reflection and action through which team members interactively acquire, share, refine, and apply task-relevant knowledge and skills (Edmondson, 1999). This process is characterized by activities including asking questions, seeking different perspectives and feedback, challenging assumptions, discussing errors or unexpected outcomes, experimenting, evaluating alternatives, and reflecting on past actions (Van der Vegt & Bunderson, 2005). Following Edmondson (1999), we used the term "team learning behavior" to avoid confusion with the notion of learning outcome as team learning is sometimes also referred to knowledge being embedded within the team (e.g., Argote & Olivera, 1999), which represents a state that indicates what a team has learned at a given time (Cohendet & Steinmueller, 2000). In this study, team learning behavior "reflects an active set of team processes" (Mathieu et al., 2008: 431), thus can be viewed as an example of a "group action process" in Marks and colleagues' (2001) team effective framework, during which teams conduct activities leading to goal accomplishment (Van der Vegt & Bunderson, 2005).

Team learning behavior is a collective process (Savelsbergh, van der Heijden, & Poell, 2009). The role of team discussion of and experimentation on the task in question and reflection on it is a prerequisite for a team's ability to convert an individual's skills and knowledge into team knowledge (Drach-Zahavy & Somech, 2001). In addition, team learning behavior may encourage social learning process such that team members engage in learning activities when they observe their peers engaging in the process and perceive learning as valuable and supported (Hirst, Van Knippenberg, & Zhou, 2009). When team members observe their teammates' engagement in the learning processes (e.g., asking challenging questions, criticizing each others' ideas, or evaluating alternatives) that can lead a team to achieve creative outcomes, they will engage in the similar learning activities as these processes create a context in which it is easier to learn and reduce the psychological risks related to learning (Hirst, Van Knippenberg, & Zhou, 2009).

Extensive evidence indicates that a team leader's behavior is a salient factor influencing whether and the extent to which team members pay attention to what other members say and do, and the ways in which they work together to solve problems (Srivastava, Bartol, & Locke, 2006). Empowering leader behaviors such as coaching help team members take collective and appropriate action and encourage them to exchange information and solve problems together (Dovey, 2002). In the process, they actively share ideas and utilize different opinions to improve overall team effectiveness. Coaching-oriented leaders help teams to become self-reliant by encouraging team members to build strong relationships with each other and work collaboratively to achieve collective goals (Arnold et al., 2000). Similarly, team leaders facilitate participative decision making by encouraging team members to openly express ideas and suggestions, which can ultimately influence decisions that affect the team and provide opportunities for team members to collaboratively evaluate each other's suggestions (Locke, Alavi, & Wagner, 1997).

In addition, by conveying a clear compelling mission, empowering leaders provide teams with access to information and a collective goal, which can reduce insecurity and defensiveness among team members (Edmondson, 1999). Members then feel psychologically safe to freely challenge the assumptions underlying each other's ideas and perspectives, and openly discuss differences of opinion. Empowering leaders show their respect for team members by recognizing their individual inputs to the team, which encourages the latter to contribute their knowledge and skills, provides them with the opportunity to learn from each other and facilitates the collaborative learning process (Srivastava, Bartol, & Locke, 2006). These empowering leader behaviors collectively encourage team members to engage in learning by increasing the knowledge and information available to team members, creating a safe and fair environment in which it is easier for team members to help one another and learn collaboratively (Hirst, Van Knippenberg, & Zhou, 2009). In sum, empowering leadership encourages team members to engage in team learning behavior, which in turn, promotes team creativity.

Another necessary building block for facilitating creativity, according to Amabile's componential theory, is task motivation. Efficacy beliefs have long been regarded as one of the most important determinants of task motivation (Bandura, 1986). Self-efficacy nourishes intrinsic motivation by enhancing the perceptions of self-competence (Bandura, 1986), thus creative self-efficacy is argued to reflect intrinsic motivation to engage in creative activities (Gong, Huang, & Farh, 2009). Empirical evidence indicates that creative self-efficacy is a crucial factor that drives employee creativity (Gong, Huang, & Farh, 2009; Tierney & Farmer, 2011).

Team efficacy is an essential motivational factor that influences goal setting and commitment among team members, their initiation of and persistence in activities, and how they deal with challenging situations (Bandura, 1986, 1997). Previous studies have emphasized the importance of team efficacy to team performance (Lindsley, Brass, & Thomas, 1995). A meta-analysis of 67 empirical studies indicated that team efficacy is positively related to team performance (Gully et al., 2002). Whereas team efficacy refers to a team's collective belief in its ability to perform a task successfully (Bandura, 1997), team creative efficacy concerns a team's shared belief in its ability to perform a *specific* task—producing new and useful ideas. Research suggests that a domain-specific efficacy belief (i.e., team creative efficacy) is necessary in predicting a specific outcome (i.e., team creativity) (Shin & Zhou, 2007).

Studies suggest that team leaders often strongly influence the efficacy perception of team members (Kozlowski et al., 1996). Thus, we argue that empowering leadership plays a key role in enhancing team creative efficacy because it is likely to influence the four sources of efficacy beliefs identified by Bandura (1986) observational learning, verbal persuasion, enactive mastery, and physiological arousal. Specifically, by showing commitment to the work and to the team itself, empowering leaders act as role models for subordinate team members; that is, team members learn to commit to their work through *observational learning*. This makes team members more confident in their team's ability to challenge the status quo and develop new ideas. By disseminating information throughout the company and clarifying expectations, empowering leaders can *verbally persuade* team members to coordinate their efforts to achieve collective goals such as team creativity. Kirkman and Rosen (1999) suggested that giving information about where an organization is going can help motivate team members to engage in actions that are aligned with collective goals.

In addition, by showing care and consideration for team members, empowering leaders encourage them to perform tasks without fear or anxiety, which increases the level of collective efficacy and can inspire team members to try different things. Research shows that support from leaders encourages team members to be more creative (Hülsheger, Anderson, & Salgado, 2009). In addition, such consideration and care can help team members understand that the leader values and appreciates their efforts to achieve collective goals, which causes *physiological arousal* among team members and strengthens their shared creative efficacy belief. Lastly, through coaching and the delegation of authority, empowering leaders help team members become more efficient and self-dependent in accomplishing tasks and help the team act autonomously. Team members are then likely to have successful *enactive mastery* experiences, thereby increasing the level of team efficacy related to creative outcomes. Thus, we offer the following hypothesis:

> *Hypothesis 2:* Team learning behavior and team creative efficacy mediate the positive relationship between empowering leadership and team creativity.

The Moderating Role of Team Task Complexity

The contingency perspective of leadership (Liden & Antonakis, 2009; Yukl, 2013) holds that a team leader's influence depends on certain conditions. Leadership is found to have a greater impact on team processes, team emergent states, and team outcomes when the context requires a greater role to be played by team leaders (Yukl, 2013). Team behavior and the need for leadership depend on the demands of the task (McGrath, 1984). Under simple and routine task conditions, teams have less need for leadership because of the familiarity of the task environment (Zaccaro, Rittman, & Marks, 2001). However, it is important for team leaders to facilitate the team to function effectively when tasks are complex, creating novel environments for which teams do not have preexisting responses (Marks, Zaccaro, & Mathieu, 2000).

Team task complexity refers to the extent of the difficulty and/or complexity of the team task, characterized by more information-processing requirements and few set procedures, which require the use of a variety of complex and high-level skills (Man & Lam, 2003; Pelled, Eisenhardt, & Xin, 1999). According to Wood (1986), compared with simple tasks, complex ones contain more distinct informational cues that must be processed, placing substantial cognitive demands in terms of comprehension and execution on the people carrying them out, and requiring task doers to adapt more frequently to changes in the process of task execution. In contrast, simple and routine tasks create a relatively familiar and consistent task environment and thus place minimum cognitive demands on task doers, who develop routines that specify precise actions and whose information processing and behavior become automatic (Gersick & Hackman, 1990).

When the team task is complex, discussing competing perspectives is essential for team members to identify appropriate strategies to assess the situation and solve the problem (Jehn, Northcraft, & Neale, 1999). Also, there is a greater need for team members to pool their expertise and resources, exchange opinions, and challenge each other openly to accomplish the task (Pelled, Eisenhardt, & Xin, 1999; Wood, 1986); hence, higher levels of empowering leadership are required. Such leadership, as noted, provides team members with considerable latitude and facilitates interactions among them in the accomplishment of tasks. In contrast, when tasks are simple/routine and well-defined teams have less need for empowering leadership. This is because when the level of team task complexity is low, team members only need to follow standard procedures, the discussion of work methods and the exchange of opinions may not be necessary or essential, as the tasks are generally familiar and performed the same way each time (Jehn, Northcraft, & Neale, 1999). As a result, team leaders' empowering leadership may be less effective in encouraging team members to engage in team learning behavior and team creative efficacy. Accordingly,

Hypothesis 3a: Team task complexity moderates the relationship between empowering leadership and team learning behavior in such a way that empowering leadership has a stronger and positive relationship with team learning behavior when the level of team task complexity is high, while empowering leadership has a weaker impact on team learning behavior when the level of team task complexity is low.

Hypothesis 3b: Team task complexity moderates the relationship between empowering leadership and team creative efficacy in such a way that empowering leadership has a stronger and positive relationship with team creative efficacy when the level of team task complexity is high, while empowering leadership has a weaker impact on team creative efficacy when the level of team task complexity is low.

In addition, based on the notion that team learning behavior and team creative efficacy mediate the relationship between empowering leadership and team creativity, it is logical to argue that the enhanced team learning behavior and team creative efficacy resulting from the positive interaction between empowering leadership and team task complexity will in turn contribute to team creativity. Hence, we advance a mediated moderation model and propose:

Hypothesis 4: The interaction between empowering leadership and team task complexity is mediated by team learning behavior and team creative efficacy, as related to team creativity.

Method

Sample and Procedures

We collected the data from 102 R&D teams in three Chinese information technology (IT) companies. The participants were professional-level employees who were members on these teams and the corresponding external team leaders. Team members' tasks are in areas including cell phone design, software development, and integrated network system design. With the assistance of the human resource managers from the three companies, a list of 113 teams, randomly selected, was compiled. These were intact teams in which members worked interactively to develop new products and services. All 866 team members (the number of team members ranged from 5 to 14 with an average of 8) and 113 external team leaders were invited to participate in the survey. Team leaders are the external leaders of these teams. They are not part of the team, as all of them supervise more than one team (ranging from two to four teams). We randomly chose one team for each team leader to prevent the design effect (Kaiser et al., 2006).

Separate questionnaires were administered to team leaders and team members. The survey questionnaires were coded before being distributed, and the human resource departments assisted in the recording of the identification numbers to match team leader and team member responses. Following the commonly used back translation procedure, the scales were translated from English into Chinese and then back translated into English by two independent bilingual individuals to ensure equivalency of meaning (Brislin, 1980). The respondents were informed that the survey aimed to examine human resource practices and assured of the confidentiality of their data. Each respondent placed his or her completed survey in a sealed envelope and returned it to a box in the human resource department in each company.

To reduce the potential common method bias, three waves of data collection from two different sources took place over eight months (Podsakoff et al., 2003). In wave one, we administered questionnaires to all 866 team members, in which respondents were asked to give their demographic information and perceptions of empowering leadership and team task complexity. We received usable survey responses from 729 team members affiliated with 110 teams, with a response rate of 84.2%. Four months later, in wave two, questionnaires were distributed to the targeted 729 team members asking them to evaluate their team learning behavior and team creative efficacy. As 10 team members had either changed their team affiliation or left the company, only 719 team members received the questionnaires. We received usable survey responses from 628 team members affiliated with 107 teams, with a response rate of 87.3%. After deleting those teams with fewer than three team members, 105 teams with 624 team members remained in the wave-two sample. All remaining participants were affiliated with the same team across times one and two. Finally, four months after the second-wave survey, in wave three, questionnaires were distributed to the 105 external team leaders asking them to rate team creativity and provide information on their own and team demographics. We confirmed with the human resource departments in all three companies that none of the teams had had a change in leader across times one, two, and three. One hundred and two team leaders returned the questionnaires. After matching leader-team pairs and deleting eight individuals who had either changed their team affiliation or left the company during the last four months, the final sample of this study consisted of 102 teams, which included 102 team leaders and 598 team members. All participants in the final sample, including team leaders and members, were affiliated with the same team across times one, two, and three.

Among the 102 teams, the average number of team members was 7.65 (s.d. = 2.07) and the average duration of the team (team age) was 7.58 years (s.d. = 2.26). Among the 102 external team leaders, 80.4 % were men, the average age was 36.06 years (s.d. = 5.82), and all held a bachelor's degree or above (51.0%, bachelor's degree; 49.0%, postgraduate degree). Among the 598 team members, 65.1% were men, the average age was 32.89 years (s.d. = 4.98), and most held a bachelor's degree or above (2.5%, high school degree; 29.1%, associate's degree; 36.6%, bachelor's degree; 31.8%, postgraduate degree).

Measures

Six-point Likert-type scales ranging from 1 "strongly disagree" to 6 "strongly agree" were used for all measures in this study, except for team creativity.

Empowering Leadership

Arnold et al. (2000) constructed and empirically validated a scale for measuring empowering leadership in teams that has five dimensions: leading by example, participative decision making, coaching, informing, and showing concern/interacting with the team. Following Srivastava, Bartol, and Locke (2006), we adopted three items for each of the five dimensions as listed in Arnold et al. (2000). Confirmatory factor analysis (CFA) showed that the fit indices for a single second-order factor fell within a good range: χ^2 (85) = 154.04, $p \leq 0.01$; comparative fit index (CFI) = 0.96, Tucker-Lewis Index (TLI) = 0.96; and root mean square error of approximation (RMSEA) = 0.09.

Team Learning Behavior

A four-item scale developed by Van der Vegt and Bunderson (2005) was used to measure team learning behavior.

Team Creative Efficacy

We used the three-item scale developed by Shin and Zhou (2007) to measure team creative efficacy.

Team Task Complexity

Following Gladstein (1984) and Man and Lam (2003), team task complexity was measured using a three-item scale.

Team Creativity

We used the four-item scale developed by Shin and Zhou (2007) to measure team creativity in R&D settings. The team leader completed the scale, which ranged from 1 "poor" to 6 "very much."

Control Variables

Following previous research (e.g., Hülsheger, Anderson, & Salgado, 2009; Shalley, Zhou, & Oldham, 2004; Shin & Zhou, 2007), we controlled for several key variables that are likely to be associated with team processes, team emergent states, and team outcomes. First, we controlled for team age diversity, gender diversity, educational background diversity, and team member mean education level. Data on age (years), gender (0 = male; 1 = female), educational background (1 = Arts; 2 = Law; 3 = Humanities; 4 = Sciences; 5 = Engineering; 6 = Agriculture; 7 = Medicine; 8 = Business and Economics), and education level (1 = high school degree or below; 2 = associate's degree; 3 = bachelor's degree; 4 = postgraduate degree) were obtained from each team member. Following Allison (1978) and Cannella, Park, and Lee (2008), we measured age diversity using the coefficient of its variation (standard deviation divided by the mean). As gender and educational background are categorical variables, following Shin and Zhou (2007) and Wiersema and Bantel (1992), we measured gender and educational background diversity using Blau's (1977) index of heterogeneity calculated as $1-\sum Si^2$, where Si is the portion of a team's members in the *i*th category. The team member mean education level was obtained by averaging the education level scores of team members.

Second, we controlled for team size (the number of members in a team), team age (years since the team was formed), and team interdependence to parcel out their potential influence on the team process, the emergent state, and the outcome (Hülsheger, Anderson, & Salgado, 2009). Team interdependence is a defining team characteristic (Barrick, Bradley, & Colbert, 2007). As a team-level input (Mathieu et al., 2008), team interdependence describes the extent to which team members cooperate and work interactively to accomplish team tasks (Steward & Barrick, 2000). It consists of task, goal, and outcome interdependence (Campion, Medsker, & Higgs, 1993), each of which is a key determinant of team effectiveness (for a review, see Gully et al., 2002). Team interdependence was measured using a nine-item scale developed by Campion and colleagues (1993).

Third, as our sample was taken from three companies, we created two company dummies and added them as control variables in the regression model to rule out the potential company effect. Finally, we controlled for leader education level and uncertainty avoidance orientation to rule out the potential confounding effect of these leader differences on team learning behavior, team creative efficacy, and team creativity. Uncertainty avoidance orientation reflects the willingness of people to take risks and accept uncertainty (Hofstede, 1980), and thus may influence a team leader's willingness to support team members to engage in creative activities. Uncertainty avoidance was measured using a five-item scale developed by Dorfman and Howell (1988).

Results

Preliminary Analyses

Attrition Analysis

Because data were collected from team members in two waves, we followed Goodman and Blum's (1996) approach to test for systematic differences in responses between the first and the second wave of data collection. The results indicated that there were no significant mean differences among these variables.

Confirmatory Factor Analysis

As the data on empowering leadership, team task complexity, team learning behavior, team creative efficacy, and team interdependence were collected from the same source (team member), we conducted CFA at the team level to evaluate the distinctiveness of these variables. For each of the single dimensional constructs, we created a first-order construct using the aggregated items as indicators. For empowering leadership, we first created five first-order constructs and each construct consists of three aggregated items. We then created a second-order construct representing empowering leadership and linked it to the five first-order constructs. All indicator means at the team level were then included in the CFA model. We first examined a five-factor model, which included empowering leadership, team task complexity, team learning behavior, team creative efficacy, and team interdependence. The model yielded an acceptable fit to the data: χ^2 (509) = 764.60, $p \leq 0.01$; CFI = 0.94; TLI = 0.94; RMSEA = 0.07; and Akaike's information criterion (AIC) = 936.60. In addition, all the factor loadings were significant, which indicates convergent validity.

The discriminant validity of the five constructs was tested by contrasting the five-factor model with one-factor and four-factor models. The one-factor model was obtained by loading all items measured into a "grand" latent factor. The four-factor model was obtained by combining team learning behavior and team creative efficacy into one-factor while keeping the other three constructs separate. We combined these two variables because correlation analysis showed that their correlation was the highest among the five constructs (r = 0.52, $p \leq 0.01$). The one-factor and four-factor models yielded a poor fit to the data: χ^2 (527) = 3095.43, $p \leq 0.01$; CFI = 0.41; TLI = 0.38; RMSEA = 0.22; and AIC = 3231.43 for the former and χ^2 (513) = 986.62, $p \leq 0.01$; CFI = 0.89; TLI = 0.88; RMSEA = 0.10; and AIC = 1150.62 for the latter model. Chi-square difference and AIC difference tests indicated that the hypothesized five-factor model fit the data better than either the one-factor model ($\Delta\chi^2$ (18) = 2330.83, $p \leq 0.01$; ΔAIC = 2294.83) or the four-factor model ($\Delta\chi^2$ (4) = 222.02, $p \leq 0.01$; ΔAIC = 214.02). Thus, the discriminant validity of these constructs was confirmed.

Level of Analysis and Data Aggregation

The hypothesized model was tested at the team level. Although the scales comprised team-level items, we empirically examined the appropriateness of aggregating the responses of individual team members by determining the level of inter-member agreement (r_{wg}) and the intra-class correlation coefficients, ICC (1) and ICC (2) (Bliese, 2000; James, Demaree, & Wolf, 1984). The results are presented in Table 6.1.

As shown in Table 6.1, all teams had r_{wg} values equal or greater than 0.70 for empowering leadership (100%), with a median r_{wg} of 0.94, for team task complexity (100%), with a median r_{wg} of 0.93, and for team task interdependence (100%), with a median r_{wg} of 0.95. All teams except one had r_{wg} values equal or greater than 0.70 for team learning behavior (99%), with a median r_{wg} of 0.94, and all teams except two had r_{wg} values equal or greater than 0.70 for team creative efficacy (98.1%), with a median r_{wg} of 0.95. The levels of inter-member agreement within teams thus justify our aggregation of individual-level data. In addition, the results showed that the ICC (1) values ranged from 0.15 to 0.25 (0.15 for empowering leadership, 0.18 for team task complexity, 0.18 for team learning behavior, 0.24 for team creative efficacy, and 0.25 for team interdependence, values greater than the conventional cutoff value of 0.05), and all were significant, indicating that between-team variance was greater than within-team variance (James, 1982). Finally, the ICC (2) values were 0.50 for empowering leadership, 0.57 for team task complexity, 0.56 for team learning behavior, 0.64 for team creative efficacy, and 0.66 for team interdependence. All of these values are higher than the conventional cutoff value of 0.50 (James, 1982). These results indicate that it was appropriate to average the scores provided by team members to obtain team-level scores.

Descriptive Statistics

Table 6.2 presents the means, standard deviations, zero-order Pearson correlations, and scale reliabilities for all key variables in this study.

Bracketed values on the diagonal are the Cronbach's alpha value of each scale at the team level.

Hypothesis Testing

We conducted hierarchical multiple regression analysis (Baron & Kenny, 1986) to test Hypotheses 1 and 2. As shown in Table 6.3 (see Model 10), empowering leadership was positively related to team creativity ($\beta = 0.24$, $p \leq 0.05$, $\Delta R^2 = 0.05$); thus, Hypothesis 1 was supported.

Hypothesis 2 predicted that team learning behavior and team creativity efficacy mediate the positive relationship between empowering leadership and team creativity. The results in Table 6.3 show that (1) empowering leadership was positively related to team learning behavior ($\beta = 0.43$, $p \leq 0.01$, $\Delta R^2 = 0.15$, Model 2) and team creative efficacy ($\beta = 0.37$, $p \leq 0.01$, $\Delta R^2 = 0.11$, Model 6), (2) empowering leadership was significantly related to team creativity ($\beta = 0.24$, $p \leq 0.05$, $\Delta R^2 = 0.05$, Model 10), (3) team learning behavior ($\beta = 0.28$, $p \leq 0.05$, $\Delta R^2 = 0.14$, Model 11) and team creative efficacy ($\beta = 0.25$, $p \leq 0.05$, $\Delta R^2 = 0.14$, Model 11) were positively related

Table 6.1 Information for Justifying Aggregation of Individual Measurements to the Team Level

	Variance analysis across team (ANOVA test)	$ICC_{[1]}$	$ICC_{[2]}$	R_{wg}				
				Median	*Minimum*	*Maximum*	*Number of teams below 0.70*	*Percentage of total teams above 0.70*
1. Empowering leadership	F (101, 496)[a] = 9.84	0.15	0.50	0.94	0.73	1.00	0	100%
2. Team task complexity	F (101, 496)[a] =11.41	0.18	0.57	0.93	0.72	1.00	0	100%
3. Team learning behavior	F (101, 496)[a] =11.22	0.18	0.56	0.94	0.68	1.00	1	99.0%
4. Team creative efficacy	F (101, 496)[a] =13.81	0.24	0.64	0.95	0.58	1.00	2	98.1%
5. Team interdependence	F (101, 496)[a] =14.61	0.25	0.66	0.95	0.83	1.00	0	100%

Note: N = 102 [a] “significant” means that

Table 6.2 Means, Standard Deviations, and Correlations

Variables	*1*	*2*	*3*	*4*	*5*	*6*	*7*	*8*	*9*	*10*	*11*	*12*	*13*	*14*
1. Age diversity														
2. Gender diversity	0.13													
3. Education background diversity	0.19	0.02												
4. Member mean education level	0.16	0.10	0.14											
5. Team size	0.07	0.30**	0.18	0.12										
6. Team age	−0.19	−0.14	−0.20*	0.02	0.14									
7. Leader education level	−0.06	−0.00	−0.09	−0.03	0.04	0.09								
8. Leader uncertainty avoidance	0.08	−0.08	−0.08	−0.22*	0.04	−0.05	0.02	*(0.86)*						
9. Team interdependence	−0.11	−0.03	−0.15	0.05	0.02	−0.02	−0.02	−0.25*	*(0.97)*					
10. Empowering leadership	−0.16	0.15	−0.10	0.04	0.07	0.05	−0.03	−0.24*	0.26**	*(0.97)*				
11. Team task complexity	−0.08	0.08	−0.11	0.15	−0.05	0.08	−0.01	−0.07	0.19	0.19	*(0.93)*			
12. Team learning behavior	0.02	0.08	0.01	0.07	0.13	0.13	0.05	−0.17	0.20*	0.44**	0.25*	*(0.94)*		
13. Team creative efficacy	−0.03	0.23*	−0.04	0.05	0.13	0.10	0.07	−0.20*	0.21*	0.43**	0.28**	0.52**	*(0.93)*	
14. Team creativity	−0.12	−0.08	−0.05	0.12	0.01	0.21*	0.18	−0.08	0.21*	0.26**	0.21*	0.44**	0.40**	*(0.74)*
Mean	0.14	0.39	0.52	3.97	7.65	7.58	4.49	2.87	4.58	4.65	4.75	4.63	4.50	4.54
SD	0.05	0.13	0.15	0.36	2.07	2.26	0.50	0.98	0.67	0.64	0.62	0.70	0.70	0.91

Notes: $N = 102$; ** $p \leq 0.01$; * $p \leq 0.05$ (two-tailed).

Table 6.3 Results of Hierarchical Regression Analysis

	Team learning behavior				*Team creative efficacy*				*Team creativity*					
	M1	*M2*	*M3*	*M4*	*M5*	*M6*	*M7*	*M8*	*M9*	*M10*	*M11*	*M12*	*M13*	*M14*
Control variables														
Company 1	−0.03	−0.04	−0.02	−0.06	0.09	0.09	0.11	0.07	−0.02	−0.02	−0.04	−0.01	−0.05	−0.06
Company 2	−0.03	−0.13	−0.08	−0.14	0.08	0	0.06	0.01	0.04	−0.01	0.02	−0.03	−0.03	0.02
Age diversity	0.07	0.13	0.14	0.16	-0.01	0.05	0.05	0.07	−0.08	−0.04	−0.09	−0.04	−0.02	−0.07
Gender diversity	0.06	0	−0.02	−0.01	0.22*	0.17†	0.15	0.17†	−0.07	−0.1	−0.14	−0.12	−0.09	−0.15
Education background diversity	0.03	0.07	0.08	0.11	-0.01	0.03	0.03	0.06	0.03	0.05	0.02	0.05	0.08	0.05
Member mean education level	0	−0.02	−0.04	−0.07	0	−0.02	−0.04	−0.06	0.13	0.13	0.13	0.11	0.08	0.15
Team size	0.14	0.14	0.14	0.13	0.07	0.07	0.08	0.06	0.02	0.02	−0.04	0.02	0.01	−0.04
Team age	0.16	0.13	0.13	0.06	0.13	0.1	0.1	0.05	0.20†	0.18†	0.12	0.18†	0.12	0.11
Leader education level	0.05	0.08	0.07	0.09	0.06	0.09	0.08	0.1	0.16†	0.18†	0.13	0.17†	0.19*	0.15
Leader uncertainty avoidance	-0.12	−0.06	−0.06	−0.04	−0.14	−0.08	−0.09	−0.06	0.01	0.04	0.08	0.04	0.07	0.11
Team interdependence	0.19†	0.1	0.08	0.1	0.18†	0.1	0.07	0.09	0.21†	0.16	0.1	0.14	0.15	0.12
Independent variable														
Empowering leadership		0.43**	0.40**	0.35**		0.37**	0.34**	0.29**		0.24*	0.02	0.21*	0.16	−0.05
Moderator														
Team task complexity			0.17†	0.05			0.20*	0.1				0.14	0.03	0.02

Interaction				0.29*				0.24*					0.26*	0.12
Empowering leadership × Team task complexity														
Mediators														
Team learning behavior											0.28*			0.26*
Team creative efficacy											0.25*			0.25*
Interactions (control)														
Team learning behavior × Team task complexity														0.08
Team creative efficacy × Team task complexity														0.12
Adjust R^2	0	0.16	0.18	0.23	0.04	0.16	0.19	0.22	0.04	0.08	0.22	0.08	0.12	0.23
ΔR^2	0.11	0.15	0.03	0.05	0.15	0.11	0.03	0.04	0.14	0.05	0.14	0.02	0.04	0.12
F	0.98	2.61**	2.67**	3.14**	1.41	2.60**	2.82**	3.06**	1.34	1.69†	2.99**	1.72†	2.03*	2.63**
ΔF	0.98	18.45**	2.85†	6.87**	1.41	13.63**	4.26*	4.67*	1.34	4.95*	8.95**	1.8	4.90*	3.84**

Notes: $N = 102$; ** $p \leq 0.01$, * $p \leq 0.05$, † $p \leq 0.10$ (two-tailed). Company 3 as the reference.

to team creativity, and (4) the relationship between empowering leadership and team creativity became nonsignificant ($\beta = 0.02$, *n.s.*, Model 11) when both mediators were present. Thus, team learning behaviors and team creative self-efficacy were full mediators in the relationship between empowering leadership and team creativity, thus supporting Hypothesis 2.

To examine the moderating and mediated moderating effects predicted by Hypotheses 3 and 4, respectively, we adopted the moderated causal steps approach to regression analysis (Muller, Judd, & Yzerbyt, 2005). All interaction variables were mean centered to minimize multicollinearity (Aiken & West, 1991).

Hypotheses 3a and 3b predicted that team task complexity moderates the relationship between empowering leadership and team learning behavior, and between empowering leadership and team creative efficacy, respectively. As shown in Table 6.3, the interaction between empowering leadership and team task complexity was positively related to team learning behavior ($\beta = 0.29, p \leq 0.05, \Delta R^2 = 0.05$, Model 4) and team creative efficacy ($\beta = 0.24$, $p \leq 0.05$, $\Delta R^2 = 0.04$, Model 8). We plotted the interaction using Aiken and West's (1991) procedure: compute slopes one standard deviation above and below the mean of the moderating variable. Figures 6.1 and 6.2 show that the interaction patterns are consistent with the hypothesized relationships. Specifically, the slope test results show that empowering leadership had a

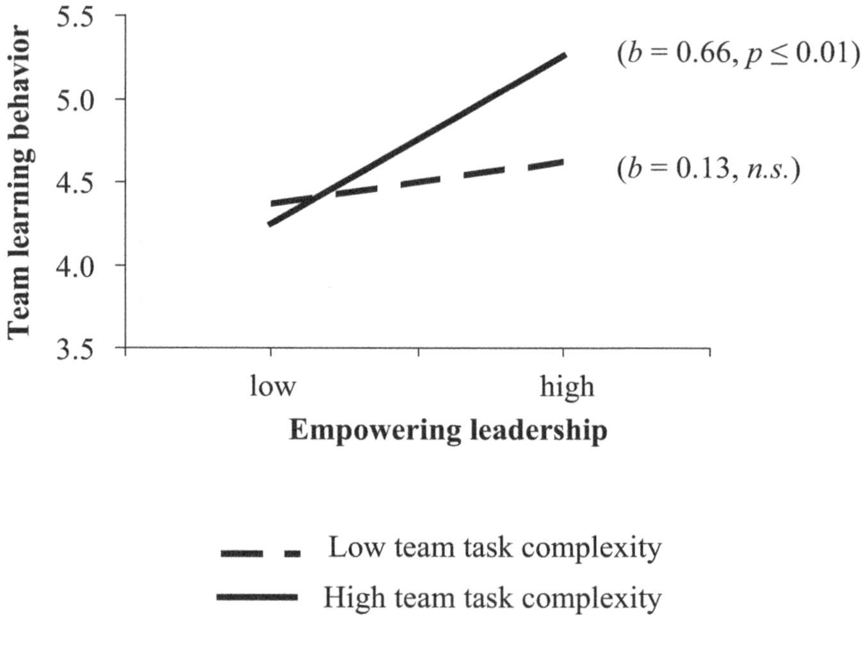

Figure 6.1 Interactive Effect of Empowering Leadership and Team Task Complexity on Team Learning Behavior

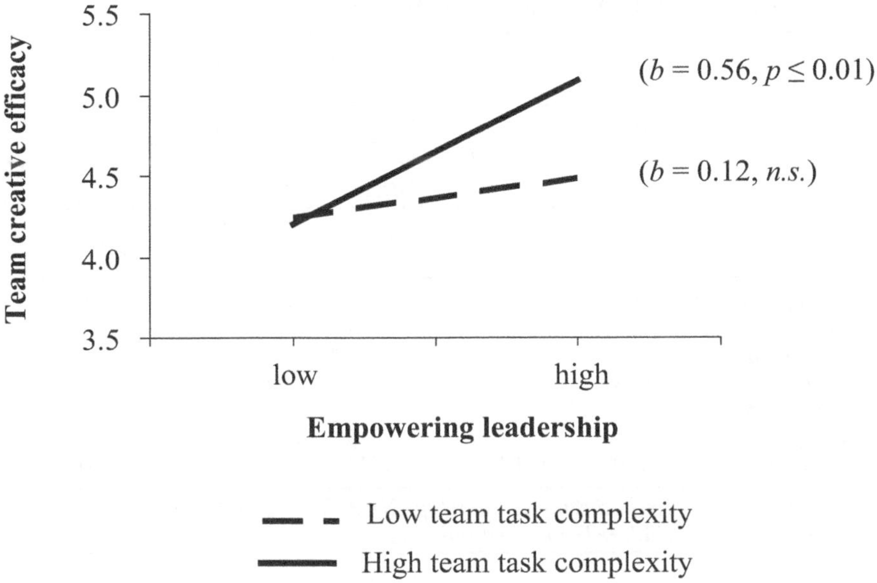

Figure 6.2 Interactive Effect of Empowering Leadership and Team Task Complexity on Team Creative Efficacy

positive and stronger effect on team learning behavior when the level of team task complexity was high ($\beta = 0.66$, $p \leq 0.01$), but its effect on team learning behavior was weaker when the level of team task complexity was low ($\beta = 0.13$, *n.s.*). Similarly, empowering leadership had a positive and stronger effect on team creative efficacy when the level of team task complexity was high ($\beta = 0.56$, $p \leq 0.01$), but its effect on team creative efficacy was weaker when the level of team task complexity was low ($\beta = 0.12$, *n.s.*). In addition, we performed moderated path analysis (Edwards & Lambert, 2007), bootstrapping 1,000 samples to compute bias-corrected confidence intervals. The results presented in Table 6.4 support first-stage moderating effects ($\Delta\beta = 0.80$, $p \leq 0.05$ for team learning behavior; $\Delta\beta = 0.69$, $p \leq 0.05$ for team creative efficacy). Thus, Hypotheses 3a and 3b were supported.

The mediated moderations were tested further based on Muller and colleagues' (2005) procedures. Supporting Hypothesis 4, the results showed that (1) empowering leadership × team task complexity was significantly related to both mediators as indicated earlier for Hypotheses 3a and 3b; (2) empowering leadership × team task complexity was significantly related to team creativity ($\beta = 0.26$, $p \leq 0.05$, $\Delta R^2 = 0.04$, Model 13); (3) after controlling for the interactions between team task complexity with the two mediators and other predictors, team learning behavior ($\beta = 0.26$, $p \leq 0.05$, $\Delta R^2 = 0.12$, Model 14) and team creative efficacy ($\beta = 0.25$, $p \leq 0.05$, $\Delta R^2 = 0.12$, Model 14) were positively related to team creativity; and (4)

Table 6.4 Results of the Moderated Path Analysis

Moderator Variable	*Empowering Leadership (X)→ Team Learning Behavior (M1)→Team Creativity (Y)*				
	Stage		*Effect*		
	First	*Second*	*Direct Dffects*	*Indirect Effects*	*Total Effects*
	P_{M1X}	P_{YM1}	(P_{YX})	$(P_{YM1}P_{M1X})$	$(P_{YX}+P_{YM1}P_{M1X})$
Simple paths for low team task complexity	−0.02	0.35	−0.33	−0.01	−0.34
Simple paths for high team task complexity	0.78**	0.53*	0.41*	0.41**	0.82**
Differences	0.80*	0.18	0.74*	0.42*	1.16*
Moderator Variable	*Empowering Leadership (X)→ Team Creative Efficacy (M2)→Team Creativity (Y)*				
	Stage		*Effect*		
	First	*Second*	*Direct effects*	*Indirect Effects*	*Total effects*
	P_{M2X}	P_{YM2}	(P_{YX})	$(P_{YM2}P_{M2X})$	$(P_{YX}+P_{YM2}P_{M2X})$
Simple paths for low team task complexity	0.02	0.27	−0.37	0.01	−0.37
Simple paths for high team task complexity	0.71**	0.51**	0.47*	0.36**	0.83**
Differences	0.69*	0.24	0.84*	0.35*	1.20*

Notes: $N = 102$; ** $p \leq 0.01$, * $p \leq 0.05$ (two-tailed).

P_{MX1}: path from empowering leadership to team learning behavior. P_{YM1}: path from team learning behavior to team creativity. P_{MX2}: path from empowering leadership to team creative efficacy. P_{YM2}: path from team creative efficacy to team creativity. P_{YX}: path from empowering leadership to team creativity.

Low team task complexity refers to one standard deviation below the mean of team task complexity; high team task complexity refers to one standard deviation above the mean of team task complexity.

Tests of differences for the indirect and total effect were based on bias-corrected confidence intervals derived from bootstrap estimates.

the interaction effect of empowering leadership and team task complexity on team creativity became nonsignificant after entering the two mediators and controlling for the interactions between team task complexity with the two mediators and other predictors ($\beta = 0.12$, *n.s.*, Model 14). Therefore, the interactive effect of empowering leadership and team task complexity on team creativity was fully mediated by team learning behavior and team

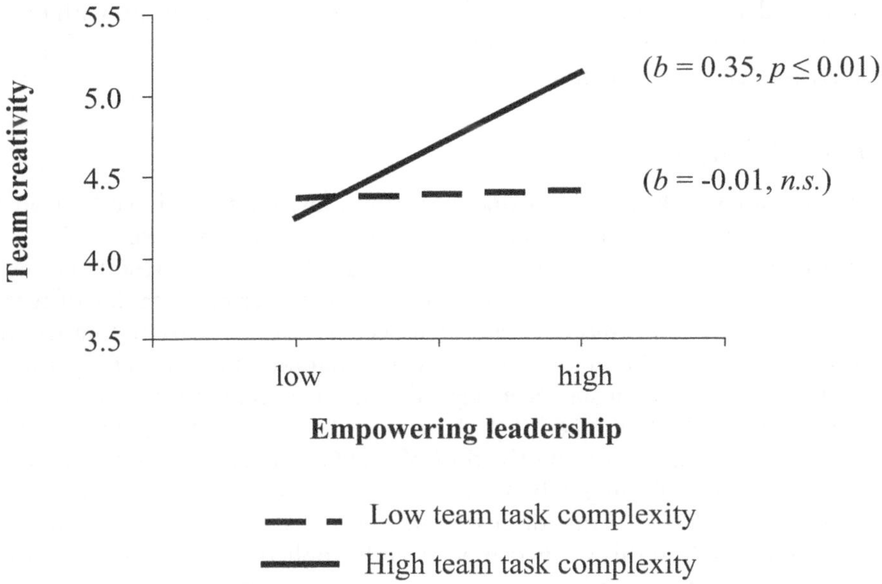

Figure 6.3 Interactive Effect of Empowering Leadership and Team Task Complexity on Team Creativity

creative efficacy. We plotted the interactive effect of empowering leadership and team task complexity on team creativity and conducted simple slope tests. Figure 6.3 shows that the interaction pattern is consistent with our arguments; that is, empowering leadership had a positive and stronger effect on team creativity when the level of team task complexity was high ($\beta = 0.35$, $p \leq 0.01$), but its effect on team creativity was weaker when the level of team task complexity was low ($\beta = -0.01$, *n.s.*).

To provide more robust support for our results, we performed moderated path analysis (Edwards & Lambert, 2007), bootstrapping 1,000 samples to compute bias-corrected confidence intervals. An indirect effect is considered to be statistically significant if the 95% confidence interval excludes zero. Our results, which are summarized in Table 6.4, show that the size of the indirect effect of team learning behavior and team creative efficacy was 0.42 and 0.35, respectively. The 95% confidence intervals computed using the bootstrap estimates exclude zero. Therefore, the indirect effects of team learning behavior and team creative efficacy were significant, providing further support for Hypotheses 2 and 4.

Discussion

We theorized, and found, that empowering leadership positively influences creativity in R&D teams through team learning behavior and team creative efficacy. In addition, when the level of team task complexity is high, empowering leadership is found to have a stronger, positive relationship with team learning behavior and team creative efficacy, which in turn, are both positively related to team creativity.

Theoretical Implications

Our research makes three distinct contributions. First, we have built and empirically tested a conceptual model that integrates empowering leadership theory with creativity theories at the team level. Our results empirically demonstrate for the first time that the empowering behavior of team leaders effectively promotes creativity in R&D teams. Due to the changes in communication technology and the social dynamics of a new generation of young professionals, it has been argued that most teams today are to some degree virtual (Kirkman & Mathieu, 2005). As a result, delegating authority to and enhancing the motivation of team members who interact with each other virtually might be different from the influence of empowering leadership on R&D teams discussed in this study. Because the theoretical framework built in this study can be broadly applied to other job categories (e.g., service), it is thus interesting to extend the current research model to other types of team to investigate.

Second, building on Amabile's (1983, 1996) componential model and Amabile and Pratt's (2016) dynamic componential theory of creativity, our study contributes to the empowering leadership and creativity literatures by theorizing and empirically testing that both team learning behavior (the team process) and team creative efficacy (the team emergent state), representing a team's learning of domain-relevant and creativity-relevant skills and team intrinsic motivation, are necessary building blocks for enhancing team creativity. In this way, we extend Amabile's solid componential model from individual employees to teams, thus building a theoretical framework that help bridge empowering leadership with creativity in teams.

Finally, based on the contingency perspective of leadership (Yukl, 2013), we further established the relationship between empowering leadership and team creativity by identifying the boundary condition. Our results are consistent with and provide empirical support for the contingency perspective. That is, leadership has a greater impact on team processes, emergent states, and outcomes when teams face demanding situations (e.g., high level of task complexity), which require team leaders to play a greater role (Morgeson, 2005).

Managerial Implications

Our theoretical model and empirical findings have important implications for managers. As an increasing number of organizations rely on team creativity to maintain competitive advantages in the face of global competition (Shin & Zhou, 2007), it is important for companies to keep in mind that the empowering behavior of team leaders can promote team creativity. Empowering leadership not only facilitates interaction and cooperation among team members in acquiring task-relevant knowledge (i.e., team learning behavior) but also creates favorable conditions that promote the shared belief of team members in their ability to produce something new and useful (i.e., team creative efficacy). Thus, those organizations and teams whose survival and competitiveness depend extensively on creative outcomes may benefit from leader selection and training to ensure that team leaders demonstrate empowering behaviors including leading by example, coaching, facilitating participative decision making, informing, and showing concern.

The study findings also indicate that managers need to consider task complexity when empowering teams. Specifically, managers may find that empowering behaviors are more effective in facilitating the team learning process and boosting team creative efficacy when teams face complex, as opposed to simple, tasks. Highly complex tasks require a high level of team collaboration to refine task-relevant knowledge and increase the inherent interest of team members in the task. Thus, when the level of team task complexity is high, leaders may need to engage in more empowering behaviors to help teams build stronger collaborations and to enhance the shared belief of team members in their creative capabilities.

Conclusion

This study integrates empowering leadership and creativity theories to further develop and test a theoretical model that connects empowering leadership and team creativity. Including both team learning behavior (the team process) and team creative efficacy (the team emergent state) in the model, we find that they fully mediate the influence of empowering leadership on team creativity. Furthermore, the moderating effect of team task complexity helps identify a critical boundary condition for the aforementioned relations. We hope that our study will stimulate future research to advance the theoretical understanding of how empowering leadership can promote team creativity in the workplace.

References

Aiken, L. S., & West, S. G. 1991. *Multiple regression: Testing and interpreting interactions*. Newbury Park: Sage Publications.

Allison, P. D. 1978. Measures of inequality. *American Sociological Review*, 43: 865–880.

Amabile, T. M. 1983. *The social psychology of creativity*. New York: Springer-Verlag New York Inc.

Amabile, T. M. 1996. *Creativity in context*. Boulder, CO: Westview Press.

Amabile, T. M., & Pratt, M. G. 2016. The dynamic componential model of creativity and innovation in organizations: Making progress, making meaning. *Research in Organizational Behavior*, 36: 157–183.

Amabile, T. M., Schatzel, E. A., Moneta, G. B., & Kramer, S. J. 2004. Leader behaviors and the work environment for creativity: Perceived leader support. *Leadership Quarterly*, 15: 5–32.
Argote, L., & Olivera, F. 1999. Organizational learning and new product development: CORE processes. In L. L. Thompson, J. M. Levine, & D. M. Messick (Eds.), *Shared cognition in organizations: The management of knowledge*: 297–325. Mahwah, NJ: Lawrence Erlbaum Associates.
Arnold, J. A., Arad, S., Rhoades, J. A., & Drasgow, F. 2000. The empowering leadership questionnaire: The construction and validation of a new scale for measuring leader behaviors. *Journal of Organizational Behavior*, 21: 249–269.
Bandura, A. 1986. *Social foundations of thought and action: A social cognitive theory*. Englewood Cliffs, NJ: Prentice-Hall.
Bandura, A. 1997. Collective efficacy. In A. Bandura (Ed.), *Self-efficacy: The exercise of control*: 477–525. New York: Freeman.
Baron, R. M., & Kenny, D. A. 1986. The moderator-mediator variable distinction in social psychological research: Conceptual, strategic, and statistical considerations. *Journal of Personality and Social Psychology*, 51: 1173–1182.
Barrick, M. R., Bradley, B. H., & Colbert, A. E. 2007. The moderating role of top management team interdependence: Implications for real teams and working groups. *Academy of Management Journal*, 50: 544–557.
Bass, B. M. 1985. *Leadership and performance beyond expectations*. New York: Free Press.
Blau, P. M. 1977. *Inequality and heterogeneity*. New York: Free Press.
Bliese, P. D. 2000. Within-group agreement, non-independence, and reliability: Implications for data aggregation and analysis. In K. J. Klein & S. W. J. Kozlowski (Eds.), *Multilevel theory, research, and methods in organizations: Foundations, extensions, and new directions*: 349–381. San Francisco, CA: Jossey-Bass.
Brislin, R. W. 1980. Translation and content analysis of oral and written material. In H. C. Triandis & J. W. Berry (Eds.), *Handbook of cross-cultural psychology*: 389–444. Boston, MA: Allyn & Bacon.
Campion, M. A., Medsker, G. J., & Higgs, A. C. 1993. Relations between work group characteristics and effectiveness: Implications for designing effective work groups. *Personnel Psychology*, 46: 823–855.
Cannella, A. A., Park, J., & Lee, H. 2008. Top management team functional background diversity and firm performance: Examining the roles of team member co-location and environmental uncertainty. *Academy of Management Journal*, 51: 768–784.
Cohendet, P., & Steinmueller, W. E. 2000. The codification of knowledge: A conceptual and empirical exploration. *Industrial and Corporate Change*, 9: 195–209.
Dorfman, P. W., & Howell, J. P. 1988. Dimensions of national culture and effective leadership patterns: Hofstede revisited. In R. N. Farmer & E. G. McGoun (Eds.), *Advances in international comparative management*, Vol. 3: 127–150. Greenwich, CT: JAI Press.
Dovey, K. 2002. Leadership development in a South African health service. *International Journal of Public Sector Management*, 15: 520–533.
Drach-Zahavy, A., & Somech, A. 2001. Understanding team's innovation: The role of team processes and structures. *Group Dynamics*, 5: 111–123.
Edmondson, A. 1999. Psychological safety and learning behavior in work teams. *Administrative Science Quarterly*, 44: 350–383.

Edwards, J. R., & Lambert, L. S. 2007. Methods for integrating moderation and mediation: A general analytical framework using moderated path analysis. *Psychological Methods*, 12: 1–22.

Gersick, C. J. G., & Hackman, J. R. 1990. Habitual routines in task-performing groups. *Organizational Behavior and Human Decision Processes*, 47: 65–97.

Gilson, L. L., & Shalley, C. E. 2004. A little creativity goes a long way: An examination of teams' engagement in creative processes. *Journal of Management*, 30: 453–470.

Gladstein, D. L. 1984. Groups in context: A model of task group effectiveness. *Administrative Science Quarterly*, 29: 499–517.

Gong, Y., Huang, J., & Farh, J. 2009. Employee learning orientation, transformational leadership, and employee creativity: The mediating role of employee creative self-efficacy. *Academy of Management Journal*, 52: 765–778.

Goodman, J. S., & Blum, T. C. 1996. Assessing the non-random sampling effects of subject attrition in longitudinal research. *Journal of Management*, 22: 627–652.

Gully, S. M., Incalcaterra, K. A., Joshi, A., & Beaubien, J. M. 2002. A meta-analysis of team-efficacy, potency, and performance: Interdependence and level of analysis as moderators of observed relationships. *Journal of Applied Psychology*, 87: 819–832.

Hirst, G., Van Knippenberg, D., & Zhou, J. 2009. A cross-level perspective on employee creativity: Goal orientation, team learning behavior, and individual creativity. *Academy of Management Journal*, 52: 280–293.

Hofstede, G. 1980. *Culture's consequences: International differences in work-related values*. Beverly Hills, CA: Sage Publications.

Hülsheger, U. R., Anderson, N., & Salgado, J. F. 2009. Team-level predictors of innovation at work: A comprehensive meta-analysis spanning three decades of research. *Journal of Applied Psychology*, 94: 1128–1145.

James, L. R. 1982. Aggregation bias in estimates of perceptual agreement. *Journal of Applied Psychology*, 67: 219–229.

James, L. R., Demaree, R. G., & Wolf, G. 1984. Estimating within-group interrater reliability with and without response bias. *Journal of Applied Psychology*, 69: 85–98.

Jehn, K. A., Northcraft, G. B., & Neale, M. A. 1999. Why differences make a difference: A field study of diversity, conflict, and performance in workgroups. *Administrative Science Quarterly*, 44: 741–763.

Kaiser, R., Woodruff, B. A., Bilukha, O., Spiegel, P. B., & Salama, P. 2006. Using design effects from previous cluster surveys to guide sample size calculation in emergency settings. *Disasters*, 30: 199–211.

Kirkman, B. L., & Mathieu, J. E. 2005. The dimensions and antecedents of team virtuality. *Journal of Management*, 31: 700–718.

Kirkman, B. L., & Rosen, B. 1999. Beyond self-management: Antecedents and consequences of team empowerment. *Academy of Management Journal*, 42: 58–74.

Kozlowski, S. W. J., Gully, S. M., Salas, E., & Cannon-Bowers, J. A. 1996. Team leadership and development: Theory, principles, and guidelines for training leaders and teams. In M. Beyerlein (Ed.), *Advances in interdisciplinary studies of work teams: Team leadership*, Vol. 3: 253–291. Greenwich, CT: JAI Press.

Liden, R. C., & Antonakis, J. 2009. Considering context in psychological leadership research. *Human Relations*, 62: 1587–1605.

Lindsley, D. H., Brass, D. J., & Thomas, J. B. 1995. Efficacy-performance spirals: A multilevel perspective. *Academy of Management Review*, 20: 645–678.

Liu, D., Gong, Y., Zhou, J., & Huang, J-C. 2017. Human resource systems, employee creativity, and firm innovation: The moderating role of firm ownership. *Academy of Management Journal*, 60: 1164–1188.

Locke, E. A., Alavi, M., & Wagner, J. 1997. Participation in decision-making: An information exchange perspective. In G. Ferris (Ed.), *Research in personnel and human resources management*: 293–331. Greenwich, CT: JAI Press.

Man, D., & Lam, S. S. K. 2003. The effects of job complexity and autonomy on cohesiveness in collectivistic and individualistic work groups: A cross-cultural analysis. *Journal of Organizational Behavior*, 24: 979–1001.

Marks, M. A., Mathieu, J. E., & Zaccaro, S. J. 2001. A temporally based framework and taxonomy of team processes. *Academy of Management Review*, 26: 356–376.

Marks, M. A., Zaccaro, S. J., & Mathieu, J. E. 2000. Performance implications of leader briefings and team-interaction training for team adaptation to novel environments. *Journal of Applied Psychology*, 85: 971–986.

Mathieu, J. E., Maynard, M. T., Rapp, T., & Gilson, L. 2008. Team effectiveness 1997–2007: A review of recent advancements and a glimpse into the future. *Journal of Management*, 34: 410–476.

McGrath, J. E. 1984. *Groups: Interaction and performance*. Englewood Cliffs, NJ: Prentice-Hall.

Morgeson, F. P. 2005. The external leadership of self-managing teams: Intervening in the context of novel and disruptive events. *Journal of Applied Psychology*, 90: 497–508.

Muller, D., Judd, C. M., & Yzerbyt, V. Y. 2005. When moderation is mediated and mediation is moderated. *Journal of Personality and Social Psychology*, 89: 852–863.

Paulus, P. B. 2008. Fostering creativity in groups and teams. In J. Zhou & C. E. Shalley (Eds.), *Handbook of organizational creativity*: 165–188. New York: Lawrence Erlbaum Associates.

Pelled, L. H., Eisenhardt, K. M., & Xin, K. R. 1999. Exploring the black box: An analysis of work group diversity, conflict, and performance. *Administrative Science Quarterly*, 44: 1–28.

Podsakoff, P. M., MacKenzie, S. B., Lee, J. Y., & Podsakoff, N. P. 2003. Common method biases in behavioural research: A critical review of the literature and recommended remedies. *Journal of Applied Psychology*, 88: 879–903.

Savelsbergh, C. M. J. H., van der Heijden, B. I. J. M., & Poell, R. F. 2009. The development and empirical validation of a multidimensional measurement instrument for team learning behaviors. *Small Group Research*, 40: 578–607.

Shalley, C. E., & Gilson, L. L. 2004. What leaders need to know: A review of social and contextual factors that can foster or hinder creativity. *The Leadership Quarterly*, 15: 33–53.

Shalley, C. E., Zhou, J., & Oldham, G. R. 2004. The effects of personal and contextual characteristics on creativity: Where should we go from here? *Journal of Management*, 30: 933–958.

Shin, S. J., & Zhou, J. 2007. When is educational specialization heterogeneity related to creativity in research and development teams? Transformational leadership as a moderator. *Journal of Applied Psychology*, 92: 1709–1721.

Srivastava, A., Bartol, K., & Locke, E. A. 2006. Empowering leadership in management teams: Effects on knowledge sharing, efficacy, and performance. *Academy of Management Journal*, 49: 1239–1251.

Stewart, G. L., & Barrick, M. R. 2000. Team structure and performance: Assessing the mediating role of intrateam process and the moderating role of task type. *Academy of Management Journal*, 43: 135–148.

Tierney, P., & Farmer, S. M. 2011. Creative self-efficacy development and creative performance over time. *Journal of Applied Psychology*, 96: 277–293.

Van der Vegt, G. S., & Bunderson, J. S. 2005. Learning and performance in multidisciplinary teams: The importance of collective team identification. *Academy of Management Journal*, 48: 532–547.

Wang, X. H., Kim, T. Y., & Lee, D. R. 2016. Cognitive diversity and team creativity: Effects of team intrinsic motivation and transformational leadership. *Journal of Business Research*, 69: 3231–3239.

Wiersema, M. F., & Bantel, K. A. 1992. Top management team demography and corporate strategic change. *Academy of Management Journal*, 35: 91–121.

Wood, R. E. 1986. Task complexity: Definition of the construct. *Organizational Behavior and Human Decision Processes*, 37: 60–82.

Yukl, G. 2013. *Leadership in organizations* (8th ed.). Essex, UK: Pearson.

Zaccaro, S. J., Rittman, A. L., & Marks, M. A. 2001. Team leadership. *The Leadership Quarterly*, 12: 451–483.

Zhang, X., & Bartol, K. M. 2010. Linking empowering leadership and employee creativity: The influence of psychological empowerment, intrinsic motivation, and creative process engagement. *Academy of Management Journal*, 53: 107–128.

Zhang, X., & Zhou, J. 2014. Empowering leadership, uncertainty avoidance, trust, and employee creativity: Interaction effects and a mediating mechanism. *Organizational Behavior and Human Decision Processes*, 124: 150–164.

Zhou, J., & Hoever, I. J. 2014. Research on workplace creativity: A review and redirection. *Annual Review of Organizational Psychology and Organizational Behavior*, 1: 333–359.

7 Fostering the Creativity of Work Teams

Creative Leadership in the Midst of Diversity

Maria Kakarika

Introduction

Creative work—the joint novelty and usefulness of ideas about products, processes and services—is vital to organizational success and often done in teams (Amabile, 1988). However, the conditions that foster it are not very well understood, as it is associated with complex interpersonal processes between leaders and followers who interact in the creative process. Team diversity—"the distribution of differences among the members of a unit with respect to a common attribute such as tenure, ethnicity" (Harrison & Klein, 2007: 1200) has been argued to increase creativity because members have non-overlapping knowledge and resources (e.g., Milliken, Bartel, & Kurtzberg, 2003; Williams & O'Reilly, 1998). However, a considerable number of studies have yielded inconsistent empirical results (Hoever et al., 2012) with diversity sometimes improving and other times hindering creative outcomes (Bantel & Jackson, 1989; Choi, 2007; Sethi, Smith, & Park, 2001). These mixed results suggest that main effect diversity models are not sufficient (van Knippenberg & Schippers, 2007) and that scholars need to consider more complex models and pay closer attention to at least two issues. First, they need to carefully select the appropriate diversity variable, given that the effects of diversity attributes vary greatly (Harrison & Klein, 2007; Horwitz & Horwitz, 2007; Joshi & Roh, 2009). Second, they need to further understand the conditions under which team diversity exerts the expected positive influence on creativity (Mannix & Neale, 2005; Williams & O'Reilly, 1998) by capturing moderator variables (van Knippenberg, De Dreu & Homan, 2004) such as leadership (e.g., Pieterse et al., 2010; Redmond, Mumford, & Teach, 1993; Shin & Zhou, 2003; Somech, 2006; Wang, Kim, & Lee, 2016; Wang et al., 2013). Despite significant progress in understanding creativity of diverse teams, we still lack an overall framework that can be used to better understand how to foster creativity and predict the conditions under which team diversity will be beneficial.

To address these calls, I draw on a recently published metatheory of team diversity (Mayo et al., 2017) and consider the effects of four different types of diversity on team creativity, while proposing that Facilitating forms of creative leadership (Mainemelis, Kark, & Epitropaki, 2015) may moderate this relationship. In so doing, I first consider the main theories of diversity: the predominant two-theory framework of information processing and social categorization (see the categorization-elaboration model [CEM]; van Knippenberg et al., 2004; van Knippenberg, van Ginkel, & Homan, 2013) and two additional theoretical lenses, disparity/(in)justice and access to external networks, thus taking a detailed look at the concept (see Mayo et al., 2017). Second, I explain the role of Facilitative creative leadership, defined as leading toward stimulating and strengthening the creative contributions of the team members, viewing team members as the primary actors within the creativity process (Mainemelis, Kark, & Epitropaki, 2015). Finally, I develop a conceptual integrative framework of creative leadership in the context of diverse work teams that takes into account complex interactions among various team diversity dimensions. That is, the framework is constructed around the mutual reinforcement of various diversity types and outlines the joint effects of leadership and diversity on team creativity.

The proposed framework contributes to the literature in several ways. First, it integrates different perspectives on team diversity and creative leadership that have developed independently with little theoretical synthesis into a unified framework. It thus contributes to the diversity literature by reconciling contradictory findings and extending the attempts to better understand the conditions under which team diversity has more or less positive effects on team creativity. Second, it contributes to the leadership literature that studies its effect on creativity (Redmond, Mumford, & Teach, 1993; Shin & Zhou, 2003, 2007) by contextualizing it in a more systematic way, capturing a wider range of diversity types and their tradeoffs. It thus builds upon past typologies (Mayo et al., 2017) and encourages future ongoing research on the complexity and specificity of creative leadership in terms of differences among followers and contexts (Hunter et al., 2011). Finally, by shedding light on how leaders can increase the creativity of diverse work teams in such a fine-grained, multi-dimensional manner, the proposed framework may prove useful to leaders and managers who strive to improve divergent processes in teams, and help diverse teams to converge around creative ideas.

This chapter proceeds through the following sections. First, I briefly overview the main four diversity theories and associated diversity types. Next, I propose an integrative framework of team diversity and leadership leading to team creativity as the dependent variable. In the final section, I discuss how this multi-lens conceptualization can help improve creative leadership research and practice in the context of team diversity.

Four Theories of Diversity in Teams and the Role of Creative Leadership

Diversity effects are explained by considering four basic theories of team diversity (see Mayo et al., 2017), as summarized in Figure 7.1 and described next.

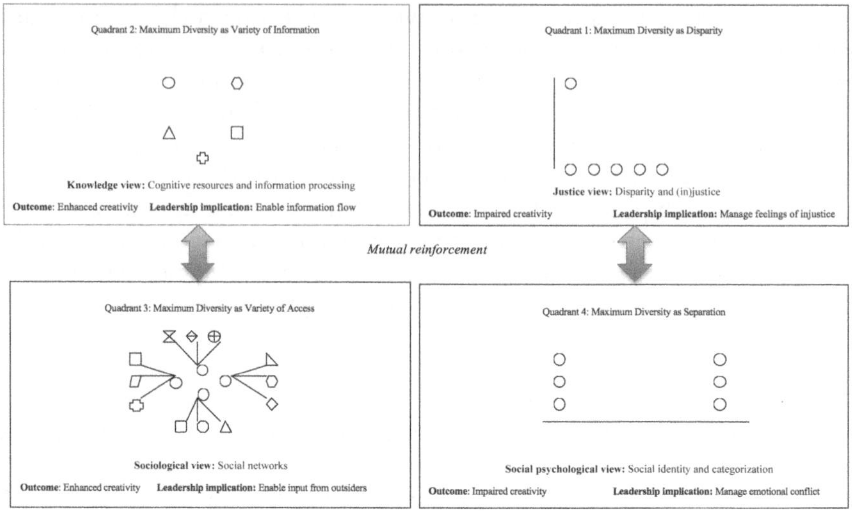

Figure 7.1 A Framework of Creative Leadership in Diverse Organizational Teams

Social Categorization (Diversity as Separation)

Much of team diversity research is based on a social psychological view—i.e., on social categorization and social identity theory (Tajfel, 1981; Turner, 1987). According to these theories, individuals define themselves against others using easily observable generic social categories such as sex and race (e.g., Stangor et al., 1992). This perspective views groups as open entities, because group members identify primarily not with the work team but with a larger social group outside it. Tajfel (1981) and his associates showed that perception of belonging to a psychological group resulted in in-group favoritism and out-group discrimination (e.g., Brewer, 1979), socio-emotional and behavioral biases that divide teams into subgroups and create 'separation.' This field of research mostly studies differences in attitudes and beliefs derived from differences in category membership. Maximum diversity as separation (see Figure 7.1, Quadrant 4) refers to perfect disagreement between subgroups with different values, attitudes or beliefs (Harrison & Klein, 2007), which significantly hinder team performance.

This type of diversity is therefore expected to impair team creativity because of possible emotional or relational conflict and distrust resulting from being different (cf. Jehn, Northcraft, & Neale, 1999), as confirmed by past studies. For example, Baer et al. (2008) found that demographic diversity was negatively related to team creativity and became nonsignificant over time. Similarly, Pearsall, Ellis, and Evans (2008) found that the activation of gender faultlines negatively affected the number and overall creativity of ideas, and Choi (2007) found that gender dissimilarity hindered creativity.

In such contexts, leaders may facilitate the creative performance of their teams primarily by managing emotional conflict management and creating a superordinate group identity that minimizes subgroup polarization.

Information Processing (Diversity as Variety of Information)

In contrast, the knowledge or information processing view explains that a diverse configuration of individuals feeds the team with a variety of knowledge, perspectives and skills that can render it more productive and creative (van Knippenberg & Schippers, 2007; see also meta-analyses by Bell et al., 2011). Maximum variety of information (see Figure 7.1, Quadrant 2) is present when each member has unique expertise (Harrison & Klein, 2007). The key idea is that a group that conducts complex tasks needs a large amount of cognitive resources for effective information processing, debate, problem solving and team performance (Simons, Pelled, & Smith, 1999).

This type of diversity should therefore increase creative performance of teams, because of idea variety and increased task conflict, as generally confirmed by past studies (e.g., Jackson, Joshi, & Erhardt, 2003; Kurtzberg & Amabile, 2001). For instance, both educational heterogeneity (Thornburg, 1991) and functional heterogeneity (Somech & Drach-Zahavy, 2013) have been found to increase group creativity. In such team contexts leaders may enable information flow by promoting healthy degrees of cognitive conflict and idea-challenging in order to spark and maintain creativity within a team (Hunter et al., 2011). They may thus support and empower followers, providing them with generous degrees of autonomy, because close monitoring has been found to have detrimental effects on employee creativity (Amabile et al., 2004; Zhou, 2003).

Disparity/(In)Justice (Diversity as Disparity)

The justice view or disparity and (in)justice approach explains how increasing heterogeneity in status, prestige and power harms the group and its members. Maximum disparity (see Figure 7.1, Quadrant 1) is present when one team member significantly outranks all other members in terms of a socially valued asset or desired resource. The resulting comparisons among team members lead to 'internal competition, suppression of voice, reduced (quality of) communication, and interpersonal undermining' (Harrison & Klein, 2007: 1201). Perceptions of 'nonlegitimate' asymmetry may cause feelings of injustice that distract members from key tasks and hinder group cohesion and performance (Greenberg, 1987).

It is thus expected that this type of diversity and the resulting competition and deviance will suppress team creativity because of reduced member input and withdrawal. Research shows that team members' knowledge sharing, participation in discussions and experimentation is proportionate to their status and power in the team (e.g., Bunderson & Reagans, 2011;

Cohen & Zhou, 1991). Those with higher status tend to dominate the discussion, whereas members with lower status are less influential, and mixed-status groups make poorer decisions (e.g., Hollingshead, 1996). In support of this reasoning, Choi (2007) found that hierarchical status diversity was negatively related to employee creative behavior. In such contexts, leaders may manage emotions and reduce feelings of injustice in order to avoid suppressing the input of low-status members and facilitate creativity within the team.

External Networks (Diversity as Variety of Access)

Team members may differ not only in skills and knowledge (i.e., individual human capital) but also in social connections to other individuals outside the group, both within and outside the organization (i.e., social capital) (Oh, Chung, & Labianca, 2004). The sociological or 'variety of access' view of diversity thus treats teams as open systems. Maximum variety of access (see Figure 7.1, Quadrant 3) occurs when each member's social network is unique (Mayo et al., 2017). A large distribution of external ties can improve group effectiveness (Burt, 1992; Nahapiet & Ghoshal, 1998). Such external ties offer instrumental resources (e.g., technical support, money, partnerships, projects), socio-emotional resources (e.g., social support; see Swann, Johnson, & Bosson, 2009) and legitimacy (i.e., political support), because having *diverse* external ties, as opposed to having just lots of external ties, makes it easier to manage impressions, lobby and appear legitimate and credible to outsiders (Ancona & Caldwell, 1992; Perry-Smith & Mannucci, 2015).

Past research has confirmed that social networks are especially important for creativity and that this type of diversity can enhance creativity (e.g., Baer, 2010; Brass, 1995; Burt, 2004; Perry-Smith, 2006; Perry-Smith & Shalley, 2003; Perry-Smith & Mannucci, 2015; Zhou et al., 2009). For example, when members bridge structural holes their capacity for creative action is enhanced (Ancona & Caldwell, 1992; Burt, 2002; Hansen, 1999; Reagans & Zuckerman, 2001). In such contexts, leaders may adopt an external focus, encourage the use of external networks, foster coalitions and political support and, ultimately, enable the team to connect with various external sources of information (Mumford et al., 2002, 2014; Rickards & Moger, 2000) in order to increase input and facilitate the creative processes within their teams.

An Integrative Framework of Creative Leadership in Diverse Teams

The large number of studies developed within the four diversity lenses has greatly enriched our understanding of the effects of team diversity on team creativity but has also led to contradictory findings (Mayo et al., 2017). An important reason is that in most studies diversity was conceptualized as a unitary concept and operationalized in inconsistent ways (Harrison & Klein, 2007), failing to capture other perspectives. This lack of conceptual distinction between diversity types has therefore led to unspecified models, limiting valid comparisons across studies and cumulative knowledge. The Integrative framework, discussed next, addresses to an extent this theoretical limitation. It provides conceptual clarity and exploits the underlying synergies of the four diversity perspectives in order to provide a more comprehensive understanding of why diversity can increase creativity in some cases and decrease it in other cases.

Figure 7.1 depicts the proposed framework that can be used as a general conceptual springboard for developing a larger set of more specific investigations of how leaders can facilitate team creativity. The framework advanced here first melds the two schools of thought of information processing and external networks. As Figure 7.1 shows, information and access diversity types can reinforce one another in affecting the team's creative potential. The cognitive diversity resulting from different knowledge, skills and abilities coming from both inside and outside the group is likely to boost task conflicts (i.e., disagreement on task-related issues: Jehn, 1995) toward creative performance (Pelled, Eisenhardt, & Xin, 1999). In support of this reasoning, Han, Han and Brass (2014) found that team-level human capital diversity (knowledge, skills and abilities) is one of the potential antecedents of social capital for team creativity. Similarly, Perry-Smith (2014) found that tie strength influences creativity through processing of non-redundant knowledge.

Leaders may thus improve synergy among team members, ease coordination and encourage participation with the external environment via communication with non team members in order to improve divergent idea generation and elaboration. For example, by intellectually stimulating their team members, transformational leaders can direct their attention to divergent ideas and urge them to experiment with new perspectives (Gong, Huang, & Farh, 2009; Kearney & Gebert, 2009; Shin & Zhou, 2007; Wang, Kim, & Lee, 2016). They can develop a climate of psychological safety that allows them to share their ideas and experiences freely, and engage in interpersonal risk taking that is important for team creative outcomes (e.g., Lee, Choi, & Kim, 2018; Nishii & Goncalo, 2008; Oldham & Cummings, 1996). They may encourage some conflict and idea challenging in order to spark creativity (Hunter et al., 2011; Nemeth, 1997). They may also connect the team with various external entities to build support for their new ideas (Mumford et al., 2002) and act as a critical liaison in order to increase their creativity (see Venkataramani, Richter, & Clarke, 2014). These ideas are summarized in the following guideline.

Guideline 1. Leaders of diverse teams may explicitly consider the mutual positive reinforcement of information and access diversity types on team creativity. In such teams, leaders may encourage the autonomy of followers and the open nature of the team in order to facilitate information exchange, and the use of external networks and creative input from outside the team.

The framework next melds the two schools of thought of social categorization and disparity/(in)justice. As Figure 7.1 shows, separation and disparity diversity types can reinforce each other and crucially influence team creativity. As previously discussed, diversity as separation creates polarized subgroups in conflict, with in-group members being biased against out-group ones. This bias is likely to intensify the negative effects of disparity and members may perceive more injustice and discrimination when power and status are concentrated in one or few members. That is, polarized values, attitudes and beliefs within the team may reinforce status or power differences, and vice versa (Mayo et al., 2017).

It is therefore pivotal for leaders to minimize the rise of social categorization and injustice processes. They may integrate the psychological subgroups that oppose one another within the work team in terms of values and beliefs, and manage intragroup conflict. For example, they may intervene to emphasize a superordinate identity and commonalities among members, which have been found to lead to recategorization, reduced bias and improved relations within teams (see Gaertner et al., 1993; Gaertner & Dovidio, 2000). Supporting this idea, Salazar, Feitosa, and Salas (2017) recently found that team identity salience reduces subgroup categorization and moderates the relationship between team diversity and idea novelty. In parallel, leaders may manage status differences, experienced inequities and resulting feelings of injustice, in order to enable followers to use each other's creative inputs of each other and converge around creative ideas. This reasoning justifies the following guideline.

Guideline 2. Leaders of diverse teams may explicitly consider the mutual negative reinforcement of separation and disparity diversity types on team creativity. In such teams, leaders may focus on interpersonal relationships within the team and actively manage emotional conflict and feelings of injustice among followers in order to create a superordinate team identity and encourage follower creative contributions.

Although the aforementioned two guidelines provide insight into the team diversity-creativity linkage, they are clearly incomplete because all four types of diversity likely co-exist within a team. For example, even though a team may be composed of members with non-overlapping knowledge and external ties, concurrent status disparity and social categorization may cause members to contribute less to the discussion, neglect the value of certain knowledge areas, neglect to bridge across different knowledge pools and underutilize external networks. Therefore, the effect of team diversity on creativity becomes difficult to predict and likely depends on whether the potential positive effects of diversity (i.e., information processing and external networks) are maximized and, at the same time, the potential negative effects of diversity (i.e., social categorization and disparity processes) are minimized (see Mayo et al., 2017).

The proposed framework is designed to explain how leaders of diverse teams can have this dual effect and enhance team creativity. Leaders may consider all four theoretical lenses in unison and manage both internal and external social relationships in order to provide to team members a common base from which to integrate diversified ideas and perspectives and develop a creative final output. That is, leaders may actively promote a superordinate team identity in order to bridge polarized beliefs and manage emotional conflict stemming from status differences, while encouraging the active exchange of non-overlapping information stemming from the team's human and social capital. These relationships are captured in the following guideline.

> *Guideline 3: Leaders of diverse teams may explicitly consider the nested interrelationships of information, access, separation and disparity diversity types in order to foster team creativity. In such teams, the positive effects of diversity as variety of information and/or access on team creativity will be jointly weakened by diversity as separation and disparity. Leaders may thus strive to reduce polarized beliefs and status differences within the team in order to enable the beneficial effects of the team's human and social capital on creativity.*

Discussion

This chapter began with acknowledging that although it is usually assumed that diversity is beneficial for creativity because of increased knowledge pools and networks, research did not always support this hypothesis and results have been inconclusive (van Knippenberg & Schippers, 2007; Williams & O'Reilly, 1998). It then proposed an answer to this puzzle, by arguing that Facilitative creative leadership moderates the relationship between four types of diversity and team creativity. The framework developed here provides new insight on the issue of boosting creativity by reaching out to multiple strands of diversity and contributes to the literature in the fields of team diversity and creative leadership in the following three ways.

This chapter's primary contribution is integrating the four diversity theories with creative leadership, which brings together two research strands into a common conceptual framework for connecting their perspectives. It is broad enough to apply to different types of team diversity and specific enough to explain the role of creative leadership in diverse teams. It thus facilitates theorizing on creative leadership in organizations without compromising its contextual sensitivity and can stimulate a cross-fertilization of knowledge.

Second, by developing a common multi-lens framework that encompasses distinct diversity types, this chapter offers a more nuanced, more synthetic theoretical explanation of how leaders can pursue creative outcomes in team settings. It can be used to study the tradeoffs involved in leading diverse teams toward creativity and thus encourages research that approaches team diversity and creative leadership in a more holistic way. This framework can thus help scholars extend their understanding of team creativity and stimulate multi-theoretical research of creative leadership.

Third, future research can draw on this multi-lens perspective to develop novel empirical studies. With few exceptions (e.g., Shin & Zhou, 2007; Somech, 2006), there is little scholarly work on how interactions between leadership and diversity affect creativity. By adopting this framework, scholars can develop fine-grained hypotheses to move beyond main effects models, and consider more complex models that can be normatively useful. Cumulative empirical research based on a solid integrative framework is the only way to answer the question of how leaders can increase creative outcomes of diverse teams.

Although the framework presented here answers some questions, it also underlines questions that have not yet been addressed. One such question pertains to the effects of specific forms of leadership, such as transformational leadership. Even though intuition suggests that transformational leadership may make an important contribution to team creativity, empirical evidence on its role in fostering team creativity and innovation is scarce and mixed (Anderson, Potočnik, & Zhou, 2014; Eisenbeiss, van Knippenberg, & Boerner, 2008). Studies have either failed to find support for the relationship of transformational leadership and team creativity (e.g., Jaussi & Dionne, 2003) or found positive effects (e.g., Eisenbeiss et al., 2008; Gumusluoglu & Ilsev, 2009; Jung, 2001; Shin & Zhou, 2003, 2007; Sosik, Kahai, & Avolio, 1998, 1999) or curvilinear effects (Eisenbeiss & Boerner, 2010). The role of transformational leadership as moderator of the diversity-creativity relationship thus deserves more research attention.

Another unanswered question refers to which leadership styles and associated theories may explain how leaders can obtain creative outcomes in organizations and at which stage. For example, Mainemelis, Kark and Epitropaki (2015) proposed examining the social identity theory of leadership and Neubert et al. (2008) proposed examining servant leadership in relation to creative behavior. In addition, Rosing, Frese and Bausch's (2011) meta-analysis suggested that leadership is more effective at the initial stage of the creative process, and past research supports this finding (e.g., Kanter, 1988; Mumford et al., 2002). Future research may thus delve deeper into this question and examine time-based dynamics and more complex interactions between time or stage of the creative process and various leadership styles. I hope researchers will use the framework to further refine future research and explore potential curvilinear effects of creative leadership in diverse teams.

Finally, while the posited framework has focused on Facilitative creative leadership as an act of fostering the creativity of others, diverse teams may also exist in Directing and Integrating contexts of creative leadership (see Mainemelis, Kark, & Epitropaki, 2015). For example, when teams are high on separation/disparity and low on information/access, emotional conflict may further shadow the existing overlapping input, and thus directing the materialization of a leader's creative vision may be more effective for creative outputs. In another example, research that examines teams led by top chefs that are high on all diversity types may further examine how Integrative creative leadership synthesizes the creative vision of the top chef with diverse inputs from team members to achieve creative performance. Consideration of such additional context-dependent manifestations of creative leadership uncovers a new set of ways to apply the framework application.

Conclusion

How can highly diverse teams increase their creativity? I suggest that leadership is one important answer. The framework developed here supports the idea that leaders of such teams need to step back to get the overall picture. It outlines the role of leadership in orchestrating team members to use their resources optimally for higher creativity, while managing emotions and related conflict. It can be seen as a tool through which leaders can view the patterns of diversity through multiple lenses and act accordingly. In sum, this integrative framework suggests interesting avenues for future research and offers a basis for understanding how diversity can lead to creativity and thus can be turned into an asset rather than a liability.

References

Amabile, T. M. 1988. A model of creativity and innovation in organizations. In B. M. Staw & L. L. Cummings (Eds.), *Research in organizational behavior*, Vol. 10: 123–167. Greenwich, CT: JAI Press.

Amabile, T. M., Schatzel, E. A., Moneta, G. B., & Kramer, S. J. 2004. Leader behaviors and the work environment for creativity: Perceived leader support. *Leadership Quarterly*, 15: 5–32.

Anderson, N., Potočnik, K., & Zhou, J. 2014. Innovation and creativity in organizations: A state-of-the-science review, prospective commentary, and guiding framework. *Journal of Management*, 40(5): 1297–1333.

Ancona, D. G., & Caldwell, D. F. 1992. Demography and design: Predictors of new product team performance. *Organization Science*, 3: 321–341.

Baer, M. 2010. The strength-of-weak-ties perspective on creativity: A comprehensive examination and extension. *Journal of Applied Psychology*, 95(3): 592–601.

Baer, M., Oldham, G. R., Jacobsohn, G. C., & Hollingshead, A. B. 2008. The personality composition of teams and creativity: The moderating role of team creative confidence. *Journal Creative Behavior*, 42.

Bantel, K. A., & Jackson, S. E. 1989. Top management and innovations in banking: Does the composition of the top team make a difference? *Strategic Management Journal*, 10: 107–124.

Bell, S. T., Villado, A. J., Lukasik, M. A., Belau, L., & Briggs, A. L. 2011. Getting specific about demographic diversity variable and team performance relationships: A meta-analysis. *Journal of Management*, 37(3): 709–743.

Brass, D. J. 1995. Creativity: It's all in your social network. In C. M. Ford & D. A. Gioia (Eds.), *Creative action in organizations*: 94–99. London: Sage Publications.

Brewer, M. B. 1979. Ingroup bias in the minimal intergroup situation: A cognitive—motivational analysis. *Psychological Bulletin*, 86: 307–324.

Bunderson, J. S., & Reagans, R. E. 2011. Power, status, and learning in organizations. *Organization Science*, 22(5): 1182–1194.

Burt, R. S. 1992. *Structural holes: The social structure of competition*. Cambridge, MA: Harvard University Press.

Burt, R. S. 2002. The social capital of structural holes. In M. F. Guillén, R. Collins, P. England, & M. Meyer (Eds.), *The new economic sociology*: 148–192. New York: Russell Sage Foundation.

Burt, R. S. 2004. Structural holes and good ideas. *The American Journal of Sociology*, 110: 349–399.

Choi, J. N. 2007. Group composition and employee creative behaviour in a Korean electronics company: Distinct effects of relational demography and group diversity. *Journal of Occupational and Organizational Psychology*, 80: 213–234.

Cohen, B. P., & Zhou, X. 1991. Status processes in enduring work groups. *American Sociological Review*, 56: 179–188.

Eisenbeiss, S. A., & Boerner, S. 2010. Transformational leadership and R&D innovation: Taking a curvilinear approach. *Creativity and Innovation Management*, 19(4): 364–372.

Eisenbeiss, S. A., van Knippenberg, D., & Boerner, S. 2008. Transformational leadership and team innovation: Integrating team climate principles. *Journal of Applied Psychology*, 93(6): 1438–1446.

Gaertner, S. L., & Dovidio, J. F. 2000. *Reducing intergroup bias: The common ingroup identity model*. Philadelphia, PA: Psychology Press.

Gaertner, S. L., Dovidio, J. F., Anastasio, P. A., Bachman, B. A., & Rust, M. C. 1993. The common ingroup identity model: Recategorization and the reduction of intergroup bias. *European Review of Social Psychology*, 4: 1–26.

Gong, Y., Huang, J-C., & Farh, J-L. 2009. Employee learning orientation, transformational leadership, and employee creativity: The mediating role of employee creative self-efficacy. *Academy of Management Journal*, 52: 765–778.

Greenberg, J. 1987. A taxonomy of organizational justice theories. *Academy of Management Review*, 12: 9–22.

Gumusluoglu, L., & Ilsev, A. 2009. Transformational leadership, creativity, and organizational innovation. *Journal of Business Research*, 62: 461–473.

Han, J., Han, J., & Brass, D. J. 2014. Human capital diversity in the creation of social capital for team creativity. *Journal of Organizational Behavior*, 35(1): 54–71.

Hansen, M. T. 1999. The search-transfer problem: The role of weak ties in sharing knowledge across organization subunits. *Administrative Science Quarterly*, 44: 82–111.

Harrison, D. A., & Klein, K. J. 2007. What's the difference? Diversity constructs as separation, variety, or disparity in organizations. *Academy of Management Review*, 32(4): 1199–1228.

Hoever, I. J., van Knippenberg, D., van Ginkel, W. P., & Barkema, H. G. 2012. Fostering team creativity: Perspective taking as key to unlocking diversity's potential. *Journal of Applied Psychology*, 97: 982–996.

Hollingshead, A. B. 1996. Information suppression and status persistence in group decision making: The effects of communication media. *Human Communication Research*, 23: 193–219.

Horwitz, S. K., & Horwitz, I. B. 2007. The effects of team diversity on team outcomes: A meta-analytic review of team demography. *Journal of Management*, 33(6): 987–1015.

Hunter, S. T., Thoroughgood, C. N., Myer, A. T., & Ligon, G. S. 2011. Paradoxes of leading innovative behaviors: Summary, solutions, and future directions. *Psychology of Aesthetics, Creativity, and the Arts*, 5: 54–66.

Jackson, S. E., Joshi, A., & Erhardt, N. L. 2003. Recent research on team and organizational diversity: SWOT analysis and implications. *Journal of Management*, 29: 801–830.

Jaussi, K. S., & Dionne, S. D. 2003. Leading for creativity: The role of unconventional leader behavior. *Leadership Quarterly*, 14: 475–498.

Jehn, K. A. 1995. A multimethod examination of the benefits and detriments of intragroup conflict. *Administrative Science Quarterly*, 40: 256–282.

Jehn, K. A., Northcraft, G. B., & Neale, M. A. 1999. Why differences make a difference: A field study of diversity, conflict, and performance in workgroups. *Administrative Science Quarterly*, 44(4): 741–763.

Joshi, A., & Roh, H. 2009. The role of context in work team diversity research: A meta-analytic review. *Academy of Management Journal*, 52(3): 599–627.

Jung, D. 2001. Transformational and transactional leadership and their effects on creativity in groups. *Creativity Research Journal*, 13: 185–195.

Kanter, R. M. 1988. When a thousand flowers bloom structural, collective and social conditions for innovation in organization. *Research in Organizational Behavior*, 10: 169–211.

Kearney, E., & Gebert, D. 2009. Managing diversity and enhancing team outcomes: The promise of transformational leadership. *Journal of Applied Psychology*, 94: 77–89.

Kurtzberg, T. R., & Amabile, T. M. 2001. From Guilford to creative synergy: Opening the black box of team-level creativity. *Creativity Research Journal*, 13: 285–294.

Lee, H. W., Choi, J. N., & Kim, S. 2018. Does gender diversity help teams constructively manage status conflict? An evolutionary perspective of status conflict, team psychological safety, and team creativity. *Organizational Behavior and Human Decision Processes*, 144: 187–199.

Mainemelis, B., Kark, R., & Epitropaki, O. 2015. 'Creative leadership: A multi-context conceptualization. *Academy of Management Annals*, 9(1): 393–482.

Mannix, E., & Neale, M. A. 2005. What differences make a difference? The promise and reality of diverse teams in organizations. *Psychological Science in the Public Interest*, 6: 31–55.

Mayo, M., Kakarika, M., Mainemelis, C., & Deuschel, N. T. 2017. A metatheoretical framework of diversity in teams. *Human Relations*, 70(8): 911–939.

Milliken, F. J., Bartel, C. A., & Kurtzberg, T. R. 2003. Diversity and creativity in work groups: A dynamic perspective on the affective and cognitive processes that link diversity and performance. In P. B. Paulus & B. A. Nijstad (Eds.), *Group creativity: Innovation through collaboration*: 32–62. New York: Oxford University Press.

Mumford, M. D., Scott, G. M., Gaddis, B., & Strange, J. M. 2002. Leading creative people: Orchestrating expertise and relationships. *Leadership Quarterly*, 13: 705–750.

Nahapiet, J., & Ghoshal, S. 1998. Social capital, intellectual capital and organizational advantage. *Academy of Management Review*, 23(2): 242–266.

Nemeth, C. J. 1997. Managing innovation: When less is more. *California Management Review*, 40: 59–74.

Neubert, M. J., Kacmar, K. M., Carlson, D. S., Chonko, L. B., & Roberts, J. A. 2008. Regulatory focus as a mediator of the influence of initiating structure and servant leadership on employee behavior. *Journal of Applied Psychology*, 93(6): 1220–1233.

Nishii, L. H., & Goncalo, J. A. 2008. *Demographic faultlines and creativity in diverse groups*. CAHRS Working Paper #08–04. Ithaca, NY: Cornell University, School of Industrial and Labor Relations, Center for Advanced Human Resource Studies.

Oh, H., Chung, M-H., & Labianca, G. 2004. Group social capital and group effectiveness: The role of informal socializing ties. *Academy of Management Journal*, 46: 860–875.

Oldham, G. R., & Cummings, A. 1996. Employee creativity: Personal and contextual factors at work. *Academy of Management Journal*, 39(3): 607–634.

Pearsall, M. J., Ellis, A. P. J., & Evans, J. M. 2008. Unlocking the effects of gender faultlines on team creativity: Is activation the key? *Journal of Applied Psychology*, 93(1): 225–234.

Pelled, L. H., Eisenhardt, K. M., & Xin, K. R. 1999. Exploring the black box: An analysis of work group diversity, conflict and performance. *Administrative Science Quarterly*, 44: 1–28.

Perry-Smith, J. E. 2006. Social yet creative: The role of social relationships in facilitating individual creativity. *Academy of Management Journal*, 49: 85–101.

Perry-Smith, J. E. 2014. Social network ties beyond nonredundancy: An experimental investigation of the effect of knowledge content and tie strength on creativity. *Journal of Applied Psychology*, 99(5): 831–846.

Perry-Smith, J., & Mannucci, P. 2015. Social networks, creativity, and entrepreneurship. In *The Oxford handbook of creativity, innovation, and entrepreneurship*: 205–224. New York: Oxford University Press.

Perry-Smith, J. E., & Shalley, C. E. 2003. The social side of creativity: A static and dynamic social network perspective. *Academy of Management Review*, 28: 89–106.

Pieterse, A. N., van Knippenberg, D., Schippers, M., & Stam, D. 2010. Transformational and transactional leadership and innovative behavior: The moderating role of psychological empowerment. *Journal of Organizational Behavior*, 31(4): 609–623.

Reagans, R., & Zuckerman, E. W. 2001. Networks, diversity, and productivity: The social capital of corporate R & D teams. *Organization Science*, 12(4): 502–517.

Redmond, M. R., Mumford, M. D., & Teach, R. 1993. Putting creativity to work: Effects of leader behavior on subordinate creativity. *Organizational Behavior and Human Decision Process*, 55: 120–151.

Rickards, T., & Moger, S. 2000. Creative leadership processes in project team development: An alternative to Tuckman's stage model. *British Journal of Management*, 11: 273–283.

Rosing, K., Frese, M., & Bausch, A. 2011. Explaining the heterogeneity of the leadership-innovation relationship: Ambidextrous leadership. *The Leadership Quarterly*, 22(5): 956–974.

Salazar, M. R., Feitosa, J., & Salas, E. 2017. Diversity and team creativity: Exploring underlying mechanisms. *Group Dynamics: Theory, Research, and Practice*, 21(4): 187–206.

Sethi, R., Smith, D. C., & Park, C. W. 2001. Cross-functional product development teams, creativity, and the innovativeness of new consumer products. *Journal of Marketing Research*, 38(1): 73–85.

Shin, S. J., & Zhou, J. 2003. Transformational leadership, conservation, and creativity: Evidence from Korea. *Academy of Management Journal*, 46: 703–714.

Shin, S. J., & Zhou, J. 2007. When is educational specialization heterogeneity related to creativity in research and development teams? Transformational leadership as a moderator. *Journal of Applied Psychology*, 92: 1709–1721.

Simons, T., Pelled, L. H., & Smith, K. A. 1999. Making use of difference: Diversity, debate, and decision comprehensiveness in top management teams. *Academy of Management Journal*, 42: 662–673.

Somech, A. 2006. The effects of leadership style and team process on performance and innovation in functionally heterogeneous teams. *Journal of Management*, 32: 132–157.

Somech, A., & Drach-Zahavy, A. 2013. Translating team creativity to innovation implementation: The role of team composition and climate for innovation. *Journal of Management*, 39: 684–708.

Sosik, J. J., Kahai, S. S., & Avolio, B. J. 1998. Transformational leadership and dimensions of creativity: Motivating idea generation in computer-mediated groups. *Creativity Research Journal*, 11(2): 11–12.

Sosik, J. J., Kahai, S. S., & Avolio, B. J. 1999. Leadership style, anonymity and creativity in group decision support systems. *Journal of Creative Behavior*, 33: 227–257.

Stangor, C., Lynch, L., Duan, C., & Glass, B. 1992. Categorization of individuals on the basis of multiple social features. *Journal of Personality and Social Psychology*, 2: 207–218.

Swann, W. B., Jr., Johnson, R. E., & Bosson, J. 2009. Identity negotiation in the workplace. *Research in Organizational Behavior*, 29: 81–109.

Tajfel, H. 1981. *Human groups and social categories*. Cambridge: Cambridge University Press.

Thornburg, T. H. 1991. Group size & member diversity influence on creative performance. *The Journal of Creative Behavior*, 25(4): 324–333.

Turner, J. C. 1987. *Rediscovering the social group: A self-categorization theory*. New York: Basil Blackwell.

Van Knippenberg, D., De Dreu, C. K. W., & Homan, A. C. 2004. Work group diversity and group performance: An integrative model and research agenda. *Journal of Applied Psychology*, 89(6): 1008–1022.

Van Knippenberg, D., van Ginkel, W. P., & Homan, A. C. 2013. Diversity mindsets and the performance of diverse teams. *Organizational Behavior and Human Decision Processes*, 121(2): 183–193.

Van Knippenberg, D., & Schippers, M. C. 2007. Work group diversity. *Annual Review of Psychology*, 58: 515–541.

Venkataramani, V., & Richter, A., & Clarke, R. 2014. Creative benefits from well-connected leaders? Leader social network ties as facilitators of employee radical creativity. *Journal of Applied Psychology*, 99: 966–975.

Wang, X. H. F., Kim, T. Y., & Lee, D. R. 2016. Cognitive diversity and team creativity: Effects of team intrinsic motivation and transformational leadership. *Journal of Business Research*, 69: 3231–3239.
Wang, P., Rode, J. C., Shi, K., Luo, Z., & Chen, W. 2013. A workgroup climate perspective on the relationships among transformational leadership, workgroup diversity, and employee creativity. *Group & Organization Management*, 38(3): 334–360.
Williams, K. Y., & O'Reilly, C. A. 1998. Demography and diversity in organizations. In B. M. Staw & R. M. Sutton (Eds.), *Research in organizational behavior*, 20: 77–140.
Zhou, J. 2003. When the presence of creative coworkers is related to creativity: Role of supervisor close monitoring, developmental feedback, and creative personality. *Journal of Applied Psychology*, 88: 413–422.
Zhou, J., Shin, J., Brass, D., Choi, J., & Zhang, Z. 2009. Social networks, personal values, and creativity: Evidence for curvilinear and interaction effects. *Journal of Applied Psychology*, 94(6): 1544–1552.

Part III

Creative Leadership in Directive Contexts

8 Creativity Is Not Enough

The WICS Model of Leadership

Robert J. Sternberg

Introduction

On January 30, 1933, Adolph Hitler became the new chancellor of Germany. Some people dreaded the thought of such a man in charge of one of the most powerful countries in the world; other people welcomed the fresh ideas he would bring to leadership. In terms of the standard definition of creativity (Runco & Jaeger, 2012), they saw Hitler as both an original and effective thinker. Some people—not just Germans—became disillusioned. Others, however, continued to believe that Hitler was both original (certainly no one had planned a mass genocide on such a scale before) and effective (he carried out the genocide with astonishing effectiveness), despite his total moral disengagement (Bandura, 2015). I will argue in this chapter that leaders such as Hitler can be charismatic—they can even be creative—but they never display creativity mediated by wisdom as well as intelligence.

Today, scholars of creativity recognize that creativity has a dark side (Cropley et al., 2010; Runco, 2017; Sternberg, 2010). What matters with creativity is not only whether it is used but also how it is used. Creativity was represented then, and is represented today, by demagogic leaders on every continent of the world. One might think that these leaders are ones who take power through the means of a coup d'état or otherwise by force. On the contrary, most of them originally are elected (Levitsky & Ziblatt, 2018). But if people are willing to elect demagogic, darkly creative individuals as leaders, perhaps creativity, in and of itself, is not as good as it is cracked up to be. Or rather, perhaps it is a *necessary but not sufficient condition* for an individual to be a great leader. What characteristics, in addition to creativity, are needed to protect against dangerous leaders? That discussion is the focus of this chapter.

The goal of this chapter is to argue that leadership that is both good and effective is, in large part, a function of *creativity* in generating ideas, but also of *analytical intelligence* in evaluating the quality of these ideas, *practical intelligence* in implementing the ideas and convincing others to value and follow the ideas, and *wisdom* to ensure that the decisions and their implementation help to achieve a common good for all stakeholders. The model is referred to as WICS—*w*isdom, *i*ntelligence, *c*reativity, *s*ynthesized (Sternberg, 2003a, 2003b, 2012; Sternberg & Vroom, 2002). It applies to any leadership at all, but especially to leadership where the stakes are high—where good leadership makes a big positive difference and where bad leadership is potentially very harmful.

Leadership involves both skills—how well people do things—and attitudes—their views on what they and others do. The attitudes are at least as important to leadership as are the underlying skills. One needs creative skills and attitudes to generate fresh and good ideas for leadership (Sternberg & Davidson, 1982); one needs analytical intellectual skills and attitudes to decide whether they are good ideas as well as practical-intellectual skills and attitudes to implement the ideas and convince others of the value of the ideas, and one needs wisdom-related skills and attitudes to assess the long- as well as short-term impacts of these ideas on other individuals and institutions as well as on oneself. One also needs basic critical literacy—some leaders today appear not to read, either through lack of skill or desire (see Spear-Swerling & Sternberg, 1994; Sternberg, 1985c).

The chapter considers the elements of creativity, intelligence, and wisdom, in that order, because it represents the order in which the elements often are initially used, although as leadership decisions evolve, the elements become interactive, and so order becomes less relevant.

Creativity

Creativity in this chapter refers to the skills and attitudes needed for generating ideas and products that are (a) relatively novel, (b) high in quality, and (c) appropriate to the task at hand (Niu & Sternberg, 2003; Sternberg & Lubart, 1995). Creativity is important for leadership because it is the component of leadership whereby one generates the ideas that others will follow. A leader who lacks creativity may get along with others and get others to go along with the leader's plans—but he or she may get others to go along with inferior, stale, or even harmful ideas.

Leadership as a Confluence of Skills and Attitudes

A confluence model of creativity (Sternberg & Lubart, 1995) suggests that creative people show a variety of characteristics. These characteristics represent not only abilities but also decisions (Sternberg, 2000). In other words, to a large extent, people decide to be creative rather than merely being born creative. People who decide for creativity display a creative attitude toward leadership. The decisions reflect the *attitudinal component* of leadership discussed earlier. There is also an *abilities component* of leadership which includes, but is not limited to, creative leadership. Deciding to be creative will go a long way toward encouraging and even producing creative thinking. But this decision will not go all the way, because people may or may not have fully developed the abilities component in addition to the attitudinal one. Without the decision to be creative, however, an individual will not be creative, no matter what the abilities, because the individual will not adopt the mindset, discussed next, that is required for creative thinking.

What are the elements of a creative attitude toward leadership? The empirical bases for these aspects of the creative attitude, including the research supporting them, are summarized in Kaufman and Sternberg (in press) and Plucker (2017).

1. ***Problem redefinition.*** Creative leaders do not define problems the way everyone else does simply because everyone else defines the problems in that way. They decide on the exact nature of the problems confronting them, using their own judgment. Most importantly, they are willing to defy the crowd in defining problems differently from the ways others do (Sternberg, 2002a; Sternberg & Lubart, 1995). But problem redefinition is not enough, because the redefinitions may be inadequate or even wrong.
2. ***Problem analysis.*** Creative leaders are willing to analyze whether their solutions to problems are the best ones possible—that is, they not only come up with new ideas but also evaluate the feasibility of those ideas.
3. ***Selling solutions.*** Creative leaders realize that creative ideas do not sell themselves; rather, creative leaders have to decide to sell their ideas and then decide to put in the effort to do so. Their effort may or may not succeed. If it does not succeed, they may find themselves out of a job.
4. ***Recognizing how knowledge can both help and at the same time hinder creative thinking.*** Creative leaders realize that knowledge can hinder as well as facilitate creative thinking (see also Adelson, 1984; Frensch & Sternberg, 1989; Sternberg, 1985a). Sometimes leaders allow themselves to become entrenched and thus become susceptible to tunnel vision. They let their expertise hinder rather than facilitate their exercise of creative leadership.
5. ***Willingness to take sensible and worthwhile risks.*** Creative leaders recognize that they must decide to take sensible and worthwhile risks. These risks can not only lead them to succeed but also lead them, from time to time and more often than they would like, to fail (Lubart & Sternberg, 1995).
6. ***Willingness to surmount challenging obstacles.*** Creative leaders are willing to surmount the challenging obstacles that confront anyone who decides to be creative and thus defy the crowd. Such obstacles result when those who accept current ways of doing things confront those who do not (Sternberg & Lubart, 1995).
7. ***Belief in one's ability to accomplish the tasks that need to get done.*** Creative leaders believe in their ability to get the job done, no matter how challenging the tasks are. This belief is sometimes referred to as representing feelings of self-efficacy (Bandura, 1996).

8. ***Willingness to tolerate periods of ambiguity.*** Creative leaders recognize that there may be long periods of time in which they feel a great deal of uncertainty. During these periods, they cannot be certain that they are doing the right thing or that what they are doing will have the outcome they hope for.
9. ***Willingness to discover extrinsic rewards for the things one is intrinsically motivated to accomplish.*** Creative leaders almost always are intrinsically motivated to do the work they do (Amabile, 1996; Hennessey, in press). Creative leaders look for and ultimately find environments in which they receive extrinsic rewards for the things they like to do anyway, regardless of the extrinsic rewards.
10. ***Continuing to grow creatively rather than to stagnate.*** Creative leaders do not get stuck in their old and somtimes outdated patterns of leadership. Their leadership skills and methods evolve as they accumulate experience and expertise. They learn from experience rather than simply letting the lessons of experience pass them by.

Types of Creative Leadership

The creative ideas leaders propose can be of different types (Sternberg, 1999; Sternberg, Kaufman, & Pretz, 2002). Consider each of the types of leadership in turn (Sternberg, Kaufman, & Pretz, 2003). These types were identified as different types of "propulsion" that can occur in a conceptual space.

Conceptual Replication

Conceptual relication as a form of leadership is an attempt to show that a field or organization is in the right place at the right time. The leader therefore attempts to keep it in that place at that time. The leader views the organization as being where it needs to be. The leader's role is to keep it there and prevent changes that could be harmful to the organization. This type of leadership is only minimally creative. It represents a limiting case of creativity. The creativity in this form of leadership is in dealing with applying a past model to an ever-changing environment.

Replicative leadership is likely to be most successful during time periods of relative stability in an organization. However, in times of flux, the kind of leader that worked before may not work again, and so a replicative leader may cause the organization to lose preeminence because he or she represents the past, not the future.

Redefinition

Redefinition in leadership is the attempt to show that a field or organization is in the right place at the right time, but not precisely for the reason(s) that others, including previous leaders, think it is. The current status of the organization thus is reconceived from a new point of view. Redefiners may end up getting credit for the ideas of other people because they find a better reason to implement the others' ideas, or at least, they say they do. The creativity in this type of leadership is in realizing how to redefine what the previous leader did.

Forward Incrementation

Forward incrementation in leadership is an attempt to lead a field or an organization forward in the direction that it already is moving. Most leadership in fields and organizations is probably forward incrementation. In such leadership, a leader takes on the helm with the idea of moving forward with the leadership program of the individual one has succeeded. The promise is of progress through continuity with the past. Creativity through forward incrementation is usually the kind that is most easily recognized and appreciated by most people as creative. Because forward incrementation extends existing ideas forward, it is seen as creative. Because it does not threaten the assumptions of such previous ideas, it is not rejected as useless or even threatening or harmful. Forward incrementations tend to be most successful when times are changing in relatively predictable and minor incremental ways. The times thus match the forward-incremental leadership strategy. When times change quickly and unpredictably, leaders may find that this strategy no longer works and even may backfire.

Advance Forward Incrementation

Advance forward incrementation in leadership is the attempt to move an organization or field forward in the direction it is already going, but by moving very quickly and often beyond where others are ready for it to go. The leader moves the organization ahead at a very fast pace. Advance forward incrementations often are not altogether successful at the time they are attempted. The reason is that followers in fields and organizations are not ready to go where the leader wants to lead the followers. Or significant number of followers may not wish to go to the point they are at, in which case followers may form an organized and sometimes successful resistance movement.

Redirection

Redirection in leadership is an attempt to redirect an organization or field from where it has been and is headed toward a new and different direction. The leader decides that the direction in which the organization currently is moving is not adaptive to modern needs and so redirects the organization elsewhere. Redirective leaders need to match to environmental circumstances to succeed (Sternberg & Vroom, 2002). If the leaders do not have the luck to have closely matching environmental conditions, even their best intentions may go awry. Leaders who are creative redirectors often are perceived negatively by followers, as the followers may not be ready for their redirections (see Mueller, Goncalo, & Kamdar, 2011). People often admire, but also fear, and may even rebel against, creative leaders (Mainemelis, Kark, & Epitropaki, 2015).

Reconstruction/Redirection

Reconstruction/redirection in creative leadership is an attempt to move a field or an organization back to where it was in the past so that it may move forward from that point, but in a direction different from the one it took from that point in the past, onward. Reconstruction/redirection tends to be successful when an organization once had strong, capable leadership, then has gotten a weak leader who has taken the organization in the wrong direction. The new leader then reconstructs and redirects. The reconstruction/redirection becomes an attempt to return to a safe direction.

Reinitiation

Reinitiation in leadership is an attempt to move a field or organization to a different and as yet unreached starting point; the leader then moves forward from that point. Reinitiation is appropriate when an organization must either entirely transform itself, or else die. For example, an organization that at one time made buggy whips probably would have had to reinitiate itself or die in the face of modern modes of transportation.

Synthesis

Synthesis is a type of creative leadership in which the creator integrates two ideas regarding leadership that previously were seen as unrelated or even as opposed. What formerly were viewed as distinct and possibly conflicting ideas now are viewed as related, integrable, and capable of being unified. Synthesis is an important means by which progress is made in the sciences. It represents neither an acceptance of existing paradigms nor a rejection of them, but rather a merger between them.

Implications

Different forms of creative contributions produce different kinds of leadership. Some leaders transform the essence of an organization or other institution; others do not. At a given time, in a given place, transformation may or may not be necessary or even desirable. So transformation is not necessarily needed in or appropriate for every leadership situation. But the leaders who tend to be remembered over the course of time are probably, at least in many cases, those who transform organizations or, more generally, organizational ways of thinking.

The reader can compare the current view regarding types of creative leadership to that of transactional and transformational leadership. Transactional leaders generally emphasize the contractual relationship between leaders and followers. For example, an employee might agree to engage in certain job-related actions in exchange for certain rewards from the leadership of the organization by which he or she is employed (Sashkin, 2004). Transformational leaders emphasize higher needs and a relationship in which followers may become leaders and leaders become moral agents (Burns, 1978; Sashkin, 2004). In the terms of Bass and Avolio (Bass, 2002; Bass, Avolio, & Atwater, 1996), transactional leaders are more likely to pursue options that preserve current paradigms. Transformational leaders, on the other hand, are more likely to pursue any of options that reject current paradigms. They are crowd defiers simply because they are certain to encounter resistance from those followers (and other leaders) who are convinced that the present way of doing things, whatever it is, is the best way, indeed, perhaps the only way. In terms of Kuhn's (2012) theory of scientific revolutions, which applies to ideas outside the sciences as well, these are the leaders who revolutionize ways of thinking. In other words, transformational leaders typically exhibit a more creative leadership style than do transactional leaders. The transactional leaders rely more on adaptive, practical-intellectual skills in determining what constitutes appropriate kinds and levels of exchange of rewards.

Of course, there are also pseudo-transformational leaders—leaders who emulate or pretend to be transformational leaders. For example, an organization might not need or be ready for change but acquire a leader who wants to transform the organization not because the organization needs change, but because the leader wants to leave his or her mark, even if it is through transformations that are not what the organization needs or wants at a given time (Bass & Steidlmeier, 1999).

Just as there are pseudo-transformational leaders, so can there be pseudo-creative leaders—leaders who give the impression of being creative but actually are merely charismatic. Charismatic leaders may seem creative but actually be merely enacting the role of a creative leader.

Our research on creativity (Lubart & Sternberg, 1995; Sternberg, 2018a, 2018b; Sternberg & Lubart, 1995) has led to several conclusions regarding creative leadership. First, creativity often involves defying the crowd, or, as Todd Lubart and I have stated it, buying low and selling high in the world of ideas. Creative leaders are like good investors in that they do what needs to be done. They do not do merely what other people or polls tell them to do. Second, creativity is relatively domain specific, with creative skills varying widely across domains. Third, creativity is only weakly related to traditional intelligence, and certainly is not the exact same thing as academic intelligence.

I have further suggested that creativity and creative leadership involve not only defying the crowd but also defying oneself and the prevailing Zeitgeist (Sternberg, 2018a, 2018b). Creative leaders do not get stuck in their old ways of doing things; they recognize that times change, situations change, even people and their tastes change. Such leaders need to be flexible rather than dogmatic, recognizing that what worked before may not work anymore or in the future (Ambrose & Sternberg, 2012a, 2012b). Creative leaders further recognize the need at times to defy conventional Zeitgeists—ways of doing things that are just taken for granted. Several watch companies, such as E. Howard & Co., went out of business early in the 20th century because they thought the pocket watch was forever. Control Data Corporation went out of business because they bet on the permanency of the mainframe computer (the type that filled a room) and lost. When times change, if leaders do not change, they and their companies, countries, or other entities get left behind.

Intelligence

Intelligence in the conventional sense would seem to be important to leadership, but how important is it really? Indeed, if the conventional intelligence of a leader is too much higher than that of his or her followers, the leader may not connect with those people and thereby become ineffective (Williams & Sternberg, 1988). Intelligence, as conceived of here, is not just intelligence in its conventional narrow sense—some kind of general factor (*g*) (Sternberg, 1985b; see essays in Sternberg & Kaufman, 2011; Sternberg & Grigorenko, 2002) or as IQ (Willis, Dumont, & Kaufman, 2011) with more specific factors below *g* in some kind of hierarchy. Rather, it is conceived of in terms of the theory of successful intelligence (Sternberg, 1997a, 1997b, 1997c, 2002b, 2015). Successful intelligence is defined as the skills and attitudes an individual needs to succeed in life, given that individual's own conception of success, and within the individual's sociocultural environment. Two particular aspects of the theory of successful intelligence are particularly relevant: what are sometimes called academic and practical intelligence.

It should be clear how intelligence, however defined, would have aspects of skill. But how would it also have aspects of an attitude? The main way it is attitudinal is through the decision to apply it. Many leaders know to do better than they do, but they do so anyway. Their minds tell them what they should be doing as leaders, but their motives—for power, for fame, for money, for possessions, for sex, or for whatever—lead them away from their proper path. Leaders often fail not through lack of intelligence, but rather through their choice not to use properly the intelligence they have.

Academic Intelligence

Academic intelligence refers to the combination of memory and analytical skills and attitudes that, in combination, largely contribute to the conventional notion of intelligence. These are the intellectual skills and attitudes needed not only to recall and recognize information, but also to analyze, evaluate, and judge that information. There is a long history of research on the relation between these intellectual skills and attitudes, on the one hand, and leadership, on the other. This history harks back at least to the work of Stogdill (1948). But the results of the research are ambiguous. On the one hand, there seems to be a modest correlation between conventionally defined intelligence and leadership effectiveness (Stogdill, 1948; see also essays in Riggio, Murphy, & Pirozzolo, 2002). The correlation is moderated by a number of factors, such as the level of stress experienced by the leader (Fiedler, 2002). These moderator variables apparently even can change the direction, not just the magnitude of the correlation.

These skills and attitudes matter for leadership, because leaders need to be able to retrieve information that is relevant to leadership decisions (memory) and to analyze and evaluate different courses of action, whether proposed by themselves or by others (analysis). But a good analyst does not necessarily make for a good leader.

The long-time heavy emphasis on *academic* intelligence (IQ) in the literature relating intelligence to leadership has been, in some ways, unfortunate. Indeed, recent theorists of intelligence have emphasized other aspects of intelligence, such as emotional intelligence (e.g., Mayer et al., 2011; Goleman, 1998) or multiple intelligences (Gardner, 2011), in their theories of intelligence. In this chapter, the emphasis is on practical intelligence (Sternberg et al., 2000; Sternberg & Hedlund, 2002; Sternberg & Smith, 1985), which has a distinctly different focus from emotional intelligence. Practical intelligence is only a part of successful intelligence, as described below.

Practical Intelligence

Practical intelligence involves those skills and attitudes used to solve everyday problems. Practical intelligence utilizes knowledge and skills acquired from experience in order purposefully to adapt to, shape, and select real-world environments. Practical intelligence thus involves modifying oneself to fit the environment (adaptation to the environment), modifying the environment to fit oneself (shaping of the environment), or finding a new and different kind of environment within which to function (selection of an environment). One uses these skills to (a) manage oneself, (b) manage others, and (c) manage tasks.

Effectiveness in "transactional leadership" (Avolio, Bass, & Jung, 1999; Bass, 2002; Bass, Avolio, & Atwater, 1996) derives, in large part, although not exclusively, from the adaptive function of practical intelligence—changing oneself to fit the environment. Transactional leaders usually are largely adapters themselves; at the very least, they want their followers to be adapters: they work with their followers toward the mutual fulfillment of what amount to contractual obligations. Transactional leaders typically provide contingent rewards, specifying role and task requirements. Then they reward desired performances. Or transactional leaders may manage by exception. In this case they monitor the meeting of previously set standards and intervene when these standards are not adequately met.

Sternberg and his colleagues (Hedlund et al., 2003; Sternberg et al., 2000) have argued that much of the knowledge associated with successful practical problem solving is tacit. Tacit knowledge is knowledge that typically is not openly expressed or explicitly stated; thus, people can acquire tacit knowledge only through their own personal experiences. Furthermore, although people's actions may reflect their tacit knowledge, the people may find it difficult to articulate verbally what they know.

Several main findings (reviewed in Sternberg et al., 2000) have emerged from tacit-knowledge research. First, tacit knowledge tends to increase with increasing amounts of experience. Second, levels of tacit knowledge correlate minimally and sometimes not at all with scores on conventional tests of academic intelligence. Third, levels of tacit knowledge do not correlate with personality. Fourth, levels of tacit knowledge significantly predict job performance. Fifth and finally, levels of tacit knowledge provide significant incremental prediction of job performance over and above scores on conventional academic intelligence measures.

Different combinations of intellectual skills tend to lead to different kinds of leadership. Leaders, of course, vary greatly in their memory skills, analytical skills, and practical skills. A leader who is particularly adept in memory skills but not in the other kinds of skills may be highly knowledgeable but be unable to use his or her knowledge effectively. A leader who is particularly adept in analytical skills as well as in memory skills may be able to retrieve information and analyze that information effectively, but may be unable to persuade others that his or her analysis is useful or even correct. A leader who is adept in memory, analytical, and practical skills is most likely to be effective in influencing other people. But, of course, there are leaders who are adept in practical skills but not in memory and analytical skills (Sternberg, 1997a, 1997b; Sternberg et al., 2000). In conventional terms, these leaders are "shrewd" but not "smart." They may be effective in getting others to go along with them, but they may end up leading these others down garden paths.

Wisdom

A leader can have all the aforementioned skills and attitudes and still lack an additional quality that, arguably, is the most important quality a leader can have, but perhaps, also the rarest. This additional quality is wisdom (see also Baltes & Staudinger, 2000; Sternberg & Glueck, in press). Wisdom is viewed here according to a proposed balance theory of wisdom (Sternberg, 1998, in press), according to which an individual is wise to the extent he or she uses successful intelligence, creativity, and knowledge as moderated by values to (a) seek to reach a common good; (b) by balancing intrapersonal (one's own), interpersonal (others'), and extrapersonal (organizational/institutional/spiritual) interests; (c) over the short and long terms; and (d) adapt to, shape, and select environments. Wisdom, then, is in large part a decision to use one's intelligence, creativity, and experience in a balanced way to help achieve a common good.

Wise leaders neither ignore nor focus exclusively on their own interests. Rather, they reflectively and skillfully balance their own interests, the interests of their followers, and the interests of the organization or other grouping for which they are responsible. They further recognize that, to be wise leaders, they must align the interests of their group or organization with the interests of other groups or organizations for the simple reason that no organization or group operates within a vacuum. Wise leaders realize that what may appear to be a prudent and useful course of action over the short term does not necessarily appear to be prudent or even useful over the long term.

Leaders who have been unsuccessful often ignore one or another set of stakeholder interests. For example, some presidents of the United States, including recently, have tried appealing only to their "base" of supporters, ignoring other groups because they know that they will never get the votes of members of these other groups.

Intelligent and creative leaders are not necessarily wise. Indeed, probably very few leaders at any level of leadership are particularly wise. Yet the few leaders who have been notably wise, such as Nelson Mandela, Martin Luther King, Mahatma Gandhi, Winston Churchill, and Eleanor Roosevelt, have left and will leave an indelible mark not only on the people they lead but also on the world. Wise leaders often are charismatic, but unfortunately, the reverse is not necessarily true. Charismatic leaders are not necessarily wise, as Hitler, Stalin, Mao, and many other charismatic leaders have demonstrated over the course of time.

Unsuccessful leaders often show in their leadership certain stereotyped cognitive fallacies. These fallacies represent not lack of intelligence but rather foolishness. Consider five such fallacies (Sternberg, 2002a, 2002b). The first fallacy, called the *unrealistic-optimism fallacy*, appears when leaders think they are so smart and so effective that they can do essentially whatever they want. The second fallacy, called the *egocentrism fallacy*, appears when leaders think that they and perhaps their family and close friends are the only ones who matter, not the followers who rely on them for leadership. The third fallacy, called the *omniscience fallacy*, is displayed when leaders think that they know everything and lose sight of the limitations and especially the narrowness of their own knowledge. People who commit this fallacy may be experienced, but they do not learn from their experience and they often ignore or actively work against the advice of knowledgeable others. The fourth fallacy, called the *omnipotence fallacy*, occurs when leaders think they are all-powerful and as a result can do whatever they please. And the fifth fallacy, called the *invulnerability fallacy*, is displayed when leaders think they can get away with anything. They believe they are too clever to be caught, and even if they are caught, they expect they can figure that how they can get away with much or all of what they have done because of who they imagine themselves to be.

Much of the empirical data regarding wisdom has been collected by the late Paul Baltes and his colleagues. Over time, Baltes and his colleagues (e.g., Baltes, Smith, & Staudinger, 1992) showed the relevance of wisdom for effective performance. For example, Staudinger, Lopez, and Baltes (1997) discovered that measures of intelligence and personality as well as of their interface overlap with, but are non-identical to, measures of wisdom in terms of what the constructs measure. Staudinger, Smith, and Baltes (1992) showed that successful human-services professionals outperformed a control group (nonprofessionals) on wisdom-related tasks. They also demonstrated that older adults performed as well on wisdom-related tasks as did younger adults. However, older adults scored better on such tasks if there was a match between their age and the age of the fictitious characters about whom they made wisdom judgments. In a further set of studies, Staudinger and Baltes (1996) showed that settings that were ecologically relevant to the lives of participants and that provided for actual or "virtual" interaction of people's minds substantially increased wisdom-related performance.

Synthesis

One of the most admired and successful leaders of the 20th century was Nelson Mandela. Mandela transformed South Africa, at least temporarily, from a repressive Apartheid state into a model of modern democracy. It did not become a country free of problems, and those problems have worsened since Mandela's stepping down from power. But the alternative model provided by his contemporary, Robert Mugabe in Zimbabwe, was far worse in almost every respect. Economically, politically, and morally, Zimbabwe became a failed state, much as Venezuela is today. It was not until 2017 that Robert Mugabe was ousted from power.

What made Nelson Mandela such a successful leader? For one thing, he had the creativity to envision the transformation of South Africa from a repressive state that deprived the large majority of its citizens of human rights to a state that would embrace human rights for all, even the former oppressors. He had the analytical intelligence to evaluate his plan for transformation and to fine-tune it as the plan was implemented. Mandela had the practical intelligence to implement the plan successfully and to convince a wide range of constituencies that his plan was workable. Such persuasion was no small feat. It largely prevented a massive exodus of white people and convinced many black people that reconciliation rather than retribution was the road to achieving success in a newly democratic state. And Mandela had the wisdom to put behind him the gross abuse of human rights to which he himself had been subjected in prison and to propose a plan that represented the common good of all stakeholders.

Without creativity, leaders cannot truly be successful. Leaders continually confront novel and unexpected tasks and situations. If the leaders lack the creativity to deal with them effectively, they fail as leaders. Mugabe, in place of creating a new and better vision for his country, essentially replicated the leadership model of divisive dictators such as Stalin and Mussonlini, pitting one group against another. He presided over a state that entered into radical decline on all measures of well-being.

Although the elements of WICS discussed in this chapter typically work together, they also can work in tension or even at odds with each other. For example, creativity is not always associated with wisdom. Creative leaders also may have ideas for making changes for which their followers are not ready. Or creative leaders may have ideas that are appropriate for the times but whose values they are unable to demonstrate to their followers. Without wisdom, creativity can be less than helpful and it even can be harmful to an organization and the individuals in it.

Conclusion

An effective leader needs creative skills and attitudes to come up with ideas, academic analytic skills and attitudes to decide whether the ideas are good ideas, practical skills and attitudes to render the ideas effective and to convince other people of the value of the ideas, and wisdom-based skills and attitudes to ensure that the ideas are in the service of the common good of all rather than just the good of the leader and perhaps some family members and cronies. A leader lacking in creativity will be unable and probably unwilling to deal with novel and challenging situations, such as a new and unanticipated source of hostility. A leader lacking in academic analytic intelligence will be unable to decide whether his or her ideas are viable and realistic for their time and place, and a leader lacking in practical intelligence will be unable to implement his or her ideas effectively and in a persusasive manner. An unwise leader may succeed in implementing ideas that are indifferent or even contrary to the best interests of the people he or she leads.

The model presented here is of course related to many other models. It incorporates elements of transformational leadership within the creative domain as well as transactional leadership (Bass & Avolio, 1994; Bass, Avolio, & Atwater, 1996) within the practical-intellectual domain. It includes aspects of emotionally intelligent leadership (Goleman, 1998) in the practical-intellectual and wisdom domains. And it includes visionary leadership (Northouse, 2016; Sashkin, 2004) and charismatic leadership (Conger & Kanugo, 1998) in the creative domain. Thus, the model discussed in this chapter provides a start toward integrating some previous models of leadership and also toward conceptualizing them under one theoretical umbrella.

The world in 2018, when this chapter is being published, is in something of a mess. War with North Korea could break out any day. Income inequality exceeds that of the gilded age and is getting worse. Pollution is killing millions of people worldwide and in many places is getting worse. Climate change is wreaking havoc throughout the entire world and already has almost destroyed entire islands. We need more creative leaders. But we also need leaders with academic analytical intelligence, common sense, and wisdom. We have relatively few of those. If the world does not acquire more of them soon, our future will be compromised or, perhaps worse, eliminated altogther. We can find better leaders. But will we?

References

Adelson, B. 1984. When novices surpass experts: The difficulty of a task may increase with expertise. *Journal of Experimental Psychology: Learning, Memory, & Cognition*, 10: 483–495.

Amabile, T. M. 1996. *Creativity in context*. Boulder, CO: Westview Press.

Ambrose, D., & Sternberg, R. J. (Eds.). 2012a. *How dogmatic beliefs harm creativity and higher level thinking*. New York: Taylor & Francis.

Ambrose, D., & Sternberg, R. J. 2012b. Overview of a collaborative, interdisciplinary exploration. In D. Ambrose & R. J. Sternberg (Eds.), *How dogmatic beliefs harm creativity and higher level thinking*: 3–8. New York: Taylor & Francis.

Avolio, B. J., Bass, B. M., & Jung, D. I. 1999. Reexamining the components of transformational and transactional leadership using the Multifactor Leadership Questionnaire. *Journal of Occupational and Organizational Psychology*, 72: 441–462.

Baltes, P. B., Smith, J., & Staudinger, U. M. 1992. Wisdom and successful aging. In T. Sonderegger (Ed.), *Nebraska symposium on motivation*, Vol. 39: 123–167. Lincoln, NE: University of Nebraska Press.

Baltes, P. B., & Staudinger, U. M. 2000. Wisdom: A Metaheuristic to orchestrate mind and virtue towards excellence. *American Psychologist*, 55: 122–136.

Bandura, A. 1996. *Self-efficacy: The exercise of control*. New York: Freeman.

Bandura, A. 2015. *Moral disengagement: How people do harm and live with themselves*. New York: Worth.

Bass, B. M. 2002. Cognitive, social, and emotional intelligence of transformational leaders. In R. E. Riggio, S. E. Murphy, & F. J. Pirozzolo (Eds.), *Multiple intelligences and leadership*: 105–118. Mahwah, NJ: Lawrence Erlbaum Associates.

Bass, B. M., & Avolio, B. J. (Eds.). 1994. *Improving organizational effectiveness through transformational leadership*. Thousand Oaks, CA: Sage Publications.

Bass, B. M., Avolio, B. J., & Atwater, L. 1996. The transformational and transactional leadership of men and women. *International Review of Applied Psychology*, 45: 5–34.

Bass, B. M., & Steidlmeyer, P. 1999. Ethics, character, and authentic transformational leadership. *Leadership Quarterly*, 10: 181–217.

Burns, J. M. 1978. *Leadership*. New York: Harper & Row, Publishers, Inc.

Conger, J. A., & Kanugo, R. N. 1998. *Charismatic leadership in organizations*. Thousand Oaks, CA: Sage Publications.

Cropley, D. H., Cropley, A. J., Kaufman, J. C., & Runco, M. A. (Eds.). 2010. *The dark side of creativity*. New York: Cambridge University Press.
Fiedler, F. E. 2002. The curious role of cognitive resources in leadership. In R. E. Riggio, S. E. Murphy, & F. J. Pirozzolo (Eds.), *Multiple intelligences and leadership*: 91–104. Mahwah, NJ: Lawrence Erlbaum Associates.
Frensch, P. A., & Sternberg, R. J. 1989. Expertise and intelligent thinking: When is it worse to know better? In R. J. Sternberg (Ed.), *Advances in the psychology of human intelligence*. Hillsdale, NJ: Lawrence Erlbaum Associates.
Gardner, H. 2011. *Leading minds*. New York: Basic Books.
Goleman, D. 1998. What makes a good leader? *Harvard Business Review*, November–December, 93–102.
Hedlund, J., Forsythe, G. B., Horvath, J. A., Williams, W. M., Snook, S., & Sternberg, R. J. 2003. Identifying and assessing tacit knowledge: Understanding the practical intelligence of military leaders. *Leadership Quarterly*, 14: 117–140.
Hennessey, B. A. In Press. Motivation and creativity. In J. C. Kaufman & R. J. Sternberg (Eds.), *Cambridge handbook of creativity*. New York: Cambridge University Press.
Kaufman, J. C., & Sternberg, R. J. (Eds.). In Press. *Cambridge handbook of human creativity* (2nd ed.). New York: Cambridge University Press.
Kuhn, T. S. 2012. *The structure of scientific revolutions* (4th ed.). Chicago, IL: University of Chicago Press.
Levitsky, S., & Ziblatt, D. 2018. *How democracies die*. New York: Crown.
Lubart, T. I., & Sternberg, R. J. 1995. An investment approach to creativity: Theory and data. In S. M. Smith, T. B. Ward, & R. A. Finke (Eds.), *The creative cognition approach*: 269–302. Cambridge, MA: MIT Press.
Mainemelis, C., Kark, R., & Epitropaki, O. 2015. Creative leadership: A multicontext conceptualization. *Academy of Management Annals*, 9: 393–482.
Mayer, J. D., Salovey, P., Caruso, D. R., & Cherkasskiy, L. 2011. Emotional intelligence. In R. J. Sternberg & S. B. Kaufman (Eds.), *Cambridge handbook of intelligence*: 538–549. New York: Cambridge University Press.
Mueller, J. S., Goncalo, J. A., & Kamdar, D. 2011. Recognizing creative leadership: Can creative idea expression negatively relate to perceptions of leadership potential? *Journal of Experimental Social Psychology*, 47: 494–498.
Niu, W., & Sternberg, R. J. 2003. Societal and school influences on student creativity: The case of China. *Psychology in the Schools*, 40(1): 103–114.
Northouse, P. G. 2016. *Leadership: Theory and practice* (7th ed.). Thousand Oaks, CA: Sage Publications.
Plucker, J. A. (Ed.). 2017. *Creativity & innovation*. Waco, TX: Prufrock Press.
Riggio, R. E., Murphy, S. E., & Pirozzolo, F. J. 2002. *Multiple intelligences and leadership*. Mahwah, NJ: Lawrence Erlbaum Associates.
Runco, M. A. 2017. The dark side of creativity: Potential better left unfulfilled. In J. A. Plucker (Ed.), *Creativity and innovation*: 49–59. Waco, TX: Prufrock Press.
Runco, M. A., & Jaeger, G. J. 2012. The standard definition of creativity. *Creativity Research Journal*, 24: 92–96.
Sashkin, M. 2004. Transformational leadership approaches: A review and synthesis. In J. Antonakis, A. Cianciolo, & R. J. Sternberg (Eds.), *The nature of leadership*: 171–196. Thousand Oaks, CA: Sage Publications.
Spear-Swerling, L., & Sternberg, R. J. 1994. The road not taken: An integrative theoretical model of reading disability. *Journal of Learning Disabilities, 27*(2): 91–103.

Staudinger, U. M., & Baltes, P. M. 1996. Interactive minds: A facilitative setting for wisdom-related performance? *Journal of Personality and Social Psychology*, 71: 746–762.
Staudinger, U. M., Lopez, D. F., & Baltes, P. B. 1997. The psychometric location of wisdom-related performance: Intelligence, personality, and more? *Personality & Social Psychology Bulletin*, 23: 1200–1214.
Staudinger, U. M., Smith, J., & Baltes, P. B. 1992. Wisdom-related knowledge in life review task: Age differences and the role of professional specialization. *Psychology and Aging*, 7: 271–281.
Sternberg, R. J. 1985a. *Beyond IQ: Toward a triarchic theory of intelligence*. New York: Cambridge University Press.
Sternberg, R. J. 1985b. Human intelligence: The model is the message. *Science*, 230: 1111–1118.
Sternberg, R. J. 1985c. Teaching critical thinking, Part 1: Are we making critical mistakes? *Phi Delta Kappan*, 67: 194–198.
Sternberg, R. J. 1997a. Managerial intelligence: Why IQ isn't enough. *Journal of Management*, 23(3): 475–463.
Sternberg, R. J. 1997b. *Successful intelligence*. New York: Plume.
Sternberg, R. J. 1997c. What does it mean to be smart? *Educational Leadership*, 54(6): 20–24.
Sternberg, R. J. 1998. A balance theory of wisdom. *Review of General Psychology*, 2(4): 347–365.
Sternberg, R. J. 1999. A propulsion model of types of creative contributions. *Review of General Psychology*, 3: 83–100.
Sternberg, R. J. 2000. Creativity is a decision. In B. Z. Presseisen (Ed.), *Teaching for intelligence II: A collection of articles*: 83–103. Arlington Heights, IL: Skylight Training and Publishing Inc.
Sternberg, R. J. (Ed.). 2002a. *Psychologists defying the crowd*. Washington, DC: American Psychological Association.
Sternberg, R. J. 2002b. Successful intelligence: A new approach to leadership. In R. E. Riggio, S. E. Murphy, & F. J. Pirozzolo (Eds.), *Multiple intelligences and leadership*: 9–28. Mahwah, NJ: Lawrence Erlbaum Associates.
Sternberg, R. J. 2003a. WICS: A model of leadership in organizations. *Academy of Management Learning and Education*.
Sternberg, R. J. 2003b. *Wisdom, intelligence, and creativity, synthesized*. New York: Cambridge University Press.
Sternberg, R. J. 2010. The dark side of creativity and how to combat it. In D. H. Cropley, A. J. Cropley, J. C. Kaufman, & M. A. Runco (Eds.), *The dark side of creativity*: 316–328. New York: Cambridge University Press.
Sternberg, R. J. 2012. The WICS model of leadership. In M. Rumsey (Ed.), *The Oxford handbook of leadership*: 47–62. New York: Oxford University Press.
Sternberg, R. J. 2015. Successful intelligence: A new model for testing intelligence beyond IQ tests. *European Journal of Education and Psychology*, 8: 76–84.
Sternberg, R. J. 2018a. The triangle of creativity. In R. J. Sternberg & J. C. Kaufman (Eds.), *The nature of human creativity*: 318–334. New York: Cambridge University Press.
Sternberg, R. J. 2018b. A triangular theory of creativity. *Psychology of Aesthetics, Creativity, and the Arts*, 12, 50–67.
Sternberg, R. J. In Press. Why people often prefer wise guys to guys who are wise: An augmented balance theory of the production and reception of wisdom. In R. J. Sternberg & J. Glueck (Eds.), *Cambridge handbook of wisdom*. New York: Cambridge University Press.

Sternberg, R. J., & Davidson, J. E. 1982. The mind of the puzzler. *Psychology Today*, June, 16: 37–44.
Sternberg, R. J., Forsythe, G. B., Hedlund, J., Horvath, J., Snook, S., Williams, W. M., Wagner, R. K., & Grigorenko, E. L. 2000. *Practical intelligence in everyday life*. New York: Cambridge University Press.
Sternberg, R. J., & Glueck, J. In Press. *Cambridge handbook of wisdom*. New York: Cambridge University Press.
Sternberg, R. J., & Grigorenko, E. L. (Eds.). 2002. *The general factor of intelligence: How general is it?* Mahwah, NJ: Lawrence Erlbaum Associates.
Sternberg, R. J., & Hedlund, J. 2002. Practical intelligence, *g*, and work psychology. *Human Performance*, 15: 143–160.
Sternberg, R. J., Kaufman, J. C., & Pretz, J. E. 2002. *The creativity conundrum: A propulsion model of kinds of creative contributions*. Philadelphia, PA: Psychology Press.
Sternberg, R. J., Kaufman, J. C., & Pretz, J. E. 2003. A propulsion model of creative leadership. *Leadership Quarterly*, 14: 453–473.
Sternberg, R. J., & Lubart, T. I. 1995. *Defying the crowd: Cultivating creativity in a culture of conformity*. New York: Free Press.
Sternberg, R. J., & Smith, C. 1985. Social intelligence and decoding skills in nonverbal communication. *Social Cognition*, 2: 168–192.
Sternberg, R. J., & Vroom, V. H. 2002. The person versus the situation in leadership. *Leadership Quarterly*, 13: 301–323.
Stogdill, R. M. 1948. Personal factors associated with leadership: A survey of the literature. *Journal of Psychology*, 25: 35–71.
Williams, W. M., & Sternberg, R. J. 1988. Group intelligence: Why some groups are better than others. *Intelligence*, 12: 351–377.
Willis, J. O., Dumont, R., & Kaufman, A. S. 2011. Factor-analytic models of intelligence. In R. J. Sternberg & S. B. Kaufman (Eds.), *Cambridge handbook of intelligence:* 39–57. New York: Cambridge University Press.

9 The Creative Leadership Practices of Haute Cuisine Chefs

Isabelle Bouty, Marie-Léandre Gomez, and Marc Stierand

Introduction

This chapter aims at unveiling specific creative leadership practices that contribute to leading as Directing. We present some aggregate insights of our joint learning from researching the leadership practices of highly creative chefs, and offer a nuanced and contextual sensitive account of creative leadership in haute cuisine. We define creative leadership as the practice of "leading others in thinking innovatively together" (Basadur, 2004: 103) and understand 'thinking together' more broadly as a 'knowing in practice' (Gomez, Bouty, & Drucker-Godard, 2003), because in the context of haute cuisine, creative cooking may involve more than just the cognitive function of thinking (Glăveanu, 2011), as it also requires playing (Mainemelis & Dionysiou, 2015), touching, seeing, smelling, tasting, and hearing (Ewenstein & Whyte, 2007). From our numerous inquiries with some of the best chefs in the world, we assess that creative leadership emerges within and is a facet of the sphere of practices (Schatzki, 2001) and, consequently, as a practice, creative leadership is "something that is routinely made and remade in practice using tools, discourse, and our bodies" (Nicolini, 2012: 2).

Whilst the socio-economic significance of creative leadership, in general, is widely acknowledged by the academic community (Amabile et al., 2004; Mumford et al., 2002; Shalley & Gilson, 2004; Tierney, 2008), the question as to what leaders can do *in practice* to enhance team creativity *in context*, however, remains an unresolved issue for two main reasons (Murphy & Ensher, 2008; Osborn, Hunt, & Jauch, 2002; Shamir & Howell, 1999; Shin & Zhou, 2003; To, Herman, & Ashkanasy, 2015). First, creative leadership research is really just beginning (Hunter, Thoroughgood, Myer, & Ligon, 2011; Vessey et al., 2014), and its theoretical foundation is disconcerting, lacking definitional clarity, nuanced theories, and contextual sensitivity (Mainemelis, Kark, & Epitropaki, 2015). Second, the samples used in most studies of leadership and creativity have been focused on leaders who consult their team on working more creatively in contexts that may not essentially depend on creativity. This brought forth theories that focus more on the average person's engagement in a creative task rather than on the practices of highly creative leaders in work contexts requiring creativity (Dörfler & Stierand, 2009; Stierand & Dörfler, 2011, 2011, 2014; Vessey et al., 2014). So far, only very few studies have explored in a contextually sensitive manner what publicly recognized and highly creative leaders actually do to enhance team creativity and what can be learned from their practices (e.g., Epitropaki & Mainemelis, 2016; Stierand, 2015; Vessey et al., 2014).

We aim to help building a more robust theoretical foundation for creative leadership research and better understand the practices of highly creative leaders in work contexts requiring creativity. We contribute to this project in an inductive way by aggregating insights from our empirical research in haute cuisine kitchens. Haute cuisine is such a context that attracts the human intellect through esthetic and essentially non-practical means of expression (Hegarty & O'Mahony, 1999; Stierand et al., 2016). Most of this expression originates from highly creative chefs (Stierand, 2015) who claim their distinctive creative identity largely through recognition in the leading restaurant guides, the Michelin and Gault Millau, which are the institutionalized guardians of the field's tradition of creative progress (Ferguson, 1998; Stierand, Dörfler, & MacBryde, 2014).

The creative leadership in this type of work context typically manifests as *Directing* for it is essentially about "materializing [the] leader's creative vision through other people's work" (Mainemelis, Kark, & Epitropaki, 2015). That is, the Directing leader is typically the 'primary creator', but may consider creative inputs from followers (Mainemelis, Kark, & Epitropaki, 2015). This has already been articulated by Bouty and Gomez (2010), who describe that top chefs foster creativity predominantly within the circle of their chosen sous-chef 'chef mentees' whilst leaving reproduction of their creations to their cooks. Stierand (2015) has added to this line of research by providing empirical evidence showing how 'chef mentees' often develop their creativity in a master-apprentice relationship in which they learn bridging the open-endedness of creative work and the social appropriateness of the final product.

Team creativity, the process by which people jointly work together in a team to produce novel and useful output (Amabile, 1988, 1996; Oldham & Cummings, 1996; Woodman, Sawyer, & Griffin, 1993), has therefore a long tradition in haute cuisine. Moreover, today, top chefs also frequently collaborate with creative professionals from other fields—for example, industrial design (Svejenova, Mazza, & Planellas, 2007)—who have different knowledge and skill sets (Paulus & Nijstad, 2003; Reiter-Palmon, Herman, & Yammarino, 2008; West et al., 2004), and together may produce a higher level creative synthesis (Mainemelis, Kark, & Epitropaki, 2015) with a strategic dimension (Bouty & Gomez, 2013) that goes beyond the development of a creative dish, focusing more on the creative progress of cuisine at large (Svejenova, Mazza, & Planellas, 2007).

The creative process, however, has long been viewed as asocial and individualistic, led by a lone effort of personal creativity (Jung, 2001; Runco, 2007), and it is only very recently that research findings consistently suggest that effective leadership can significantly proliferate team creativity and, as a result, enhance the creative output produced by a team (Lingo & O'Mahony, 2010; Stenmark, Shipman, & Mumford, 2011; Thomson, Jones, & Warhurst, 2007). Shalley and Gilson (2004), for example, note that leaders who engage in supportive high quality exchanges with their team members increase team creativity. Furthermore, Amabile et al. (2004) showed that team members perceive leaders to be supportive through both their instrumental (or task-oriented) and socio-emotional (or relationship-oriented) behavior. Whether team creativity is fostered or hindered, is therefore determined by how well leaders can motivate team members and nurture a work climate that is conducive to team creativity (Anderson, Potočnik, & Zhou, 2014; Heinze et al., 2009; Hunter, Bedell-Avers, & Mumford, 2007; Stenmark, Shipman, & Mumford, 2011; Tierney & Farmer, 2011), and how well leaders can mobilize individual, organizational, and institutional forces in the overall creative process (Bouty & Gomez, 2015).

Our analysis is inductively based on our long-standing empirical investigations in the life-world of haute cuisine. This study is based on reflexive interpretation in a data-driven perspective as defined by Alvesson and Sköldberg (2009: 283), which grants particular weight to the capacity of researchers highly acquainted with their empirical field to construct new interpretations (Alvesson & Sköldberg, 2009: 313). The first- and second-named authors have conducted in-depth longitudinal studies of several two and three-Michelin-star restaurants, their chefs, teams, and organizations; the last-named author has been a chef in haute cuisine and explored, together with various collaborators, the creative process of over three dozen Michelin-starred chefs and half a dozen expert chefs carrying titles such as 'Meilleurs Ouvrier de France'. Only because we were able to go in between the leadership practices of creative teams in haute cuisine, either through insider interviews (Stierand & Dörfler, 2014), or through case studies, observation, and interviews with chefs and their teams (Bouty & Gomez, 2010, 2015; Gomez, Bouty, & Drucker-Godard, 2003; Gomez & Bouty, 2011) were we able to unearth how creative leadership practices are made and re-made (Stierand et al., 2017). We completed a reflexive transversal analysis that allowed us to compare our cases and group similar elements regarding Directing as creative leadership that we synthesized into three practices. As a matter of fact, the output of our joint learning from researching highly creative chefs is that they direct their team through **enabling** (configuring the creative space to set the conditions of creative work), **orientating** (managing creative work to keep it abounded and focused), and **complying** (assessing ideas to select those that fit), that we detail in the following pages.

1. Enabling: Configuring the Creative Space

Chefs first direct creativity by enabling it: they make it possible and sustained. In other words, creativity in high-end restaurants is not merely based on serendipity, even if this dimension is not absent. Chefs and their teams work long hours and within this sustained rhythm of activity, they need to organize creative work. A three-star chef assesses,

> *The really great idea is a rarity, and anyway, I don't view cooking in terms of ideas. I don't ask myself, "What new thing I am going to do?" on getting out of bed in the morning. But if I manage still to have the energy, freshness and time, my culinary story and thought continue [. . .], necessity serves me notice to create,*

Enabling creativity pertains to several aspects, among which the configuration of creative space, by granting time and space for creative work. Chefs favor specific occasions for individual creativity: quiet hours in the morning or between sittings in their personal offices as well as outside of their restaurants, in cafés, farmer's market, or gardens, for example.

Chefs also set the conditions of creative teamwork: they confine it to the restaurant's kitchen and separate it from other kitchen activities, set it up aside of the rush periods and service time. Besides, enabling creativity involves selecting whom to involve into the creative process. Chefs perform creative work both with external and internal partners, whom they select and do not mix with each other. Partners for individual creative brainstorming are for example other haute cuisine chefs, painters, designers, and other artists whom chefs work with because of personal affinities and friendship: "*I would not say we have chosen each other. Rather, we found each other*" says a three-star chef about his external creativity-mate (a scientist for that matter). They keep these actors apart from those involved in creative teamwork, whom they also carefully select. Most chefs pick their sous-chefs and some station chefs to participate to creative teamwork, a type of work that is not based on open contribution by any cook; who can contribute is the chef's decision. This reflects the highly hierarchical and formal organization of haute cuisine kitchens in which chefs have prominence and unquestioned authority over their sous-chefs, who themselves command to station chefs, who are eventually also of differentiated importance, with the meat and fish stations traditionally more valued.

Last, enabling creativity involves proposing products, tools, and spurs for creativity. We recorded that these stimuli are selected and proposed exclusively by chefs, especially for creative teamwork. As chefs confine creative teamwork to the restaurants' kitchens, some of the creative resources are limited to those available in these kitchens: existing equipment, appliances, and products. In this perspective, the way kitchens are organized and equipped play a significant role. We also observed that chefs select additional elements, products, and ideas to be introduced into their kitchens. For example, one of them brings selected vegetables and herbs from his kitchen garden in addition to those daily delivered. Chefs' choices vary according to their individual tastes, inclinations, current interests, and to organizational considerations. Chefs can select regional ingredients in coherence with the location of their restaurants or with the region they originate from. Besides, these ingredients need not be sophisticated or expensive; they rather have caught the chefs' attentions because of their taste, austerity, or meaning. Chefs also bring various sources of inspiration for creative teamwork in the form of music, drawings, and literature. One of them for example uses notes, pictures, and sketches he took and drew when traveling around the world to evoke an inspiring expression or a color that moved him and that he wants to convey in his cuisine.

Besides, chefs de facto exclude various elements from the creative space they so configure, such as the experience and sensitivity of other cooks (those who do not participate to creative teamwork), and other products than those selected. These restrictions create constrains that manifest as positive influences over creativity in haute cuisine restaurants: "*I always thought that the more limited the means, the stronger the expression*" says a chef. Another three-Michelin-star chef explains,

> *Tough constrains stimulate great creativity. Therefore, we perhaps need restrictions more than total freedom [. . .] Take the Oulipo movement in the years 1950's for instance; they used constraining writing techniques. That can be it: impose tough [. . .] constrains upon yourself and team.*

Altogether, chefs direct creativity through enabling it by configuring the creative space in many regards, from the spatiotemporal conditions of creative work, to the actors involved, and the products and sources of inspirations that are mobilized. However, since each of these elements largely involves individual appreciation by the chefs, each chef configures unique conditions in his restaurant and at a given moment.

2. *Orientating: Managing Topics and Themes*

Chefs also direct creativity by orientating creative work as it happens in the creative space defined, as well as in more mundane everyday kitchen work. We observed that quite often, when chefs and their teams work on a new dish, most chefs do not properly participate to the trials: they explain their ideas, sometimes work on a very first draft, and then let selected cooks at creative teamwork. For example, a chef explains,

> *I prepare the dish with one of my chefs, he decodes my "message", understands it and does it over again, like a musician playing a piece. Then we taste it together, make comments, change things [. . .] and the dish either works or it doesn't.*

In particular, we observed that each creative development brought about by a team member is systematically considered with reference to the chef's idea or to the themes and topics the chef wants central in his cuisine. The following excerpt recounts a creative teamwork session in a three-star restaurant:

> The chef, sous-chef and two station chefs are working inside the quiet kitchen, notebooks spread on the counters, pencils in hands.
>
> > —*The idea is to revamp a traditional dish the chef explains. Sole with chives [. . .] That's our base but we don't want to copy it. Let's start with how to cook the sole. Then we'll cover it completely in chives and see how it tastes, see what the relationship is between sole and chives.*
>
> The sous-chef and station chefs steam sole filets, thinly cut chives, and roll sole filet in chives. They and the chef take notes. The chef comments,
>
> > —*Both sides . . . and set it onto a plate with cooked shallots.*
>
> They taste carefully; the chef adds,
>
> > —*[. . .] The chives are bland. There is not enough of a link between the new and the old. We need to rework the taste of the chives. I remember the sauce was full of chives, but we need to do something different.*
>
> They start over, and prepare a chive pesto and a juice. They coat a steamed sole filet in pesto and set it onto a dish. [. . .] The sous-chef and station chefs do not seem fully convinced:
>
> > —*It's not the same; it's totally different, a different dish . . .*
> >
> > —*It tastes fresher*, says the chef. . . *I miss the breadcrumbs though.*
> >
> > —*How about sliced almonds?* the sous-chef suggests.
>
> The chef weighs the idea and carries on, thinking aloud,
>
> > —*There's a problem with breadcrumbs . . . They don't fit in, and how it looks! We have to get rid of it in our new concept . . . [. . .]; maybe not in the dish but on the side* [. . .]
>
> The sous-chef and station chefs return to cooking. [. . .] The pesto is now spread between two slices of steamed sole filet like a long thin sandwich, and the fried chives, breadcrumbs, and shallots are mixed together next to the filet.

> —*We're getting closer*, the chef comments. *This might be it . . .*

They taste once again; he still seems skeptical.

> —*It's just cooked in butter,* says a station chef. *You don't like the inside?*

> —*Not really . . .* replies the chef. *It's too technical, too sleek . . .*

Orientating creative work, as it appears in this illustration, is implicit and latent though highly salient in creative work as it happens. Creative work is permanently driven back to the matter of being faithful to the spirit of the original signature dish, though without reproducing it. Furthermore, orientating creative work generates exchanges and debates within the creative team, as is further exemplified by a dialog between a chef and his sous-chef over a lobster dish:

> —*The overall presentation is rough, [. . .] and the langouste is tasteless* [. . .]
> —*What if we made a cream of lobster?* asks the sous-chef
> —*No, no, because langouste is so subtly-flavored . . .*
> —*It needs to be left as it is . . .*
> —*Yes, leave it as it is. The butter is not bad, but it needs to be much sharper, with lemon rinds* [. . .]
> —*It also needs a potato, a starch . . .* suggests the sous-chef -chef
> —*The tiny, very thin pasta we used to make, do you remember?* [. . .]
> —*I remember vaguely* [. . .]
> —*Well, do that instead, Eh?*

The dialog carries on with questions about ingredients and their preparation, and the chef and his sous-chef progressively agree on ingredients, techniques, and visual effects. The chef concludes, "*The important thing* [. . .] *is the extent to which [the sous-chef] knows how to ask*, [. . .] *was moving along with me, and even prompting me along with a real line of questioning*".

As illustrated earlier, through orientating creativity, chefs channel work but also challenge those involved (including themselves) to go further with their efforts and confront their contributions on a topic. It keeps creativity abounded and intense though focused.

3. Complying: Assessing Ideas

Last, chefs direct creativity, as they are the only ones validating (or not) creative ideas and trials. They specifically assess and bound creative ideas so that they comply with their unique cooking style and with the restaurant's position and conditions. To do so, chefs continually appreciate the ideas, trials, and propositions with regard to a variety of elements. In the first place, chefs grant major importance to keeping their personal cuisine style central to creative ideas at the restaurant. Talking about the creativity of cooks, one of them, for example, states, "*If they wish, they too can become composers themselves, once we have jointly set bounds to that together. Then can express their own know-how and sensibility while keeping to my story*". The unique 'story' or cooking universe of the chef is one of the criteria against which creativity is assessed. This dimension is especially salient when chefs weigh how new dishes interact with the overall menu and evaluate general coherence. A menu "*tells a story*", explains a chef. "*Dishes on a menu are like pebbles in a Japanese garden*", says another one. "*It's a complete universe*", indicates yet another one. In this regard, chefs direct creativity by assessing whether a novelty will fit in. Their personal style and almost artistic expression is at stake in this regard.

Directing creativity through complying also pertains to assessing ideas against other, more external, though no less important, elements, such as the fit between novel ideas and the restaurant's location, its clients, the physical disposition of the kitchen, and the structure of the organization. For example, one of the chefs we studied disregarded some creative ideas because they encompassed technical elements that created too many difficulties in the small kitchen. Another one insists on the necessary coherence between food and location at his restaurant: "*We are in a garden here; we're in a former greenhouse. Although we do not cook vegetarian cuisine, we must serve vegetables; otherwise, it makes no sense*".

Most important, because restaurants are also businesses, chefs assess creative ideas against their potential: will they be acceptable or regarded as too wild by prospective diners? Chefs always keep in mind their business responsibilities. "*They [employees] count on me*" explains one of them. "*It's tough. We have an haute cuisine house, a business to run for a living*". Creative dishes show by definition some degree of novelty, but largely remain within the bounds of the type and degree of novelty that the clients of the respective restaurants expect. Chefs tacitly understand and perceive these boundaries; they integrate them throughout years as part of their expertise as they survey empty (or not so empty) plates at the end of meals, interact with dining-room staff, and even go around the dining-room to enquire about diners' opinions. This tacit understanding is constitutive of chefs' creative leadership within kitchens: clients both expect and bound creativity. Not fully directing creativity in this regard comes at the price of losing clients, as a now well-renowned chef experienced a few decades ago when his clients became reluctant to taste and pay high prices for a cuisine they deemed too innovative for their tastes, and he eventually went bankrupt. Another chef confessed that he kept in mind that his customers expect "*moderate extravagancy*" and somehow restrained creativity and the newness of eventually selected ideas. In other words, the chef decides on which ideas cultivated in kitchens during creative sessions will be integrated in restaurants' dishes and the menus, and, equally important, which will not (at least not directly). To direct creativity in this regard and assess whether ideas comply with these constrains chefs sometimes simply turn themselves into diners at their own restaurants: between sittings, they seat at a dining room table and go through the eating experience in context as would their clients. This can generate a variety of consequences from simply abandoning or validating an idea to pointing at directions for further creative efforts and adjustments. Actually, chefs' complying practice is not limited to a final stop/go in a linear process. Rather, and as one dimension of their creative leadership, it occurs at any moment in creative work.

Concluding Discussion

This chapter contributes to illuminate what leaders can do in practice to enhance team creativity in context and to advance our theoretical understanding of Directing as creative leadership practices. We depict how highly creative leaders have their vision materialized through other's work (Mainemelis, Kark, & Epitropaki, 2015) and highlight that even though leaders rarely perform the necessary legwork of creative production themselves, they strictly control it to be in line with their overall creative vision. We suggest that creative leadership manifests as Directing in haute cuisine restaurants through three facets: enabling, orientating, and complying. Each dimension regards distinct yet related aspects of creativity. These results are summarized in Figure 9.1.

In this chapter, we identified the existence of these three practices, yet did not address the interrelationships among them. How do the three practices of enabling, orientating, and complying intertwine into Directing remains to be further explored. As represented in Figure 9.1, the three dimensions of creative leadership do not form a linear progression: complying is not the validation that terminates creative work; rather, it is mixed with orientating and enabling in an intricate way. Enabling, orientating, and complying appear concomitantly along the numerous loops and fuzzy moments of creative work. In addition, we see no reasons why these interrelationships should be stable; they may well evolve through time. In the same vein, the respective weight of each practice in the making of Directing certainly changes over time, in coherence with the evolving focus and activities of restaurants over the year. For instance, when the kitchen team is involved in the creation of new dishes for the upcoming season, pressure can be higher on enabling and orientating.

A process ontology may help in better capturing these dynamics. Hence, we argue that the creative leadership practices of enabling, orientating, and complying can be regarded as entities of the leadership structure of Directing. We also experienced this empirically when we investigated the creative process in the kitchen using different research tools for these three entities

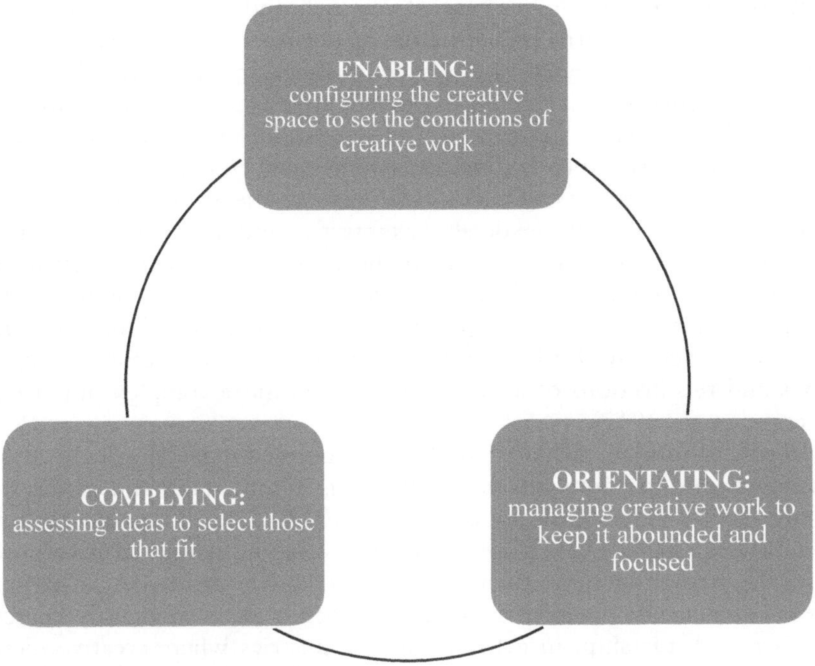

Figure 9.1 Creative Leadership as Directing

appeared to us as stable effects of the creative process, not in the sense of a 'solid rock' (see Dörfler, Stierand, & Zizka, 2017: 3), but more of a 'standing wave' (see Rescher, 2000: 13). That is, like any reality, the kitchen reality "is deemed to be continuously in flux" (Chia, 1995: 579) and therefore future research needs to get to the "emergent relational interactions and patternings that are recursively intimated in the fluxing and transforming of our life-worlds" (Chia, 1995: 581–582). Exposing the many interlocking micro-practices of creative work can provide a more nuanced yet also more essential understanding of creative leadership. As the passionate researchers of the creative process and the world of chefs that we are, we discussed over and over again how we could best go about exposing these leadership micro-practices. The only answer we have so far is that we also need to allow our research process to be in flux in order to capture the ever-becoming nature of creative process as already investigated (Bouty & Gomez, 2015) and its associated leadership. Both those practicing creativity and us researching it are faced with the reality that our theoretical knowledge of creativity, our knowing of how to create, and our knowing of how to be creative is constantly in a process of becoming (Dörfler, Stierand, & Zizka, 2017; Stierand & Zizka, 2015).

In addition, we realized with hindsight that the only reason why we were able to untangle and make sense of our rich and thick data was that we recorded, not necessarily in a structured but rather in a systematic way, the antenarratives we listened to and were engaged in during the data collection. According to Boje (2008), "antenarrative is a relational process that potentially will make future sense and eventually lead to a retrospective narrative collapsed into beginning, middle and ending" (Stierand et al., 2017: 3). In the context of chef's creativity, we therefore define antenarrative processes of creative leadership as intuitive and tacitly operating micro-practices aiming to direct others in bringing order to the messiness of creating (see Stierand et al., 2017). Hence, we argue that antenarratives of creative leadership are indispensable for our understanding of the usual narratives of creative leadership that frequently are post-factum reconstructions and recollections of a much trickier and more complex practice (see Stierand et al., 2017).

In conclusion, our insights are deeply grounded in the particular field of haute cuisine. In haute cuisine, creativity is a core stake and manifests in many aspects of work (Bouty & Gomez, 2013, 2015; Stierand, Dörfler, & MacBryde, 2014). Chefs play a key role, keep the whole creative process under control, and claim their distinctive creative identity. As a matter of fact, haute cuisine provides a particularly rich context to identify Directing as creative leadership. In other creative industries where creative identity claims are not as strong, Directing may not be as important as the other two creative leadership practices, or may simply not be as visible, and the balance between enabling, orientating, and complying may also differ. For example, enabling may be open to a greater number of actors in the organization, whereas in haute cuisine it is fully controlled by the chef. The way the practices are materialized into specific activities may also well differ. For example, chefs permanently orientate creativity by intervening directly and continually, whereas in other fields, creative leaders may control as directly but in a discrete manner. Future research will be beneficial to illuminate these nuances. In haute cuisine restaurants, leading creativity as Directing is also particularly salient and, as we outlined earlier, high-end restaurants form an empirical field well suited to investigate this facet of creative leadership. However, how Directing interweaves with other facets of creative leadership—namely, Facilitating and Integrating—remains an open question that further research could fruitfully address, in general, but also with regard to the three specific practices that we highlighted.

References

Alvesson, M., & Sköldberg, K. 2009. *Reflexive methodology, new vistas for qualitative research*. London: Sage Publications.

Amabile, T. M. 1988. A model of creativity and innovation in organizations. In B. Staw & L. Cummings (Eds.), *Research in Organizational Behavior*, 10: 123–167. Greenwich: JAI Press.

Amabile, T. M. 1996. *Creativity in context: Update to the social psychology of creativity*. Boulder, CO: Westview Press.
Amabile, T. M., Schatzel, E. A., Moneta, G. B., & Kramer, S. J. 2004. Leader behaviors and the work environment for creativity: Perceived leader support. *The Leadership Quarterly*, 15(1): 5–32.
Anderson, N., Potočnik, K., & Zhou, J. 2014. Innovation and creativity in organizations a state-of-the-science review, prospective commentary, and guiding framework. *Journal of Management*, 40(5): 1297–1333.
Basadur, M. 2004. Leading others to think innovatively together: Creative leadership. *The Leadership Quarterly*, 15(1): 103–121.
Boje, D. 2008. Antenarrative. In R. Thorpe & R. Holt (Eds.), *The Sage dictionary of qualitative management research*: 28–30. London: Sage Publications.
Bouty, I., & Gomez, M-L. 2010. Dishing up individual and collective dimensions in organizational knowing. *Management Learning*, 41(5): 545–559.
Bouty, I., & Gomez, M-L. 2013. Creativity in Haute cuisine: Strategic knowledge and practice in Gourmet kitchens. *Journal of Culinary Science & Technology*, 11(1): 80-95.
Bouty, I., & Gomez, M-L. 2015. Creativity at work: Generating useful novelty in haute cuisine restaurants. In R. Garud, B. Simpson, A. Langley, & H. Tsoukas (Eds.), *The emergence of novelty in organizations*: 216–241. Oxford: Oxford University Press.
Chia, R. C. H. 1995. From modern to postmodern organizational analysis. *Organization Studies*, 16(4): 579–604.
Dörfler, V., & Stierand, M. 2009. *Investigating the extraordinary*. Paper presented at the British Academy of Management (BAM) Annual Conference, Brighton.
Dörfler, V., Stierand, M., & Zizka, L. 2017. *Studying reflecting on becoming: Some philosophical reference points*. Paper presented at the British Academy of Management (BAM) Annual Conference, University of Warwick, UK.
Epitropaki, O., & Mainemelis, C. 2016. The "genre bender": The creative leadership of Kathryn Bigelow. In C. Peus, S. Braun, & B. Schyns (Eds.), *Leadership lessons from compelling contexts*, 8: 275–300. Bingley: Emerald.
Ewenstein, B., & Whyte, J. 2007. Beyond words: Aesthetic knowledge and knowing in organizations. *Organization Studies*, 28(5): 689–708.
Ferguson, P. 1998. A cultural field in the making: Gastronomy in the 19th century France. *American Journal of Sociology*, 104(3): 597–641.
Glăveanu, V. P. 2011. Is the lightbulb still on? Social representations of creativity in a western context. *The International Journal of Creativity and Problem Solving*, 21(1): 53–72.
Gomez, M-L., & Bouty, I. 2011. The emergence of an influential practice: Food for thought. *Organization Studies*, 32(7): 921-940.
Gomez, M-L., Bouty, I., & Drucker-Godard, C. 2003. Developing knowing in practice: Behind the scenes of haute cuisine. In D. Nicolini, S. Gherardi, & D. Yanow (Eds.), *Knowing in organizations—a practice-based approach*. New York: M.E. Sharpe.
Hegarty, J., & O'Mahony, G. 1999. Gastronomy: A phenomenon of cultural expressionism and an aesthetic for living. *Journal of Hospitality & Tourism Education*, 11(4): 25–29.
Heinze, T., Shapira, P., Rogers, J. D., & Senker, J. M. 2009. Organizational and institutional influences on creativity in scientific research. *Research Policy*, 38(4): 610–623.

Hunter, S. T., Bedell-Avers, K. E., & Mumford, M. D. 2007. The typical leadership study: Assumptions, implications, and potential remedies. *Leadership Quarterly*, 18(5): 435–446.

Hunter, S. T., Thoroughgood, C. N., Myer, A. T., & Ligon, G. S. 2011. Paradoxes of leading innovative endeavors: Summary, solutions, and future directions. *Psychology of Aesthetics, Creativity, and the Arts*, 5(1): 54.

Jung, D. I. 2001. Transformational and transactional leadership and their effects on creativity in groups. *Creativity Research Journal*, 13(2): 185–195.

Lingo, E. L., & O'Mahony, S. 2010. Nexus work: Brokerage on creative projects. *Administrative Science Quarterly*, 55: 47–81.

Mainemelis, C., & Dionysiou, D. 2015. Play, flow, and timelessness. In C. Shalley, M. Hitt, & J. Zhou (Eds.), *The oxford handbook of creativity, innovation, and entrepreneurship*: 121–140. New York: Oxford University Press.

Mainemelis, C., Kark, R., & Epitropaki, O. 2015. Creative leadership: A multi-context conceptualization. *Academy of Management Annals*, 9(1): 393–482.

Mumford, M. D., Scott, G. M., Gaddis, B., & Strange, J. M. 2002. Leading creative people: Orchestrating expertise and relationships. *Leadership Quarterly*, 13: 705–750.

Murphy, S. E., & Ensher, E. A. 2008. A qualitative analysis of charismatic leadership in creative teams: The case of television directors. *The Leadership Quarterly*, 19(3): 335–352.

Nicolini, D. 2012. *Practice theory, work, and organization: An introduction*. Oxford: Oxford University Press.

Oldham, G. R., & Cummings, A. 1996. Employee creativity: Personal and contextual factors at work. *Academy of Management Journal*, 39(3): 607–634.

Osborn, R. N., Hunt, J. G., & Jauch, L. R. 2002. Toward a contextual theory of leadership. *The Leadership Quarterly*, 13(6): 797–837.

Paulus, P., & Nijstad, L. 2003. Group creativity: An introduction. In P. Paulus & B. Nijstad (Eds.), *Group creativity: Innovation through collaboration*: 110–136. New York: Oxford University Press.

Reiter-Palmon, R., Herman, A., & Yammarino, F. 2008. Creativity and cognitive processes: Multi-level linkages between individual and team cognition. *Multi-Level Issues in Creativity and Innovation*, 7: 203–267.

Rescher, N. 2000. *Process philosophy: A survey of basic issues*. Pittsburgh: University of Pittsburgh Press.

Runco, M. A. 2007. To understand is to create: An epistemological perspective on human nature and personal creativity. In R. Richards (Ed.), *Everyday creativity and new views of human nature: Psychological, social, and spiritual perspectives*: 91–107. Washington, DC: American Psychological Association.

Schatzki, T. R. 2001. Introduction: Practice theory. In T. R. Schatzki, K. Knorr-Cetina, & E. von Savigny (Eds.), *The practice turn in contemporary theory*: 1–14. London: Routledge.

Shalley, C. E., & Gilson, L. L. 2004. What leaders need to know: A review of social and contextual factors that can foster or hinder creativity. *Leadership Quarterly*, 15: 33–53.

Shamir, B., & Howell, J. M. 1999. Organizational and contextual influences on the emergence and effectiveness of charismatic leadership. *The Leadership Quarterly*, 10(2): 257–283.

Shin, S. J., & Zhou, J. 2003. Transformational leadership, conservation, and creativity: Evidence from Korea. *Academy of Management Journal*, 46(6): 703–714.

Stenmark, C. K., Shipman, A. S., & Mumford, M. D. 2011. Managing the innovative process: The dynamic role of leaders. *Psychology of Aesthetics, Creativity, and the Arts*, 5(1): 67.

Stierand, M. 2015. Developing creativity in practice: Explorations with world-renowned chefs. *Management Learning*, 46(5): 598–617.

Stierand, M., Boje, D. M., Glăveanu, V., Dörfler, V., Haley, U. C., & Feuls, M. 2017. Paradoxes of "creativity": Examining the creative process through an antenarrative lens. *The Journal of Creative Behavior*. Published online ahead of print. doi.org/10.1002/jocb.224

Stierand, M., & Dörfler, V. 2011a. Methods against methods. In A. Mesquita (Ed.), *Technology for creativity and innovation: Tools, techniques and applications*: 121–134. Hershey, PA: IGI Global.

Stierand, M., & Dörfler, V. 2011b. *Revising the notion of sample representativeness*. Paper presented at the British Academy of Management (BAM) Annual Conference, Birmingham.

Stierand, M., & Dörfler, V. 2014a. Researching intuition in personal creativity. In M. Sinclair (Ed.), *Handbook of research methods on intuition*: 249–263. Cheltenham, UK: Edward Elgar Publishing.

Stierand, M., & Dörfler, V. 2014b. *Studying the practice of apprenticeship through insider interviews*. Paper presented at the British Academy of Management (BAM) Annual Conference, Belfast, UK.

Stierand, M., Dörfler, V., & MacBryde, J. 2014. Creativity and innovation in haute cuisine: Towards a systemic model. *Creativity and Innovation Management*, 23(1): 15–28.

Stierand, M., Mainemelis, C., Dörfler, V., & Sadler-Smith, E. 2016. *The role of aesthetic knowledge in the creative process of expert chefs*. Paper presented at the 32nd EGOS Colloquium, Naples, IT.

Stierand, M., & Zizka, L. 2015. Reflecting on hospitality management education through a practice lens. *Quality Assurance in Education*, 23(4): 353–363.

Svejenova, S., Mazza, C., & Planellas, M. 2007. Cooking up change in haute cuisine: Ferran Adrià as an institutional entrepreneur. *Journal of Organizational Behavior*, 28(5): 539–561.

Thomson, P., Jones, M., & Warhurst, C. 2007. From conception to consumption: Creativity and the missing managerial link. *Journal of Organizational Behavior*, 28: 625–640.

Tierney, P. M., & Farmer, S. M. 2011. Creative self-efficacy development and creative performance over time. *Journal of Applied Psychology*, 96(2): 277.

Tierney, P. M. 2008. Leadership and employee creativity. In C. E. Shalley & J. Zhou (Eds.), *Handbook of organizational creativity*: 95–123. New York: Lawrence Erlbaum Associates.

To, M. L., Herman, H. M., & Ashkanasy, N. M. 2015. A multilevel model of transformational leadership, affect, and creative process behavior in work teams. *Leadership Quarterly*, 26(4): 543–556.

Vessey, W. B., Barrett, J. D., Mumford, M. D., Johnson, G., & Litwiller, B. 2014. Leadership of highly creative people in highly creative fields: A historiometric study of scientific leaders. *The Leadership Quarterly*, 25(4): 672–691.

West, M., Hirst, G., Richter, A., & Shipton, H. 2004. Twelve steps to heaven: Successfully managing change through developing innovative teams. *European Journal of Work and Organizational Psychology*, 13(2): 269–299.
Woodman, R., Sawyer, J., & Griffin, R. 1993. Toward a theory of organizational creativity. *Academy of Management Review*, 18(2): 293–321.

10 "It Must Give Birth to a World"

Temporality and Creative Leadership for Artistic Innovation

Silviya Svejenova

I regard the past and I work with the future in mind as well.

—Joan Miró (1947–1948), in Rowell (1992: 202)

Even more important than the painting itself is what it gives off, what it projects. . . . One must not worry about whether a painting will last, but whether it has planted seeds. . . . A painting must be fertile. It must give birth to a world . . . it must fertilize the imagination.

—Joan Miró (1959), in Rowell (1992: 252)

Introduction

This chapter elaborates the notion of creative leadership—the collective phenomenon of leading others toward the attainment of creative outcomes through Facilitating, Directing, or Integrating (Mainemelis, Kark, & Epitropaki, 2015)—in the context of artistic innovation. Radical innovation in the arts, as in other domains, comes about rather rarely and its success is hard to foresee. Whereas original and distinctive forms of expression may abound, only a limited number of artists or social groups, usually denoted as avant-garde (Crane, 1987; Vickery, 2007), mavericks (Becker, 1982; Jones et al., 2016), precursors (Kubler, 1962), or rebels (Jones et al., 2012), achieve breakthrough novelty and open up new domains of knowledge through their work. These can include conceiving and introducing radically new forms, easthetics, techniques, or subject matters. Similar to other contexts of creative leadership, artistic innovation is a collective endeavor. Artists develop new esthetic ideas not in isolation but as a practiced social process (Fortwengel, Schüßler, & Sydow, 2017), embedded in collaborative circles, communities, and magnetic places, which offer inspiration, comparison, and validation for the novel approaches (Crane, 1987; Farrell, 2001; Grandadam, Cohendet, & Simon, 2013).

This chapter suggests that the meaning of creative leadership in contexts of radical artistic innovation extends Mainemelis, Kark, and Epitropaki's (2015) definition that emphasizes different collective aspects of leading others for the realization of creative work or the attainment of creative outcomes to entail leading in time. This leading in time is about "giv[ing] birth to a world", as the opening quote suggests. It is a *creative world* in that it offers inspiration for others and, thereby, projects the novel artwork into the future. Thus, while acknowledging creative leadership's innate collective aspect (i.e., leading others), the chapter argues that in the context of radical artistic innovation the emphasis is on *leading in time*. Leading in time involves *time patterning*, i.e., activities that entail organizing time in relation to different tensions, and *temporality work*, i.e., work that engages with distant and nearer pasts and futures. The former enables the attainment of a creative outcome by providing a scaffolding for steady creative work and experimentation, whereas the latter ensures the materialization of a *creative world*. The chapter suggests that patterning time is a precondition for any creative endeavor, whereas temporality work is of particular relevance for the pursuit of artistic innovation (Table 10.1 compares the two perspectives

Table 10.1 Two Perspectives of Creative Leadership: Leading Others Versus Leading in Time

Perspective	*Approach*	*Enactment of Creative Leadership*	*Outcome*
Leading *others**	Combining leader's and followers' creative contributions	*Facilitating* employee creativity *Directing* the materialization of a leader's creative vision *Integrating* heterogeneous creative contributions	Creative work
Leading *in time*	Organizing temporal structures	*Time patterning (iterational)* Temporal organizing along different tensions - solitary and collective creation - artistic work and social interactions - routine practice and serendipitous discoveries	Scaffolding for steady creative work and experimentation
	Addressing different depths of past and future horizons	*Temporality work (projective)* Cultivating serendipity and surprise Extending events' duration Stepping into new temporalities Considering potentiality	Artistic innovation (creative world as a universe of new signs and symbols)

* Creative leadership as outlined by Mainemelis, Kark, & Epitropaki, 2015

of creative leadership—leading others and leading in time—in terms of their approach, enactment, and outcomes).

A *creative world* is a distinctive universe of signs and symbols that is fertile—i.e., able to inspire others. It differs from Becker's (1982) notion of art world, which focuses on the collaborations supporting the realization of a work of art, emphasizing the temporality work that enables semiotic innovation—i.e., the creation of new signs and symbols through which a new language of expression comes into being. This creative world is shaped in what Bakken, Holt, and Zundel (2013: 13) denote as "world time", the time that gives managers and, one can argue, creative leaders new possibilities for experimentation and play, "in which the future and past are open to subjects' imagination and interpretation".

The research question that guides this exploration is, "How does creative leadership unfold in time in contexts of artistic innovation?" Empirically, I investigate these issues in the context of a critical case, that of Catalan artist Joan Miró (1893–1983), who has been recognized among the greatest innovators of 20th-century art for establishing a new visual language and esthetics. The study delves into a wealth of public sources to shed light on the artist's creative leadership depicted as time patterning and temporality work. The chapter is organized as follows. First, it offers some background on the theoretical and research approach. Second, it highlights theoretical reflections on and illustrations with texts by and on Miró of different enactments of creative leadership in the context of radical artistic innovation, distinguishing between time patterning and temporality work. It concludes by discussing implications for creative leadership.

Theoretical Approach

Highly innovative art as a social accomplishment takes place in time. It is often depicted as a rebellion against tradition (Farrell, 2001), a rupture from the past and a progression toward a new future, as avant-garde movements' manifestos tend to claim. Radically new ideas seems to settle when they come along "at the right time" (i.e., right opportunity structure), for example, as with Cubism and Picasso, whose novel language was launched at a moment of fragmented market with multiple niches that had made the mainstream more open to new ideas from the periphery (Sgourev, 2013). Such novel ideas may also come to being serendipitously, "as a consequence of recombining observations into unusual but meaningful associations" (Morley & de Rond, 2009: 3) and get realized in a dynamic relationship with time, reacting to ideas with different depths of past and future. Their persistence in the future requires preservation and consecration in the collective memory (Lang & Lang, 1988; Jones & Massa, 2013).

Time is, thus, "a crucial variable in leading innovation initiatives" (Halbesleben et al., 2003: 34). Actors make sense of novelty in the flow of time (Fortwengel, Schüßler, & Sydow, 2017), their novel projects carrying "shadows" of past exchanges and future possibilities in terms of ideas and relationships (Stjerne & Svejenova, 2016). Yet social scientists have also recognized the "messiness" of time and the "challenges that temporality poses to received conceptualizations, analyses, and explanations of social action and social structure" (Griffin, 1992: 403), as well as the risks of over-emphasizing fluidity and under-appreciating stabilizing infrastructures (Schreyögg & Sydow, 2010; Schoeneborn, Vásquez, & Cornelissen, 2016). Overall, however, whereas creative leadership's multiple dimensions (Facilitating, Directing, and Integrating) and temporal complexity have been acknowledged (Bluedorn & Jaussi, 2008; Mainemelis, Kark, & Epitropaki, 2015), a temporality perspective on creative leadership has yet to be articulated.

The temporality perspective advanced in this chapter responds to recent calls for paying "more attention to the temporal dimensions" of creative leadership (Mainemelis, Kark, & Epitropaki, 2015: 457). Yet it goes beyond the suggested exploration of long-term effects to emphasize the connection between structural and dynamic aspects of time in the emergence and stabilization of novelty, and its materialization into a "creative world". A temporality perspective (Schultz & Hernes, 2013; Reinecke & Ansari, 2016) draws the attention to how different pasts and futures are ongoingly mobilized in the achievement of artistic novelty in the present, in an entanglement of events (Hernes, 2014; Hussenot & Missonier, 2016). It conceives of leadership as "the ability to change the vector of the present-past-future relationship" (Hernes, 2014: 163). Last, but not least, it allows to expand the definition of creative leadership to incorporate "leading in time", capturing the importance and meaning of dynamic time in artistic innovation.

Research Approach

This research was initiated in a series of informal meetings with the Director and the Communications Head of the Miró Foundation in Barcelona that took place in 2009, organized by my colleagues at the time at ESADE Business School, with the idea to explore the idea of a case on Miró that could be of interest to business students. It was further inspired by a subsequent conversation with Joan Gardy Artigas, the son of Josep Llorens Artigas, who, together with his father, had collaborated with Miró in his ceramics works. Data was further gathered over time and rather serendipitously: at exhibitions, meetings, or chance encounters. I visited the permanent collections of Miró's work in the Barcelona and Mallorca foundations (and his studios, as part of the latter) on a number of occasions, as well as temporary exhibitions focusing on facets of his work in Spain and abroad. I also explored exhibits on the work of his closest collaborators (e.g., ceramist Josep Llorens Artigas). In addition, I collected catalogues of exhibitions, published collections of Miró's letters, working notes, and interviews (a number of these sources were received as a generous gift by the Miró foundation in

Barcelona during the informal exploration in 2009, for which I am grateful). It is worth noting that the case I examine is among those that "have withstood the assaults of time" and the "chancy adjustments between the individual and his moment" (Kubler, 1962: 86). Further, my knowledge of Miró's artistic work is amateurish, and my exploration of the artist's trajectory is from an organizational perspective with an interest in leadership, innovation, and temporality.

An interest in a temporality perspective of creative leadership has guided my examination of Miró's creative process and artistic innovation. Thus, while other perspectives could have been possible and informative, I have particularly looked for references to social time (e.g., rhythms, cycles) and time dynamics (e.g present-past-future, events), as suggested in the literature on time, temporality, and organizing (Hassard, 1990; Hernes, 2014; Reinecke & Ansari, 2015; Granqvist & Gustafsson, 2016; Hussenot & Missonier, 2016). I have also sought to distinguish between surface and deeper temporal structures (Rowell, Gustafsson, & Clemente, 2016). The overall approach is qualitative, drawing inspiration from hermeneutics in seeking the coalescence of ideas into insights (Klag & Langley, 2013). The engagement with hermeneutics thought (Kinsella, 2006) involves interpretations of parts of texts, which constitute reflections of and on Miró in order to come up with an understanding of the "whole", in this case, the artist's creative leadership in the context of artistic innovation in relation to temporality. As noted by Gadamer (1996: 388), the interpreters' own thoughts go into "re-awakening the texts" meaning. In that, my hope has been to discover ideas related to creative leadership and artistic innovation in time that, while escaping the conventional meaning of usefulness, can be generative of new ways for seeing or understanding (Gabriel, 2013; March, 2013).

Miró's Leading in Time

Miró's public texts reveal "an artist who constantly revised his work" (Col. leccio Joan Miró, 2016: 6). They give numerous hints of his awareness and, at times, proactive work with different temporal aspects in developing his novel work. These texts give an impression of an artist constantly "on the move", at the junction of multiple events (e.g., commissions, canvasses, exhibitions) and mediums (not only painting but also ceramics, textile, sculpture, etc.), trying to articulate their meaning for his work and the tensions encountered. In this process, Miró acknowledges, lies the creation of his distinct universe—a world of signs and symbols in constant becoming:

> Forms give birth to other forms, constantly changing into something else. They become each other and in this way create the reality of a universe of signs and symbols in which figures pass from one realm to another.
>
> (Miró, 1957, Arken Exhibition, 2010, Denmark)

Overall, Miró's texts offer reflections not only on the temporal patterning of his creative practices (i.e., his surface temporal structures) but also on his deep temporal structures (Rowell, Gustafsson, & Clemente, 2016)—e.g., how he values past, present, and future; what his temporal horizons are; and his more abstract conceptions of time and his work in time. In addition, he also offers reflections on temporal agency, acknowledging the sensing of appropriate moments to wait or to strike (Hernes, 2014: 165), extending the duration of events to prolong the possibility for surprises to happen or initiating new events through orchestrated or serendipitous encounters. This awareness of temporality in the creation of his creative universe is also found in reflections, in which the artist acknowledges influences coming from different depths of art's past, as well as from the temporalities of the different materials and art forms with which he engages. Next, I organize these reflections by and on the artist's creative work into two main and interconnected ways of enacting his creative leadership from a temporality perspective, which I denote as time patterning and temporality work.

Time Patterning

Temporal patterns capture surface temporal structures, revealing positioning of activities and events with regard to time (Rowell, Gustafsson, & Clemente, 2016). Different sources by and on Miró recognize a distinctive time patterning of his creative work, which can be understood as temporal organizing characterized by different tensions—e.g., between solitary and collective creation, between artistic work and social interactions, and between routine practice and serendipitous discoveries. These tensions can be considered both a source of energy and a stabilizing infrastructure in a process of creation in a constant flow of events—i.e., of a "*becoming, without denying the being*: without denying that there are . . . stable entities on each side of the fold" (Ortmann & Sydow, 2017: 13, italics in original). Whereas they may not be directly conducive to artistic innovation, they provide the scaffolding for steady creative work and experimentation, upon which a new creative world can be envisioned and attained.

For example, in the following quote, Miró (1959, in Gether, Høholt, & Rygg Karberg, 2010) accounts for the speed of creation (e.g., things coming slowly), sequencing (e.g., the garden analogy, which captures a "natural course" of growing and ripening), and timing (e.g., pruning at the "right moment"):

> I consider my studio as a kitchen garden. Here, there are artichokes. There, potatoes. Leaves must be cut so that the fruit can grow. At the right moment, I must prune. I work like a gardener. . . . Things come slowly. . . . Things follow their natural course. They grow, they ripen. I must graft. I must water. . . . Ripening goes on in my mind. So I'm always working at a great many things at the same time.

Miró also refers to periods of working "furiously", thereby revealing an ability to create in different rhythms, which in turn imply different approaches—e.g., slowly, by "ripening" (the previous quote):

> If I sometimes work very quickly, letting myself be carried away by the purest and most disinterested mental impulse, at other times I work very slowly. . . . This procedure allows me to work without interruption and without feeling excessive fatigue.
>
> (Miró, 1937, in Rowell, 1992: 148)

Another important distinction is between self- and interaction-time (Lewis & Weigart, 1990)—i.e., the artist's experiences between solitary and collective creative work, and what each of these approaches allows for. For example, self-time and regular, disciplined work allow for balancing acts, such as between creation and being, or between different emotional states—e.g., panic and optimism:

> I have been working a lot, especially on the early stages of my canvasses, and this demands a great effort—to capture the total idea of the painting. During my off-hours I lead a primitive existence. . . . I do exercises, run like a madman out in the sun, and jump rope. In the evening, after I've finished my work, I swim in the sea. I am convinced that one's serious work begins in maturity, and to get to that point of development, we must lead a good life. . . . I see no one here (Montroig), and my chastity is absolute. Quite a change from my busy social life in Paris.
>
> (Miró, 1922, in Rowell, 1992: 79)

> I am working really a lot, with absolute regularity and method. . . . I know that I am following very dangerous paths, and I confess that at times I am seized with a panic like that of the hiker who finds himself on paths never before explored, but this doesn't last, thanks to the discipline and seriousness with which I am working and, a moment later, confidence and optimism push me onward once again.
>
> (Miró, 1923, in Rowell, 1992: 82)

Miró's self-time accounts point to the importance of concentration and solitude in clarifying ideas, whereas the interaction-time accounts reveal the vitality in creative processes brought by a collectivity. This interaction-time requires renouncing oneself and allowing everyone to "do what he wants":

> I do my prints with a team of master printers and assistants. They give me ideas, and I have complete confidence in them, but all this is impossible if you want to be a star. By working in a group this way, I am not

> creating my own little country, or, if I am, it is a universal country. . . . The world is moving toward collectivity. . . . Anonymity allows me to renounce myself, but in renouncing myself I come to affirm myself even more.
>
> (Miró, 1959, in Rowell, 1992: 253)

Interaction-time can also influence self-time, inspiring new ways of work discovered in conversation:

> You and all my other writer friends have given me much help and improved my understanding of many things. I think about our conversation, when you told me how you started with a word and watched to see where it would take you. I have done a series of small things on wood, in which I take off from some form in the wood.
>
> (Miró, 1924, in Rowell, 1992: 86)

Interaction-time is also revealed in the accounts of the relationships Miró maintained with his art dealers (e.g., Pierre Matisse, his New York City dealer), exhibitors at museums and galleries internationally, or commissioners of public work, as well as particularly with his personal friends, such as the architect Josep Lluis Sert, who was the creator of the buildings of the Miró foundations. Given distances (both Matisse and Sert lived and worked in the United States) and the available at the time means of communication, the interaction-time encompasses not only face-to-face interactions but also primarily the extensive number of letters' exchanges, which serve as "acts of articulation" (Hernes, 2014), used to set the stage for future events and encounters and in that connects creative work with artistic innovation. Further, distance is not a deficiency (Ibert, 2010) and through the medium of the letters contributes to copresence-as-perception (Grabher et al., 2018).

Temporality Work

Cultivating serendipity and surprise. An important aspect of creative leadership for artistic innovation is the cultivation of serendipity and surprise. This cultivation is related to "the active roles that actors play in making something out of what they 'stumble upon'" (Garud, Kumaraswamy, & Karnøe, 2010: 762), thereby initiating action and generating meaning. This stumbling upon has a very material origin and, through the shock it produces, leads to a transformation of the encountered objects into a new work of art, making them part of Miró's "world". As one of Miró's friends and supporters Joan Prats noted, "When I pick up a stone it's a stone; when Miró picks up a stone it's a Miró".

According to Jacques Dupin, poet, art critic and close friend of Miró, the artist was a "hunter of images and objects and sudden discoveries" (Jeffett, 2002: 33). In a number of sources, Miró reflects on surprise and serendipitous discoveries as a starting point for an artwork—e.g., using "stains on paper and imperfections in canvases" (Miró, in Rowell, 1992). Writing to his US dealer Pierre Matisse, Miró explains,

> You speak to me of my objects and ask how I conceive of them. I never think about it in advance. I feel myself attracted by a magnetic force toward an object, and then I feel myself being drawn toward another object which is added to the first, and their combination creates a poetic shock—not to mention their original formal physical impact—which makes the poetry truly moving, and without which it would have no effect.
>
> (Miró, 1936, in Rowell, 1992: 126)

Overall, Miró is known for having "sought inspiration in what he called the shock or 'spark' of a chance encounter with objects in the outside world" (Jeffett, 2002: 33):

> Use things found by divine chance, bits of metal, stone, etc., the way I use schematic signs drawn at random on the paper or an accident . . . that is the only thing-this magic spark-that counts in art.
>
> (Miró, in Coyle, 2002: 83)

> I always begin a painting immediately after receiving a shock from something material, such as for example the weave of a canvas, the very matter of which the weave is formed, or whatever triggers something in me without my knowing why. This is what Rimbaud calls the spark.
>
> (Miró, in Malet, 2003: 59)

He clarifies in another source, "When I go for a stroll, I don't search for things like one searches for mushrooms. There is a force—clack!—that makes me bend my head downward, a magnetic force" (Miró, in Jeffett, 2002: 33). The cultivation of serendipity could be seen in the artist's ability of being "attracted by" or "drawn toward" objects, generating meaning (poetic shock) around these serendipitous combinations, which in itself can be an event that can alter in some way the future of the artist as well as the meaning created by audiences exposed to the shock.

In addition to stumbling upon, Miró also orchestrates shock and surprise, for example, to "[m]elt down the metal of my empty paint tubes and use the resulting shapes as my starting point" (Miró, in Jeffett, 2002: 40). As the artist elaborates, "If I frequently integrate the objects as they are, with raw materials, it is not to obtain a plastic effect but by necessity. It is in order to produce the shock of one reality against another" (Joan Miró, L'Humanité, 1974—in Coyle, Jeffett, & Punyet Miró, 2002). Another variation of shock comes from the use of different media and instruments, as revealed in the following quotes (Miró, 1959 in Rowell, 1992: 250–251):

> The medium and the instrument I am using dictate my technique, which is a way of giving life to a thing. If I attack a piece of wood with a gouge, that puts me in a certain frame of mind. If I attack a lithographer's stone with a brush, or a copper plate with an etching needle, that puts me in another frame of mind. The encounter between the instrument and the material produces a shock, and this is a live thing, something that I think will have an effect on the viewer.
>
> The brightness of ceramics appeals to me: it seems to produce sparks. And then there is the struggle with the elements—clay and fire. As I said before, I am a fighter. You have to know how to control fire when you do ceramics. And it's unpredictable! That, too, is very seductive. Even when you use the same formula, the same kiln temperature, you do not get the same result. Unpredictability causes a shock, and that is something that appeals to me now.

Cultivating serendipity and surprise is not only about the role played by luck, chance or coincidence, but also about the ability to "spark", to initiate action (e.g., to begin a painting), and to envision unusual yet meaningful associations and combinations (Morley & de Rond, 2009). In the case of Miró, this ability is revealed not only in chance encounters with objects but also through provoked incidents, which are expected to shock and in this way could become what Morley and de Rond call "magic moments" where possibilties for turning points appear.

Extending Events' Duration

Kubler (1962: 19) suggests that "any work of art is actually a portion of arrested happening, or an emanation of past time. It is a graph of an activity now stilled, but a graph made visible like an astronomical body, by a light that originated with that activity". One of the aspects of creative leadership for artistic innovation understood as temporality work is how Miró seeks to extend events' duration, not only as a trajectory traceable to the past but also as one that extends into the future and 'projects' new possibilities, planting seeds and fertalizing the imagination. For example, each canvas can be considered an event that takes place over years and alongside other artworks; it can be left waiting, re-worked, and even burnt down. Miró (1958, in Thailandier, 2017: 36) seems to find himself in the flow of multiple canvas events:

> If a canvas remains in progress for years in my studio, that doesn't worry me. On the contrary, when I'm rich in canvases which have a point of departure vital enough to set off a series of rhythms, a new life, new living things, I'm happy.

These canvases, however, have to have vital point of departure that can bring new life, i.e., to be fertile, generative. By having canvasses remain "in progress", Miró stretches the duration of these events. Thus, "by letting time pass, other possible events may appear on the horizon that enable a different meaning to be made of events that have already happened" (Hernes, 2014: 165). In addition, translating emergent ideas into actions (e.g., the drawing of line with a brush) can also be stretched through multiple reiterations of reflection:

> It took me only a moment to draw this line with my brish. But it took me months, perhaps even years of reflection to form the idea of it.
>
> (Miró, in Rowell, 1992: 275)

This extended reflection leaves an event (artwork) open to new influences and further rethinking of the present-past-future. It is revealed, for example, in Miró's approach to sculpture, in which he casts in bronze assemblages of everyday materials. According to Rygg Karberg (2010: 17), in doing that "he manages to say something of lasting importance about the transient. He creates a timeless monument to the now".

A different way of thinking about extending duration, not only of artworks but also of the artist's trajectory and legacy, is through specific forms of temporary and permanent organizing, such as exhibitions and foundations. Exhibitions, organized during an artist's time and subsequently, bring together work conceived at different moments in time and with different duration of the creative process that has brought it to being. This bringing together of multiple events allows the creation of new meaning in relation to the artist's work, which in itself extends the duration of the artist's trajectory.

Similarly, the foundations that have been established in Barcelona and Mallorca seek to keep alive—i.e., extend the duration- of Miró's legacy by ensuring the visibility of and keeping the interest in his work, as well as expanding the audiences exposed to it. For example, Marko Daniel, the recently hired director of the Miró Foundation in Barcelona stated in an interview that he will seek to find new ways of presenting and communicating the foundation's collection:

> . . . in surprising ways, working with the holdings and the archive, which richness perhaps is not exploited as much as it could be. Today more than never the way in which an artist works and thinks, the processes he uses to arrive at the final work are important and useful in order to make comprehend the relevance and urgency of art in our daily lives.
>
> (Daniel, in Sesé, 2017, author's translation from Spanish)

This quote suggests the importance of revisiting the artist's past (from holdings and archive) and bringing it into the concerns of the present.

Stepping Into New Temporalities

During his creative trajectory, Miró worked not only in painting but also—through collaborations—in a number of other art forms and mediums, such as sculpture, ceramics, etchings, or textile. Entering a new art form could be considered as "stepping into new and often unknown temporalities" (Hernes, 2014: 154)—i.e., the temporalities of the specific art forms and their distinctive norms and practices. This stepping into new temporalities is captured by Miró's confession at the age of 81: "I am an established painter but a young sculptor" (in Punyet Miró, 2002: 15). In the words of a critic, through the sculptures, Miró has launched "a second artistic career", as the exhibition "'Miró's sculptures' is the budding of a talent that—however much nourished by experience—has all the best qualities of youth: inquisitiveness, energy, dedication, flexibility, and freshness" (in Coyle, 2002: 82). This new career can be considered as an instance of what Said has denoted as a "late style", a "new idiom" that some great artists acquire close to the end of their lives, "not as harmony and resolution but as intransigence, difficulty, and unresolved contradiction" (Said, 2006: 7). What Said finds paradoxical is "how essentially unrepeatable, uniquely articulated aesthetic works written not at the beginning but at the end of a career can never the less have influence on what comes after them" (17–18).

Significant world events could be another source of stepping into new temporalities or stretching the duration of certain events. As Rowell (1992: 145) notes,

> In January 1937, Miró began to realize that his hopes for returning to Barcelona and continuing his works in progress would not be fulfilled for some time. Since he was unable to find either a frame of mind or working conditions that would allow him to elaborate his earlier ideas, he decided to embark on a series of works that were entirely different in concept.

Exiled in France, Miró writes to his dealer Pierre Matisse from Hötel Récamier on January of 1937:

> I left all my work material in Barcelona—about a hundred things in progress—that was where I was living in an atmosphere of work. . . . Given the impossibility of going on with my works in progress, I have decided to do something absolutely different; I am going to begin doing *very realistic* still lifes. . . . I am now going to attempt to draw out the deep and poetic reality of things, but I can't say whether I will succeed to the degree I wish. We are living through a terrible drama, everything happening in Spain is terrifying in a way you could never imagine (italics in original).
>
> (In Rowell, 1992: 146)

A year later, in another letter to Matisse, Miró shares that "I am going to etch on copper now, something that will open up new possibilities for me" (in Rowell, 1992: 158). One could imagine these are new possibilities for creation. Later on in 1938, writing again to him, Miró notes,

> This method of work—alternating between very tight execution, things done quickly, and manual work allows me to stay in good shape and at the same time opens up new avenues to me and enriches me with new possibilities and expressive resources.
>
> (in Rowell, 1992: 159)

Another way to capture the stepping into new temporalities is by "escaping" reality, particularly at a time of dramatic events with historical significance. This escape is achievable through finding other sources of inspiration, which in turn bring novel ideas. As related by Miró in a comment and interview (Malet, 2003: 51),

> At Varengeville-sur-Mer, in 1939 there began a new stage in my work which had its source in music and nature. It was about the time the war broke out. I felt a deep desire to escape. I closed myself within myself purposely. The might, music and the stars began to play a major role in suggesting my paintings. Music had always appealed to me, and now music in this period began to take the role poetry had played in the early twenties, especially Bach and Mozart.

Stepping into new temporalities has implications not only for creative work and leadership but also for creatives' careers and identities, offering possibilities for rethinking one's past and envisioning alternative futures. It can also be a way of orchestrating surprises for oneself, as creator, as well as for the audiences, accustomed to experience a creator within a given medium.

Considering Potentiality

Another line of Miró's reflection on temporality is about the potentiality of events pointing toward possible distant events. Hernes (2014), from Heidegger, suggests that the being of an entity exists ahead of itself and reveals itself though its projection onto (future) possibilities. Similarly, an artwork is important for its potentiality, "what it would allow others to do at a more or less distant point in time", thereby implying its generativity for different futures and time horizons:

> It is not an artwork that matters but the trajectory of the spirit in life's totality, not what has been done in the span of life, but what it hints to and what it would allow others to do at a more or less distant point in time
>
> (Miró, in Picon, 2002: 146, author's translation from Spanish)

> Even more important than the painting itself is what it gives off, what it projects. . . . One must not worry about whether a painting will last, but whether it has planted seeds that give brith to other things.
>
> (Miró, 1959, in Rowell, 1992: 252)

Envisioning potentiality becomes particularly important at times of crises and dramatic historic events that challenge the role of the creative act. For example, Rowell (1992: 165) notes,

> In the spring of 1939, Cahiers d'art published a short survey based on the following question: "Is the creative act affected by contemporary events, when these events involve no less than the destruction of the forms of that very civilization which the painter or the sculptor was consciously trying to enrich at the beginning of his career?" The dominant realities in European minds in 1939 were the rise of fascism, the Spanish civil war, and impending war.

In responding to Cahiers d'art's inquiry, Miró emphasized,

> The forms expressed by an individual who is part of society must reveal the movement of a soul trying to escape the reality of the present . . . in order to approach new realities, to offer other men the possibility of rising above the present.
>
> (In Rowell, 1992: 166)

This could be interpreted as awareness of the potentiality of art to allow the possibility of a different future.

Considerations of potentiality could also involve negation—i.e., as with the artist's contempt for his own work—or, alternatively, the negation of the negation, in a quest for oppositions:

> For a whole year I went about systematically destroying everything I'd done. My inner rebellion was just beginning. There is absolutely nothing left from that period.
>
> (Miró, 1928, in Rowell, 1992: 94)

> The same process makes me look for the noise hidden in silence, the movement in immobility, life in inanimate things, the infinite in the finite, forms in a void, and myself in anonymity. This is the negation of the negation that Marx spoke of.
>
> (Miró, 1959, in Rowell, 1992: 253)

The potentiality consideration is also present in the establishment of Barcelona-based Miró foundation, which had been done on the initiative of the artist, in a building created by his close friend, the architect Josep Lluis Sert. In a letter to Sert, Miró shares some ideas of how the foundation could look like, emphasizing among other aspects that in creating its design, he should "think of the man of the future" and the possibility for "lectures and debates about all current issues and problems, needless to say with a broad scope, and apart from work".

Creative Leadership for Artistic Innovation: Toward a Temporality Perspective

It could be argued that the time patterning and temporality work identified in the analysis of texts on and by Miró contribute differently toward the stabilization and ongoing transformation of the artist's work, paving the way to the creation of a creative world of novel signs, symbols, and forms. Time patterning could be interpreted as the iterational agency (Emirbayer and Mische, 1998: 971, italics in original), which depicts action and thought that continuously and selectively reactivate past patterns, "giving stability and order to social universes and helping to sustain identities, interactions, and institutions over time". It constitutes a temporal infrastructure of the artist's creative practice, which gives both energy and stability to his artwork by ensuring a rhythm that enables holding polarizing tensions. These tensions could be seen as providing a scaffolding for steady creative work and ongoing experimentation upon which a new creative world can be envisioned and attained. As captured in the illustrations, these tensions involve not only individual but also collective aspects of creative work (e.g., conversations with writer friends, collaboration with printers) as well as not only self- but also interaction-time. In that, the time patterning aspect of leading in time shares ground with general depictions of creative leadership as leading others for the attainment of creative outcome.

Temporality work, which involves cultivating serendipity and surprise, extending events' duration, stepping into new temporalities, or considering potentiality, concerns events and, as such, is essential for allowing novelty to come into being and stabilize in (relation to) time. It could be seen as what Emirbayer and Mische (1998: 971, italics in original) depict as projective agency, which entails "*the imaginative generation by actors of possible future trajectories of action, in which received structures of thought and action may be creatively reconfigured in relation to actors' hopes, fears, and desires for the future*". For example, cultivating serendipity and surprise allows incorporating the unexpected by changing the trajectory of events, benefitting from the resulting sparks and shocks, which brings an emotional response to the novel work. Extending the events' duration can be interpreted as prolonging the trajectory of an event to allow more opportunities to redefine the future and the past by incorporating new elements and surprises. Stepping into new temporalities, as in the case of new art forms, their respective materials, and collaborations, enables exploring different futures and re-defining the artist's past. Lastly, considering potentiality captures the artist's own ideas for and imagination of how his work could extend to and influence the future. With these kinds of projective action (not only by the artist but also by those involved in preserving and propagating his legacy, e.g. through foundations, temporary exhibitions), the artist's creative world constitutes a continuously emergent event (Mead, referred to in Emirbayer and Mische, 1998) that influences its own temporality as well as the audiences' orientations towards past, present, and future.

In conclusion, this study took the case of Joan Miró as a point of departure to advance reflections on creative leadership in the context of artistic innovation from a temporality perspective. As such, it is part of a larger effort to explore the nature and meaning of creative leadership in different contexts. This contextual diversity was originally acknowledged by Mainemelis, Kark, and Epitropaki (2015) and has subsequently been extended to other specific contexts, such as for example artistic innovation (this chapter) or social purpose (Svejenova & Christiansen, 2018). Further research needs to explore if and how creative leadership as leading in time could extend the understanding of innovation in contexts other than art.

Acknowledgments

These ideas are part of an ongoing (wider) project on the temporality of creativity and innovation at the Centre for Organisational Time, Copenhagen Business Schools, Denmark. The author is thankful to Olga Epitropaki, Tor Hernes, Babis Mainemelis, and Jonathan Smith for helpful comments and suggestions provided to earlier drafts of this chapter, and to Marcel Planellas and the late Montse Ollé with whom the project on Joan Miró was initiated at ESADE Business School in Barcelona, Spain. It is dedicated to the memory of Montse Ollé.

References

Bakken, T., Holt, R., & Zundel, M. 2013. Time and play in management practice: An investigation through the philosophies of McTaggart and Heidegger. *Scandinavian Journal of Management*, 29: 13–22.

Becker, H. 1982. *Art worlds*. Berkeley, CA: University of California Press.

Bluedorn, A. C., & Jaussi, K. S. 2008. Leaders, followers, and time. *The Leadership Quarterly*, 19: 654–668.

Col.leccio Joan Miró. 2016. *Press kit* (April 8). Barcelona, Spain: Fundació Joan Miró.

Coyle, L., Jeffett, W., & Punyet Miró, J. (Eds.). 2002. *The shape of color: Joan Miró's painted sculpture*: 21–65. Washington, DC: Corcoran Gallery of Art. in association with Scala Publishers Ltd., London.

Crane, D. 1987. *The transformation of the avant-garde: The New York art world, 1940–1985*. Chicago, IL: University of Chicago Press.

Emirbayer, M., & Mische, A. 1998. What is agency? *American Journal of Sociology*, 103(4): 962–1023.

Farrell, M. P. 2001. *Collaborative circles: Friendship dynamics and creative work*. Chicago, IL: University of Chicago Press.

Fortwengel, J., Schüßler, E., & Sydow, J. 2017. Studying organizational creativity as process: Fluidity or duality? *Creativity and Innovation Management*, 26(1): 5–16.

Gabriel, Y. 2013. Surprises: Not just the spice of life but the source of knowledge. *M@n@gement*, 16(5): 719–731.

Gadamer, H. G. 1996. *Truth and method* (2nd rev. ed.). New York: Continuum.

Garud, R., Kumaraswamy, A., & Karnøe, P. 2010. Path dependence or path creation? *Journal of Management Studies*, 47: 760–774.

Gether, S., Høholt, & A. Rygg Karberg (Eds.). 2010. *Miró: I work like a gardener*. Ishøj, Denmark: Arken Museum of Modern Art.

Grabher, G., Melchior, A., Schiemer, B., Schüßler, E., & Sydow, J. 2018. From being there to being aware: Confronting geographical and sociological imaginations of copresence. *Environment and Planning A*, published online on November 24, 2017, http://journals.sagepub.com/doi/pdf/10.1177/0308518X17743507.

Grandadam, D., Cohendet, P., & Simon, L. 2013. Places, spaces and the dynamics of creativity: The video game industry in Montreal. *Regional Studies*, 47(10): 1701–1714.

Granqvist, N., & Gustafsson, R. 2016. Temporal institutional work. *Academy of Management Journal*, 59(3): 1009–1035.

Griffin, L. J. 1992. Temporality, events, and explanation in historical sociology. *Sociological Methods & Research*, 20(4): 403–427.

Halbesleben, J. R. B., Novicevic, M. M., Harvey, M. G., & Buckley, M. R. 2003. The influence of temporal complexity in the leadership of creativity and innovation: A competency-based model. *Leadership Quarterly*, 14: 433–454.

Hassard, J. 1990. Introduction. In J. Hassard (Ed.), *The sociology of time*: 1–28. London: Palgrave Macmillan.

Hernes, T. 2014. *A process theory of organization*. Oxford: Oxford University Press.

Hussenot, A., & Missonier, S. 2016. Encompassing stability and novelty in organization studies: An events-based approach. *Organization Studies*, 37(4): 523–246.

Ibert, O. 2010. Relational distance: Sociocultural and time-spatial tensions in innovation practices. *Environment and Planning A*, 42: 187–204.

Jeffett, W. 2002. The shape of color: Joan Miró's painted sculpture, monumentality, metaphor. In L. Coyle, W. Jeffett, & J. Punyet Miró (Eds.), *The shape of color: Joan Miró's painted sculpture*: 21–65. Washington, DC: Corcoran Gallery of Art. in association with Scala Publishers Ltd., London.

Jones, C., Maoret, M., Massa, F. G., & Svejenova, S. 2012. Rebels with a cause: Formation, contestation, and expansion of the de novo category "Modern Architecture," 1870–1975. *Organization Science*, 23(6): 1523–1545.

Jones, C., & Massa, F. G. 2013. From novel practice to consecrated exemplar: Unity Temple as a case of institutional evangelizing. *Organization Studies*, 34(8): 1099–1136.

Jones, C., Svejenova, S., Strandgaard Pedersen, J., & Townley, B. 2016. Misfits, mavericks and mainstreams: Drivers of innovation in the creative industries. *Organization Studies*. Special issue introduction, 37(6): 751–768.

Kinsella, E. A. 2006. Hermeneutics and critical hermeneutics: Exploring possibilities within the art of interpretation. *Forum: Qualitative Social Research/Sozialforschung*, 7(3): Art. 19.

Klag, M., & Langley, A. 2013. Approaching the conceptual leap in qualitative research. *International Journal of Management Reviews*, 15(2): 149–166.

Kubler, G. 1962. *The shape of time*. New Haven: Yale University Press.

Lang, G. E., & Lang, K. 1988. Recognition and renown: The survival of artistic reputation. *American Journal of Sociology*, 94(1): 79–109.

Lewis, D. J., & Weigart, A. J. 1990. The structures and meanings of social-time. In J. Hassard (Ed.), *The sociology of time*: 77–101. London: Palgrave Macmillan.

Mainemelis, C., Kark, R., & Epitropaki, O. 2015. Creative leadership: A multi-context conceptualization. *Academy of Management Annals*, 9(1): 393–482.

Malet, R. M. 2003. *Joan Miró: Notes on a collection*. Barcelona, Spain: Fundació Joan Miró.

March, J. G. 2013. In praise of beauty. *M@n@gement*, 16(5): 732–738.

Morley, I., & de Rond, M. 2009. Introduction: Fortune and the prepared mind. In M. de Rond & I. Morley (Eds.), *Serendipity: Fortune and the prepared mind*: 1–10. Cambridge: Cambridge University Press.

Ortmann, G., & Sydow, J. 2017. *Dancing in chains: Creative practices in/of organizations*. Organization Studies, first published online on August 19, 2017, https://doi.org/10.1177/0170840617717096.

Picon, G. 1980/2002. *Joan Miró: Los cuadernos catalanes (Spanish edition)*. Valencia-Murcia, Spain: IVAM and Colegio Oficial de Aparejadores y Arquitectos Técnicos de la Región de Murcia.

Reinecke, J., & Ansari, S. 2015. When times collide: Temporal brokerage at the intersection of markets and developments. *Academy of Management Journal*, 58: 618–648.

Reinecke, J., & Ansari, S. 2016. Time, temporality and process studies. In A. Langley & H. Tsoukas (Eds.), *The Sage handbook of process organization studies*. London: Sage Publications.

Rowell, C., Gustafsson, R., & Clemente, M. 2016. How institutions matter "in time": The temporal structures of practices and their effects on practice reproduction". *Research in the Sociology of Organizations*, 48A: 303–327.

Rowell, M. (Ed.) 1992. *Joan Miró: Selected writings and interviews*. Cambridge, MA: Da Capo Press.

Rygg Karberg, A. 2010. The gardener of art—the late miró. In C. Gether, S. Høholt, & A. Rygg Karberg (Eds.), *Miró: I work like a gardener*. Ishøj, Denmark: Arken Museum of Modern Art.

Said, E. W. 2006. *On late style: Music and literature against the grain*. New York: Vintage Books.

Schoeneborn, D., Vásquez, C., & Cornelissen, J. 2016. Imagining organization through metaphor and metonymy: Unpacking the process-entity paradox. *Human Relations*, 69: 915–944.

Schreyögg, G., & Sydow, J. 2010. Organizing for fluidity? On the dilemmas of new organizational forms. *Organization Science*, 21: 1251–1262.

Schultz, M., & Hernes, T. 2013. A temporal perspective on organizational identity. *Organization Science*, 24(1): 1–21.

Sesé, T. 2017. Una apuesta por revitalizar la figura de Miró: El nuevo director de la Fundació Miró, Marko Daniel desvela los ejes de su programa. *La Vanguardia*, November 23, 2017, www.lavanguardia.com/cultura/20171123/433089891940/marko-daniel-nuevo-director-fundacio-miro.html, accessed on January 6, 2017.

Sgourev, S. 2013. How Paris gave rise to cubism (and Picasso): Ambiguity and fragmentation in radical innovation. *Organization Science*, 24(6): 1601-1617.

Stjerne, I. S., & Svejenova, S. 2016. Connecting temporary and permanent organizing: Tensions and boundary work in sequential film projects. *Organization Studies*, 37(12): 1771–1792.

Svejenova, S., & Christiansen, L. 2018. Creative leadership for social impact. *Research in the Sociology of Organizations*, 55: 47–72.

Thailandier, Y. 2017. *Joan Miró: I work like a gardener*. Hudson, NY: Princeton Architectural Press.

Vecchierini, P. J. 2008. *Miró Sert in their own words, correspondence 1937–1980*. Palma de Mallorca and Murcia, Spain: Fundació Pilar i Joan Miró a Mallorca & CENDEAC.

Vickery, J. 2007. Avant-garde organization: Understanding radical art practice as management and organizational investigation. *Aesthesis: International Journal of Art and Aesthetics in Management and Organizational Life*, 1(2): 112–127.

Part IV

Creative Leadership in Integrative Contexts

11 Leading for Creative Synthesis

A Process-Based Model for Creative Leadership

Sarah Harvey, Chia-yu Kou and Wenxin Xie

Introduction

Organizations rely on groups and teams to come up with breakthrough new ideas. This is particularly evident in creative industries like product design, filmmaking, television and music where groups of professionals work together to come up with creative art and music, consumer products, policy recommendations, research projects and a variety of other innovative outputs (Elsbach & Flynn, 2013; Elsbach & Kramer, 2003; Harvey & Kou, 2013; Hargadon & Bechky, 2006; Long-Lingo & O'Mahony, 2010; Sutton & Hargadon, 1996). Those groups display distinct characteristics that create challenges for the process of developing new ideas. Creative groups work on non-routine tasks, group members are highly skilled experts with unique abilities and knowledge to contribute to the project, and they have to work in a highly interdependent fashion despite their novel tasks evolving and emerging over time. As a result of the nature of this work, creative groups face a variety of coordination challenges (Harrison & Rouse, 2014). Yet perhaps because of the importance of creative professionals to producing new ideas and the critical need for them to have freedom in the creative process, researchers have often studied these groups as if they are leaderless (e.g., Reiter-Palmon, Herman, & Yammarino, 2008; Shalley, 1991).

Research has begun to unpick the processes through which creative professionals can work together (Bechky & Hargadon, 2006; Harvey, 2014; Harrison & Rouse, 2015), building an understanding of how creativity is embedded within a social context (Amabile, 1996; Csikszentmihalyi, 1999; Drazin, Glynn, & Kazanjian, 1999; Ford, 1996; Hennessey, 2004). However, we know relatively less about how leaders can facilitate that process (Mainemelis, Kark, & Epitropaki, 2015). One reason for the disconnection between research on creative processes and leadership may be that we assume that leaders will constrain a creative process that is expected to be free-flowing, autonomous, chaotic and iterative. Leaders of creative teams have been advised to minimize power and status differences (Galinsky, Magee, Gruenfeld, Whitson, & Liljenquist, 2008) so that all members of the group can contribute their unique and diverse resources and inputs.

However, evidence increasingly suggests that creativity also benefits from constraint (Binyamin & Carmeli, 2010; Gilson et al., 2005; Goldenberg, Mazursky, & Solomon, 1999). Leaders may therefore play a vital role in setting and enforcing boundaries on the collective creative process.

In this chapter, we build on a process-based view of collective creativity to suggest one set of leader behaviors that can facilitate creativity. Specifically, we extend one process for collective creativity—the process of creative synthesis (Harvey, 2014)—to the domain of leadership to develop a model of leading for creative synthesis. Creative synthesis is a dialectic process in which group members integrate their diverse inputs to develop a shared understanding of a task that guides future idea generation and enables the group to recognize highly creative ideas when they arise. We suggest that leaders can play a critical role in guiding and facilitating creative synthesis. Mainemelis, Kark, and Epitropaki (2015) have suggested that leading for creativity can be conceptualized in three ways: facilitating employees' (or group members') creativity, materializing the leader's vision and integrating heterogeneous contributions. Our model draws on all three conceptualizations to describe how leaders can shape and help materialize a vision by drawing out and then enabling integration of group members' diverse inputs.

An Overview of the Process of Creative Synthesis

The idea-generation paradigm views breakthrough ideas as resulting from a combination of diverse inputs (Staw, 2009). It assumes that creative products triumph when leaders can include more diverse individuals with different background and experiences (Muira & Hida, 2004; Watson, Kumar, & Michaelson, 1993). Introducing diverse perspectives into the creative process, however, is costly. It is difficult and time consuming for group members to appreciate, understand and use one another's diverse knowledge and ideas (Nembhard & Edmondson, 2006; Edmondson & Nembhard, 2009; Srikanth, Harvey, & Peterson, 2016; Harvey, Currall, & Hammar, 2017). As a result, groups with diverse perspectives can struggle to develop integrated creative products (Harvey, 2013). Therefore, understanding the process through which divergent perspectives are combined is critical for understanding collective creativity.

Harvey (2014) proposed a dialectic process for integrating diverse group resources into breakthrough creative output in groups. In the process of creative synthesis, group members integrate their individual ideas, information and perspectives into a shared understanding that draws uniquely on those individual inputs to enable group members to commonly interpret their task or problem. Integrated understanding can guide collective idea generating efforts to facilitate the development of radically new ideas. As specific ideas develop, they also reveal problems and inconsistencies with the shared understanding that prompts the group to continue evolving how they think about the task or problem so that the shared understanding developed by a group is dynamic over time.

Synthesis unfolds as groups iterate between three process facilitators. To develop shared understanding, groups (a) enact ideas by making them concrete (for example, through sketches, drawings, prototypes, or conversations about implementation); (b) focus their collective attention on joint creative products; and (c) build on the similarities or overlaps within their diverse perspectives. Underlying that process are the diverse resources available to the group (Amabile, Conti et al., 1996; Woodman, Sawyer, & Griffin, 1993) and external feedback (e.g., Harrison & Rouse, 2015). Once a shared understanding develops, it forms the basis for a new process of synthesis that occurs when the group's view is challenged by novel diverse inputs or feedback from the external environment. In this way, creativity is conceptualized as a continuous dialectic process of building then rebuilding shared understanding and transforming it into creative output.

Contexts for Creative Synthesis and the Role of Leadership

The creative synthesis process relies on two broad assumptions. The first is that group members have unique and diverse inputs to contribute to the process, so that new perspectives and new ideas can be crafted from those different views. Without those inputs, there is nothing for the group to integrate. The second assumption is that it occurs during what could be described as intense collective creative work, in which group members (i) work together over a significant period of time, (ii) work jointly to develop creative output through both idea generation and implementation and (iii) engage in deep dialogues that reveal and reconcile perspectives. Those are groups such as teams working on films at Pixar, dance troupes (Harrison & Rouse, 2014), entrepreneurial start up teams (e.g., Forbes et al., 2006) or management consulting project teams (e.g., Wer & Stjernberg, 2003). We suggest that intense collective creative work is necessary to give group members the opportunity to uncover and understand one another's perspectives, identify similarities and develop a shared understanding that is unique to the group. Creative synthesis is likely to be less productive in more dispersed networks like those studied by Lingo and O'Mahony (2010) or in short-term, generation-focused teams, such as brainstorming groups. Those teams are unlikely to spend enough time together to develop a sufficiently deep understanding of one another's perspectives, for a variety of reasons. For instance, in dispersed networks, members of the creative project may spend a significant portion of their time working individually, whereas in brainstorming groups, members work together over a short period of time and have relatively superficial level dialogues.

Since Fiedler (1978) first proposed the contingency model of leadership, scholars have agreed that context can influence the type of leadership that emerges and it effectiveness (Oc, 2018). Therefore, leaders need adjust their leadership behaviors according to the context. For example, prior research suggests that delegative leadership is more effective for helping groups to diverge whereas providing Directive leadership is more effective for helping groups to converge (Gebert, Boerner, & Kearney, 2010). Leaders also need different conflict management styles at different points in the creative processes (Farh, Lee, & Farh, 2010). The contingency view therefore suggests that leaders will need to adjust to the features of the context for creative synthesis described earlier. For more dispersed networks or for brainstorming groups, leaders may need to directly intervene in the process of integrating perspectives by making decisions and resolving conflicts, reducing the negative consequences of political negotiation, status conflicts and dysfunctional interpersonal interactions (Edmondson, 1999; Marks et al., 2001; Zaccaro, Rittman, & Marks, 2001). Indeed, prior literature often recommends relying on leaders to engage in creative synthesis themselves by collecting ideas and perspectives from organizational members, integrating them and using them to set the creative direction of the organization (Lewis et al., 2002; Mainemelis, Kark, & Epitropaki, 2015).

For creative synthesis in teams involved in intense creative work, we propose a different solution. We suggest that leaders can direct and facilitate the processes that will enable groups to engage in the process of creative synthesis. Prior literature shows that leaders can fulfil the leadership functions with structure, schedules, monitoring and motivating group members to wisely spend time and effort to combine different perspectives (Morgeson, DeRue, & Karam, 2010; Reiter-Palmon & Illies, 2004). We apply the insight that leaders can facilitate creative processes to the process of creative synthesis next.

A Model of Leading Through Creative Synthesis

We extend the model of creative synthesis by suggesting that leaders can facilitate that process in three ways. We conceptualize creative work as unfolding through cycles of initial preparation, generating synthesis and ideas, and then obtaining feedback, which triggers another cycle of creative work. In the initial phase, leaders can marshal the appropriate resources that form productive inputs into the synthesis process. In the next phase of generating synthesis and ideas, leaders can help groups to engage in each of the three process facilitators. In the final phase, leaders can help groups to obtain and productively use external feedback to trigger the next cycle. We summarize our model of leading for synthesis in Figure 11.1.

Phase I: Marshalling Resources

Our model is consistent with prior research that focuses on how leaders compile collective resources to support creativity. To lead for synthesis, leaders must also establish a positive interpersonal environment in which

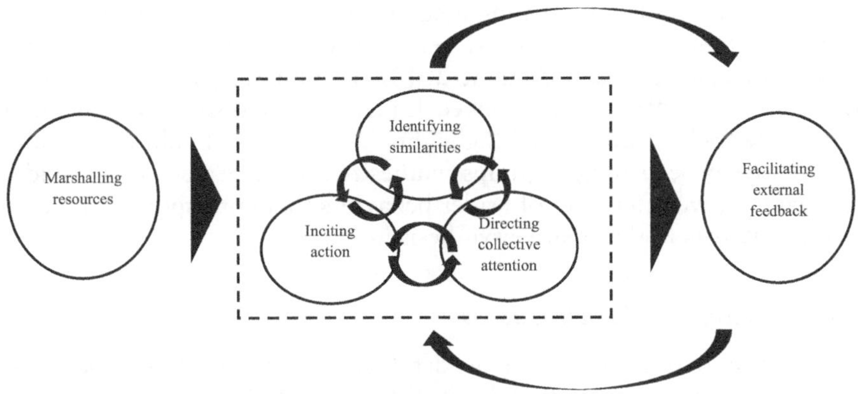

Figure 11.1 Leading for Creative Synthesis

group members feel motivated to contribute and comfortable drawing on one another's contributions (Amabile et al., 1996), and compile a group of people whose individual creative thinking skills can contribute to the group (Amabile, 1988; Taggar, 2002).

Of particular importance to the model of leading for synthesis is composing the group for creativity. This is a tricky leadership task. Variety between group members in terms of the perspectives and knowledge triggers the creative synthesis process by producing conflict and dissent, and prevents groups from reaching consensus prematurely (Harvey, 2014). Therefore, diversity in group composition is critical. Yet at the same time, synthesis is not possible if group members' knowledge structures are too distant from one another or incompatible (Cronin & Weingart, 2007). Therefore, getting the right mix of diverse group members, with an underlying thread of common interest through which to connect those diverse perspectives, is a fundamental function of leadership in the creative synthesis model.

A further critical resource for groups engaged in this process is time. Process facilitators like searching for similarities and integrating ideas takes a significant amount of cognitive effort and engagement with other group members. Therefore, leading for creative synthesis requires leaders to manage their time in two ways—leaders need to give the group adequate time to engage in the creative process as well as ensure that group members spend enough of that time working together to help build shared understanding.

Phase II: Helping Groups to Engage in the Process Facilitators Through Leader Behaviors

To help groups deeply engaged in collective creative work to achieve creative synthesis, leaders should facilitate the process of integrating perspectives into collective output. This is perhaps the most important way that our model departs from prior work. Whereas research has traditionally emphasized the importance of creating a supportive environment, such as establishing a climate for creativity (Eisenbeiss, van Knippenberg, & Boerner, 2008; Somech & Drach-Zahavy, 2013) or building psychological safety (Edmondson, 1999), or has viewed leaders as responsible for integrating inputs themselves, our model highlights how leaders should aim to direct the creative process to help groups synthesize diverse perspectives and ideas. To that end, we offer a set of leader behaviors that corresponds to the process facilitators in the creative synthesis model.

Inciting Action for Enacting Ideas

We suggest that a first set of leader behaviors involves inciting action. Groups follow a variety of styles in their early development, often beginning with planning activities (Marks, Mathieu, & Zaccaro, 2001; Gersick, 1988). However, the creative synthesis model suggests that groups should begin instead by discussing ideas in detail, making them concrete, and realizing them in some physical form like drawings, sketches, or PowerPoint documents. Those physical artefacts are likely to be basic and provisional, yet they can help groups to reveal and build collective knowledge, communicate more easily and generate positive affect. Enacting ideas also helps leaders to construct a problem in a way that group members could reconcile multiple and even competing goals and understanding (Reiter-Palmon & Illies, 2004). For instance, Harvey and Kou (2013) found that one path for collective creativity was to generate and discuss a small number of ideas in concrete detail at the beginning of a group interaction. They suggested that doing so helped groups to establish a problem framework and evaluation criteria that could be used to consider subsequent ideas.

Leaders can help groups to enact ideas in two ways. The first is to directly begin to enact ideas themselves through physical objects such as drawings, prototypes, or performances (e.g., role plays). Leaders can initiate those physical artefacts themselves. For instance, collecting pictures to develop design mood boards or opening role playing conversations. Doing so can help group members begin to visualize output and set a group norm for enacting or physically representing ideas.

However, getting group members involved in enacting ideas themselves is also critical; otherwise, the group may simply rely on the leader to enact ideas and limit their own engagement in the creative process. Therefore, a second way leaders can help groups to enact ideas is to incite action, so that group members themselves begin to move ideas toward physical representation. This could occur by promoting conversations around specific ideas or objects, asking for visualizations or requesting performances like presentations of ideas. At the same time, leaders must be careful not to allow the discussion to focus on personal and affective aspects, but rather focus on the problem at hand and its conceptualizations (Reiter-Palmon & Illies, 2004).

Alternatively, however, a variety of contextual factors can also promote action in a way likely to lead groups to enact ideas without direct intervention. In particular, leaders can influence group creativity by providing appropriate physical spaces to enable the creative process. For instance, one study found that having group members move around while generating new ideas increased information elaboration and reduced territoriality over ideas (Knight & Baer, 2014). Thus, to the extent that leaders can provide non-sedentary work spaces, they may help groups to enact ideas. Other work has associated work spaces that can act as physical representations of ideas themselves with creativity (e.g., Sutton & Hargadon, 1996; Stigliani & Ravasi, 2012). Being able to pin things on walls or reconfigure the work space allows creative groups to move around in the process of making connections between ideas, visualize and externalize their thoughts, and remember ideas that may otherwise be lost. For leaders, these contextual factors are more than simple fixes that can be easily instituted, however. They require leaders to both establish stimulating physical spaces and build a culture in which creators feel comfortable and free to move around and play with ideas. Leaders can also go a step beyond this by providing resources to begin implementing ideas early in the creative process. Idea implementation can then act as an indispensable part of idea generation (Škerlavaj et al., 2014). For instance, experimenting by implementing an idea with a small critical target population can provide feedback that facilitates further idea generation.

Directing Collective Attention

A second set of leader behaviors centers on directing collective attention toward the group's shared understanding or dominant paradigm. Focusing collective attention helps group members to cognitively engage with and develop new ideas, facilitates interaction and can help to create psychological meaning in new ideas. The advice to focus collective attention appears to run counter to the traditional idea generating approach of diverging in many directions (e.g., Paulus, 2002). What we propose is a more focused path for diverging (e.g., Cropley, 2006). Leaders are critical for facilitating that focus.

Leaders can facilitate collective attention by directing group members' attention toward collective products. During idea generation, this amounts to controlling the divergent processes of group members. We propose two ways that leaders may facilitate collective attention during idea generation. The first way is to frame ideas and cues from the group discussion to draw attention to those things that may be most engaging for the group, helping to create and sustain attention. People tend to pay more creative attention to opportunities than to threats, so framing information and tasks in terms of opportunities can help to direct members' collective attention. For instance, when leaders classify strategic issues as opportunities, it encourages subordinates to think freely, resulting in a more creative outcomes (Naidoo, 2016). People also tend to notice and attend to novel stimuli (Wu & Huberman, 2007). However, people can also overlook novel ideas that are generated by others, particularly if those ideas do not fit with their own understanding of the problem, evaluation criteria or information that is relevant for the task (Stasser & Titus, 1985; Harvey, 2013). Therefore, the leader can highlight unique ideas or contributions that have not been previously discussed by the group. Research suggests that even straightforward, explicit instructions are enough to improve creative problem solving (Reiter-Palmon, Mumford, & Threlfall, 1998), so simple directions are likely to shift collective attention.

A second way that leaders can promote collective attention is directing group members' attention toward their shared (or emerging) framework. Leaders can use the conflicting goals between group members to restrict how issues are framed (Butler & Scherer, 1997; Stokes, 1999). Evidence from a study by Mumford et al. (1996) suggests that people who focus on factual information and ignore irrelevant data produce higher quality, and more original solutions on the creative tasks. That focusing on relevant factual data serves as the benchmark to identify alternative perspectives. In other words, by creating a new framework, group members may become more adept at identifying and using alternative concepts, and leading to better collective focus and more original solutions (Baughman & Mumford, 1995).

Finally, a third way that leaders can direct collective attention during idea evaluation is by creating an environment that encourages shared emotion and protects the group from distraction (Metiu & Rothbard, 2013). Shared emotion develops through close interaction, routines and rituals (Collins, 2005). Shared emotion can be enhanced by, for instance, sharing and celebrating successes or by working together to overcome problems. Leaders can therefore manage shared emotion by creating rituals or imposing challenges that provide opportunities for groups to pull together. When groups share experiences, it can focus their attention internally to the group task.

Identifying Overlaps for Building on Similarities

A final set of leader behaviors involves helping group members to identify overlaps between their divergent perspectives and ideas. According to the creative synthesis model, building on similarities is the beginning of synthesis; groups develop those ideas they are commonly attracted to as they integrate ideas. Building on similarities facilitates creativity because similarities form the foundation for new connections, ease group interactions and provide opportunities for group members to become affectively attracted or attached to ideas.

Leaders can help groups to build on members' similarities by establishing clear goals that can be assessed with transparent evaluation standards.

Transparent evaluation criteria make it easier for group members to know how to plug their own ideas and perspectives into the collective task (Faraj & Xiao, 2006; Harvey & Mueller, 2018). Restricting the problem framework in this way has been linked to more creative solutions, because it channels group members' divergent inputs. The existence of multiple and conflicting goals places a restriction on how a problem can be framed and the type of solutions that are appropriate, as multiple goals need to be integrated and satisfied (Butler & Scherer, 1997; Stokes, 1999). The need to integrate multiple goals and take into account the restrictions that are placed because of conflicting goals may result in a more complex and innovative problem construction, leading to higher quality and more original solutions.

Alternatively, leaders can help groups to establish the common framework by encouraging group members to discuss their different perspectives to identify similarities. For ambiguous creative ideas, this task is non-trivial—on creative tasks, it is unclear how to judge what is a good idea and defining idea quality requires input from multiple stakeholders (Long-Lingo & O'Mahony, 2010). Leaders can provide that judgment, but without explicitly deciding on evaluation standards for the group. For instance, leaders can be attuned to similarities in group members' ideas and opinions, so that they can direct the group toward those overlaps. To be effective at this, leaders may need a mix of both broad and deep technical competence in the group task. Leaders need broad enough experience so that they can identify important contributions from a range of perspectives and see overlaps between group members' diverse ideas. Yet they may also need sufficiently deep technical competence for group members to view their direction as legitimate (Kacperczyk & Younkin, 2017).

Leaders can also help group members to identify similarities by encouraging group members to take on the perspectives of other group members (Hoever, Van Knippenberg, Van Ginkel, & Barkema, 2012) and to construct multiple different problem frames (Reiter-Palmon et al., 1998). They can also prompt group members to open up their thinking by giving individual members a variety of assignments, increasing the diversity within each person, which facilitates cross-domain understanding (Bunderson & Sutcliffe, 2002; Reiter-Palmon et al., 1998). Leaders can help groups to identify similarities by encouraging group members to search for other's unique and unshared information, which may provide the basis for making novel connections (Stasser & Birchmeier, 2003).

Finally, helping groups to identify overlaps and similarities may involve strategically excluding the views of some group members at different points in the creative process if their perspective is preventing integration between other group members. Long-Lingo and O'Mahony (2010) found that excluding members of the creative network from certain periods during the process was critical for synthesizing diverse inputs. We extend this notion to suggest that in closer creative teams, even some views may be temporarily excluded in order to achieve a temporary synthesis and move group discussion forward. This is helpful because not all perspectives can be reconciled (Cronin & Weingart, 2007), particularly at a given point in time (whereas, for instance, deeper interrelationships may emerge over a longer time frame; Putnam et al., 2016). However, temporarily excluding a group members' viewpoint takes significant skill to ensure that person does not feel sidelined or left out. On the contrary, their contribution is actually critical to maintaining the synthesis process. If a member of the group has been excluded at one stage, their perspective can be brought back in after a temporary synthesis is achieved so that they trigger a new dialectic process aimed at integrating their perspective with the rest of the group. That can help the group's synthesized understanding to remain dynamic.

Phase III: Feedback

Finally, the creative synthesis model relies on feedback from the external environment to fuel new conflicts that help groups to renew their shared understandings continuously over time. Feedback, therefore, forms a critical link between one dialectic process of synthesizing diverse inputs and the next dialectic process of revising and redeveloping the synthesis. Since leaders are the group's most critical link to the external environment, facilitating external feedback is an important facet of leading for synthesis. Leaders can act as brokers (Lingo & O'Mahony, 2010) or boundary spanners (Marrone, 2010) to connect groups to external parties. In particular, we propose that leaders can use their status and influence to find opportunities for the group to present emerging ideas to a variety of stakeholder audiences. Prior research has found that a leader's centrality within her network of peers is associated with higher group creativity (Venkataramani, Richter, & Clarke, 2014). Recent research further suggests that in obtaining external feedback, a critical task for leaders is to establish the appropriate social frame for interaction to take place (Fisher, Pillemer, & Amabile, 2017).

How Might Leaders Achieve These Behaviors?

Some evidence suggests that leadership itself benefits from a dialectic process (Kearney and Gebert, 2009; Kazanjian et al., 1999; Smith & Tushman, 2005). Leaders may need to embody different ends of a spectrum to successfully engage in leading for synthesis—they need to encourage conflict and divergence and bring group members together, to help groups enact ideas and to build new ways of understanding problems and to develop an internally cohesive problem framework while continuously exposing that framework to external feedback. Leading creative teams may therefore require a combination of different leadership styles. For example, inspiring members to generate novel ideas and challenging existing paradigms may require transformational leadership style. Listening to members' ideas, helping members when they need aid and creating a positive atmosphere for all group members may require a servant leadership style. Therefore, leading for synthesis requires contextual leadership, which allows the leaders to engage in different ends of the spectrum as necessary. Here we suggest that different characteristics of the creative practices itself also influence which type of leadership behaviors or leadership styles can be most effective.

We suggest that another avenue to achieve the balance of skills necessary for leading for synthesis is through shared leadership. Sharing leadership does not mean the group is leaderless, but that different group members with different skills and leadership styles could have the opportunities to provide leadership functions when the context requires so. In shared leadership, leadership functions can be distributed among team members regardless of their official role (Gibb, 1954; Pearce & Conger, 2002). With shared leadership, different leadership styles and different leadership behaviors can occur simultaneously or sequentially. That means that leaders can engage in different ends of the spectrum as necessary, but also that in doing so, they can iterate back and forth between those ends in a way that promotes synthesis at the leadership level. Sharing leadership requires the team to commit to the same goal, trust and support each other (Carson, Tesluk, & Marrone, 2007). That also suggests that shared leadership could help build shared understanding by helping to find similarities between group members. Sharing leadership could maximize the utilization of group members' skills and expertise (Friedrich et al., 2009). That means group members with different perspectives and ideas have opportunities to influence the team processes so that group members are more motivated to pay collective attentions. Moreover, sharing leadership could stimulate members to be more sensitive to the context requirements. Because in shared leadership, it is critical to justify who will emerge as a leader, who will be perceived to be a legitimate leader or who may succeed (Derue & Ashford, 2010). The context requirements provide legitimate reasons for who shall provide leadership in a given situation(Aime et al., 2013). Therefore, shared leadership may help group members deal with the ambiguity of the creative processes and have a better judgment of when to do what. Shifting roles is a form of sharing leadership (Contractor et al., 2012). It may also drive leaders to stand in each other's shoes to understand situations, prompting more perspective taking and helping them to see connections between diverse inputs.

Conclusion

Leading for creativity may be unlike other forms of leadership. It requires leaders to both encourage group members to diverge and contribute their unique perspectives and ideas, and to gently bring group members together to move their ideas forward in a common collective direction. In this chapter, we have set out a process model of leading for creative synthesis and some associated leader behaviors to facilitate that process.

Our model reiterates some aspects of leadership that have been highlighted in prior research. For instance, we suggest that leading for creative synthesis involves providing groups with resources of sufficient time and a positive group environment and establishing clear and transparent goals. We also elevate and elaborate the importance of some aspects of leadership. For example, our model emphasizes the careful management of group composition for both diversity and overlap, and engaging feedback from external audiences. These are both fundamental to creative synthesis, and so prioritized over environment and goals in our model. Finally, our model introduces some new leadership behaviors. Those include inciting action, encouraging shared emotion and carefully excluding group members at different points of the creative process.

Our model is also most relevant to teams engaged in the context of intense collective creative work—those who collectively engage with creative products over some period of time, working closely together. Teams who do not have those characteristics are likely to lack the time and resources to synthesize their diverse perspectives in a way that is productive for creativity. They may therefore require more Directive leadership in the form of setting the vision for the group. From our perspective, leading for synthesis may be seen more as a process of continuously managing uncertainty and ambiguity (Long-Lingo & O'Mahony, 2010) by allowing group members to diverge but also helping them to converge periodically. Rather than emphasizing how leaders can set the vision themselves, or create an environment where new ideas arise or a context where new ideas are resourced and implemented, our model focuses on the way that leaders can help others to integrate and synthesize ideas as they engage in a messier middle process that takes them between idea generation and idea selection.

References

Aime, F., Humphrey, S., DeRue, D. S., & Paul, J. B. 2013. The riddle of heterarchy: Power transitions in cross-functional teams. *Academy of Management Journal*, 57(2): 327–352.

Amabile, T. M. 1988. A model of creativity and innovation in organizations. In B. M. Staw & L. L. Cummings (Eds.), *Research in organizational behavior*, 10: 123–167. Greenwich, CT: JAI Press.

Amabile, T. M., Conti, R., Coon, H., Lazenby, J., & Herron, M. 1996. Assessing the work environment for creativity. *Academy of Management Journal*, 39(5): 1154–1184.

Baughman, W. A., & Mumford, M. D. 1995. Process-analytic models of creative capacities: Operations influencing the combination-and-reorganization process. *Creativity Research Journal*, 8(1): 37–62.

Binyamin, G., & Carmeli, A. 2010. Does structuring of human resource management processes enhance employee creativity? The mediating role of psychological availability. *Human Resource Management*, 49: 999–1024.

Butler, A. B., & Scherer, L. L. 1997. The effects of elicitation aids, knowledge, and problem content on option quantity and quality. *Organizational Behavior and Human Decision Processes*, 72(2): 184–202.

Bunderson, J. S., & Sutcliffe, K. M. 2002. Comparing alternative conceptualizations of functional diversity in management teams: Process and performance effects. *Academy of Management Journal*, 45(5): 875–893.

Carson, J. B., Tesluk, P. E., & Marrone, J. A. 2007. Shared leadership in teams: An investigation of antecedent conditions and performance. *Academy of Management Journal*, 50(5): 1217–1234.

Collins, R. 2005. *Interaction ritual chains*. Princeton, NJ: Princeton University Press.

Contractor, N. S., DeChurch, L. A., Carson, J., Carter, D. R., & Keegan, B. 2012. The topology of collective leadership. *Leadership Quarterly*, 23(6): 994–1011.

Cronin, M. A., & Weingart, L. R. 2007. Representational gaps, information processing, and conflict in functionally diverse teams. *Academy of Management Review*, 32: 761–773.

Cropley, A. 2006. In praise of convergent thinking. *Creativity Research Journal*, 18(3): 391–404.

Csikszentmihalyi, M. 1999. Implications of a systems perspective for the study of creativity. In R. J. Sternberg (Ed.), *Handbook of creativity*: 313–335. Cambridge: Cambridge University Press.

DeRue, D. S., & Ashford, S. J. 2010. Who will lead and who will follow ? A social process of leadership identity construction in organizations. *Academy of Management Review*, 35(4): 627–647.

Drazin, R., Glynn, M. A., & Kazanjian, R. K. 1999. Multilevel theorizing about creativity in organizations: A sensemaking perspective. *Academy of Management Review*, 24: 286–307.

Edmondson, A. 1999. Psychological safety and learning behavior in work teams. *Administrative Science Quarterly*, 44(2): 350–383.

Edmondson, A. C., & Nembhard, I. M. 2009. Product development and learning in project teams: The challenges are the benefits. *Journal of Product Innovation Management*, 26(2): 123–138.

Eisenbeiss, S. A., van Knippenberg, D., & Boerner, S. 2008. Transformational leadership and team innovation: Integrating transformational leadership and team climate models. *Journal of Applied Psychology*, 93: 1438–1446.

Elsbach, K. D., & Flynn, F. J. 2013. Creative collaboration and the self-concept: A study of toy designers. *Journal of Management Studies*, 50(4): 515–544.

Elsbach, K. D., & Kramer, R. D. 2003. Assessing creativity in Hollywood pitch meetings: Evidence for a dual-process model of creativity judgments. *Academy of Management Journal*, 46: 283–301.

Faraj, S., & Xiao, Y. 2006. Coordination in fast-response organizations. *Management Science*, 52(8): 1155–1169.

Farh, J. L., Lee, C., & Farh, C. I. C. 2010. Task conflict and team creativity: A question of how much and when. *Journal of Applied Psychology*, 95(6): 1173–1180.

Fiedler, F. E. 1978. The contingency model and the dynamics of the leadership process1. In *Advances in experimental social psychology* (Vol. 11, pp. 59–112). Academic Press.

Forbes, D. P., Borchert, P. S., Zellmer-Bruhn, M. E., & Sapienza, H. J. 2006. Entrepreneurial team formation: An exploration of new member addition. *Entrepreneurship Theory and Practice*, 30(2): 225–248.

Ford, C. M. 1996. A theory of individual creative action in multiple social domains. *Academy of Management Review*, 21(4): 1112–1142.

Fisher, C. M., Pillemer, J., & Amabile, T. M. 2017. Deep help in complex project work: Guiding and path-clearing across difficult terrain. *Academy of Management Journal*. https://doi.org/10.5465/amj.2016.0207

Friedrich, T. L., Vessey, W. B., Schuelke, M. J., Ruark, G. A., & Mumford, M. D. 2009. A framework for understanding collective leadership: The selective utilization of leader and team expertise within networks. *Leadership Quarterly*, 20(6): 933–958.

Galinsky, A. D., Magee, J. C., Gruenfeld, D. H., Whitson, J. A., & Liljenquist, K. A. 2008. Power reduces the press of the situation: Implications for creativity, conformity, and dissonance. *Journal of Personality and Social Psychology*, 95(6): 1450.

Gebert, D., Boerner, S., & Kearney, E. 2010. Fostering team innovation: Why is it important to combine opposing action strategies? *Organization Science*, 21(3): 593–608.

Gersick, C. J. G. 1988. Time and transition in work teams: Toward a new model of group development. *Academy of Management Journal*, 31(1): 9–41.

Gibb, C. A. 1954. Leadership. In G. Lindzey (Ed.), *Handbook of social psychology*, 2: 877–917. Reading, MA: Addison-Wesley.

Gilson, L. L., Mathieu, J. E., Shalley, C. E., & Ruddy, T. M. 2005. Creativity and standardization: Complementary or conflicting drivers of team effectiveness? *Academy of Management Journal*, 48(3): 521–531.

Goldenberg, J., Mazursky, D., & Solomon, S. 1999. The fundamental templates of quality ads. *Marketing Science*, 18: 333–351.

Hargadon, A. B., & Bechky, B. A. 2006. When collections of creatives become creative collectives: A field study of problem solving at work. *Organization Science*, 17: 484–500.

Harrison, S. H., & Rouse, E. D. 2014. Let's dance! Elastic coordination in creative group work: A qualitative study of modern dancers. *Academy of Management Journal*, 57(5):1256–1283.

Harrison, S. H., & Rouse, E. D. 2015. An inductive study of feedback interactions over the course of creative projects. *Academy of Management Journal*, 58(2): 375–404.

Harvey, S. 2013. A different perspective: The multiple effects of deep level diversity on group creativity. *Journal of Experimental Social Psychology*, 49: 822–832.

Harvey, S. 2014. Creative synthesis: Exploring the process of extraordinary group creativity. *Academy of Management Review*, 39(3): 324–343.

Harvey, S., Currall, S. C., & Helland Hammer, T. 2017. Decision diversion in diverse teams: Findings from inside a corporate boardroom. *Academy of Management Discoveries*, 3(4): 358–381.

Harvey, S., & Kou, C. Y. 2013. Collective engagement in creative tasks: The role of evaluation in the creative process in groups. *Administrative Science Quarterly*, 58: 346–386.

Harvey, S., & Mueller, J. 2018. Staying alive: Towards a diverging consensus model for keeping novel ideas alive over the course of group discussion. Working paper.

Hennessey, B. A. 2004. The social psychology of creativity: The beginnings of a multicultural perspective. In *Creativity: When east meets west* (pp. 201–226).

Hoever, I. J., Van Knippenberg, D., Van Ginkel, W. P., & Barkema, H. G. 2012. Fostering team creativity: Perspective taking as key to unlocking diversity's potential. *Journal of Applied Psychology*, 97(5): 982.

Kacperczyk, A., & Younkin, P. 2017. The paradox of breadth: The tension between experience and legitimacy in the transition to entrepreneurship. *Administrative Science Quarterly*, 62(4): 731–764.

Kearney, E., & Gebert, D. 2009. Managing diversity and enhancing team outcomes: The promise of transformational leadership. *Journal of Applied Psychology*, 94(1): 77.

Knight, A. P., & Baer, M. 2014. Get up, stand up: The effects of a non-sedentary workspace on information elaboration and group performance. *Social Psychological and Personality Science*, 5(8): 910–917.

Lingo, E. L., & O'Mahony, S. 2010. Nexus work: Brokerage on creative projects. *Administrative Science Quarterly*, 55: 47–81.

Mainemelis, C., Kark, R., & Epitropaki, O. 2015. Creative leadership: A multi-context conceptualization. *The Academy of Management Annals*, 9(1): 393–482.

Marks, M. A., Mathieu, J. E., & Zaccaro, S. J. 2001. A temporally based framework and taxonomy of team processes. *Academy of Management Review*, 26(3): 356–376.

Marrone, J. A. 2010. Team boundary spanning: A multi-level review of past research and proposals for the future. *Journal of Management*, 36(4): 911–940.

Metiu, A., & Rothbard, N. P. 2013. Task bubbles, artifacts, shared emotion, and mutual focus of attention: A comparative study of the microprocesses of group engagement. *Organization Science*, 24(2): 455–475.

Morgeson, F. P., DeRue, D. S., & Karam, E. P. 2010. Leadership in teams: A functional approach to understanding leadership structures and processes. *Journal of Management*, 36(1): 5–39.

Muira, A., & Hida, M. 2004. Synergy between diversity and similarity in group idea generation. *Small Group Research*, 35: 240–264.

Mumford, M. D., Baughman, W. A., Threlfall, K. V., Supinski, E. P., & Costanza, D. P. 1996. Process-based measures of creative problem-solving skills: I. Problem construction. *Creativity Research Journal*, 9(1): 63–76.

Naidoo, L. J. 2016. Leader opportunity versus threat verbal framing and nonverbal emotional expressions impact followers' creative performance. *The Leadership Quarterly*, 27(6): 869–882.

Nembhard, I. M., & Edmondson, A. C. 2006. Making it safe: The effects of leader inclusiveness and professional status on psychological safety and improvement efforts in health care teams. *Journal of Organizational Behavior*, 27(7): 941–966.

Oc, B. 2018. Contextual leadership: A systematic review of how contextual factors shape leadership and its outcomes. *Leadership Quarterly*, 29(1): 218–235.

Paulus, Paul B. 2002. Different ponds for different fish: A contrasting perspective on team innovation. *Applied Psychology: An International Review*, 51(3): 394–399.

Pearce, C. L., & Conger, J. A. 2002. *Shared leadership: Reframing the hows and whys of leadership*. Thousands Oaks, CA: Sage Publications.

Putnam, L. L., Fairhurst, G. T., & Banghart, S. 2016. Contradictions, dialectics, and paradoxes in organizations: A constitutive approach. *The Academy of Management Annals*, 10(1): 65–171.

Reiter-Palmon, R., Herman, A. E., & Yammarino, F. J. 2008. Creativity and cognitive processes: Multi-level linkages between individual and team cognition. In *Multi-level issues in creativity and innovation*: 203–267. Bingley: Emerald Group Publishing Limited.

Reiter-Palmon, R., & Illies, J. J. 2004. Leadership and creativity: Understanding leadership from a creative problem-solving perspective. *Leadership Quarterly*, 15(1): 55–77.

Reiter-Palmon, R., Mumford, M. D., & Threlfall, K. V. 1998. Solving everyday problems creatively: The role of problem construction and personality type. *Creativity Research Journal*, 11(3): 187–197.

Shalley, C. E. 1991. Effects of productivity goals, creativity goals, and personal discretion on individual creativity. *Journal of Applied Psychology*, 76(2): 179.

Škerlavaj, M., Černe, M., & Dysvik, A. 2014. I get by with a little help from my supervisor: Creative-idea generation, idea implementation, and perceived supervisor support. *The Leadership Quarterly*, 25(5): 987–1000.

Smith, W. K., & Tushman, M. L. 2005. Managing strategic contradictions: A top management model for managing innovation streams. *Organization Science*, 16(5): 522–536.

Somech, A., & Drach-Zahavy, A. 2013. Translating team creativity to innovation implementation: The role of team composition and climate for innovation. *Journal of Management*, 39(3): 684–708.

Srikanth, K., Harvey, S., & Peterson, R. 2016. A dynamic perspective on diverse teams: Moving from the dual-process model to a dynamic coordination-based model of diverse team performance. *The Academy of Management Annals*, 10(1): 453–493.

Stasser, G., & Birchmeier, Z. 2003. Group creativity and collective choice. Group creativity: Innovation through collaboration, pp.85–109.

Stasser, G., & Titus, W. 1985. Pooling of unshared information in group decision making: Biased information sampling during discussion. *Journal of Personality and Social Psychology*, 48(6): 1467.

Stasser, G., & Titus, W. 1987. Effects of information load and percentage of shared information on the dissemination of unshared information during group discussion. *Journal of Personality Social Psychology*, 53(1): 53–81.

Staw, B. M. 2009. Is group creativity really an oxymoron? Some thoughts on bridging the cohesion-creativity divide. In Elizabeth A. Mannix, Jack A. Goncalo, & Margaret A. Neale (Eds.), *Creativity in groups: Research on managing groups and teams*, 12: 311–323. Bingley: Emerald Group Publishing Limited.

Stigliani, I., & Ravasi, D. 2012. Organizing thoughts and connecting brains: Material practices and the transition from individual to group-level prospective sensemaking. *Academy of Management Journal*, 55(5): 1232–1259.

Stokes, P. 1999. Novelty. In M. Runco & S. Pritzker (Eds.), *Encyclopedia of creativity*, vol. 2: 297–304. London: Academic Press.

Sutton, R. I., & Hargadon, A. 1996. Brainstorming groups in context: Effectiveness in a product design firm. *Administrative Science Quarterly*, 41: 685–718.

Taggar, S. 2002. Individual creativity and group ability to use individual creative resources: A multilevel model. *Academy of Management Journal*, 45: 315–220.

Venkataramani, V., Richter, A. W., & Clarke, R. 2014. Creative benefits from well-connected leaders: Leader social network ties as facilitators of employee radical creativity. *Journal of Applied Psychology*, 99(5): 966–375.

Watson, W. E., Kumar, K., & Michaelson, L. K. 1993. Cultural diversity's impact on interaction process and performance: Comparing homogeneous and diverse task groups. *Academy of Managment Journal*, 36: 590–603.

Werr, A., & Stjernberg, T. 2003. Exploring management consulting firms as knowledge systems. *Organization Studies*, 24(6): 881–908.

Woodman, R. W., Sawyer, J. E., & Griffin, R. W. 1993. Toward a theory of organizational creativity. *Academy of Management Review*, 18: 293–322.

Wu, F., & Huberman, B. A. 2007. Novelty and collective attention. *PNAS*, 104: 17599–17601.

Zaccaro, S. J., Rittman, L. A., & Marks, M. A. 2001. Team leadership. *Leadership Quarterl*, 12: 451–483.

12 Brokerage and Creative Leadership

Process, Practice, and Possibilities

Elizabeth Long Lingo

Introduction

> *The label wanted one thing; the artist another. . . . So I found myself acting as the referee. . . . It's tricky, if I butt heads with the artist, I get fired. If I don't butt heads with the artist, the label fires me. I was up a creek. I also have allegiance to me, where I don't believe this is a good song. That's the hardest part, as producer, you're hired to have a strong musical opinion and with three points of view, none of them lining up. . . . I didn't know what to do.*
>
> —*Nashville Music Producer*

What do leaders developing global climate change solutions, scientists translating their scientific discoveries into viable enterprises, and music producers creating billion-dollar global cultural products have in common? These individuals are navigating and advancing a new form of creative leadership—one that involves not only guiding and eliciting creative ideas from others but also integrating differing contributions, perspectives, and interests—including their own. As the opening quote suggests, Integrative creative leadership differs in important ways from creative leadership focused on facilitating or fostering the creativity of subordinates, or directing others to advance one's own creative ideas (Mainemelis, Kark, & Epitropaki, 2015). First, Integrative creative leadership focuses on the interplay between generating creative ideas *and* synthesizing those ideas into an implementable, cohesive whole (Harvey, 2014). Integration demands subtle negotiation, and leaders must strategically finesse how they edit and winnow ideas while also maintaining the creative energy and commitment necessary to co-create and implement novel outcomes. Second, Integrative creative leaders often need to bring together a constellation of content creators, technical experts, clients, stewards, and resource gatekeepers from across a network, rather than from within a single organization (Lundin et al., 2015). As a result, competing interests, assumptions, and perspectives driven by differing occupational and organizational affiliation may further complicate both the co-creation and integration of ideas. Finally, Integrative creative leaders often lack formal authority over those involved (Mainemelis, Kark, & Epitropaki, 2015). The roles each party plays are ambiguous and integrative leaders play a central role in helping experts carve out these roles as the venture evolves (Lingo & O'Mahony, 2010). Not all contributors are involved in all aspects of the creative process and so Integrative creative leaders must also navigate the fluid and evolving involvement of parties.

Integrative creative leaders can have a range of titles—project or country managers, producers, directors, entrepreneurs, event planners, or VP of policy development. What is the nature of the collective creative process they lead? What challenges do these leaders face in their work? How do Integrative creative leaders navigate the challenges of eliciting and synthesizing resources, expertise, and commitment from across a network? In this chapter, I bring insights from research on creative brokerage in networks to inform our understanding of Integrative creative leadership. In the following sections, I first provide a brief theoretical introduction to creative brokerage and how it might inform Integrative creative leadership. I then animate the nature of Integrative creative leadership by presenting findings from my three-year ethnographic study of music producers working within the Nashville country music industry. I illustrate the collective creative process that producers navigate, the challenges they face, and the creative brokerage practices they use to respond to these challenges. I conclude the chapter by looking forward—offering several streams of future research possibilities.

What Is Creative Brokerage?

Scholars have long been interested in the network, or structure of relationships, among individuals and organizations (Borgatti & Foster, 2003; Burt, 2000; Fombrun, 1982; Granovetter, 1973; Kilduff & Tsai, 2003; Powell, 1990; Tichy, 1980). Within these networks, "brokers" play an especially important role since they are the unique link—or "span structural holes"—between unconnected actors (Burt, 1992, 2000). Scholars have conceived of brokers as the *tertius gaudens*, or the "third who benefits" (Simmel, 1950) or extracts advantage by spanning structural holes (Burt, 1992, 2000). As a *tertius gaudens*, brokers advance creativity through extracting good ideas from others, while only selectively sharing information with unconnected parties (Burt, 2004). While the *tertius gaudens* can enjoy career advancement, power, and control by leveraging their position in this way, they often fail to develop the commitment and trust needed to foster *collective* creativity and implementation of good ideas (Fleming, Mingo, & Chen, 2007; Fleming & Waguespack, 2007; Ibarra, Kilduff, & Tsai, 2005; Obstfeld, 2005).

Brokers can also span structural holes by being the "third who joins," or *tertius iungens* (Obstfeld, 2005). In this form of brokerage, the *tertius iungens* develops and advances innovative ideas by combining and recombining existing technology (Hargadon & Sutton, 1997), or by connecting people and ideas (rather than keeping them apart) to create new possibilities (Obstfeld, 2005, 2017). Brokers enacting a *tertius iungens* approach need not garner distrust from those they connect as their reputation and power comes from successfully bridging and bringing together "combinations of people, ideas, and resources" (Obstfeld, 2005: 103). While the *tertius gaudens* conception of brokerage focuses on the advantages enjoyed by brokers who extract unique information and leverage the disconnect between social contacts, the *tertius iungens* perspective emphasizes how creative inputs can be brought together to forge new creative outcomes.

Both conceptions on their own, however, fail to convey the challenges faced by Integrative creative leaders. The *tertius gaudens* fails to develop the trust and commitment necessary for collective creativity and implementation, while the *tertius iungens* fails to address the negotiated nature of integrating the differing interests and perspectives of those involved. Further, while both approaches involve translating network position into power for creative ends, neither resolves a fundamental interdependence faced by integrative creative leaders. Even as they exercise power, these leaders cannot benefit from their position on their own and must harness others' ideas, resources, and expertise. Individual advantage and the collective creative outcome are inextricably intertwined. As described by Ibarra, Kilduff, and Tsai (2005: 367), "The individual pursuit of network advantage detracts from or contributes to the emergence of public [collective] goods."

Burt (2004) identified four types of creative brokerage that could foster collective value: (1) making parties on either side of the structural hole aware of the other, (2) transferring knowledge from one group to another, (3) drawing analogies from one group to another and (4) synthesizing ideas from multiple sources (355). This fourth level of creative brokerage most closely informs our understanding of Integrative creative leadership. However, for several reasons, it is the most difficult to achieve. For example, translation of knowledge is necessary to enable different specialists to understand, absorb, and put others' ideas into practice (Barley, 2015; Bechky, 2003a, b; Hargadon & Bechky, 2006). Yet moving from knowledge transfer to synthesis is much more difficult as specialists need to improvise, transform, and build upon each other's expertise and ideas (Carlile & Rebentisch, 2003; Kaplan, 2011; Murray & O'Mahony, 2007). Thus, Integrative creative brokerage requires fostering an environment that encourages collective experimentation and risk-taking even as ideas are being evaluated (Harrison & Rouse, 2015; Harvey & Kou, 2013), and prevents the premature discarding of potentially fruitful alternatives. Integrative creative brokerage is also difficult to achieve because it involves the negotiation of conflicting interests (Carlile, 2004), and as described by Uzzi and Spiro in their study of Broadway musicals (2005: 458), "Full days of collaborative brainstorming, the sharing of ideas, joint problem-solving, difficult editing as well as flashpoints of celebration and commiseration." Integrative brokerage, then, requires deft management of egos and expectations so that people will remain engaged, even after their ideas are left behind.

In their analysis of Nashville country music producers, Lingo and O'Mahony (2010) offered insight into how creative brokers might use their role to navigate these tensions and advance creative ideas from initial conception to final synthesis. They detail the challenges inherent to integrative brokerage work, and the practices producers use to respond. More specifically, they find that integrative creative brokers face three forms of ambiguity in their work: (1) ambiguity over quality, or what constitutes success; (2) ambiguous occupational jurisdictions, or control over decisions or whose expertise should prevail; and (3) ambiguity regarding process, or how the collective creative work should proceed. Further, they show how over the course of the collective creative process, producers engage in a distinct form of relational integration work that weaves together both *tertius gaudens* and *tertius iungens* approaches to manage these three types of ambiguity, elicit creative contributions, and maintain the commitment of those involved. In the next section, I provide excerpts from Lingo and O'Mahony's (2010: 57–74) findings to illuminate how integrative creative brokerage unfolds in practice.

Integrative Creative Brokerage in Action

Independent producers are central players within the Nashville country music industry, brokering interactions among an array of parties—record label personnel, songwriters and song publishers, artists, their managers and family, engineers, and musicians. The producers' goal? To take the singer-songwriters' "three chords and the truth" and turn it into gold- or platinum-selling records or songs. Producers advance their projects through four primary phases of the collective creative process, including (1) *resource gathering*, (2) *defining project boundaries*, (3) *creative production* and (4) *final synthesis*, each with their own constellation of participants (as shown in Figure 12.1). While the process model may suggest a linear progression through these phases, producers found themselves repeatedly circling back to prior stages throughout the project when new songs or performances were needed.

Lingo and O'Mahony (2010) found that as producers guide their projects from resource gathering and generating ideas to final synthesis, they encounter the three forms of ambiguity inherent to the collective creative process. Managing these forms of ambiguity are a central part of their integrative brokerage work. Unlike uncertainty, ambiguity is not resolved by more information, but rather is a negotiated resolution process. "The problem in ambiguity is not that the real world is imperfectly understood and that more information will remedy that. The problem is that information may not resolve misunderstandings" (Weick, 1995: 92). While ambiguity can be used strategically to allow multiple simultaneous interpretations

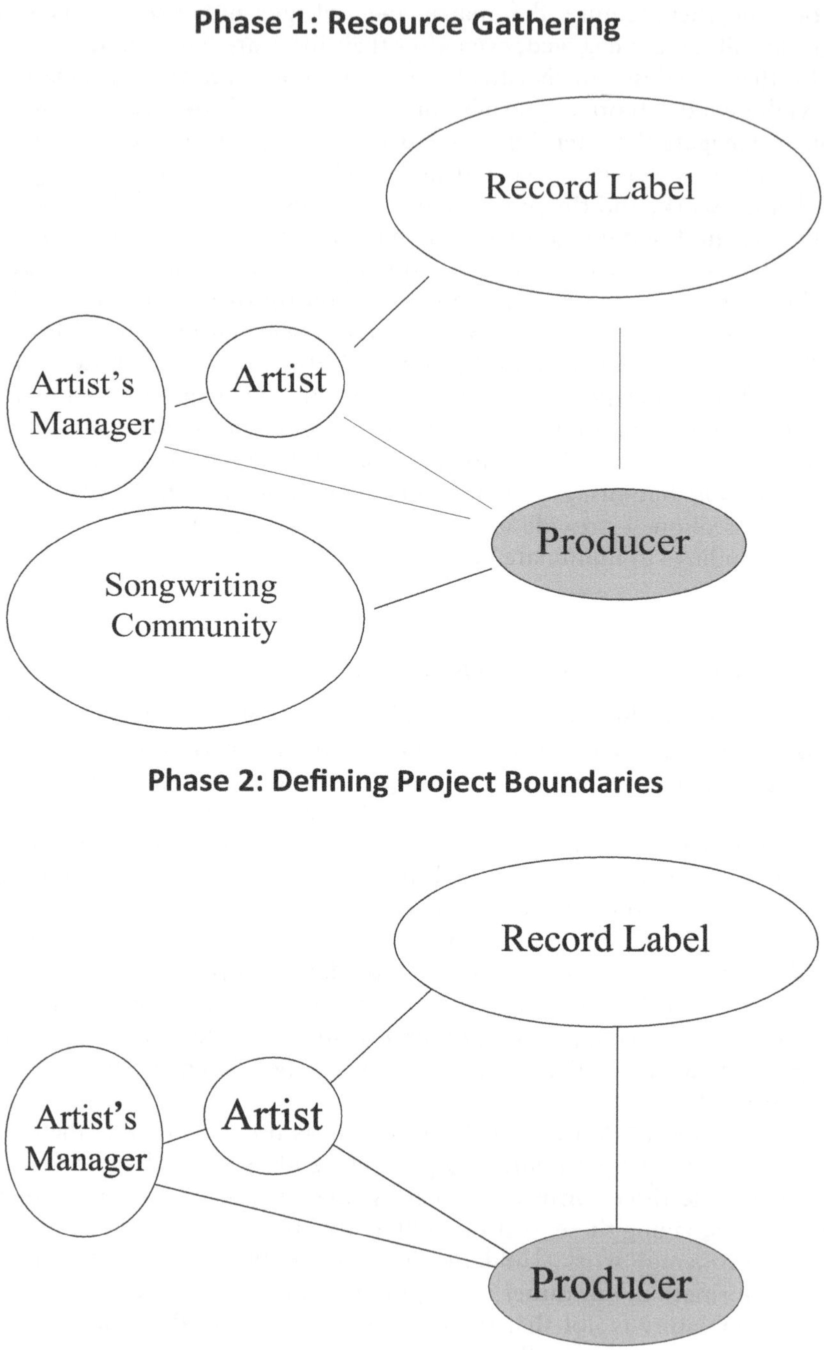

Figure 12.1 Participants by Project Phase

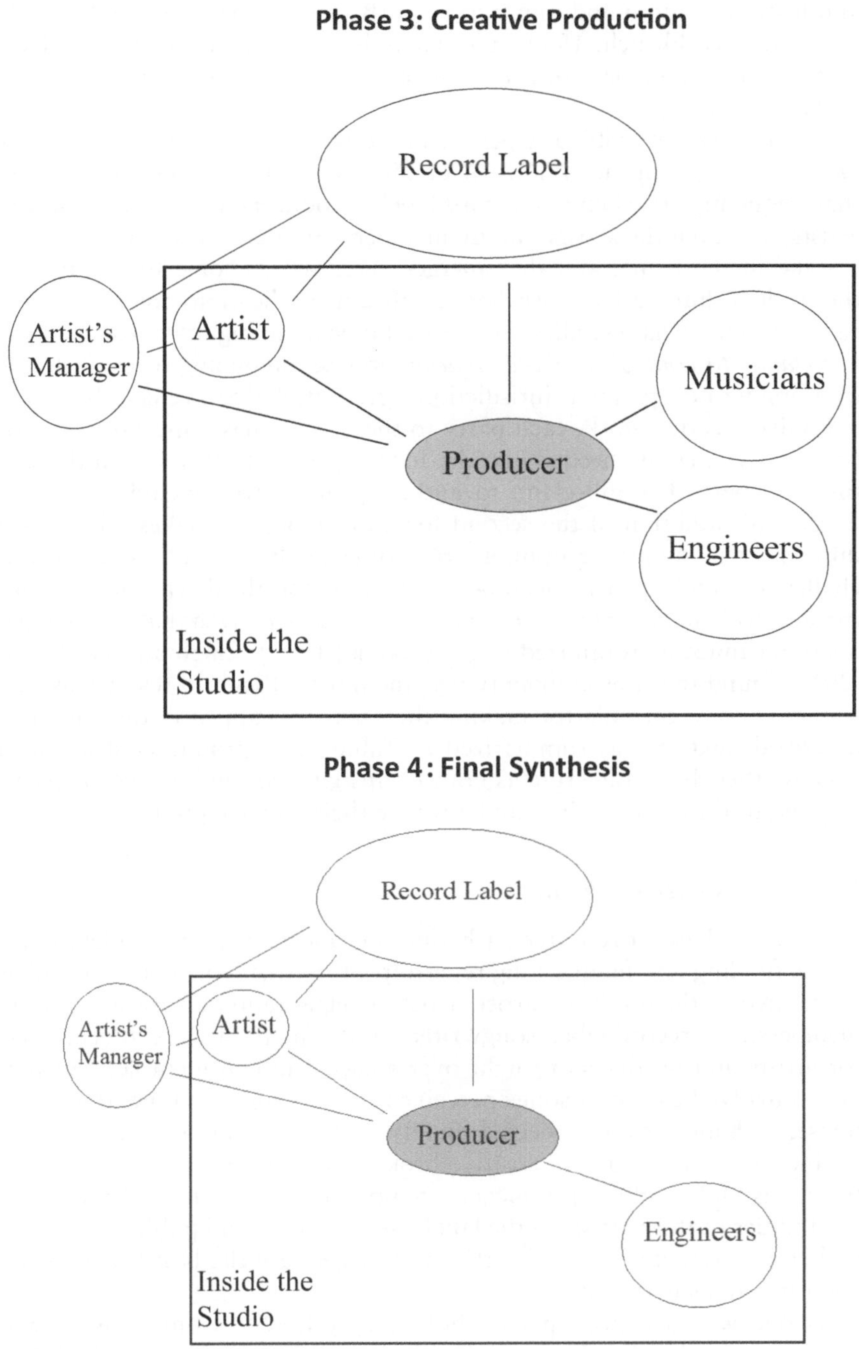

Figure 12.1 (Continued)

and foster invention and improvization (Barley, Leonardi, & Bailey, 2012; Contractor & Ehrlich, 1993), ultimately leaders need to develop a shared understanding and plan for action as part of the integration process (Weick, 1995, 1998).

The first type of ambiguity pertains to *what the creative process will produce*, or competing definitions of quality or what will constitute success, that frequently arise between record labels, producers, musicians, engineers, artists, and even the artists' family members and managers. Each party has a stake in the game, and the emergent creative outcome forged through the leaders' Integrative work has significant implications for each party's career and financial viability. The second type of ambiguity pertains to *who has claims to control over the creative process*, stemming from unclear or overlapping occupational jurisdictions (Abbott, 1988; Bechky, 2003a). In collective creative work, each party to the process has important expertise or resources that are needed in order for the project to succeed. At the same time, no party has full claim to authority or control, including the producer. This addition of the second form of ambiguity makes adjudicating differences in subjective opinions regarding quality or success even more challenging and open to negotiation. Finally, the third type of ambiguity pertains to *how the creative work is to be achieved*, given that creative production cannot be routinized (e.g., Amabile, 1996). Lingo and O'Mahony (2010) found that this ambiguity was the most difficult to resolve, as there simply is not a formula for making the "magic" happen in the studio. As described next and as summarized in Table 12.1, producers strategically exercise their brokerage role as both *tertius gaudens* and *tertius iungens* to respond to these ambiguities and advance their creative projects.

Phase 1: Resource Gathering

In the first phase of resource gathering, producers attempt to identify and secure funding and unique song repertoires for artists to record. This phase could involve the producer, artist, artist manager (and perhaps artist family members), the record label, songwriters, and song publishers. It is common for artists and producers to fight over songs, and considerable maneuvering is involved to access songs perceived to have high hit potential. In this phase, ambiguity over perceived quality and what will be a "hit" is most problematic for integrative creative brokers. Given the intense competition for songs and funding, producers attempt to identify and sell the unique capabilities of their artists to the labels, songwriters, and publishing houses, and convince them why their artist and project are the best bet for scarce and often treasured resources.

As one would expect, parties hold very different estimations of what is quality or what would create success—both in terms of the viability of potential artists, and the chemistry between artists and certain songs. For

Table 12.1 Integrative Creative Brokerage as Integrative Creative Leadership: Process and Practice

	Phase 1: Resource Gathering	*Phase 2: Defining Project Boundaries*	*Phase 3: Creative Production*	*Phase 4: Final Synthesis*
Key challenge in phase	Assemble set of songs and build perception that the artist will be commercially successful	Winnow down set of songs to be recorded without disenfranchising parties needed for project	Foster and elicit extraordinary creative contributions with commercial potential	Harvest, synthesize, and modify creative contributions into coherent, commercially viable final product
Result that triggers next phase	Song portfolio and label backing	Loose agreement on set of songs that are worth recording	Set of recorded tracks	Artist and label approval
Types of Ambiguity Present				
	Ambiguous quality metrics	**Ambiguous quality metrics**	**Ambiguous quality metrics**	**Ambiguous quality metrics**
		Ambiguous occupational jurisdictions	**Ambiguous occupational jurisdictions**	**Ambiguous occupational jurisdictions**
			Ambiguous transformation process	
Integrative Creative Brokerage Practices				
	TI* practices bring people together to develop shared understanding of quality and success	TI practices bring people together to develop shared understanding of quality and success	TI practices bring people together to develop shared aesthetic and foster environment that encourages creative risk-taking, collective experimentation, and transformation of ideas	TI practices build shared understanding of what will foster commercial success
	TG practice proactively attempts to limit negative perceptions of the project in case of unexpected difficulties	TG practices manage differing perceptions of quality and competing claims to control over creative decisions	TG practices manage competing claims to control over creative decisions and threats to creative energy	TG practices manage competing claims to control over creative decisions and buffer final synthesis

*TI = practices consistent with the *tertius iungens* approach; TG = practices consistent with the *tertius gaudens* approach.

Source: Adapted from Lingo and O'Mahony (2010: 59).

example, Sarah describes how she works with her artists to understand what songs would work best for them:

> [The artist] might be looking at it in terms of . . . what song they like to sing the most, but I'm looking at it as more of a business proposition. What will the market bear? What will the label get the most excited about? If the label already has three people on their roster who have these kinds of singles out right now, they aren't going to be as interested. What they don't have is someone who did a ballad like you just did.

Producers use both *tertius iungens* and *tertius gaudens* practices to manage this first form of ambiguity, bringing people together and proactively acting to keep them apart to shape and maintain a shared understanding of merit and possibility.

Building Legitimacy

Hank discovered his latest top-five act through a friend who is a booking agent. After seeing the artist play live in concert, he approached the artist's manager after the show to communicate his enthusiasm for the act and to offer his services and influence in securing a contract for the artists with a major label. To obtain a label deal, Hank needed to intrigue the labels in the artist and enhance the artist's credibility, or legitimacy, as a worthwhile risk. Here he describes how he strategically uses the *tertius iungens* practice of building legitimacy to get the artist a label deal:

> I got the showcase moved to a larger club. I got the head of the [Century] record label and the head of A&R and another label [Fantasy Records] to the showcase. And the band was smart enough to bring a truckload of fans to plant in the crowd. So when they hit the stage the place went unglued.
>
> And the [century] record label people are going, "What the hell is this?"
>
> And I'm just chuckling to myself, "This is amazing."
>
> The head of A&R, he said to me, "Who else is here?" Then he looked back at [Fantasy label head who was also present].

Hank carefully orchestrates a showcase, where the artist can perform live, as a means to establish legitimacy for his artist. He brings together the previously unconnected artist and label personnel in a way that highlights the artist's talent and "allure." Bringing together multiple label personnel to the same event also allows the label personnel to see how others are reacting to the artist. Hank further enhances this effect by talking to label personnel one-on-one and communicating that other parties are involved and interested. Once another label is involved, the urgency to sign an act increases.

The band putting on a great show and bringing its fan club to the showcase only intensifies this dynamic.

Fostering a Generative Network

Producers also need to ensure a strong pipeline of songs and funding for their projects, amidst fierce competition from other artists, labels, and producers in the network. To build and maintain a generative network with label personnel, song publishers, songwriters, and musicians who might be sources of the "best songs" and funding, producers put considerable effort into the *tertius iungens* practice of fostering a generative network. Producers meet with their network constantly and wine and dine songwriters and publishers to share their latest artists and what they may be looking for in songs in the future. The goal is to be the first to be called when a hit song is in the works. If producers decide not to use a particular song, they make a special point of connecting with the writer to explain why the producer, label, or the artist did not choose that song for the project. As Hank continues, "So I need to call the [songwriters and publishers] back personally. Say, 'I played it for her [the artist], but it didn't ring her bell. Keep them coming.' I have to. It's the relationship." Even as he turns songs down, Hank strokes the egos of his songwriting network, and asks them to continue to share new songs with him. This level of follow-up involves considerable time and energy given the thousands of songs that cross Hank's desk for each project he is working on. As Hank explains, "I have to go through thousands of junk. And I have to write nice things to people, when maybe I don't feel like it." Hank fears that if he does not do this, he will be cut off from the future supply of "good" songs.

Creating Slack

As they secure resources for their projects, producers also keep in mind future negotiations over quality and success that might unfold during later phases of the creative production and synthesis. Any signal that the project was not thriving could lead fickle investors or marketers to get cold feet, or to want more creative control over the project. As a result, producers proactively engage in the *tertius gaudens* practice of creating slack so that they will have the buffer needed to maintain the positive spin around their projects. As one star producer describes,

> You want to be in a situation where, "I over budgeted this thing by a third. They're a great artist, the selecting went well, they got in and out of the studio in record time." Those are the stories that we want to tell. Not that "we're struggling with the vocals; we've had a cold; we've had to dump all the vocals we've got; we're starting over, and we're flying to

> Key West next week to do vocals to dry this artist out since they've had a cold for six weeks."

After securing songs to be recorded and funding for their project, producers move onto the next stage of defining project boundaries.

Phase 2: Defining Project Boundaries

Defining project boundaries comprises casting musicians and engineers for recording sessions, and sometimes winnowing more than 3,000 songs down to the 15 songs recorded in the studio. Defining project boundaries involves producers, artists, artist managers, and if labels are involved, heads of label, and artists and repertoire (A&R) persons. During this phase a second form of ambiguity arises pertaining to who should have control over creative decisions and whose expertise should prevail. As one major-label producer describes,

> Even this last record, there was a song the label head wanted [the artist] to cut, and nobody liked it. Nobody, except the label head. . . . It was like, what was he thinking? Plus he's not a music guy; he's a marketing guy. . . . In that case, [the producer] just said, "I'm not recording this. The artist hates it. Nobody likes it but you."

In the end, this particular song was not recorded but the producer went back to the record label and allowed them to include another song on the album in order to retain their support for the project. As this example makes clear, integrative creative brokerage is much more than simply generating ideas. It involves leveraging the temporal nature of the collective creative process, and both *tertius gaudens* and *tertius gaudens* practices to effectively negotiate differences without undermining the commitment and imagination parties bring to the process, as further described next.

Bracketing and Checking In

The veneer of checking in belies producers' perceptions of expertise and control vis-à-vis other participants, particularly label personnel. Producers use the *tertius gaudens* practice of bracketing and checking in to make label personnel feel included when in fact they are excluded from interactions over the emergent esthetic. Producers might check in with the labels solely to provide status details or incidental information, rather than engaging them in the decision-making process. As one producer describes,

> It's important to be very proactive in including them [the label] in the process. At least to the point of giving them information if not involving

> them in the actual creative process itself. At least keep them informed of the progress.

Producers bracket and check in with labels to manage their impression of the project and maintain their enthusiasm for the project.

Deferring Decisions

At some point, the producers do need to bring all the parties together to make decisions over which songs would be recorded. Even then, producers utilize the *tertius iungens* practice of deferring decisions to strategically delay choices in order to avoid conflict, help parties save face, and maintain as many creative options as possible. For example, Larry, an up-and-coming producer brought together the artist and label personnel to select songs to be recorded. They agreed on six songs, but could not reach agreement on three particular songs that the artist felt strongly about. At this point, Larry stepped in and said, "Let's keep these on the table and revisit it later." This allowed time for everyone to work toward a more shared understanding of quality, without raising the stakes over who would control the decision. As another producer recalls, a song may be in the "deferred pile" for a "long, long time. It was one of the artist's least favorite but the A&R person and I loved it. Now that song is one of the artist's favorites."

Once songs are chosen, producers work with labels and artists to decide on the choice of musicians, engineers, and recording studio that would work best for each of the songs and the project overall. Once these decisions have been made, the project moves into the next phase of creative production and synthesis.

Phase 3: Creative Production

In creative production, the producer may bring together upward of 20 people in the recording studio, including the artist and their family and/or managers, engineers, lead and bass guitarists, fiddlers, pianists, drummers, background vocalists, and label personnel, each with their own agenda and sense of what will make a hit. The producer's goal is to elicit creative ideas, encourage others to perform their best without overpowering each other, and guide performances toward a cohesive whole. As Sarah explains,

> You don't want the players stepping on each other's toes playing. If I don't want the musicians getting in the way of the vocal here I have to bring them down in the right spot to let the vocalist shine. I need certain instrumentation in certain places so it creates the attitude needed for the song and doesn't destroy something else. . . . A lot of it is directing

> which instrumentation is going to happen where in the song and what impact it [a particular player's performance] is going to have.

In creative production, ambiguity over quality and claims to expertise continues, while a third type of ambiguity arises: ambiguity regarding how creative work should be achieved. As one producer describes,

> Sometimes you get in the studio and for whatever reason the song's not the magic you thought it was going to be. The song can still be wonderful; the artist can still be wonderful. . . . If there was a formula, we'd all be doing it more often. But there's another element to the room that you can't always control.

Producers use both *tertius gaudens* and *tertius iungens* practices in rapid combination during this phase to achieve generation and synthesis of ideas.

Crafting Role Boundaries

As they elicit and synthesize creative contributions amidst the increasingly complex web of ambiguity, producers attempt to prevent unintended slights or conflict that may undermine the creative energy and willingness of participants to collectively experiment and improvise off each other. To manage this dynamic, producers proactively engage in the *tertius gaudens* practice of crafting role boundaries, especially with participants who might undermine the emotional vibe of the recording session. As this producer describes:

> With the artist, I have to be clear with them. They have their time. When I'm working with them beforehand, that's their time. But when I'm in the studio, I tell them upfront, "You don't say anything to the musicians. I'm going to be thinking about what you want, but it's for your own good. When we're in the tracking session, it's not about you. I need to be able to focus on the players and what is going on. I have to be able to keep the energy up." And they might have their idea of, "Well, I came down here, and I have played in concerts so I'm just going to come down here and run the session. And my brother, he's a guitarist, and he said I should do this, so that's what I want to tell the session player." Oh no. That's not going to happen.

Affirming Direction

Even as they limit communication between participants, producers provide in-the-moment critical feedback on performances—encouraging artists and musicians to refine their performances, while also helping them save face and remain open to new creative suggestions. To achieve this, producers engage in the *tertius iungens* practice of publicly affirming the contributions and expertise of contributors while also guiding them toward a shared aesthetic. Affirming direction involves providing musical direction through public praise rather than criticism. For an example, Josh learned from the legendary producer Chet Atkins how to provide feedback to his musicians, and then publicly praise and credit them for those same ideas. Josh recalls how he first became aware of this technique when it was used on him as a session musician: "I played what he showed me, and when I did that, he said over the speaker, 'I love what you're doing. . . . That's great'—as if I had come up with the idea myself." Josh later applied this practice in his own work as a producer: "You want to make the musicians look good to each other. You have the best and most respected musicians in the world."

Absorbing Challenges

Producers use the *tertius gaudens* practice of absorbing challenges when their proactive efforts to reduce tension are not successful. Producers absorb tension when participants' comments challenge other musicians' expertise or threaten the positive dynamic fostered among session participants. Producers might also act as emotional and informational gatekeepers to prevent potentially problematic comments made by one participant from being heard by other participants. As this producer describes, she leverages the setup of the recording space and available technology to achieve this *tertius gaudens* practice:

> Well, I let the artist tell me things if they have to in the control booth, in between takes. And he might say, well the guitar player isn't doing this . . . and I'll say to him, 'Well I'll go out and talk to him,' and then I go out and I don't say anything of the sort. . . . I don't let the artist know if the musicians don't think something's great about the artist. Plus, when it comes right down to it, I've got the talk-back button. I'm the only one who can use it. And if I do have something to say to a player, I always do it in a private conversation.

During creative production, producers proactively and strategically weave together *tertius iungens* and *tertius gaudens* in rapid iteration to deftly manage the intertwined process of generating and integrating creative possibilities to achieve the best possible collective creative outcome and, hopefully, submit hit records to their artists and labels.

Phase 4: Final Synthesis

During final synthesis, producers work with artists, engineers, and record labels to select the individual performances that will be included in the final creative product and how they will sound in relation to each other. Decisions are made regarding particular aesthetic treatments—foregrounding or backgrounding certain performances, adding sonic treatments such as reverb—and deciding which songs will be chosen as promotional "singles." The challenge of implementation, or in this case, creating a record that would be enthusiastically distributed and promoted when handed off, casts a long shadow over the entire collective creative process. Nevertheless, final synthesis involves time consuming effort and precise focus, and so producers use their brokerage role to buffer this process from artist and record label involvement as needed.

Without using the creative brokerage practices deftly, parties critical to implementation could feel disenfranchised and that their creative contributions are not represented in the final outcome. As this producer describes,

> Ultimately, we made the record without much input from the label. At least one of the dissenters was out of the way, and so it was just between me and the artist. But what ended up happening was that the label was out of the way for the production, and she got the songs she wanted, but the label obviously won, because *they didn't sell it.*

Integrative Creative Brokerage and Leadership: Process, Practice, and Future Possibilities

Drawing from insights from the integrative creative brokerage work of Nashville country music producers, this chapter sheds light on Integrative creative leadership as leading an emergent, multi-phase, and iterative collective creative process that stretches well beyond initial ideation to final synthesis and, ultimately, implementation. As Integrative creative leaders guide a collective creative process of securing, generating, transforming, and synthesizing resources and creative ideas into a cohesive whole, they must also be cognizant of three forms of ambiguity that may complicate their work. As described in this chapter, a creative brokerage perspective offers insight into how Integrative creative leaders may leverage their brokerage role to strategically bring people together or keep them apart to maintain creative energy and commitment, and ensure the best possible collective creative outcome. This perspective also highlights the negotiated nature of Integrative creative leadership and the need to deftly manage the competing interests and claims to control of creative experts and resource gatekeepers throughout the creative process.

The creative brokerage model of Integrative creative leadership can extend beyond the Nashville country music industry to inform the work of leaders who must not only guide and elicit creative ideas from others but also integrate the differing contributions, perspectives, and interests of everyone involved (Mainemelis, Kark, & Epitropaki, 2015). Creative brokerage is most generalizable to leaders who bring together technical experts, clients, and resource gatekeepers from across networks, rather than single organizations. As such, this model can inform the work of producers and directors in other project-based creative industries, entrepreneurs, policy leaders tackling global, wicked problems (such as poverty, climate change, or immigration), and individuals leading large-scale development projects. Across these contexts, leaders may face differing degrees of the three forms of ambiguity, which may in turn shape the nature and extent of strategic brokerage work required. For example, music producers lack formal authority over those involved, thus requiring them to pay close attention to competing claims to expertise and control alongside negotiations over the emergent creative outcome. In other contexts, creative and technical experts may enjoy permanent rather than temporary employment relationships, and organizational norms and defined roles may shape and define perceptions of quality, occupational jurisdictions, and the creative process itself. In sum, the roles that parties play, the definitions of what will constitute success, and understandings of how work should proceed, may be more or less ambiguous across contexts, and the nature and extent of strategic brokerage required will differ.

These dynamics might also be shaped by the extent to which Integrative creative leaders have worked previously with contributors. Even as music producers brokered relationships across unconnected individuals, they also engaged trusted partners to contribute to multiple projects over time. For example, Lingo (2010) found that some music producers, especially those coming from engineering backgrounds, rely on "creative foils" to help manage the complex web of socio-emotional and task-related dynamics in creative production. Other creative industries such as film, haute cuisine, and Broadway, have signature partnerships that span multiple projects and years (Mainemelis, Nolas, & Tsirogianni, 2016; Simonton, 2002, 2004; Svejenova, Mazza, & Planellas, 2007). These relationships can both constrain or enable collective creativity (Perretti & Negro, 2007; Uzzi & Spiro, 2005). Integrative creative leaders who utilize long-term collaborators may do so in order to focus their brokerage work on those who are "outsiders" to the creative process—such as record label personnel or artists new to the industry. Future research could examine how repeat collaborations within the constellation of contributors shapes creative brokerage, and the viability of outcomes created.

Several additional possibilities for future research follow from this chapter. First, research could explore how Integrative creative leadership may differ for those working in the core, middle, and periphery of their networks. For example, on the one hand, those in the periphery may bring a fresh perspective and innovative ideas to their respective industries or organizations, but may have more difficulty establishing their claims to expertise and control over the creative process and performances of seasoned experts (Faulkner, 1983). On the other hand, established creative leaders may find themselves bound by convention and desires for consistency and the status quo (Patriotta & Hirsch, 2016; Svejenova, Mazza, & Planellas, 2007). We need to better understand the challenges and opportunities of Integrative creative leaders working across the core, middle, and periphery of a network, both in terms of advancing innovative ideas and individual careers (Baker & Faulkner, 1991; Sgourev, 2013; Uzzi & Spiro, 2005). Such research can also inform our understanding of women and minority Integrative creative leaders, who may often find themselves stuck in the middle and periphery of their industry networks. How does the ambiguity inherent to creative brokerage make their work as leaders more or less difficult? How might these leaders leverage their brokerage role, perhaps in different ways, to respond to ambiguity as well as advance their careers?

A second stream of research could take a longitudinal perspective on creative brokers' career development as they move from the periphery to the core. In addition, this research can extend work highlighting the roller-coaster nature of boundaryless careers, which vacillate between success and failure over time (Mainemelis, Nolas, & Tsirogianni, 2016). Such research could shed light on the role of project failure, as well as success, for Integrative creative leaders and how that informs the careers of all parties involved. Similarly, the model could be refined by comparing how novice and veteran leaders orchestrate creative brokerage. Do the challenges presented, and ability to successfully utilize both *tertius gaudens* and *tertius iungens* practices, change as creative brokers advance their careers? Might some practices work better for veteran versus novice producers at different phases of the collective creative process, as research on networks and creativity suggest (Perry-Smith & Mannucci, 2017)? Taken together, this stream of future research can provide invaluable insight into how Integrative creative leaders develop the "social skill" needed to develop and advance novel and transformative ideas (Fligstein, 2001).

Third, how might big data technology change the nature of creative brokerage? Technology plays a role in producers' efforts to absorb challenges to expertise. Could big data also help reconcile challenges and debates over quality or process? Big data is also becoming more central to the recording and editing work within video game, film, and music industries. Future research could explore how big data impacts the collective creative process, and Integrative creative leadership. For example, as the volume and granularity of creative ideas expands when using big data, do creative production and final synthesis become more recursive and intertwined? How might leaders utilize their brokerage role to respond to the challenges and opportunities presented by big data in collective creative work?

Finally, future research could explore connections between Integrative creative brokerage and Facilitative and Directive creative leadership (Mainemelis, Kark, & Epitropaki, 2015). For example, how may Integrative creative brokerage be interwoven with Facilitative and Directive creative leadership over various phases of the collective creative process, or across one's career? How does the ambiguity that features in creative brokerage work manifest in other forms of creative leadership? Could certain creative brokerage practices be useful to respond, and why? Do some occupations, industries, or types of organizations lend themselves to multiplex forms of creative leadership? Taken together, these possibilities suggest the ample opportunities emerging as disparate streams of research on creative leadership are finally brought together and synthesized into the cohesive whole that is this book.

References

Abbott, A. 1988. *The system of professions: An essay on the division of expert labor*. Chicago, IL: University of Chicago Press.

Amabile, T. M. 1996. *Creativity in context*. Boulder, CO: Westview Press.

Baker, W. E., & Faulkner, R. R. 1991. Role as resource in the Hollywood film industry. *American Journal of Sociology*, 97(2): 279–309.

Barley, W. C. 2015. Anticipatory work: How the need to represent knowledge across boundaries shapes work practices within them. *Organization Science*, 26(6): 1612–1628.

Barley, W. C., Leonardi, P. M., & Bailey, D. E. 2012. Engineering objects for collaboration: Strategies of ambiguity and clarity at knowledge boundaries. *Human Communication Research*, 38(3): 280–308.

Bechky, B. A. 2003a. Object lessons: Workplace artifacts as representations of occupational jurisdiction. *American Journal of Sociology*, 109(3): 720–752.

Bechky, B. A. 2003b. Sharing meaning across occupational communities: The transformation of understanding on a production floor. *Organization Science*, 14(3): 312–332.

Borgatti, S. P., & Foster, P. C. 2003. The network paradigm in organizational research: A review and typology. *Journal of Management*, 29(6): 991–1013.

Burt, R. S. 1992. *Structural holes: The social structure of competition*. Cambridge, MA: Harvard University Press.

Burt, R. S. 2000. The network structure of social capital. In R. I. Sutton & B. M. Staw (Eds.), *Research in organizational behavior*: 345–423. New York: Elsevier and JAI Press.

Burt, R. S. 2004. Structural holes and good ideas. *American Journal of Sociology*, 110: 349–399.

Carlile, P. R. 2004. Transferring, translating and transforming: An integrative framework for managing knowledge across boundaries. *Organization Science*, 15(5): 555–568.

Carlile, P. R., & Rebentisch, E. S. 2003. Into the black box: The knowledge transformation cycle. *Management Science*, 49(9): 1180–1195.

Contractor, N. S., & Ehrlich, M. C. 1993. Strategic ambiguity in the birth of a loosely coupled organization: The case of a $50-Million experiment. *Management Communication Quarterly*, 6(3): 251–281.

Faulkner, R. R. 1983. *Music on demand: Composers and careers in the Hollywood film industry*. New Brunswick, NJ: Transaction Books.

Fleming, L., Mingo, S., & Chen, D. 2007. Collaborative brokerage, generative creativity, and creative success. *Administrative Science Quarterly*, 52(3): 443–475.

Fleming, L., & Waguespack, D. M. 2007. Brokerage, boundary spanning, and leadership in open innovation communities. *Organization Science*, 18(2): 165–180.

Fligstein, N. 2001. Social skill and the theory of fields. *Sociological Theory*, 19(2): 105–125.

Fombrun, C. J. 1982. Strategies for network research in organizations. *Academy of Management Review*, 7: 280–291.

Granovetter, M. 1973. The strength of weak ties. *American Journal of Sociology*, 6: 1360–1380.

Hargadon, A., & Bechky, B. A. 2006. When collections of creatives become creative collectives: A field study of problem solving at work. *Organization Science*, 17(4): 484–500.

Hargadon, A., & Sutton, R. I. 1997. Technology brokering and innovation in a product development firm. *Administrative Science Quarterly*, 42(4): 716–749.

Harrison, S. H., & Rouse, E. D. 2015. An inductive study of feedback interactions over the course of creative projects. *Academy of Management Journal*, 58(2): 375–404.

Harvey, S. 2014. Creative synthesis: Exploring the process of extraordinary group creativity. *Academy of Management Review*, 39(3): 324–343.

Harvey, S., & Kou, C-Y. 2013. Collective engagement in creative tasks: The role of evaluation in the creative process in groups. *Administrative Science Quarterly*, 58(3): 346–386.

Ibarra, H., Kilduff, M., & Tsai, W. 2005. Zooming in and out: Connecting individuals and collectivities at the frontiers of organizational network research. *Organization Science*, 16(4): 359–371.

Kaplan, S. 2011. Strategy and powerpoint: An inquiry into the epistemic culture and machinery of strategy making. *Organization Science*, 22(2): 320–346.

Kilduff, M., & Tsai, W. 2003. *Social networks and organizations*. London: Sage Publications.

Lingo, E. L. 2010. The creative foil: Managing multi-disciplinary expertise. In K. D. Elsbach & B. A. Bechky (Eds.), *Qualitative organizational research: Best papers from the Davis conference on qualitative research*: 91–113. Charlotte, NC: Information Age Press.

Lingo, E. L., & O'Mahony, S. 2010. Nexus work: Brokerage on creative projects. *Administrative Science Quarterly*, 55(1): 47–81.

Lundin, R. A., Arvidsson, N., Brady, T., Ekstedt, E., Midler, C., & Sydow, J. 2015. *Managing and working in project society institutional challenges of temporary organizations*. Cambridge: Cambridge University Press.

Mainemelis, C., Kark, R., & Epitropaki, O. 2015. Creative leadership: A multi-context conceptualization. *Academy of Management Annals*, 9(1): 393–482.

Mainemelis, C., Nolas, S-M., & Tsirogianni, S. 2016. Surviving a boundaryless vreative career: The case of Oscar-nominated film directors, 1967–2014. *Journal of Management Inquiry*, 25(3): 262–285.

Murray, F., & O'Mahony, S. 2007. Exploring the foundations of cumulative innovation: Implications for organization science. *Organization Science*, 18(6): 1006–1021.

Obstfeld, D. 2005. Social networks, the *tertius iungens* orientation, and involvement in innovation. *Administrative Science Quarterly*, 50: 100–130.

Obstfeld, D. 2017. *Getting new things done: Networks, brokerage, and the assembly of innovative action*. Stanford: Stanford University Press.

Patriotta, G., & Hirsch, P. M. 2016. Mainstreaming innovation in art worlds: Cooperative links, conventions and amphibious artists. *Organization Studies*, 37(6): 867–887.

Perretti, F., & Negro, G. 2007. Mixing genres and matching people: A study in innovation and team composition in Hollywood. *Journal of Organizational Behavior*, 28(5): 563–586.

Perry-Smith, J. E., & Mannucci, P. V. 2017. From creativity to innovation: The social network drivers of the four phases of the idea journey. *Academy of Management Review*, 42(1): 53–79.

Powell, W. W. 1990. Neither market nor hierarchy: Network forms of organization. In B. M. Staw & L. L. Cummings (Eds.), *Research in organizational behavior*, Vol. 12: 295–336. Greenwich, CT: JAI Press.

Sgourev, S. V. 2013. How Paris gave rise to Cubism (and Picasso): Ambiguity and fragmentation in radical innovation. *Organization Science*, 24(6): 1601–1617.

Simmel, G. 1950. The triad. In K. Wolff (Ed.), *The sociology of Georg Simmel*: 145–169. New York: Free Press.

Simonton, D. K. 2002. Collaborative aesthetics in the feature film: Cinematic components predicting the differential impact of 2,323 Oscar-nominated movies. *Empirical Studies of the Arts*, 20(2): 115–125.

Simonton, D. K. 2004. Group artistic creativity: Creative clusters and cinematic success in feature films. *Journal of Applied Social Psychology*, 34(7): 1494–1520.

Svejenova, S., Mazza, C., & Planellas, M. 2007. Cooking up change in haute cuisine: Ferran Adrià as an institutional entrepreneur. *Journal of Organizational Behavior*, 28(5): 539–561.

Tichy, N. M. 1980. Networks in organizations. In P. C. Nystrom & W. H. Starbuck (Eds.), *Handbook of organizational design*: 225–249. New York: Oxford University Press.

Uzzi, B., & Spiro, J. 2005. Collaboration and creativity: The small world problem. *American Journal of Sociology*, 111(2): 447–504.

Weick, K. E. 1995. *Sensemaking in organizations*. Thousand Oaks, CA: Sage Publications.

Weick, K. E. 1998. Introductory essay: Improvisation as a mindset for organizational analysis. *Organization Science*, 9(5), Special Issue: Jazz Improvisation and Organizing): 543–555.

13 A Curatorial Metaphor for Creative Leadership

Robert C. Litchfield and Lucy L. Gilson

Introduction

> The technical hierarchy was so dominant that managers sometimes complained that they didn't get enough credit, because "everyone here acts like being a good designer is all that matters, like nothing else matters," even though they need us desperately.
>
> (Sutton & Hargadon, 1996: 705)

A key challenge for many creative leaders is how to resolve the tension they often face when promoting the creative work of others while, at the same time, also being creative themselves. The tension between letting others' ideas take the spotlight, but not at the expense of your contribution is a real one for many creative leaders. Hence, for the last 40 plus years, the topic of creative leadership has continued to receive a great deal of research attention (e.g., Abecassis-Moedas & Gilson, 2017; Abfalter, 2013; Andrews & Farris, 1967; Barnowe, 1975; Mainemelis, Kark, & Epitropaki, 2015). As the earlier quote suggests, leading others to be creative is almost always challenging (Mumford & Licuanan, 2004; Murphy & Ensher, 2008), but necessary if organizations are to succeed (Abfalter, 2013; Mainemelis, Kark, & Epitropaki, 2015; Mumford et al., 2002). Research on leading others to be creative further suggests that that there are specific skills necessary if one is to foster, develop, or bring to the forefront, the creativity of others in a workgroup or organization (Mainemelis, Kark, & Epitropaki, 2015; Mumford et al., 2002). In this chapter, we propose a curatorial approach to leadership as a means through which leaders can support, encourage, and showcase the creativity of their followers while at the same time, allowing their own creativity to flourish.

A curatorial perspective on creativity leverages ideas from the world of museums to consider how the creative content of idea collections might be managed in an organizational setting (Litchfield & Gilson, 2013). Recently, Mainemelis and colleagues (2015) suggested this perspective as an example of what they termed "integrating" creative leadership—where leaders synthesize their "own and others' heterogeneous creative contributions" (401). In this chapter, we elaborate upon the curatorial perspective of creative leadership by contrasting it with two alternative metaphors—the champion (Howell & Higgins, 1990) and the portfolio manager (Cooper, Edgett, & Kleinschmidt, 2001).

While creative leadership can be either Facilitative, Directive, or Integrative, research suggests that the Directive and Facilitating styles are the most common (Abecassis-Moedas & Gilson, 2017; Mainemelis, Kark, & Epitropaki, 2015). Most early research supported the Facilitating style and suggested that the role of the leader is to foster the creativity of others. Here, leaders themselves are not considered to be primary idea generators, but rather play an important role in supporting the creative endeavors of their followers through things like a climate supportive of creativity, or ensuring that creativity is appropriately rewarded. Finally, the role of Facilitative leaders also encompasses idea selection, where leaders are tasked with choosing among the creative ideas of others rather than themselves adding to idea variation (Ford, 1996). In contrast, Directive leaders are those who see themselves as the primary creator or as the individual who will have the most creative ideas, and thus their leadership style entails having others carry out their creative vision. Directive leaders are often described as charismatic and inspiring because they need to get others onboard with their ideas and elicit high-quality followership. Directive leadership is often used in the creative industries, where leaders might have more experience or expertise, and their reputation is tightly coupled with the outcome produced. For example, orchestra conductors frequently consider themselves to be primary creators; they select what music is to be played, how it should be interpreted by the musicians, and finally, patrons often attend a performance to see a specific conductor in action (e.g., Hunt, Stelluto, & Hooijberg, 2004; Marotto, Roos, & Victor, 2007). Similarly, in haute cuisine, it is often the chef who makes most of the decisions about what recipes to prepare (e.g., Bouty & Gomez, 2010), and customers go to specific restaurants based on the reputation of the chef. Lastly, a Directive style is frequently used within a context where deadlines are tight or there is not enough time to solicit and evaluate the input of others.

In contrast to the styles noted earlier, Integrative leaders are described as synthesizers who seek input from multiple others, while at the same time also playing a key creative role in the outcomes (Murningham & Conlon, 1991). Leaders are often Integrative because they realize the most creative and best overall outcomes are achieved through dialog, interaction, and by having others involved in the creative endeavor (Kramer & Crespy, 2011; Mainemelis, Kark, & Epitropaki, 2015). While the Integrative style is one that synthesizes and combines the creative contributions of both the leader and followers, many important questions emerge about the nature of Integrative leaders' contributions.

One form of Integrative leadership is to consider the leader as a curator (Litchfield & Gilson, 2013). Using a museum analogy, curators bring together the creative works of others and aggregate them into *collections*. They then take samples of these collections and present these groupings as a form of new work labeled *exhibitions*. To the extent that curators themselves are creative, their creativity lies not in the individual works, which they generally do not produce, but rather in their ability to combine works into a new (novel) and coherent (useful) exhibition. Thus, a curatorial perspective of creative leadership suggests that leaders integrate by granting others' creativity in the development of individual ideas (i.e., facilitating) while materializing the leader's vision (i.e., directing) at the level of groups of ideas. In the remainder of the chapter, we expand upon how a curatorial metaphor helps leaders to legitimize variety in both individual ideas and organizational stories, and we show why this matters to the assessment and development of ideas exhibiting different creative profiles.

The Curatorial Metaphor in Organizational Creativity

We first introduced a curatorial metaphor into the organizational creativity research lexicon as a means to explore new ways to tailor idea generation, and to better meet the needs of innovation processes (Litchfield & Gilson, 2013). In our original work, we argued that the ease with which large numbers of ideas can now be generated through technological tools has not been matched by improvements in selecting ideas for subsequent implementation. Given widespread pessimism about the prospects for improving idea selection to nurture novelty (e.g., Denrell & March, 2001; March, 1976; Osborn, 1957; Van de Ven, 1986), we proposed adopting a curatorial perspective similar to that of cultural institutions (e.g., museums) as a kind of partial workaround. The curatorial metaphor provides a new way to conceptualize the management of ideas by suggesting that a critical role of creative leadership is to group ideas into collections that might indirectly improve idea selection. Specifically, we suggest that this curatorial metaphor allows organizations and managers to improve the results of idea selection by focusing on the shaping, maintenance, and use of collections of ideas. We briefly recap each of these processes in this section with an eye toward building the leader's distinct role in operationalizing them.

Within the museum world, the reality of escalating prices for cultural works has left even top institutions on the sidelines when it comes to acquiring peak exemplars of creativity (Litchfield & Gilson, 2013). Thus, a curatorial strategy focused exclusively on known masterpieces is not particularly feasible. Fortunately, such a strategy is also generally counter to the need for museums to attract a wider audience through the development of new and diverse narratives that display an institution's holdings to diverse audiences (Halbreich, 2010). However, just as too many diverse masterpieces might function as isolated "anchors" impeding the ability to develop coherent narratives in a museum (Rugoff, 2006), too many highly novel business ideas that are very different from each other might overwhelm managers in a more traditional firm. To deal with this, we suggested that organizations, under the curator's leadership, pursue collections of ideas that fit with both their strategies and resources. Furthermore, in order to understand the ideas they collect, we suggested that organizations seek to pool their ideas according to the type of creativity they wish to exhibit. Such policies should encourage organizations to maintain both highly novel and more incremental ideas on tap with both ready to be displayed as needed.

In addition to acquisitions, a critical concern of many museums is the storage, preservation, and ongoing categorization of their existing and newly acquired works (Litchfield & Gilson, 2013). We called this "maintenance" of collections and suggested that organizations attend both to preserving their stocks of ideas *and* those who generate them. Keeping sources of creativity alive and well can be difficult in organizational life (Amabile, 1998). Amabile and Khaire (2008) describe the critical role that leaders need to play for creativity such that that when it comes to engage the right people, at the right time, leadership has already nurtured those who provide the lifeblood of innovation in the form of creative ideas. Like contemporary artists who aim to place works in museum collections, today's employee-creators also may benefit from autonomy in their work and from receiving credit for their contributions (Amabile, 1998; Sutton & Hargadon, 1996).

Lastly ideas, like pieces of art are collected so that they can be used, but leveraging idea collections can be more complex than it seems (Litchfield & Gilson, 2013). Politics, time, and poor search strategies often result in idea collections being undersampled. Extant research suggests that organizations do not do a good job of resampling from their idea collections and that over time, ideas are put into idea "freezers" where they are left and never considered or visited again (Hargadon & Bechky, 2006; Majchrzak, Cooper, & Neece, 2004). Building upon these arguments in a subsequent article (Gilson & Litchfield, 2017), we noted that because ideas are often considered as the outcome of creativity, while at the same time the starting point for innovation, preserving ideas that are unused in the short term can become problematic in many organizations. In part, this is because the tendency is to "dump" or not follow through on ideas that do not make it through the initial handoff from creativity to implementation. To begin to remedy this, we suggested that organizations need to pay more attention to the creativity profiles of ideas meaning that, for example, ideas that are relatively low in feasibility may require different developmental strategies from those suffering from low perceived value potential.

Although our prior works were not specifically about leadership, we noted that the curatorial view naturally leads to a conversation about a curatorial role (Litchfield & Gilson, 2013) which in essence is a leadership role. Using this lens, a curatorial role involves adopting multiple perspectives over time to build and sample from collections of ideas. Although there is nothing technically prohibiting curators from contributing individual ideas to the collections they manage and work with, the implication from museum studies is that curators build and exhibit from collections of ideas contributed by others. Thus, a key point of separation in the work of curators is between the individual ideas, which they typically are not directly responsible for and do not receive credit for, and the collection of ideas, which curators are directly responsible for and may receive credit for as they leverage it into exhibitions. A curator hoping for a long career cannot take only one perspective on a collection that took years or even decades to assemble. Instead, a single collection, perhaps augmented by outside loans of key works, typically becomes fodder for many exhibitions. Using the separation of levels of analysis between ideas and collections, the concept of multiple perspectives, and the processes of collecting and exhibiting, we now proceed to consider the role of a curatorial leader.

The Curatorial Leader

Leaders act in a curatorial role when they allow others to initiate, develop, and receive credit for autonomous creative contributions while they themselves initiate, develop, and take credit for organizing or collecting these contributions into coherent groupings, and sampling from these groupings to develop new contributions that reframe groups of ideas. Two fundamental insights arise from the curatorial view: (1) leaders adopting a curatorial perspective give up responsibility for individual ideas and (2) leaders take responsibility for providing creative contributions in the form of collections of individually creative ideas and exhibitions that draw on these collections. In this section, we elaborate upon each of these distinct notions by considering two common, alternative metaphors for leading creativity and innovation—the champion and the portfolio manager.

From Champion to Curator

Idea championing has long been considered a key leadership behavior in the creativity and innovation process (Howell & Higgins, 1990). In its most general form, an idea "champion" might be anyone who generates "positive behavioral support for the project . . . in the face of organizational neutrality or opposition" (Markham, 2000: 438). Although this support may take many forms, scholars have tended to agree that a key to championing involves taking responsibility for ideas (cf., Schön, 1963; Walter et al., 2011). Yet taking responsibility for individual ideas is not without risks for leaders. In addition to the myriad risks of failures associated with novel ideas and approaches, if a leader takes too much responsibility for any one idea, as part of their champion role, they risk alienating others which may ultimately reduce project success (Walter et al., 2011), or the willingness of others to bring forward new creative ideas in the future. Moreover, focusing on individual ideas may lead champions to escalate their commitment toward a particular idea even in the face of negative feedback about said idea (Walter et al., 2011). Perhaps due to these risks, research tends to suggest that championing may be most successful when leaders do not themselves get overly involved with the generation of initial ideas (Howell & Boies, 2004). Hence, championing may be characterized as an ongoing form of leader support that is executed differently at different points in the creative process (Howell & Boies, 2004), or perhaps even as a distinct stage in an idea's journey to implementation (Perry-Smith & Mannucci, 2017).

Although we, like others, certainly do not aim to argue against championing, from a leadership perspective, there appears to be a downside that needs to be given careful consideration. Specifically, when leaders champion individual ideas, the act of championing itself may serve as a constraint by committing the leader to a limited range of possibilities. This early narrowing of alternatives is contrary to the goal of developing a range and variety of ideas that creativity theorists suggest is likely to lead to successful solutions and ultimate innovation (cf., Campbell, 1960; Litchfield, 2008; Simonton, 2003, 2011). In other words, rather than hitching their proverbial wagon to what may or may not become a shooting star, leaders should aim to create conditions where range and variety can flourish by encouraging multiple perspectives. We propose that the curatorial role of creative leadership enables this flourishing of range and variety specifically by legitimizing multiple perspectives within a domain. Whereas a champion role encourages taking sides, advocating for, and the early picking of winners (and thus by default losers), a curatorial role seeks to legitimize and embrace multiple perspectives in order to build collections that contain substantial variety and then leverage these collections in different ways to foster innovation. Making space for multiple perspectives to truly be considered has long been a vexing issue in innovation research (Dougherty, 1992), and achieving significant range and variety to support multiple perspectives has been called "illegitimate" in organizational innovation (Dougherty & Heller, 1994). In short, organizations need processes that *legitimize* creativity to move beyond the championing of individual ideas and perspectives (Dougherty & Heller, 1994). We envision the curatorial leadership role as one that serves as a legitimizing mechanism that seeks out and then combines a range and variety of creative contributions.

The issue of *legitimacy* has long been discussed in both the creativity (Tierney, 2015) and leadership (DeRue & Ashford, 2010) literatures. Leaders, like other organizational actors engaged in creativity, are often driven by strong attachments to their creative self-views (for a review of identity in creativity, see Tierney, 2015). Moreover, leaders who are regarded as creative often have an advantage with followers as they better fulfill the leadership ideal held by others, especially in creative groups (van Knippenberg & Hogg, 2003). Theories of identity suggest that actions are seen as legitimate when they are consistent with maintaining or furthering a particular identity (Ashforth & Mael, 1989). From a curatorial leadership perspective, the leader's creative contributions lie beyond the generation of the ideas themselves, and in the leader's ability to combine others' diverse ideas. However, in order to engage in combinatorial acts, leaders must first acquire the necessary raw materials, which means they need to encourage and legitimize the diversity of others' ideas. From the leader's perspective, encouraging variety in subordinates' creative contributions also needs to be consistent with their creative identity. A curatorial role for creative leadership redefines what behaviors are consistent with the "creative leader" identity in a way that allows them to empower followers to make autonomous creative contributions that will ultimately foster enough variety for the leader to consider the resulting collection from multiple perspectives.

From Portfolio Manager to Curator

Although one part of a curatorial creative leadership role is to empower and recognize the autonomous creative contributions of others, curators are Integrative leaders which means that the leader also must make a distinct creative contribution. Within this framework however, their creative contribution comes at the higher level of organizing the creative ideas generated by others. When it comes to organizing, innovation research has long adopted portfolio management as its dominant metaphor for categorizing and evaluating projects (Cooper, Edgett, & Kleinschmidt, 2001). While there are many benefits to portfolio management, an acknowledged downside of this approach is that it can lead away from more strategic views of innovation and toward financial views that have the effect of often privileging the most incremental of ideas (Alexander & van Knippenberg, 2014; Cooper, Edgett, & Kleinschmidt, 2001). From a portfolio view, a leader's key creative responsibility is to either acquire or prune ideas to achieve a coherent and valuable collection. The implication is that ideas not currently proving the appropriate value (or providing an obvious "hedge" in the form of an opposing bet) are somehow a drag on the portfolio. Accordingly, while the portfolio metaphor suggests that leaders must "buy" or "sell" to diversify their portfolio, the curator metaphor suggests that leaders can and usually do, sample from their respective idea collections (portfolios). This rationale also may help to explain the inherent bias toward more incremental creativity in the portfolio approach given that the portfolio manager aims to develop resources that can spread risk and smooth the overall stream of returns. In contrast, the curator aims to develop resources that can be differently leveraged to provide value from a variety of perspectives. In the curator metaphor, the initial grouping of ideas into collections can be seen as a creative act. However, much of the curatorial leader's distinct creative contribution is found in "exhibition"—imagining and adopting multiple perspectives from which to view and sample the assembled ideas.

A curatorial metaphor allows for the divestiture of ideas, but conceptualizes such "deaccessioning" from collections as a relatively less frequent occurrence (Litchfield & Gilson, 2013).

Research on how imagining and adopting multiple perspectives might aid creativity is concentrated on imagining the alternatives, with little consideration given to whether they are adopted, or their ultimate financial value. For instance, research shows that additive counterfactual framings (Markman et al., 2007), goals in brainstorming (Litchfield, Fan, & Brown, 2011), and drawing attention to the presence of multiple identities (Gaither et al., 2015) can all lead to the generation of more diverse ideas. Unfortunately, these various research streams are only minimally informative when it comes to understanding curatorial *leaders'* creativity because, a key part of the leader's unique creative contribution—if there is to be one—arises from actually adopting one or more alternative points of view. Thus, although it is concerned with persons rather than ideas per se, the concept of *perspective-taking* offers a relatively clean analogy to the task facing the curatorial leader.

Perspective-taking is a motivated process that entails imagining the views of others (Ku, Wang, & Galinsky, 2015) and has been linked to organizational creativity and innovation (Grant & Berry, 2011; Hoever et al., 2012; Litchfield, Ford, & Gentry, 2015; Litchfield & Gentry, 2010). Work by Hoever and colleagues (2012) provides specific evidence that perspective-taking in groups can lead not only to the presence of alternatives but also to the elaboration of information from multiple perspectives, and that this elaboration can constitute a mechanism through which perspective-taking translates into creativity. Where this theory fits with the ideas proposed here is that a curatorial leader's creative task is to frame collections of ideas in ways that highlight different aspects of their value, different ways of looking at their value, or different combinations of ideas that form new or improved value propositions. The fact that perspective-taking is known to be an imperfect process which only partially improves outcomes (e.g., Epley et al., 2004) also informs and bounds the view of creative leaders as curators. Just as art museums have historically underrepresented non-white and non-male creative contributions out of the failure to imagine these as important perspectives (e.g., Simpson, 2012; The Guerrilla Girls, 2004), a curatorial view of creative leadership acknowledges that the leader's creativity is bounded both by the imagination to collect and the imagination to adopt different perspectives.

To summarize, we posit curatorial creative leadership in two parts: (1) assembling collections of ideas that can, either as a whole or in part, be subjected to different, potentially valuable framing and (2) applying alternative perspectives to the collection or a sample from it. To illustrate how these assemblages and, in particular, perspectives, can work, we turn in the second part of this chapter to an extended example based on our prior work in defining profiles of creative ideas (Litchfield, Gilson, & Gilson, 2015). Our proposal is that curatorial leaders might logically aim to assemble ideas that represent different types of creativity from the perspective of their general business operations and that alternate framings may serve to alter these creative profiles in ways that can reveal new value propositions.

Using a Curatorial Lens to Classify and Reclassify Creative Ideas

Creativity is not monolithic. A long-standing trend in both the creativity and innovation literatures has been to segment the domain according to the degree of novelty present in ideas (cf., March, 1991; Mumford & Gustafson, 1988). Yet this tradition largely ignores variation in creativity's other key dimension of usefulness (see Litchfield, Gilson, & Gilson, 2015 for an exception). Usefulness itself has been defined in terms of both the feasibility of ideas and their perceived value. Reviewing and synthesizing prior definitions, we developed a set of four creative continua to capture how novelty, defined as conceptual distance from current knowledge or practice, might be differently classified depending upon the combination of feasibility and value used to define usefulness (Litchfield, Gilson, & Gilson, 2015). The continua are labeled *foolishness* (capturing variations in novelty when feasibility and value are both low), *disruptive* (feasibility is high and value is low), *radical* (low feasibility and high value), and *breakthrough* (high feasibility and high value).

To see how these continua might be used to score ideas into collections, we consider a boutique hotel chain that seeks to cross-reference ideas collected from employees by domain (e.g., lobby, bar, maid service, guest services/concierge) and creative type (i.e., foolish, disruptive, radical, or breakthrough). Table 13.1 presents a first cut at collecting ideas under these labels for the domain "lobby."

Examining this framing in more detail we see that the "breakthrough" idea is to integrate the lobby and bar due to its potential to add value (i.e., revenue from the bar) while remaining feasible (e.g., still providing space for the basic functionality of a hotel lobby). However, a curatorial leadership role proposes that leaders' creativity comes to the fore as they develop "exhibitions" (i.e., implementations of ideas from the collection) by applying different perspectives to understand and sample ideas from the

Table 13.1 Hotel Perspective

Creative Type	*Example*
Foolish	Eliminate lobby
Disruptive	Turn lobby into a meditation space with art and quiet music
Radical	Move lobby to another floor and turn entry into a bar
Breakthrough	Integrate lobby and bar

collection. For instance, two alternative perspectives for imagining what a boutique hotel can deliver in terms of an experience might be called "home" and "club." In an era where boutique hotels are striving to compete against both traditional large full-service hotels and home rentals through online outlets, such as Airbnb, alternate perspectives may be useful ways to gain new insights into how to innovate successfully.

Tables 13.2 and 13.3 illustrate, respectively, applications of the "home" and "club" perspectives to the ideas generated in Table 13.1. The first thing to notice is that changing the perspective for scoring alters the categorization of the ideas. For instance, "eliminate lobby" is a foolish idea from both a traditional hotel perspective and from a club perspective, but it arguably represents a breakthrough idea from a home perspective because a lobby is not usually a feature associated with home and, therefore, it might be possible to make the hotel more "home-like" by eliminating the lobby altogether. A second thing to notice is that the value of different combinations of ideas also begins to change. For instance, when employing the club perspective, a new kind of lobby/bar space that integrates quiet, meditative sophistication, and perhaps cocktails, emerges as potentially valuable for its exclusive connotations. In contrast, such an idea would offer less value-added in a traditional hotel framing, where the bar may be regarded as a more social, lively space seeking to attract guests and locals alike.

Building upon the examples noted earlier, but moving to larger collections of ideas, the challenge then becomes how to repeatedly leverage creativity by resampling the collection in numerous ways. As an example from the art world, the Whitney Museum of American Art mounted two major exhibitions, only two years apart, and both predicated on sampling its unique and significant collection of works by the artist Edward Hopper. The two

Table 13.2 Home Perspective

Creative Type	*Example*
Foolish	Move lobby to another floor and turn entry into a bar
Disruptive	Integrate lobby and bar
Radical	Turn lobby into a meditation space with art and quiet music
Breakthrough	Eliminate lobby

Table 13.3 Club Perspective

Creative Type	*Example*
Foolish	Eliminate lobby
Disruptive	Move lobby to another floor and turn entry into a bar
Radical	Integrate lobby and bar
Breakthrough	Turn lobby into a meditation space with art and quiet music

exhibitions were successful because they focused on different framings of his oeuvre (one on "modern life," the other on his use of preparatory drawings; see the "art and artists" tab at Whitney.org). These exhibitions, which contained overlapping works, were completely different products that each contributed to our understanding of Hopper's art due to their framing. While few would doubt the creativity of Hopper's work, of note is also the creativity of the curators in imagining the two exhibitions, organizing and sampling from the collections, and implementing their visions. Linking this back to our hypothetical boutique hotel chain, alternate framings allow leaders to design differently identifiable products to fill different niches (e.g., club vs. home) which in the long run should contribute to organizational survival and success.

Implications and Conclusion

Adopting a curatorial metaphor for creative leadership suggests that leaders can facilitate others' creativity and give full credit to the creativity of others, while concurrently contributing their own creatively at a higher level of analysis (see Table 13.4). Related to the Sutton and Hargadon (1996) quote we opened the chapter with, a curatorial leader will encourage the good designers to be creative and give them the necessary recognition for their contributions, while at the same time receiving credit and recognition because in fact, their contribution is "desperately" needed. As a form of Integrative creative leadership (Mainemelis, Kark, & Epitropaki, 2015), the curatorial metaphor addresses the paradox faced by many leaders by offering clear roles to both leaders and followers that can allow each to be creative and, as importantly, to be recognized for their creative contributions.

Table 13.4 summarizes key distinctions between the curatorial approach to creative leadership, the champion, and the portfolio manager. In adopting a curatorial role, leaders make their creative contributions through their vision and ability to assemble collections of creative ideas and subsequently, taking multiple perspectives that over time reframe and resample idea collections to create exhibitions that may take the form of products, processes, or other implementations of coherent groups of ideas. This description also implicitly identifies situations where curatorial creative leadership may be less effective. For instance, if single ideas form the main basis for innovation, require direct association with a leader (i.e., a "champion") to be implemented, and are "used up" in that process, a curatorial metaphor may provide little value. Similarly, if the main function of having collections of ideas is to spread risk, a portfolio approach may well be the most appropriate. Additionally, some good ideas may struggle to get noticed even within the "big tent" of a collection. Given that the curatorial approach focuses on groupings of ideas, a lone idea, however creative, may face an uphill battle for recognition when it is not perceived as relevant to other ideas in the collection. This is not to say it is impossible for such ideas to be used. In

Table 13.4 Contrasting Curatorial, Champion, and Portfolio Views of Creative Leadership

	Curatorial	*Champion*	*Portfolio Manager*
Creative Contribution at Level of:	Groups of Ideas	Individual ideas	Groups of Ideas
Role of Leader:	Nurtures sources of creativity, providing autonomy and credit for creative contributions by employees Legitimizes the diversity of others' ideas, creating an environment in which a wide range and variety of ideas can flourish Assembles collections of ideas that can, either as a whole or in part, be subjected to different, potentially valuable framing Applies alternative perspectives to collections or samples from them to create exhibitions (which may take the form of products, processes, or other implementations of coherent groups of ideas) Preserves stocks of ideas and who generated them	Generates positive behavioral support for a project, often by taking responsibility for ideas Takes sides quickly, advocating for early winners (and by default assigning losers)	Acquires and prunes ideas to achieve a coherent and valuable collection (portfolio) "Buys" or "sells" ideas to diversify the portfolio: ideas that do not currently add value are deemed a drag on the portfolio Aims to develop resources that can spread risk and smooth the overall stream of returns
Perspective on Assessing Ideas:	Do not discount ideas that do not presently add value, apply alternate perspectives to realize value	Find a promising idea while discounting others	Add or remove ideas from the portfolio based on their value in the current situation
View of Innovation:	Strategic	Varies	Financial
Challenges:	Limited by leader's imagination to collect and to adopt different perspectives Relies on others to provide individual ideas from which to organize/evaluate	Leader constrained by committing to single ideas May alienate others by championing an idea in the face of organizational opposition May reduce the likelihood that others will bring forward creative ideas	May lead away from more strategic views of innovation and toward financial views that privilege the most incremental of ideas

developing exhibitions, curators can and do seek outside ideas and form alliances with other institutions to supplement works from the collections they manage (Litchfield & Gilson, 2013). Nevertheless, building from a single great idea blurs the line between the curatorial and champion approaches and, to us, opens questions about this boundary of curatorial creative leadership. Moreover, it seems likely that leaders adopting a curatorial mindset are simply less likely, relative to those in a champion mindset, to be attuned to such "loner" ideas. Finally, we imagine that collections are unlikely to be static over time. Specifically, the leader often has significant power over the degree to which collections of ideas are reused, augmented, and reshaped by additional ideas, or even dissolved. Today's knowledge management tools seem to offer significant potential to keep and reuse ideas, but the limited extant research suggests that such reuse may be relatively uncommon (Majchrzak, Cooper, & Neece, 2004).

Our aim in writing this chapter is to offer a new way of looking at creative leadership that can augment and reside alongside established metaphors such as that of champion and the portfolio manager. The curatorial metaphor for creative leadership offers a perspective on leading *for* creativity that is explicitly Integrative allowing both the leaders' and others' creative contributions to make an impact. We hope that this chapter will inspire others to both consider the curatorial metaphor and to imagine other metaphors that will continue to expand our understanding of creative leadership.

Acknowledgment

We thank Hannah Bonitz for her assistance with Table 13.4.

References

Abecassis-Moedas, C., & Gilson, L. L. 2017. Drivers and levels of creative leadership: An examination of choreographers as directive and integrative leaders. *Innovation: Organization & Management*. doi:10.1080/14479338.2017.1394793.

Abfalter, D. 2013. Authenticity and suspect: Leading creative teams in the performing arts. *Creativity and Innovation Management*, 22(3): 295–306.

Alexander, L., & van Knippenberg, D. 2014. Teams in pursuit of radical innovation: A goal orientation perspective. *Academy of Management Review*, 39: 423–438.

Amabile, T. 1998. How to kill creativity. *Harvard Business Review*, 76: 76–87.

Amabile, T., & Khaire, M. 2008. Creativity and the role of the leader. *Harvard Business Review*, 86: 100–109.

Andrews, F. M., & Farris, G. F. 1967. Supervisory practices and innovation in scientific teams. *Personnel Psychology*, 20: 497–575.

Ashforth, B. E., & Mael, F. 1989. Social identity theory and the organization. *Academy of Management Review*, 14(1): 20.

Barnowe, J. T. 1975. Leadership and performance outcomes in research organizations: The supervisor of scientists as a source of assistance. *Organizational Behavior & Human Performance*, 14: 264–280.

Bouty, I., & Gomez, M. L. 2010. Dishing up individual and collective dimensions in organizational knowing. *Management Learning*, 41: 545–559.

Campbell, D. T. 1960. Blind variation and selective retention in creative thought as in other knowledge processes. *Psychological Review*, 67: 380–400.

Cooper, R., Edgett, S., & Kleinschmidt, E. 2001. Portfolio management for new product development: Results of an industry practices study. *R & D Management*, 31: 361–380.

Denrell, J., & March, J. G. 2001. Adaptation as information restriction: The hot stove effect. *Organization Science*, 12: 523–538.

DeRue, D. S., & Ashford, S. J. 2010. Who will lead and who will follow? A social process of leadership identity construction in organizations. *Academy of Management Review*, 35: 627–647.

Dougherty, D. 1992. A practice-centered model of organizational renewal through product innovation. *Strategic Management Journal*, *13*: 77–92.

Dougherty, D., & Heller, T. 1994. The illegitimacy of successful product innovation in established firms. *Organization Science*, 5: 200–218.

Epley, N., Keysar, B., van Boven, L., & Gilovich, T. 2004. Perspective taking as egocentric anchoring and adjustment. *Journal of Personality and Social Psychology*, 87: 327–339.

Ford, C. M. 1996. A theory of individual creative action in multiple social domains. *Academy of Management Review*, 21: 1112–1142.

Gaither, S. E., Remedios, J. D., Sanchez, D. T., & Sommers, S. R. 2015. Thinking outside the box: Multiple identity mind-sets affect creative problem solving. *Social Psychological and Personality Science*, 6: 596–603.

Gilson, L. L., & Litchfield, R. C. 2017. Idea collections: A link between creativity and innovation. *Innovation: Organization & Management*, 19: 80–85.

Grant, A., & Berry, J. 2011. The necessity of others is the mother of invention: Intrinsic and prosocial motivations, perspective-taking, and creativity. *Academy of Management Journal*, 54: 73–96.

The Guerrilla Girls. 2004. *The Guerilla Girls' art museum activity book*. New York: Printed Matter.

Halbreich, K. 2010. Comments in special section on the museum revisited. *Artforum*, http://artforum.com/inprint/issue=201006&id=25687, accessed on February 1, 2012.

Hargadon, A., & Bechky, B. 2006. When collections of creatives become creative collective—A field study of problem solving at work. *Organization Science*, 17: 484–500.

Hoever, I. J., van Knippenberg, D., van Ginkel, W., & Barkema, H. G. 2012. Fostering team creativity: Perspective-taking as key to unlocking diversity's potential. *Journal of Applied Psychology*, 97: 982–996.

Howell, J. M., & Boies, K. 2004. Champions of technological innovation: The influence of contextual knowledge, role orientation, idea generation, and idea promotion on champion emergence. *The Leadership Quarterly*, 15: 123–143.

Howell, J. M., & Higgins, C. A. 1990. Champions of technological innovation. *Administrative Science Quarterly*, 35: 317–341.

Hunt, J. G., Stelluto, G. E., & Hooijberg, R. 2004. Toward new-wave organizing creativity: Beyond romance and analogy in the relationship between orchestra-conducting leadership and musician creativity. *Leadership Quarterly*, 15: 145–162.

Kramer, M. W., & Crespy, D. A. 2011. Communicating collaborative leadership. *Leadership Quarterly*, 22: 1024–1037.

Ku, G., Wang, C. S., & Galinsky, A. 2015. The promise and perversity of perspective-taking in organizations. *Research in Organizational Behavior*, 35: 79–102.
Litchfield, R. C. 2008. Brainstorming reconsidered: A goal-based view. *Academy of Management Review*, 33: 649–668.
Litchfield, R. C., Fan, J., & Brown, V. R. 2011. Directing idea generation using brainstorming with specific novelty goals. *Motivation and Emotion*, 35: 135–143.
Litchfield, R. C., Ford, C. M., & Gentry, R. J. 2015. Linking individual creativity to organizational innovation. *Journal of Creative Behavior*, 49: 279–294.
Litchfield, R. C., & Gentry, R. J. 2010. Perspective-taking as an organizational capability. *Strategic Organization*, 8: 187–205.
Litchfield, R. C., & Gilson, L. L. 2013. Curating collections of ideas: Museum as metaphor in the management of creativity. *Industrial Marketing Management*, 42: 106–112.
Litchfield, R. C., Gilson, L. L., & Gilson, P. W. 2015. Defining creative ideas: Toward a more nuanced approach. *Group & Organization Management*, 40: 238–265.
Mainemelis, C., Kark, R., & Epitropaki, O. 2015. Creative leadership: A multi-context conceptualization. *Academy of Management Annals*, 9: 393–482.
Majchrzak, A., Cooper, L. P., & Neece, O. E. 2004. Knowledge reuse for innovation. *Management Science*, 50: 174–188.
March, J. G. 1976. The technology of foolishness. In J. G. March & J. P. Olsen (Eds.), *Ambiguity and choice in organizations*: 69–81. Oslo: Universitetsforlaget.
March, J. G. 1991. Exploration and exploitation in organizational learning. *Organization Science*, 2: 71–87.
Markham, S. K. 2000. Corporate championing and antagonism as forms of political behavior: An R & D perspective. *Organization Science*, 11: 429–447.
Markman, K. D., Lindberg, M. J., Kray, L. J., & Galinsky, A. D. 2007. Implications of counterfactual structure for creative generation and analytical problem solving. *Personality and Social Psychological Bulletin*, 33: 312–324.
Marotto, M., Roos, J., & Victor, B. 2007. Collective virtuosity in organizations: A study of peak performance in an orchestra. *Journal of Management Studies*, 44: 388–413.
Mumford, M. D., & Gustafson, S. B. 1988. Creativity syndrome: Integration, application, and innovation. *Psychological Bulletin*, 103: 27–43.
Mumford, M. D., & Licuanan, B. 2004. Leading for innovation: Conclusions, issues, and directions. *Leadership Quarterly*, 15: 163–171.
Mumford, M. D., Scott, G. M., Gaddis, B., & Strange, J. M. 2002. Leading creative people: Orchestrating expertise and relationships. *Leadership Quarterly*, 13: 705–750.
Murningham, J. K., & Conlon, D. E. 1991. The dynamics of intense work groups: A study of British string quartets. *Administrative Science Quarterly*, 36: 165–186.
Murphy, S. E., & Ensher, E. A. 2008. A qualitative analysis of charismatic leadership in creative teams: The case of television directors. *Leadership Quarterly*, 19: 335–352.
Osborn, A. F. 1957. *Applied imagination*. New York: Scribner's.
Perry-Smith, J., & Mannucci, P. V. 2017. From creativity to innovation: The social network drivers of the four phases of the idea journey. *Academy of Management Review*, 42: 53–79.
Rugoff, R. 2006. You talking to me? On curating group shows that give you a chance to join the group. In P. Marincola (Ed.), *What makes a great exhibition?* 44–51. Philadelphia, PA: Philadelphia Exhibitions Initiative.

Schon, D. A. 1963. Champions for radical new inventions. *Harvard Business Review*, 41: 77–86.

Simonton, D. K. 2003. Scientific creativity as constrained stochastic behavior: The integration of product, person, and process perspectives. *Psychological Bulletin*, 129: 475–494.

Simonton, D. K. 2011. Creativity and discovery as blind variation: Campbell's (1960) BVSR model after the half-century mark. *Review of General Psychology*, 15: 158–174.

Simpson, M. G. 2012. *Making representations: Museums in the post-colonial era*. New York: Routledge.

Sutton, R. I., & Hargadon, A. 1996. Brainstorming groups in context: Effectiveness in a product design firm. *Administrative Science Quarterly*, 41: 685–718.

Tierney, P. 2015. An identity perspective on creative action in organizations. In C. E. Shalley, M. A. Hitt, & J. Zhou (Eds.), *The Oxford handbook of creativity, innovation, and entrepreneurship*. Oxford: Oxford University Press.

Van de Ven, A. H. 1986. Central problems in the management of innovation. *Management Science*, 32: 590–607.

Van Knippenberg, D., & Hogg, M. A. 2003. A social identity model of leadership effectiveness in organizations. *Research in Organizational Behavior*, 25: 243–229.

Walter, A., Parboteeah, K. P., Risenhuber, F., & Hoegl, M. 2011. Championship behaviors and innovation success: An empirical investigation of university spinoffs. *Journal of Product Innovation Management*, 28: 586–598.

14 Exploring Integrative Creative Leadership in the Filmmaking Industry

Nicole Flocco, Filomena Canterino, Stefano Cirella, Jean-Francois Coget, and Abraham B. (Rami) Shani

Introduction

Creativity—defined as "the production of ideas, products, or procedures that are novel or original, and potentially useful or practical" (Amabile, 1996) or "as a continuous process of thinking innovatively, or finding and solving problems, and implementing new solutions" (Basadur, Graen, & Green, 1982)—is considered a necessary prerequisite for organizational innovation, growth, and survival. Many scholars assert that leadership plays a crucial role in managing the creative process and that it is unlikely that creative outcomes will be realized without a large degree of support from organizations and organizational leaders (Reiter-Palmon, & Illies, 2004).

Various studies have examined the relationship between *leadership* and *creativity* (e.g., Lovelace & Hunter, 2013; Mumford, Medeiros, & Partlow, 2012; Zhang & Bartol, 2010; Harris et al., 2014; Murphy & Ensher, 2008). A recent contribution about these topics came from Mainemelis, Kark, and Epitropaki (2015), who surveyed and analyzed the dispersed body of knowledge about leadership and creativity and synthesized it under the construct of *creative leadership*. In their work, Mainemelis, Kark, and Epitropaki (2015) suggest three narrow conceptualizations of creative leadership, related to (i) *Facilitating* employee creativity, (ii) *Directing* the materialization of a leader's creative vision, and (iii) *Integrating* heterogeneous creative contributions. These three manifestations of creative leadership represent *collaborative contexts* in which leaders and followers interact in the creative process. The three contexts differ in terms of *creative contributions* (e.g., generating and developing new ideas) made by the leader and those made by the followers and in terms of *supportive contributions* (e.g., providing psychological, social, and material support for creativity) made by the leader and by the followers.

In the *Facilitating* context, leaders themselves have limited creative contributions. Their focus is on supporting and enabling employee creativity. This is radically different from *Directive* contexts, in which the leader is the key creative agent, and employees' role is to facilitate and execute the leader's creative vision. *Integrating* heterogeneous creative contributions represents a third context, where non-similar professionals typically collaborate in order to integrate highly heterogeneous inputs. In this third context, both leaders and followers are creative in their own right, and play an important, distinctive, and often credited role in the creative process. However, the process is so complex that it needs to be coordinated by the leader so that the different contributions form an integrated whole. This third context is the focus of this chapter.

Filmmaking is typical of Integrative creative leadership, a context in which multiple non-similar professionals provide highly heterogeneous inputs. Films require a screenwriter, a director, a director of photography (who operates and directs camera and lighting equipment), a sound editor, actors, a music composer, a special-effects director, an editor, and many other such professionals as set designers, costume designers, assistant directors (ADs), location scouts, producers, casting directors, makeup artists, and personal assistants (PAs) (Bechky, 2006; Coget, 2004). A key role of the director is to elicit, orient, and integrate the heterogeneous inputs of these various professionals into a coherent whole, the final cut. Integrating is both a leadership and a creative activity. The director is typically the one who provides the artistic vision for the movie—a creative product itself. The creative vision is also a tool that influences and aligns other professionals' creative processes so as to prepare the integration of their products into the whole.

Integration occurs, for instance, in the collaboration between the director and his or her actors. While actors bring their own skill, training, and acting philosophy or method to the table, and are selected partly for it, the director is supposed to "direct" them. This involves having a number of preparatory discussions with them, and providing them with subtext, notes, adjustments, and other prompts, sometimes in between different takes, to bring their character to life, according to the director's vision, but also the actors' vision. Power struggles between actors and directors are not rare.

Likewise, the director works intimately with their director of photography (DP) to craft visual looks and effects. Camera angles, movement, and other choices are essential to the look of a movie. The editor is another crucial partner; selecting, cutting, and stitching together takes to create different cuts that tell the story visually. Music is essential to creating the emotional mood and tonality of a movie. Directors often collaborate with composers to craft music that reflects the mood they intend to create. The script is the core of a movie and typically written entirely prior to the filming of a movie. Sometimes the director writes the script, or collaborates with the screenwriter before, and even during, filming to rewrite the script.

Some professional inputs are arguable more important than others. The DP and principal actors, for instance, arguably weigh more heavily on the final product than makeup artists or even set and costume designers. Nonetheless, each professional has some input that needs to be integrated into the whole. Mainemelis, Kark, and Epitropaki (2015) emphasize integration as a key role of creative leaders in the "integrative leadership context." In filmmaking, this role falls upon the director.

How do directors do it? More specifically, to what extent do they involve others in the process of integration? While the final product is a collective effort, the act of integrating heterogeneous inputs itself is not necessarily so. At the limit, integration could be done solely by the director, in an autocratic manner. At the other end of the spectrum, it could be shared with others in a more democratic manner.

This chapter explores variation along these two extremes: autocratic vs. democratic integration, through examples from different, famous directors. Some directors, such as Lars Von Triers, are known to be "control freaks," who attempt to micromanage all aspects of filmmaking, and are even reluctant to credit other people's inputs. Others, such as Richard Linklater, are known to collaborate extensively with their crew and cast, often writing the script, even the concept of the movie itself, with his actors, and collaborating with the same, intimate crew repeatedly. Through a few illustrative examples, we develop hypotheses about the factors that influence the extent to which directors share the burden of integration in filmmaking.

Approach

We chose to focus our study on the filmmaking industry because, while directors are undoubtedly the leaders of the creative process, having the greatest creative influence on films, filmmaking nonetheless demands a high degree of creative collaboration, with various professionals making distinct, credited creative contributions. The job of a movie director requires strong creative skills and a creative vision. It also demands leadership skills, such as the ability to inspire and integrate high-magnitude creative contributions from various other professionals. Indeed, Mainemelis, Kark, and Epitropaki (2015) identify filmmaking as an exemplar of the Integrative context.

Having narrowed down our exploration to filmmaking, we chose to investigate movie directors that seemed to vary maximally on our variable of interest: the extent to which they integrate creative contributions among their team in an autocratic vs. a democratic manner. This led us to investigate six renowned movie directors who seem to vary considerably on that continuum: Christopher Nolan, George Lucas, John Lasseter, Lars von Trier, Quentin Tarantino, and Richard Linklater. In particular, this selection was based on three criteria: (i) we chose directors who also wrote the screenplay of their movies, so as to follow the creative process from the earliest stage of idea generation; (ii) we included directors who produced several successful, internationally recognized movies, including prequel/sequel, sagas, and animated films, which require the management and coordination of a wide range of experts; (iii) we identified directors who differed from each other in terms of attitude, personal characteristics, working habits and genres of movies they typically directed. We collected and analyzed a wide array of secondary sources about these six directors: 13 videos, 4 documentaries, 39 articles, 7 interviews, and 2 books.

Emerging Themes

Our exploration confirmed that movie directors indeed seem to vary considerably in the extent to which they integrate various contributions in an autocratic vs. a democratic manner. Furthermore, we identified seven possible factors that appear to be associated with this variation: (1) the personality of the director, in particular, their apparent need for control; (2) the temporality of involvement of others in crafting the vision: early vs. late; (3) secrecy, or the extent to which directors protect the creative process from others vs. leaving it open; (4) directors' tendency to work with the same crew and cast across different movies or not; (5) consolidation of roles by the director; (6) technology, in particular how high vs. low tech the movie is, as indicated by the extent and complexity of special effects or animation in the filmmaking process; and (7) the organization of the filmmaking process, such as whether rehearsals occur or not, or time is allotted for creative reorientation during the filmmaking. Next, we illustrate these seven factors with examples from the six directors we investigated.

Personality of the Director—Need for Control

The personality of the director seems to influence the degree to which they integrate other professionals' contributions autocratically or democratically. Some directors seem to have a higher need for control than others. Linklater and Lasseter, for instance, seem to possess a relatively lower need for control than other directors:

> Filmmakers are control freaks. For us, it's about bending the elements of a story into existence. But you had to give up full control, and admit you have a major collaborator sitting with you at all times: that's the unknown, the future. You're counting on it being there, but you don't know what it is yet.
>
> (Richard Linklater—Linklater's case)

> I still understand the need for faith in a creative context. Because we are often working to invent something that doesn't yet exist (. . .). When we trust the process, we can relax, let go, take a flyer on something radical. We can accept that any given idea may not work and yet minimize our fear of failure because we believe we will get there in the end
>
> (Co-producer—Lasseter's case)

Tarantino offers a good contrast to these, especially with respect to dialog. He insists that actors remain absolutely faithful to his scripts:

> Actors aren't there to riff. They're there to say the dialogue. If their riffing is genius, I will take credit for it
>
> (Quentin Tarantino—Tarantino's case)

Nolan and von Trier also demonstrate a high need for control:

> I almost never get to leave the set. I have to go pee sometimes, of course, but otherwise I'm there, by the camera, the whole time.
>
> (Christopher Nolan—Nolan's case)

> I like that you're at the mercy of the director and don't know where you're going.
>
> (Lars von Trier—von Trier's case)

Involving Others Early Versus Late in Crafting the Vision

Creative leadership requires awareness of the temporal complexity dimensions of creative projects (Halbesleben et al., 2003; Mainemelis, 2002). In our exploration, we found indication that temporality indeed had an influence on the Integrative process. More specifically, we hypothesize that how early directors involve others in crafting the vision influences the degree to which they integrate other professionals' contributions autocratically or democratically. The directors who involve others early tend to integrate more democratically. Linklater, for example, wrote the entire script of the movie *Before Sunset* with the two main actors, Ethan Hawke and Julie Delpy:

> Ethan and Julie brought much of themselves to [the previous] work, a lot of their ideas and story, so when the three of them [Linklater, Hawke, Deply] decided to make the second movie they wanted to come in as writers.
>
> (Co-producer—Linklater's case)

Ethan Hawke commented,

> We talked about it for years, and we realize we really had to do it, we all, for about a year, exchange emails, writing different scenes and say, 'Try to write on this subject, on that subject,' and then one day Julie posted us forty pages. . . . I was pregnant with the idea for a while.
>
> (Actor—Linklater's case)

John Lasseter, at Pixar, also integrates followers' creative contributions in the initial stages of the creative process:

> I come up with the initial concepts. We bounce the idea around with the crew we have. Most of them have computer backgrounds, but over the years they've become quite savvy with animation and stories. So we usually develop the stories together, and I'll do the storyboard. From the storyboard we define what needs to be modeled. We generally divide up

> the modeling task between the crew. I'll do some modeling, and then I'll do all the animation, generally.
>
> (John Lasseter—Lasseter's case)

Secrecy

Another factor we found associated with autocratic vs. democratic integration was secrecy. Tarantino, for example, is very secretive about his scripts and different cuts of his movies:

> The script was sent out to actors with the warning, "If you show this to anybody, two guys from Jersey [Films] will come and break your legs."
>
> (Quentin Tarantino—Tarantino's case)

Brad Pitt, in a conference presser about the movie *Inglorious Bastards*, declared,

> No one has seen the film yet, because Quentin kept it under wraps, so it could be very nice for us tonight to see all it together, because all we know is we wrapped three months ago. We shot our respective parts and, suddenly, here we are
>
> (Actor—Tarantino's case)

The same thing could be said for Nolan:

> Secrecy is less of a fact on a Christopher Nolan production than it is a working method. Michael Caine was allowed to keep his script for *Interstellar*, but each page of every copy of the script bore his name, so it could be traced back were it to go missing.
>
> (Interviewer—Nolan's case)

This need for secrecy stands in stark opposition with the collaborative and sharing practices associated with a democratic creative exchange, where leaders usually rework the story and change the plot to integrating other professionals' ideas.

Working With the Same Crew and Cast Across Movies

Although Integrative creative leadership seems to be associated with higher degree of recombination (Mainemelis, Kark, & Epitropaki, 2015), some directors seem to find benefits in working with the same crew, cast, and/or producer across projects (Alvarez et al., 2005; Alvarez & Svejenova, 2002). Additionally, even though movies are typically organized as temporary projects (Bechky, 2006), some movies, such as Pixar's animations, are produced by permanent organizations, even though they are projects within the organization. We hypothesize that working with the same team across projects helps the integration and might favor a more democratic type of integration, by reducing the need to constantly communicate and clarify expectations. Nolan, for instance, worked with the same directorial team (1st AD Nilo Otero, 2nd AD Brandon Lambdin, and 2nd 2nd Greg Pawlik) on several of his films, and said,

> I rely on Nilo to keep a quiet set with no cell phones, and hopefully without making things too tense. He does a good job making people feel at ease, while also making it clear that we're going to be extremely focused on the work that's going on.
>
> (Christopher Nolan—Nolan's case)

Linklater and Tarantino also like to work with the same crew and actors:

> His collaborators often stay with him, his assistant and office manager Kirsten McMurray answered an ad for part-time work as a college student, ten years ago, and never left. Vince Palmo has been the assistant director on almost all his features over the past decade.
>
> (Interviewer—Linklater's case)

> I had the same problem with Sam for about a decade; it's hard not to write for these guys; they say my dialogues so well . . . for seven months of the year and a half that I was writing *Kill Bill*, Bill just sounded like Sam.
>
> (Quentin Tarantino—Tarantino's case)

Directors seem to work repeatedly with people that share similar beliefs and behaviors:

> I'm very straight with the team. And if I were to get involved in a project and feel that we weren't seeing the same film, I would run a mile.
>
> (Christopher Nolan—Nolan's case)

Consolidation of Roles by the Director

Consolidating roles has been well-documented in the literature as a strategy to help integration, and for an individual to increase their power (Alvarez et al., 2005; Baker & Faulkner, 1991; Bechky, 2006; Svejenova, 2005). Our investigation yielded a number of examples of directors who consolidate different roles besides that of director, such as screenwriter or DP. Such a practice seems to favor a more autocratic approach to integration. Some directors go even further than role consolidation, and overstep the boundaries of their role into others' roles. Lars von Trier, for example, often operates the camera himself, overstepping on the responsibility of the DP. In the movie *Manderlay*, for instance, he credited himself as DP, alongside Anthony Dod Mantle, the DP he had hired. When a journalist asked him how many shots of the movie he did, he answered,

> Almost all of them, actually. Anthony did one scene, I think.
>
> (Lars von Trier—von Trier's case)

Tarantino demonstrated a similar behavior when he was reluctant to credit Roger Avary, the screenwriter, as co-writer for *Pulp Fiction*:

> "He didn't write the script," Tarantino says today. Avary contributed the story about the boxer, which is the centerpiece of the movie (. . .) After production on the movie began, Avary reportedly received a call from Tarantino's attorney, demanding that he accept a "story by" instead of a co-writer credit, so that Tarantino could say, "Written and directed by Quentin Tarantino." (. . .) Tarantino told him that if he didn't accept the "story by" credit, Tarantino would write his section out of the script and Avary would get nothing.
>
> (Interviewer—Tarantino's case)

Christopher Nolan and George Lucas tend to master other roles as well and generally are interested in minute details of the process:

> I'm interested in every different bit of filmmaking because I had to do every bit of it myself, from sound recording and ADR to editing and music. [my study] gave me a really good grounding in knowing overall what has to go into a film technically.
>
> (Christopher Nolan—Nolan's case)

> I was working with a British editor and the scenes would come back, and I'd go on the weekends and look at the scenes with the editor, and they just weren't working. I was very down about the whole situation. So I went in myself on Sundays and started re-cutting the movie. . . . As I started to cut the film together, I realized that I was making cuts that were, you know, a foot away from where the editor had been making them. And I had been using the same takes that I'd given him.
>
> (George Lucas—Luca's case)

Technology

Large, technology-intensive productions, such as Pixar's animated films, or special-effects laden movies such as *Star Wars*, require a larger crew of highly skilled individuals, as compared to lower-tech, productions more characteristic of independent movies, or European productions.

Lars von Trier and his film school colleagues specifically articulated a method of filmmaking dubbed Dogma 95—that is, low tech—including using natural light instead of lighting equipment, sound being produced at the same time as images, and handheld cameras (Lumholdt, 2003). Such rules allow for the use of a smaller crew and arguably allow the director to control more of the process than a large-scale production such as Pixar's animations, where it is impossible for the director to micromanage all aspects of the process (Catmull & Wallace, 2014).

> Because making a movie involves hundreds of people, a chain of command is essential. But in this case, we had made the mistake of confusing the communication structure with the organizational structure. Of course an animator should be able to talk to a modeler directly, without first talking with his or her manager. So we gathered the company together and said: Going forward, anyone should be able to talk to anyone else, at any level, at any time, without fear of reprimand.
>
> (Co-producer—Lasseter's case)

> We start from the presumption that our people are talented and want to contribute. We accept that.
>
> (Co-producer—Lasseter's case)

> If there was one thing we prided ourselves on at Pixar, it was making sure that Pixar's artists and technical people treated each other as equals.
>
> (Co-producer—Lasseter's case)

We therefore hypothesize that the more technologically sophisticated productions, which require more skilled technicians, are more likely to lend themselves to a democratic process of integration than smaller, low-tech productions. That said, low-tech productions are not necessarily associated with autocratic integration, as shown in Linklater's example. However, we argue that this type of production allows more variability than highly technical productions.

Organization of the Filmmaking Process

Movies are complex and expensive ventures. The number of professionals involved in creating one, and the equipment needed are critical and have an impact on the overall costs. For this reason, time is of the essence on a movie set. Directors typically do not have the luxury of extra time. Yet research on creativity has emphasized the importance of improvization (Barrett, 1998; Vera & Crossan, 2004) and play (e.g., Mainemelis & Altman, 2010;

Mainemelis & Dionysiou, 2015) in the creative process. We hypothesize that directors who build in time for rehearsal and improvization in the filmmaking process to practice integration in a more democratic manner. Linklater is a case in point: he often rewrites the entire script with his main actors during rehearsal time:

> He schedules a lot of rehearsal time—two solid weeks or so before production starts—and goes through each scene in an open-ended way, talking about character motivations and getting actors to riff. Most of the rehearsal time is spent rewriting the screenplay, line by line, drawing out and molding his work against performers' strengths and styles. "Often what I write is incredibly 'written,' pretentious" he says. "Then it's like: How do we undercut this?" The original ideas work their way into the scene, but the language changes. By the time the cameras start rolling, the screenplay is halfway between the voice of the writer-director and the voices of his actors.
>
> (Richard Linklater—Linklater's case)

> Some directors are tyrants, driving their actors with lengthy, chaotic shifts; abusing their crews; and running through assistants like silk stockings in a berry patch. This isn't Linklater's style.
>
> (Interviewer—Linklater's case)

Linklater also shot his Oscar-winning movie *Boyhood* across 12 years to follow the evolution of the main character from the age of 5–18. He did so by filming every summer with the same cast for 12 years. Such an unusual filmmaking practice is undeniably part of the movie's success. While Nolan is very demanding on set, he nonetheless tries to create a comfortable environment and leave room for experimentation:

> I really try to be different [and adapt] for every actor, I try to make them comfortable, I try to get the best out of them. You hear stories of directors deliberately making actors uncomfortable, but I always make the actors feel that they have what they need to explore a scene.
>
> (Christopher Nolan—Nolan's case)

> I learned lots of things on *Memento*, but one thing I've always adhered to since then is letting actors perform as many takes as they want. I've come to realize that the lighting and camera setups, the technical things, take all the time, but running another take generally only adds a couple of minutes. If an actor tells me they can do something more with a scene, I give them the chance, because it's not going to cost that much time. It can't all be about the technical issues.
>
> (Christopher Nolan—Nolan's case)

> With *Insomnia*, Al Pacino liked to rehearse very, very carefully, block things out, and do a lot of takes. His first take would be perfect, but he really wanted to talk about things, whereas Hilary Swank didn't want to rehearse too much. She wanted to save it, then do what she was going to do in one or two takes and no more. As a director, you have to figure out how to balance those things, because you want them both to feel that they're being given the floor in the way they need for what they're doing.
>
> (Christopher Nolan—Nolan's case)

Quentin Tarantino seems to dedicate extra time building the character with actors in order to be more effective on set:

> Quentin briefs me on my character background for many weeks; actually, he made me watch quite a few old movies, talks to me about what my character background would be.
>
> (Actress—Tarantino's case)

Other ways of organizing the filmmaking process that seem to favor more of a democratic process of integration is by establishing routines, learning routines and designing learning mechanisms. Those routines seem to enhance the collaborative context and creative output. At Pixar, for example, John Lasseter has founded a body called the Braintrust, a team of long-timer, expert Pixar filmmakers in charge of reviewing and critiquing Pixar's movies throughout the entire creative cycle:

> First, we draw storyboards of the script and then edit them together with temporary voices and music to make a crude mock-up of the film, known as reels. Then the Braintrust watches this version of the movie and discusses what's not ringing true, what could be better, what's not working at all.
>
> (John Lasseter—Lasseter's case)

The goal of the Braintrust is to give feedback about Pixar movies under development:

> The Braintrust is fueled by the idea that every note we give is in the service of a common goal: supporting and helping each other as we try to make better movies.
>
> (Co-producer -Lasseter's case)

> A good note doesn't make demands; it doesn't even have to include a proposed fix. But if it does, that fix is offered only to illustrate a potential solution, not to prescribe an answer.
>
> (Co-producer—Lasseter's case)

Quentin Tarantino also uses some learning routines, such as organizing cine-forums, in order to foster creativity and collaboration among his team:

> There is something which is quite incredible, Quentin organized a Cine-club every week, we saw lots of films from that period [World War II].
>
> (Actress—Tarantino's case)

Implications

The Integrative creative leadership conceptualization focuses on "the leader's role in integrating his or her creative ideas with the diverse creative ideas of other professionals in the work context" (Mainemelis, Kark, & Epitropaki, 2015: 398). Our investigation reveals a fairly wide continuum in the manner in which leaders combine their creative contributions with their followers.

Democratic Integration

Factors that we hypothesize are associated with a more democratic form of Integration include leaders involving followers early in the creative process, leaders demonstrating a relatively lower need for control, setting up structures and routines that enable collaboration and sharing, such as rehearsal time and Pixar's Brainstrust, tending to work with the same team across projects, and projects that are more technically complex. These findings are interesting in light of the debates in the literature about leadership styles and creativity. Some authors find that an empowering leadership style is positively linked with creativity, because it encourages employees' autonomy and freedom, while a Directive leadership style appears negatively related to followers' creativity (Zhang & Bartol, 2010). Creativity however, like many organizational phenomena, involves fundamental paradoxes (i.e., tensions between novelty and usefulness, idea generation and implementation, exploration, and exploitation). A fundamental tension for the creation of something novel and useful is the need for both freedom and stability/structure in the process (Fortwengel et al., 2017; Cirella, 2016).

Creative leadership may therefore involve not only providing freedom but also *designing and sustaining structures and routines* (Goncalo et al., 2015; Lampel, Honig, & Drori, 2014; Cirella et al., 2016; Verganti, 2016). Concerning this challenge, we observe that leaders can design, manage, and adopt a tapestry of learning mechanisms, i.e., a combination of conscious and planned engines that encourage *collective* learning and development (Popper & Lipshitz, 1998; Shani & Docherty, 2008). We also observed that utilizing design thinking is a powerful way to engage people in action by anchoring them directly into the creative process. Our findings provide an example of how this may happen. In Integrative creative practices that are democratic, leaders provide freedom to their collaborators, but they also set up purposeful learning mechanisms by design in the form of structures and routines (such as Pixar's Braintrust and Linklater's early and long rehearsals).

Autocratic Integration

Factors that we hypothesize are associated with a more autocratic form of Integration include leaders demonstrating a high need for control of the creative process, consolidating roles or master and overstepping on other professionals' roles, asking for secrecy, especially during the initial stages of the creative process, working with different crews across projects, involving others later in the process, having less time for improvization and play, and having a less technologically complex process and a smaller crew. In Integrative contexts, the creative character of the work is open to various interpretations and debates among collaborators throughout the creative process (Lampel & Shamsie, 2003). Yet our findings seem to imply that leaders on the autocratic end of the continuum seem averse to debating different creative interpretation of their work. This may be due to their high skills and competences (e.g., Tarantino on dialogs), but also their personal leadership style preference.

Conclusion

In this chapter, we have identified some relevant insights about Integrative creative leadership in the context of filmmaking. In particular, our examples highlight the likely existence of a continuum from autocratic to democratic integration and identify factors possibly associated with variations on this continuum. The Integrative context of creative leadership implies collaboration among various heterogeneous professionals, such a collaboration does not necessarily imply democracy or equality. Integration can still occur in an autocratic manner. While we are agnostic about whether a more autocratic or more democratic approach to integration lead to higher or lower quality, or more innovative products, it would be interesting to explore this question in further studies. Another possible avenue for further research revolves around collective and shared leadership (e.g., Denis, Langley, & Sergi, 2012; Friedrich et al. 2009; Pearce & Conger, 2003), which have been presented as examples of Integrative creative leadership (Mainemelis, Kark, & Epitropaki, 2015). It would be interesting to explore the relationship between formal and informal leaders (e.g., DP, screenwriter, costume designer, music composer) in the light of these theories.

References

Alvarez, J. L., Mazza, C., Pedersen, J. S., & Svejenova, S. 2005. Shielding idiosyncracy from isomorphic pressures: Towards optimal distinctiveness in European filmmaking. *Organization*, 12: 863–888.

Alvarez, J. L., & Svejenova, S. 2002. Symbiotic careers in movie making: Pedro and Augustin Almodovar. In M. Peiperl, M. Arthur, & N. Anand (Eds.), *Career creativity: Explorations in the remaking of work*: 183–208. New York: Oxford University Press.

Amabile, T. M. 1996. *Creativity in context*. Boulder, CO: Westview Press.

Baker, W. E., & Faulkner, R. R. 1991. Role as resource in the Hollywood film industry. *American Journal of Sociology*, 97: 279–309.

Barrett, F. J. 1998. Creativity and improvisation in jazz and organizations: Implications for organizational learning. *Organization Science*, 9: 605–622.

Basadur, M. S., Graen, G. B., & Green, S. G. 1982. Training in creative problem solving: Effects on ideation and problem finding in an applied research organization. *Organizational Behavior and Human Performance*, 30: 41–70.

Bechky, B. A. 2006. Gaffers, gofers, and grips: Role-based coordination in temporary organizations. *Organization Science*, 17: 3–21.

Catmull, E., & Wallace, A. 2014. *Creativity, Inc: Overcoming the unseen forces that stand in the way of true inspiration*. New York, NY: Random House.

Cirella, S. 2016. Organizational variables for developing collective creativity in business: A case from an Italian fashion design company. *Creativity and Innovation Management*, 25(3): 331–343.

Cirella, S., Canterino, F., Guerci, M., & Shani, A. B. 2016. Organizational learning Mechanisms and creative climate: Insights from an Italian fashion design company. *Creativity and Innovation Management*, 25(2): 211–222.

Coget, J. F. 2004. *Leadership in motion: An investigation into the psychological processes that drive behavior when leaders respond to "real-time" operational challenges*. Unpublished doctoral Dissertation, UCLA, Anderson School of Management.

Denis, J-L., Langley, A., & Sergi, V. 2012. Leadership in the plural. *Academy of Management Annals*, 6: 211–283.

Fortwengel, J., Schüßler, E., & Sydow, J. 2017. Studying organizational creativity as process: Fluidity or duality? *Creativity and Innovation Management*, 26: 5–16.

Friedrich, T. L., Vessey, W. B., Schuelke, M. J., Ruark, G. A., & Mumford, M. D. 2009. A framework for understanding collective leadership: The selective utilization of leader and team expertise within networks. *Leadership Quarterly*, 20: 933–958.

Goncalo, J. A., Chatman, J. A., Duguid, M. M., & Kennedy, J. A. 2015. Creativity from constraint? How the political correctness norm influences creativity in mixed-sex work groups. *Administrative Science Quarterly*, 60(1): 1–30.

Halbesleben, J. R. B., Novicevic, M. M., Harvey, M. G., & Buckley, M. R. 2003. The influence of temporal complexity in the leadership of creativity and innovation: A competency-based model. *Leadership Quarterly*, 14: 433–454.

Harris, T. B., Li, N., Boswell, W. R., Zhang, X. A., & Xie, Z. 2014. Getting what's new from newcomers: Empowering leadership, creativity, and adjustment in the socialization context. *Personnel Psychology*, 67(3): 567–604.

Lampel, J., Honig, B., & Drori, I. 2014. Organizational ingenuity: Concept, processes and strategies. *Organization Studies*, 35(4): 465–482.

Lampel, J., & Shamsie, J. 2003. Capabilities in motion: New organizational forms and the reshaping of the Hollywood movie industry. *Journal of Management Studies*, 40: 2189–2210.

Lovelace, J. B., & Hunter, S. T. 2013. Charismatic, ideological, and pragmatic leaders' influence on subordinate creative performance across the creative process. *Creativity Research Journal*, 25(1): 59–74.

Lumholdt, J. 2003. *Lars von trier: Interviews*. Jackson: University Press of Mississippi.
Mainemelis, C. 2002. Time and timelessness: Creativity in (and out of) the temporal dimension. *Creativity Research Journal*, 14: 227–238.
Mainemelis, C., & Altman, Y. 2010. Work and play: New twists on an old relationship. *Journal of Organizational Change Management*, 23: 4–9.
Mainemelis, C., & Dionysiou, D. 2015. Play, flow, and timelessness. In C. Shalley, M. Hitt, & J. Zhou (Eds.), *The Oxford handbook of creativity, innovation, and entrepreneurship*: 121–140. New York: Oxford University Press.
Mainemelis, C., Kark, R., & Epitropaki, O. 2015. Creative leadership: A multi-context conceptualization. *The Academy of Management Annals*, 9(1): 393–482.
Mumford, M. D., Medeiros, K. E., & Partlow, P. J. 2012. Creative thinking: Processes, strategies, and knowledge. *Journal of Creative Behaviour*, 46: 30–47.
Murphy, S. E., & Ensher, E. A. 2008. A qualitative analysis of charismatic leadership in creative teams: The case of television directors. *The Leadership Quarterly*, 19: 335–352.
Pearce, C. L., & Conger, J. A. 2003. *Shared leadership: Reframing the hows and whys of leadership*. Thousand Oaks, CA: Sage Publications.
Popper, M., & Lipshitz, R. 1998. Organizational learning mechanisms: A structural and cultural approach to organizational learning. *Journal of Applied Behavioral Science*, 34(2): 161–179.
Reiter-Palmon, R., & Illies, J. J. 2004. Leadership and creativity: Understanding leadership from a creative problem-solving perspective. *The Leadership Quarterly*, 15(1): 55–77.
Shani, A. B., & Docherty, P. 2008. Learning by design: Key mechanisms in organization development. In T. Cummings (Ed.), *Handbook of organizational change and development*: 499–518. Thousand Oaks, CA: Sage Publications.
Svejenova, S. 2005. "The path with the heart": Creating the authentic career. *Journal of Management Studies*, 42: 947–974.
Vera, D., & Crossan, M. 2004. Theatrical improvisation: Lessons for organizations. *Organization Studies*, 25: 727–751.
Verganti, R. 2016. *Overcrowded: Designing meaningful products in a world awashed with ideas*. Cambridge, MA: MIT Press.
Zhang, X., Bartol, K. M. 2010. Linking empowering leadership and employee creativity: The influence of psychological empowerment, intrinsic motivation, and creative process engagement. *Academy of Management Journal*, 53: 107–128.

Index